Global Perspectives on Teaching and Learning Paths in Islamic Education

Miftachul Huda
Universiti Pendidikan Sultan Idris Malaysia, Malaysia

Jimaain Safar
Universiti Teknologi Malaysia, Malaysia

Ahmad Kilani Mohamed
Universiti Teknologi Malaysia, Malaysia

Kamarul Azmi Jasmi
Universiti Teknologi Malaysia, Malaysia

Bushrah Basiron
Universiti Teknologi Malaysia, Malaysia

A volume in the Advances in Educational Technologies and Instructional Design (AETID) Book Series

IGI Global
DISSEMINATOR OF KNOWLEDGE

Published in the United States of America by
    IGI Global
    Information Science Reference (an imprint of IGI Global)
    701 E. Chocolate Avenue
    Hershey PA, USA 17033
    Tel: 717-533-8845
    Fax: 717-533-8661
    E-mail: cust@igi-global.com
    Web site: http://www.igi-global.com

Library of Congress Cataloging-in-Publication Data

Names: Huda, Miftachul, 1990- editor. | Safar, Jimaain, 1963- editor. | Ahmad
  Kilani Mohamed, editor. | Kamarul Azmi Jasmi, editor. | Basiron, Bushrah,
  editor.
Title: Global perspectives on teaching and learning paths in Islamic
  education / Miftachul Huda, Jimaain Safar, Ahmad Kilani Mohamed, Kamarul
  Azmi Jasmi, and Bushrah Basiron, editors.
Description: Hershey PA : Information Science Reference, [2020] | Includes
  bibliographical references.
Identifiers: LCCN 2018055423| ISBN 9781522585282 (hardcover) | ISBN
  9781522585299 (softcover) | ISBN 9781522585305 (ebook)
Subjects: LCSH: Islamic education. | Islamic learning and scholarship. |
  Education--Philosophy. | Islamic universities and colleges.
Classification: LCC LC903 .G56 2020 | DDC 297.7/7--dc23 LC record available at https://lccn.loc.
gov/2018055423

This book is published in the IGI Global book series Advances in Educational Technologies and Instructional Design (AETID) (ISSN: 2326-8905; eISSN: 2326-8913)

British Cataloguing in Publication Data
A Cataloguing in Publication record for this book is available from the British Library.

For electronic access to this publication, please contact: eresources@igi-global.com.

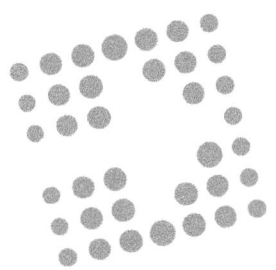

Advances in Educational Technologies and Instructional Design (AETID) Book Series

ISSN:2326-8905
EISSN:2326-8913

Editor-in-Chief: Lawrence A. Tomei, Robert Morris University, USA

MISSION

Education has undergone, and continues to undergo, immense changes in the way it is enacted and distributed to both child and adult learners. In modern education, the traditional classroom learning experience has evolved to include technological resources and to provide online classroom opportunities to students of all ages regardless of their geographical locations. From distance education, Massive-Open-Online-Courses (MOOCs), and electronic tablets in the classroom, technology is now an integral part of learning and is also affecting the way educators communicate information to students.

The **Advances in Educational Technologies & Instructional Design (AETID) Book Series** explores new research and theories for facilitating learning and improving educational performance utilizing technological processes and resources. The series examines technologies that can be integrated into K-12 classrooms to improve skills and learning abilities in all subjects including STEM education and language learning. Additionally, it studies the emergence of fully online classrooms for young and adult learners alike, and the communication and accountability challenges that can arise. Trending topics that are covered include adaptive learning, game-based learning, virtual school environments, and social media effects. School administrators, educators, academicians, researchers, and students will find this series to be an excellent resource for the effective design and implementation of learning technologies in their classes.

COVERAGE

- Classroom Response Systems
- Educational Telecommunications
- Hybrid Learning
- Online Media in Classrooms
- E-Learning
- Instructional Design Models
- Instructional Design
- Higher Education Technologies
- Bring-Your-Own-Device
- Web 2.0 and Education

IGI Global is currently accepting manuscripts for publication within this series. To submit a proposal for a volume in this series, please contact our Acquisition Editors at Acquisitions@igi-global.com or visit: http://www.igi-global.com/publish/.

Titles in this Series

For a list of additional titles in this series, please visit:
https://www.igi-global.com/book-series/advances-educational-technologies-instructional-design/73678

Handbook of Research on Diverse Teaching Strategies for the Technology-Rich Classroom
Lawrence A. Tomei (Robert Morris University, USA) and David D. Carbonara (Duquesne University, USA)
Information Science Reference • © 2020 • 450pp • H/C (ISBN: 9781799802389) • US $265.00 (our price)

Emerging Technologies in Virtual Learning Environments
Kim Becnel (Appalachian State University, USA)
Information Science Reference • © 2019 • 348pp • H/C (ISBN: 9781522579878) • US $205.00 (our price)

English Language Teaching in a Post-Method Paradigm
Paulette Joyce Feraria (The University of the West Indies, Jamaica)
Information Science Reference • © 2019 • 426pp • H/C (ISBN: 9781522592280) • US $175.00 (our price)

Cases on Digital Learning and Teaching Transformations in Higher Education
Rebecca J. Blankenship (Florida Agricultural and Mechanical University, USA) and Charlotte Baker (Virginia Polytechnic Institute and State University, USA)
Information Science Reference • © 2019 • 266pp • H/C (ISBN: 9781522593317) • US $175.00 (our price)

Handbook of Research on Innovative Digital Practices to Engage Learners
Prince Hycy Bull (Gardner-Webb University, USA) and Jared Keengwe (University of North Dakota, USA)
Information Science Reference • © 2019 • 468pp • H/C (ISBN: 9781522594383) • US $275.00 (our price)

701 East Chocolate Avenue, Hershey, PA 17033, USA
Tel: 717-533-8845 x100 • Fax: 717-533-8661
E-Mail: cust@igi-global.com • www.igi-global.com

Editorial Advisory Board

Table of Contents

Detailed Table of Contents

Chapter 1
Islamic Education Today and Yesterday: Principal Themes and their Potential
to Enlighten Western Education...1
Terence Lovat, University of Newcastle, Australia

The chapter will offer a literature review of principal themes to be found in
contemporary and earlier sources concerned with distinctive features of Islamic
education. It will be found that, among a number of themes, those concerned with
the teacher-student relationship and the holistic balance between intellectual and
spiritual/moral ends stand out as dominant. Explicit in much contemporary literature
and implicit in some earlier sources lies a critique of Western education as more
instrumental and so narrower regarding these two features. The chapter will conclude
with a summary of the distinctive contribution that Islamic education can make to a
Western education contemporaneously in search of a renewed holism and fortified
moral component.

Chapter 2
Transmitting the Teachings of Islam in Contemporary Times: Glimpses From
Prophetic Approach...20
AbdulGafar Olawale Fahm, University of Ilorin, Nigeria

There is a growing body of literature that recognizes the importance of proper approach to transmission of learning. This is because an effective method teaching always goes a long way in helping to understanding what is being taught. Contemporary discourse on teaching style often stresses either a teacher-centered or student-centered approaches. This chapter takes a critical look at the Prophet Muhammad's methods of teaching Islam to the Companions (Sahaba). This study attempts to understand the intent of these methods used by the Prophet Muhammad and investigates their possible implications. Through historical and descriptive methods examines the primary sources in Islam – the Qur'ān and the life case of the Prophet Muḥammad as presented in his sayings and teachings (Ḥadīth). The study reveals that the prophetic approach, apart from being very effective, is also a very practical method that can be used in our contemporary times and provides a better understanding of the message of Islam and prophetic heritage.

Chapter 3

Benaouda Bensaid, İstanbul Sabahattin Zaim University, Turkey
Salah Machouche, International Islamic University Malaysia, Malaysia

This chapter seeks to explore the crossroads between learning in Islam and spirituality, and also the methods according to which Muslim instructors shape students' experiences in a context of piety development. This study also examines questions pertaining to the concept of spirituality in education, methods pedagogic principles that further merge spiritual discipline with knowledge acquisition. The theoretical research draws on the textual analysis of early works of Muslim scholars, more specifically on Abdul Ibn Khaldun and Abu Hamid al-Ghazali, given their prominent positions in the history of Muslim education. This study shows that the Islamic learning has always taken students' spiritual growth for granted and has, despite differences of practices across Muslim regions, always maintained the refining of learners' spiritual character.

Chapter 4

Imran Mogra, Birmingham City University, UK

This chapter provides a synopsis of teaching techniques gleaned from traditional texts represented in Muslim canonical ḥadīth collections. To begin with, the life of Prophet Muḥammad is surveyed from a teacher's perspective. Thereafter, narratives which illuminate pedagogical strategies are analyzed to emphasize the need for teachers to have a repertoire of teaching methods. It is argued that the techniques derived from traditional texts are relevant as they resonate with contemporary educational ideas.

This chapter focuses on transformational Islamic leadership based on a case study of a madrasah in Singapore. The research findings underscore the significance of an Islamic leader in articulating and promoting a shared vision, demonstrating exemplary behavior, working towards group goals, rendering individual support, providing intellectual stimulation, and setting high expectations. A major implication is that Islamic leadership contributes to the existing literature on transformational leadership by highlighting the religious motivation, principles, and values for madrasah leaders.

The curriculum is one component that has a strategic role in the formation of graduate character. Educational institutions have the authority to develop their curriculum in accordance with the development of society (social needs), the world of work (industrial needs), the development of science and profession (professional needs), as well as the specificity and superiority of educational institutions (core character building). The curriculum of college peculiarities developed as a course of personality character forming of learners. The course of keaswajaan (Nahdlatul 'Ulama / ke-NU-an) is a study material that aims to build a normative framework and Islamic charity according to the vision and mission of each college. This chapter aims to analyze and find the concept of character values in the curriculum of keaswajaan.

This study discusses the series of life cycle rituals the people of Kluet Timur, South Aceh implement. The study focuses on five main rituals—the rituals of pregnancy, giving birth, circumcision, marriage, and death. Islamic educational values contained in each ritual are also described. To collect this data, this qualitative study applied observation and interview methodologies. The values of customary education, Tawheed, health, and correct decision making can be found in the rituals of pregnancy and childbirth. The values of responsibility and health appear in the ritual of circumcision. The people of Kluet Timur develop the values of deliberation, consensus, and togetherness in the ritual of marriage. The values of solidarity and cooperation are reflected in the implementation of the death ritual.

Chapter 8

Najwan Saada, The Mofet Institute, Israel

In this multiple case study, the authors explore the purposes and significance of Islamic religious education as it is viewed and interpreted by Arab and Muslim teachers in Arab high schools in Israel. It interrogates how the Muslim teachers locate themselves and their pedagogy within a continuum of salafi (conservative) versus liberal conceptions of tarbiyya (the spiritual aspects of Islam) and ta`dib (the moral aspects of Islam) and why they do so. The results show that teachers support the salafi rather than the liberal conceptions of Islamic education. This means that they focus on the naql (the transmission of religious knowledge) rather than aql (rational thinking) in teaching the moral aspects of Islam. Also, teachers avoid the dealing with the intellectual diversity within Islam, the discussion of contemporary issues, and the tenets of other Abrahamic religions. They conclude that this may lead to religious illiteracy and argue that liberal Islamic education with critical and reflective reasoning is much appropriate for living in multicultural and multi-faith society.

Chapter 9

Ibrahima Diallo, University of South Australia, Australia

Evidence shows that in pre-colonial West Africa, Islamic education played a significant role following conversion of West Africans to Islam because of its impact on all spheres of life. With the establishment of theocratic states and communities, Islamic learning centers emerged to spread Islamic education and consolidate the Islamic way of life in West Africa. In this vast region where people of different ethnic, linguistic, and religious backgrounds lived and interacted for trade and commerce, Islamic education fostered Islamic affinities constructed on the universalism of Islam and Islamic injunction to form Muslim brotherhood and create the Ummah.

The learning environment is defined as "external stimulants" that is exposed or reinforced in learners as a means to challenge their learning experiences. These reinforcements may include physical settings, teaching and learning endeavours, and even cultural and social determiners. This empirical study focuses on the perceived experiences that undergraduates from Brunei, Malaysia, and Indonesia experienced in their Arabic and English language learning environments. This qualitative study employed in-depth interviews with 60 informants that were selected through criterion sampling, snowballing technique. The analysis utilised template analysis. Emerging themes were compared and contrasted, to find similarities and differences. This chapter does not aim to seek the superiority of one learning environment over another but to appreciate the diversity and concord of these institutions. The findings illustrated overlapping, differentiated themes, which included the abovementioned.

Nashid is one of various teaching methods and facilitator (PdPc). Teenagers nowadays are full of interest in entertainment in the form of songs and singing, and a good alternative is to bring them to God. Thus, this paper will be debating nashid as medium of education and missionary, nashid as a method of teaching and facilitating, the effectiveness of the method, and its implementation in teaching and learning. Aspects of creativeness in education are required in the 21st century. Nashid method is able to help students memorize facts and important things, strengthen memory, create high interest, build excitement, improve motivation and concentration, and enhance the confidence level among students. It will bring about a holistic student. However, the selection of the appropriate nashid must be considered to make sure the teaching objectives are achieved. Thus, teachers in Islamic teaching must look at this method as one of the important methods and apply it in their teaching and facilitating process.

This chapter examines the distinctive point of view about moral responsibility as the main principle in maximizing the learning quality in the perspective of Islamic education. Moreover, the extensive details could be also discussed referring to the strategic comprehensive point of view to contribute into the modern age. Literature review has been adopted to critically examine the detailed overview of learning quality with a comprehensive enhancement in wide range of requirements to achieve quality learning referred to the Islamic education. The findings reveal that through addressing the contextual broad-basis in the learning process to follow up the strategic principles in the requirements combined into the modern age environment, the learning quality could be achieved through committing with the strategic comprehensive principles of moral responsibility. Those are moral responsibility as fundamental purpose of learning process, moral responsibility as strategic principles for learning quality, and moral responsibility as competence skills for learning quality. Thus, this chapter is expected to contribute into the outstanding point of view to enlarge the learning quality procedure in the context of Islamic education contribution into the modern age of education system.

    Miftachul Huda, Universiti Pendidikan Sultan Idris, Malaysia
    Khoirurrijal Khoirurrijal, State Institute for Islamic Studies (IAIN)
        Metro Lampung, Indonesia
    M. Ihsan Dacholfany, Universitas Muhammdiyah Metro Lampung,
        Indonesia
    Susminingsih Susminingsih, State Institute of Islamic Studies (IAIN)
        Pekalongan, Indonesia
    Azmil Hashim, Universiti Pendidikan Sultan Idris, Malaysia
    Nurazmalail Marni, Universiti Teknologi Malaysia, Malaysia
    Ahmad Kilani Mohamed, Universiti Teknologi Malaysia, Malaysia
    Madheil Azaeim Ahmad Puad, Universiti Kebangsaan Malaysia,
        Malaysia
    Mohd Hilmi Rozali, Universiti Teknologi Malaysia, Malaysia
    Andino Maseleno, Universiti Tenaga Nasional Malaysia, Malaysia
    Nasrul Hisyam Nor Muhamad, Universiti Teknologi Malaysia, Malaysia
    Afiful Ikhwan, Universitas Muhammadiyah Ponorogo, Indonesia

Since every deed is an inextricable link to the process which is well prepared with a goal, possessing the initiative of implementing the learning needs to have a good strategy committed into the clear determination in enabling the stakeholder to deal with in the school context. This chapter aims to critically explore learning ethics culture in Islamic education which needs to pay attention to the learning goal. A critical review from referred books and journals that are linked to the topic was employed through searching for google scholar. The finding reveals that learning ethics culture for learning achievement in Islamic education could be indicated into three core paths: achieving divine engagement-based spiritual commitment, assisting skill performance for personal capability development, and applying knowledge for active involvement in the society. This chapter is expected to enrich the conceptual framework of learning acquisition with paying particular attention to learning ethics culture.

Chapter 14
Understanding Istifadah (Utilizing Time and Chance) for Personality

    Miftachul Huda, Universiti Pendidikan Sultan Idris, Malaysia
    M.Ikhsan Nawawi, Institute for Islamic Studies Agus Salim, Indonesia
    Liberty Liberty, State Institute for Islamic Studies (IAIN) Metro
        Lampung, Indonesia
    Jarkawi Jarkawi, Universitas Islam Kalimantan Muhammad Arsyad Al
        Banjari, Indonesia
    Azmil Hashim, Universiti Pendidikan Sultan Idris, Malaysia
    Muhamad Mustaqim Ahmad, Universiti Kebangsaan Malaysia,
        Malaysia
    Mohd Hilmi Rozali, Universiti Teknologi Malaysia, Malaysia
    Nurazmalail Marni, Universiti Teknologi Malaysia, Malaysia
    Bushrah Basiron, Universiti Teknologi Malaysia, Malaysia
    Ahmad Kilani Mohamed, Universiti Teknologi Malaysia, Malaysia
    Andino Maseleno, Universiti Tenaga Nasional Malaysia, Malaysia
    Noorhaswari Ismail, Universiti Teknologi Malaysia, Malaysia

This chapter attempts to accurately investigate the conception to take a benefit as an ethical foundation of character education, known as the concept of istifādah. This refers to the insightful value of al-Zarnūjī's Ta'lim al-Muta'allim, containing fundamental principles in the context of education, which has been used by the Islamic boarding school Pesantren in Indonesia. This research is employed through literature study using descriptive analysis. The findings reveal that there four core stages to examine istifādah for personal development in Islamic education context. Those are integrating Hikmah (wisdom) based moral quality for personal development, sustaining continuous discipline, nurturing effective time management, and empowering strategic effort with experiential foundations. Moreover, this study is supposed to give the contribution mainly in supplementing the theoretical basis on personality development in Islamic education context.

Foreword

With expanding the uniquely distinctive way towards theoretical and practical based procedure, Islamic education is consistently committed with serving as providing important sources to create the human behaviour with a moral and spiritual balance assimilated into the cognitive skills. Through a comprehensive outline in the scale of individual and society concern, the primary source which IE offers in terms of knowledge and values could play a significant role in elevating the significance to sustain the inextricable link between cohesive social and universal order. This aims to strengthen both faith-based spirituality concern and knowledge transfer process as Islamic education has transformed with its distinctive point of maintaining the balance between cognitive, spiritual and moral substance.

Moreover, the advancement of technology with its newly transformed innovation has begun to give the influential parameter to offer such new paradigm shift where to adapt consequently from alive to cybernetic base in underlying the social activities. Such expansion comes not only into the society at large but also more directly into the educational setting basis where there are the number of newly developed instruction in the basis of digitalization technology. In the attempts to answer such modern learning environment (MLE), it is worthwhile to commit with an insightful value in enhancing the balance with a wise basis between ethical and professional engagement as an attempt to respond in underlying the human performance. To bring undoubtedly with committing both learning and teaching style, it is necessary to concisely convey such approaches into the universal basis in enabling the global perspective to have a look into that kind of initiative. Thus, getting a wide point of looking at the global perspectives, the balance between practical and theoretical debate of Islamic education could bring along with the approach variety of ways implemented in the basis of society and personality.

With such basis through recent studies of Islamic education, I believe that this book will give an insightful value of good references to supplement those elaborated in expanding the curriculum development and construction of Islamic education within the values transformed into teaching and learning from the global perspectives. Since the tradition on educational trends becomes a unique and valuable feature to be appropriately enhanced with expanding the embodiment process on experiential learning, the achievement could essentially be creating the outcomes with the balance not only cognitive skills quality but also good spirituality and morality.

Azmil Hashim
Universiti Pendidikan Sultan Idris, Malaysia

Foreword

In the past decades, the variety of new strategy of educational setting has been widely incorporated since the emerging trend of digitalization is also giving such advancements with offering the innovative basis on instructional method. In this view, Islamic education (IE) has consequently necessary to respond in elaborating its expansion towards developing the curriculum design. It is more directly into sustaining the existing traditional culture combined with adopting the new implementation strategy in taking the beneficial value of digital tool in particular. As a result, the wise combination of unique tradition which IE has and digital-based emerging trends would produce the useful merit of sources to give the supplement into the research and development of IE.

The pattern shift from live-based way into the virtual based instruction would potentially give a point of view in transforming the digital-based learning. It is undoubtedly to note that such emerging trends form the wide advancement into the way of Islamic education performance are necessary to reconsider its role play in driving its appropriate way to transmit the knowledge, values and spirituality basis. Responding such trend, the need to enhance the valuable strategies of the operational section within wise approach should be taken into consideration in improving the curriculum design through adopting the approach variety widely in ensuring the main concern to enhance the quality assurance of educational setting.

With providing both theoretical and practical basis of IE performance, this book will be beneficial insights in supplementing the good reference in giving the path on the curriculum enhancement by compelling the unique tradition of IE with adopting the emerging trends on digital instruction style. Moreover, expanding the curriculum transformed into teaching and learning (T&L) of Islamic education from the global perspectives is potentially a valuable insight into development of improving the instruction basis widely concerned to enhance the quality assurance in educational process. Both content and material subject in IE curriculum could be fixed into the global demands along with community's needs and demands. Particularly, the references could benefit as a supplementing source to guide in running the process wisely with developing such analysis, design, and appropriate methods with the entire process involved into expanding the embodiment process on experiential learning in resulting the outcomes with good spirituality and morality and also cognitive quality skills.

M. Ihsan Dacholfany
Universitas Muhammadiyah Metro Lampung, Indonesia

Foreword

Widely elaborating the emerging trends of the technology advancement in Islamic education, there are the numbers of initiatives with expanding the creativities to transform the curriculum design, philosophical discourse, and implementation stage by taking the beneficial value of digitalization. It is worthwhile to have a mutually inextricable link between theoretical and practical style. In making the knowledge acquisition through teaching and learning (T&L) context, the uniqueness of the virtues Islam offers through its potential benefit including the religious values and professional morality in the certain guidelines could be widely engaged into the attempts to bring along with an extensive integration of such curriculum-based integration of practice.

As such, the endeavours to ensure the global perspectives on the way to transmit the Islamic education performance are in line with committing into both sustenance and sustainability of keeping in particular of traditional based instruction and modern learning basis, which needs to have a look at a particular view into the current trends amidst the digitalization. Having to continue the advantage in assisting the instructional process, enduring to possess on bringing the main foundation with such characteristics, philosophical point of view, moral and spiritual parts and application basis might have a piece of driving the role model in extensively building Islamic education to shape the balance between moral and spiritual qualities. The certain theory and practice referring to the instructional style through bringing along with expanding the knowledge inquiry and transfer should maintain the traditional part while going to sustain the initiative of adopting the new instructional side of technology advancement. With this regard, enhancing the entire attempts to take into account of elevating the cognitive skills could be applied through empowering the personal and social personality through nurturing the Islamic values along with redesigning the curriculum construction.

Outlining this book entitled *Global Perspectives on Teaching and Learning Paths of Islamic Education*, the number of contributions are coverage into the basis of theory and practice of Islamic education including the latest update of study until taking a new look of relevance towards the indigenous theory based- study. Such initiatives with the potential values might have also combined in the attempts to provide the wide range of viewpoints in developing the curriculum design, philosophical foundation and contemporary application amidst the emerging trends on digital age.

I trust this book will have its useful point of view to those of target audience including professionals, scholars, and graduate students with their interest of research and development (R&D) of Islamic education in both school programs and tertiary education.

Mifedwil Jandra Janan
Universiti Ahmad Dahlan Yogyakarta, Indonesia

Preface

In the last decade, the emerging trends of Islamic education have been widely elaborated with the number of initiatives, one of which comes to take a benefit of digitalization. In this view, the instructional model has shifted to the new paradigm, while staying on the main foundation of the characteristics, philosophical point of view, moral and spiritual parts and application basis. As such, this played a role model in making Islamic education extensively with determining the particular concern about theoretical and practical stage within the instructional style. Through bringing along with the unique virtue Islam encourages to expand the knowledge inquiry and transfer, attempts to maintain the traditional part of foundational co-existence together with adopting new instructional side of technology advancement could be taken into consideration in enhancing the moral and spiritual qualities while also elevating the cognitive skills. With this regard, the personal and social personality's empowerment might sustain the wide integration of nurturing the Islamic values along with redesigning the curriculum construction.

The technology advancement within a new shift paradigm from live to virtual basis of social activities would lead to bring an insightful value in a wise basis as an attempt to respond in enhancing the balance between ethical and professional engagement in underlying the human performance. It is mainly in the learning and teaching style to concisely transmit into the universal basis in the sense that can be viewed referring the conditional circumstance. As such, it is useful to have a look at the global perspectives on the practical and theoretical discussion of Islamic education in bringing along with wide range of approaches and ways undertaken in the society and personality trait basis.

This book *Global Perspectives on Teaching and Learning Paths of Islamic Education* with all the chapters with the most recent studies including theoretical articles, conceptual frameworks, and review papers for Islamic education provides the wide range of points of view in developing the curriculum design, philosophical foundation and contemporary application amidst the emerging trends on digital age. These new analytical methods and emerging trends in digital age would be the significant references in giving insights on developing curriculum with the nature, and unique feature continuously enhanced in the operation in designing new operations research methods of teaching and learning on Islamic education. The wide combination of unique tradition on Islamic education curriculum and emerging trends of digital age would be appropriately engaged into the references useful for subsequent research and educational sector in the attempts to build curriculum development. The target audience of this book includes professionals, researchers, faculty, and graduate students with an interest in the research and application of Islamic education in both school programs and tertiary education. Public and private sector education institution will get a tremendous benefit through the wide applications including process, implementation stage, and evaluation analysis committed into strategic operations together with decision making in committing tradition of Islamic education and adopting the valuable insights of emerging trends on digital age. Those include stakeholder; local, state and federal governments who manage the educational institution from school to tertiary education level. The entirely valuable process of curriculum development in Islamic education refers to the attempts on the significant condition in making the transfer process of knowledge into the learners more comprehensive including moral, spiritual and cognitive side. Transmitted into the digital age, the chances will be good opportunities to transform the valuable insights to help disseminate the values within the learners. Both content and material subject in Islamic education curriculum could be fitted into the global demands along with community's needs and demands in order to guide them to run the process well and appropriately.

The book is coverage into the number of topics from Historical glance of Islamic education, Prophetic foundation style for teaching and learning, Educating Muslim pious personality, Traditional text as the curriculum resource, Islamic leadership, Curriculum development, Islamic values in ritual tradition, Reflective teaching of Islamic education, Islamic education and affinities, Arabic education, Learning strategy of Nasheed (Religious song), moral responsibility for learning quality, ethical strategy for learning, and also Islamic character education. The following is about the summary of each chapter.

Chapter 1 titled "Islamic Education Today and Yesterday: Principal Themes and Their Potential to Enlighten Western Education" by Terence Lovat (University of Newcastle, Australia) offers a literature review of principal themes to be found in contemporary and earlier sources concerned with distinctive features of Islamic education. It will be found that, among a number of themes, those concerned with the teacher-student relationship and the holistic balance between intellectual and spiritual/moral ends stand out as dominant. Explicit in much contemporary literature and implicit in some earlier sources lies a critique of Western education as more instrumental and so narrower regarding these two features. The chapter will conclude with a summary of the distinctive contribution that Islamic education can make to a Western education contemporaneously in search of a renewed holism and fortified moral component.

Chapter 2 titled "Transmitting the Teachings of Islam in Contemporary Times: Glimpses From Prophetic Approach" by Abdul Gafar Olawale Fahm (University of Ilorin, Nigeria) points out taking a critical look at the Prophet Muhammad's methods of teaching Islam to the Companions (Sahaba). This study attempts to understand the intent of these methods used by the Prophet Muhammad and investigates their possible implications. Through historical and descriptive methods examines the primary sources in Islam – the Qur'ān and the life case of the Prophet Muḥammad as presented in his sayings and teachings (Ḥadīth). The study reveals that the prophetic approach, apart from being very effective, is also a very practical method that can be used in our contemporary times and provides a better understanding of the message of Islam and prophetic heritage.

Chapter 3 titled "Education Piety a Muslim Insight" by Salah Machouche (International Islamic University-Malaysia) and Benaouda Bensaid (Effat University, Jeddah Saudi Arabia) seeks to explore the crossroads between learning in Islam and spirituality, and also the methods according to which Muslim instructors shapes students' experience in a context of piety development. This study draws also examines questions pertaining to the concept of spirituality in education, methods pedagogic principles that further merge spiritual discipline with knowledge acquisition. The theoretical research draws on the textual analysis of early works of Muslim scholars, more specifically on 'Abdul Ibn Khaldun and Abu Hamid al-Ghazali, given their prominent positions in the history of Muslim education. This study shows that the Islamic learning has always taken students' spiritual growth for granted, and has, despite differences of practices across Muslim regions, always maintained the refining of learners' spiritual character.

Chapter 4 titled "Traditional Texts and Contemporary Teaching Techniques" by Imran Mogra (Birmingham City University) provides a synopsis of teaching techniques gleaned from traditional texts represented in Muslim canonical ḥadīth collections. To begin with, the life of Prophet Muḥammad is surveyed from a teacher's perspective. Thereafter, narratives which illuminate pedagogical strategies are analysed to emphasise the need for teachers to have a repertoire of teaching methods. It is argued that the techniques derived from traditional texts are relevant as they resonate with contemporary educational ideas.

Chapter 5 titled "Transformational Islamic Leadership: A Case Study From Singapore," Diwi Abbas (Nanyang Technological University, Singapore) and Charlene Tan (Nanyang Technological University, Singapore), focuses on transformational Islamic leadership based on a case study of a madrasah in Singapore. Our research findings underscore the significance of an Islamic leader in articulating and promoting a shared vision, demonstrating exemplary behaviour, working towards group goals, rendering individual support, providing intellectual stimulation, and setting high expectations. A major implication is that Islamic leadership contributes to the existing literature on transformational leadership by highlighting the religious motivation, principles and values for madrasah leaders.

Chapter 6 titled "Development of Curriculum Keaswajaan (Nahdlatul 'Ulama) in Character Formation: Moral Study on Islamic Education" by Afiful Ikhwan (Universitas Muhammadiyah Ponorogo, Indonesia), Ju'subaidi Ju'subaidi (State Institute of Islamic Studies (IAIN) Ponorogo, Indonesia), Elfi Mu'awanah, (State Institute of Islamic Studies (IAIN) Ponorogo, Indonesia), and Ali Rohmad (State Institute of Islamic Studies (IAIN) Ponorogo, Indonesia) attempts to analyze and find the concept of character values in the curriculum of keaswajaan. The curriculum is one component that has a strategic role in the formation of graduate character. Educational institutions have the authority to develop their curriculum in accordance with the development of society (social needs), the world of work (industrial needs), the development of science and profession (professional needs) as well as the specificity and superiority of educational institutions (core character building). The curriculum of college peculiarities developed as a course of personality character forming of learners. The course of keaswajaan (Nahdlatul 'Ulama / ke-NU-an) is a study material that aims to build a normative framework and Islamic charity according to the vision and mission of each college.

Chapter 7 titled "Islamic Educational Values in Life-Cycle Rituals: An Ethnographic Study in Kluet Timur Community, Aceh, Indonesia" by Abdul Manan (The State Islamic University of Ar-Raniry Banda Aceh) discusses the series of life cycle rituals the people of Kluet Timur, South Aceh implement. The study focuses on five main rituals—the rituals of pregnancy, giving birth, circumcision, marriage, and death. Islamic educational values contained in each ritual are also described. To collect this data, this qualitative study applied observation and interview methodologies. The values of customary education, Tawheed, health, and correct decision-making can be found in the rituals of pregnancy and childbirth. The values of responsibility and health appear in the ritual of circumcision. The people of Kluet Timur develop the values of deliberation, consensus, and togetherness in the ritual of marriage. The values of solidarity and cooperation are reflected in the implementation of the death ritual.

Chapter 8 titled "Teachers' Perceptions of Islamic Religious Education in Arab High Schools in Israel" by Najwan Saada (The Mofet Institute) examined the multiple case study in exploring the purposes and significance of Islamic religious education as it is viewed and interpreted by Arab and Muslim teachers in Arab high schools in Israel. It interrogates how the Muslim teachers locate themselves and their pedagogy within a continuum of salafi (conservative) versus liberal conceptions of tarbiyya (the spiritual aspects of Islam) and taʿdib (the moral aspects of Islam) and why they do so. The results show that teachers support the salafi rather than the liberal conceptions of Islamic education. This means that they focus on the naql (the transmission of religious knowledge) rather than aql (rational thinking) in teaching the moral aspects of Islam. Also, teachers avoid the dealing with the intellectual diversity within Islam, the discussion of contemporary issues, and the tenets of other Abrahamic religions. We conclude that this may lead to religious illiteracy and argue that liberal Islamic education with critical and reflective reasoning is much appropriate for living in multicultural and multi-faith society.

Chapter 9 titled "Islamic Education and Islamic Affinities in Precolonial West Africa" by Ibrahima Diallo (University of South Australia) investigated the evidence that in pre-colonial West Africa, Islamic education played a significant role following conversion of West Africans to Islam because of its impact on all spheres of life. With the establishment of theocratic states and communities, Islamic learning centres emerged to spread Islamic education and consolidate the Islamic way of life in West Africa. In this vast region where people of different ethnic, linguistic and religious backgrounds lived and interacted for trade and commerce, Islamic education fostered Islamic affinities constructed on the universalism of Islam and Islamic injunction to form Muslim brotherhood and create the Ummah.

Chapter 10 titled "English and Arabic Language Learning Environments: Islamic Universities Undergraduates' Experiences" by Noraisikin Sabani (Curtin University, Malaysia Campus and Universiti Brunei Darussalam), Anita Jimmie (Curtin University, Malaysia Campus), and Hanin Naziha Hasnor (Curtin University, Malaysia Campus) elaborated the learning environment defined as "external stimulants" that is exposed or reinforced in learners as a means to challenge their learning experiences. These reinforcements may include physical settings, teaching and learning endeavours, and even cultural and social determiners. This empirical study focuses on the perceived experiences that undergraduates from Brunei, Malaysia and Indonesia experienced in their Arabic and English language learning environments. This qualitative study employed in-depth interviews with 60 informants that were selected through criterion sampling, snowballing technique. The analysis utilised template analysis. Emerging themes were compared and contrasted, to find similarities and differences. This paper does not aim to seek the superiority of one learning environment over another but to appreciate the diversity and concord of these institutions. The findings illustrated overlapping, differentiated themes, which included the abovementioned.

Chapter 11 titled "Understanding *Nasheed* as Learning Strategy in Islamic Education" by Muhammad Talhah Ajmain (Universiti Teknologi Malaysia), Jimaain Safar (Universiti Teknologi Malaysia), Ahmad Kilani Mohamed (Universiti Teknologi Malaysia) and, Miftachul Huda, Universiti Pendidikan Sultan Idris (UPSI),

Malaysia addressed the concern of Nashid (religious song) as one of various teaching methods and facilitator. Our teenagers nowadays full of interest in entertainment in the form of songs and singing, also good alternative to bring them to God. Thus, this concept paper will be debating about nashid as medium of education and missionary, nashid as a method of teaching and facilitating, the effectiveness of the method and its implementation in teaching and learning. Aspects of creativeness in education highly required in this 21st century. Nashid method able to help students memorise facts and important things, strengthen memory, create high interest, build excitement, improve motivation and concentration and enhance the confidence level among students. It will bring towards holistic student. However, the selection of the appropriate nashid must be in highly consideration to make sure the teaching objectives are achieved. Thus, teachers in Islamic teaching must look at this method as one of the important methods and applying it in their teaching and facilitating process along this 21st century.

Chapter 12 titled "Strengthening Moral Responsibility for Learning Quality in Islamic Education" by Miftachul Huda (Universiti Pendidikan Sultan Idris, Malaysia), Widhiya Ninsiana (State Islamic Institute of Metro Lampung Indonesia), Ulfatmi (Universitas Islam Negeri Imam Bonjol, Padang, Indonesia), Maragustam Siregar (Universitas Islam Negeri Sunan Kalijaga, Yogyakarta, Indonesia), Febriyanto (Universitas Muhammadiyah Metro, Lampung, Indonesia), Azmil Hashim (Universiti Pendidikan Sultan Idris, Malaysia), Affandi Saleh (Universiti Sultan Zainal Abidin, Malaysia), Mohd Hilmi Rozali (Universiti Teknologi Malaysia, Malaysia), Ahmad Kilani Mohamed (Universiti Teknologi Malaysia, Malaysia), Mahyuddin Hassan (Universiti Teknologi Malaysia, Malaysia), Andino Maseleno (Universiti Tenaga Nasional, Malaysia), Nasrul Hisyam Nor Muhamad (Universiti Teknologi Malaysia, Malaysia), and Kamarul Azmi Jasmi (Universiti Teknologi Malaysia, Malaysia) examines the distinctive point of view about moral responsibility as the main principle in maximising the learning quality in the perspective of Islamic education. Moreover, the extensive details could be also discussed referring to the strategic comprehensive point of view to contribute into the modern age. Literature review has been adopted to critically examine the detailed overview of learning quality with a comprehensive enhancement in wide range of requirements to achieve quality learning referred to the Islamic education. The findings reveal that through addressing the contextual broad-basis in the learning process to follow up the strategic principles in the requirements combined into the modern age environment, the learning quality could be achieved through committing with the strategic comprehensive principles of moral responsibility. Those are moral responsibility as fundamental purpose of learning process, moral responsibility as strategic principles for learning quality, and moral responsibility as competence skills for learning quality. Thus, this chapter is expected to contribute into the outstanding point of view to enlarge the learning quality procedure in the context of Islamic education contribution into the modern age of education system.

Chapter 13 titled "Empowering Learning Ethics Culture in Islamic Education" by Miftachul Huda (Universiti Pendidikan Sultan Idris, Malaysia), Khoirurrijal (State Institute for Islamic Studies (IAIN) Metro Lampung Indonesia), Ihsan Dacholfany (Universitas Muhammdiyah Metro Lampung, Indonesia), Susminingsih (State Institute of Islamic Studies (IAIN) Pekalongan, Indoneisa), Jarkawi (Universitas Islam Kalimantan Muhammad Arsyad Al Banjari, Indonesia), Azmil Hashim (Universiti Pendidikan Sultan Idris, Malaysia), Nurazmalail Marni (Universiti Teknologi Malaysia, Malaysia), Ahmad Kilani Mohamed (Universiti Teknologi Malaysia, Malaysia), Madheil Azaeim Ahmad Puad (Universiti Kebangsaan Malaysia, Malaysia), Mohd Hilmi Rozali (Universiti Teknologi Malaysia, Malaysia), Andino Maseleno (Universiti Tenaga Nasional, Malaysia), Nasrul Hisyam Nor Muhamad, (Universiti Teknologi Malaysia, Malaysia), and Kamarul Azmi Jasmi (Universiti Teknologi Malaysia, Malaysia) to critically explore learning ethics culture in Islamic education which needs to pay attention to the learning goal. A critical review from referred books and journals which are linked to the topic was employed through searching for google scholar. The finding reveals that learning ethics culture for learning achievement in Islamic education could be indicated into three core paths: achieving divine engagement-based spiritual commitment, assisting skill performance for personal capability development, and applying knowledge for active involvement in the society. This chapter is expected to enrich the conceptual framework of learning acquisition with paying particular attention to learning ethics culture.

Chapter 14 titled "Understanding *Istifādah* (Utilizing Time and Chance) for Personality Development in Islamic Education" by Miftachul Huda (Universiti Pendidikan Sultan Idris, Malaysia), M. Ikhsan Nawawi (Institute for Islamic Studies Agus Salim, Lampung, Indonesia), Liberty (State Institute for Islamic Studies (IAIN) Metro Lampung, Indonesia), Azmil Hashim (Universiti Pendidikan Sultan Idris, Malaysia), Ahmad Kilani Mohamed (Universiti Teknologi Malaysia, Malaysia), Nurazmalail Marni (Universiti Teknologi Malaysia, Malaysia), Muhamad Mustaqim Ahmad (Universiti Kebangsaan Malaysia, Malaysia), Mohd Hilmi Rozali (Universiti Teknologi Malaysia, Malaysia), Andino Maseleno (Universiti Tenaga Nasional, Malaysia), Bushrah Basiron (Universiti Teknologi Malaysia, Malaysia), Noorhaswari Ismail (Universiti Teknologi Malaysia), Afiful Ikhwan (Universitas Muhammadiyah Ponorogo, Indonesia), and Kamarul Azmi Jasmi (Universiti Teknologi Malaysia, Malaysia) attempts to accurately investigate the conception to take a benefit as an ethical foundation of character education, known as the concept of *istifādah*. This refers to the insightful value of al-Zarnūjī's *Ta'lim al-Muta'allim*, containing fundamental principles in the context of education, which has been used by the Islamic boarding school *Pesantren* in Indonesia. This research is employed through literature study using descriptive analysis. The findings reveal that there four core stages to examine *istifādah* for personal development in Islamic education context. Those are integrating *Hikmah* (wisdom) based moral quality for personal development, sustaining continuous discipline, nurturing effective time management, and empowering strategic effort with experiential foundations. Moreover, this study is supposed to give the contribution mainly in supplementing the theoretical basis on personality development in Islamic education context.

In summary, all the chapters with the most recent studies including theoretical articles, conceptual frameworks, and review papers for Islamic education provide the wide range of points of view in developing the curriculum design, philosophical foundation and contemporary application amidst the emerging trends on digital age. These new analytical methods and emerging trends in digital age would be the significant references in giving insights on developing curriculum with the nature, and unique feature continuously enhanced in the operation in designing new operations research methods of teaching and learning on Islamic education. The wide combination of unique tradition on Islamic education curriculum and emerging trends of digital age would be appropriately engaged into the references useful for subsequent research and educational sector in the attempts to build curriculum development. The target audience of this book includes professionals, researchers, faculty, and graduate students with an interest in the research and application of Islamic education in both school programs and tertiary education. Public and private sector education institution will get a tremendous benefit through the wide applications including process, implementation stage, and evaluation analysis committed into strategic operations together with decision making in committing tradition of Islamic education and adopting the valuable insights of emerging trends on digital age. Those include stakeholder; local, state and federal governments who manage the educational institution from school to tertiary education level. The entirely valuable process of curriculum development in Islamic education refers to the attempts on the significant condition in making the transfer process of knowledge into the learners more comprehensive including moral, spiritual and cognitive side. Transmitted into the digital age, the chances will be good opportunities to transform the valuable insights to help disseminate the values within the learners. Both content and material subject in Islamic education curriculum could be fitted into the global demands along with community's needs and demands in order to guide them to run the process well and appropriately.

This book provides the good reference for those involved in expanding the curriculum development and construction within the values transformed into teaching and learning of Islamic education from the global perspectives, in this digital age. The process of improving the curriculum through the various approaches is widely the main concern to enhance the quality assurance in educational process. Commonly used in developing such approaches including analysis, design, and appropriate methods, the entire process has to be involved into totally engaged formation. In Islamic education, the tradition on educational trends becomes a unique and valuable feature to be appropriately enhanced with expanding the embodiment process on experiential learning to evaluate the achievement in resulting the outcomes with balancing not only good spirituality and morality but also quality of cognitive analysis performances. In this digital age, the shift paradigm from physical to virtual basis has given a significant value to ease the process widely in digital devices. Then, the challenges come into the way of Islamic education would respond this trend through enhancing the valuable guidelines on the operational section within wise approach. This edited book will have the number of references to be the useful guidelines on giving the direction on the curriculum enhancement by committing tradition of Islamic education and adopting the valuable insights of emerging trends on digital age.

Miftachul Huda
Universiti Pendidikan Sultan Idris, Malaysia

Jimaain Safar
Universiti Teknologi Malaysia, Malaysia

Ahmad Kilani Mohamed
Universiti Teknologi Malaysia, Malaysia

Kamarul Azmi Jasmi
Universiti Teknologi Malaysia, Malaysia

Bushrah Basiron
Universiti Teknologi Malaysia, Malaysia

Acknowledgment

All editorial team would like to sincerely express our gratitude and appreciation to the Universiti Teknologi Malaysia and the Universiti Pendidikan Sultan Idris (UPSI) Malaysia for the full support. We also would like to acknowledge the constructive supports of our expert advisory panel with their very useful advice. The widely special thanks go to the anonymous referees for their valuables comments and suggestions which greatly improved all the chapter manuscript.

Chapter 1
Islamic Education Today and Yesterday:
Principal Themes and their Potential to Enlighten Western Education

Terence Lovat
University of Newcastle, Australia

ABSTRACT

The chapter will offer a literature review of principal themes to be found in contemporary and earlier sources concerned with distinctive features of Islamic education. It will be found that, among a number of themes, those concerned with the teacher-student relationship and the holistic balance between intellectual and spiritual/moral ends stand out as dominant. Explicit in much contemporary literature and implicit in some earlier sources lies a critique of Western education as more instrumental and so narrower regarding these two features. The chapter will conclude with a summary of the distinctive contribution that Islamic education can make to a Western education contemporaneously in search of a renewed holism and fortified moral component.

INTRODUCTION

Speaking at a seminal gathering of Muslim educators in Saudi Arabia in 1977, Syed Muhammad al-Attas (1979) noted the dilemma facing Muslim education everywhere at the time, namely that Muslims were at risk of losing the essence of Islamic education. So what was this essence, in his view? He spoke mainly of

DOI: 10.4018/978-1-5225-8528-2.ch001

two things: first, the central importance of the nature of the relationship between teacher and student, one characterized as close, personal and loving, so reflecting the role of the teacher as standing in the place of God in the student's formation; and, second, the need for balance between intellectual and broader developmental aims, especially those around moral and spiritual formation. Both of these essential features of Islamic education were seen as being under threat from the dominance of Western educational priorities, ones that were affecting Muslim education both directly in Western settings but also through Western influence in Muslim countries. The inference was that Western educational assumptions are built around more instrumentalist notions of teacher-student relations and more pragmatic, outcomes-based aims rather than those pertaining to holistic human achievement, both of which run counter to the essence of Islamic education. In a word, Islamic education was conceived of as being principally a form of holistic moral education, to be seen in the distinctive ambience of teacher-student relations and the balancing of intellectual with moral and spiritual ends. These principal features can be found as persistent themes among Muslim scholars, today and yesterday, addressing Islamic education's distinctiveness. They are also features that persistently arise in Western education reforms striving to overcome the narrow instrumentalism around which al-Attas's critique is focussed. Among these reforms are those centrally concerned with quality teaching and modes of moral education.

Islamic Education Today: Principal Features

Qais Faryadi (2015) refers to the essence of Islamic education as one:

… based on values and character development. As educators, we are duty bound to be attentive to the needs of students and to help develop their critical thinking and problem-solving skills so that they can shape their future meaningfully. Muslim instructors must understand the true meaning of how students learn … What is the process of moral development in our classrooms? (p. 51)

In other words, Islamic education is morally grounded, holistic and prioritizes the individual learner, rather than being overly concerned with standardized outcomes as ends in themselves, again all posited in contrast to what is seen as the dominant Western priorities. Faryadi regards education as a tool that, above all, serves as an instrument for God's plan for the individual to be dispensed. Midst this process, the teacher stands in the place of God, expressing the essence of God's love for the individual in the form of respect and mutual regard. In this relationship, the teaching-learning process is necessarily facilitative and collaborative, rather than hierarchical:

Islamic philosophy of education stresses that both the teacher and student are equally responsible for the teaching-learning process… It is a complete code of conduct and a collective system of learning and teaching, and also based on the system of justice and brotherhood. (Faryadi, 2015, p. 56)

Again, we find the implicit critique that Islamic education is, in these respects, to be held in contrast with the assumptions dominant in Western education.

Qasi Nusrat Sultana (2012) also draws a contrast between educational assumptions typically found in the West, ones alleged to concentrate principally on intellectual formation, with the main goal to be found in Islamic tradition, one said to focus on whole person development. Furthermore, Seyyed Hossein Nasr (2010) speaks of the emphasis in Islam on the balanced and comprehensive curriculum and the revered role of teaching, especially in facilitating philosophical understanding. Nasr also speaks to the misconception in the modern world about Islamic education that it is oriented to fundamentalism, with special reference to the stereotype in the West about the *madrasah* (Islamic school) being a tool of radical Islam. He outlines how in fact the *madrasah* of early and medieval Islam actually influenced many earlier forms of Western education, especially in relation to dealing positively with other religious traditions through dialogue and debate and through an overall balanced curriculum targeted at holistic development (see also Moulton, 2009).

Zahra al-Zeera (2001) challenges the kind of education most prominent in the West, one that focusses principally on the intellectual and physical aspects of human development. She compares this with what she describes as the methodological aim and structure of Islamic education where the centrality of spiritual and religious factors, along with scholarly ones, are aimed at forming a 'whole and holy' human being. Al-Zeera's philosophy of teaching seems to rest principally on the teacher's capacity to utilize 'transformative methodology', modelling and guiding the student in the kind of learning acquisition that leads to such formation: "For a student to be able to think holistically, she or he must be trained and equipped with methods that both develop the mind and discipline the soul." (p. xxvii) She criticizes the narrow intellectual focus of much education, again implicitly targeted at the dominance of Western assumptions: "By so doing, they create unbalanced human beings that have advanced intellectual abilities, yet spiritually are poor and weak." (p. xxvii) Again, the two principal features of Islamic education noted above come into focus, namely the balance of aims around intellectual through to moral and spiritual ends and the role of the teacher-student relationship in modelling and ensuring this holistic balance. In many ways echoing al-Zeera, Mark Halstead (2004) characterizes the distinctiveness of Islamic education as residing in its focus on individual development, and social and moral education, in addition to the acquisition of knowledge.

Islamic Education Yesterday: Principal Features

The principal features of contemporary Islamic education, as identified above, can be seen to have built on an educational tradition that takes us back to the earliest days of Islam and echoed especially in its medieval "Golden Age" that saw Islam as a leader in the sciences, medicine, philosophy and a raft of other enlightened reforms. Among these reforms lies its conception of the essential features of education. Abdul Fattah Ghuddah (2010) speaks to the conception from the revelation era of the Prophet as a teacher of extraordinary capacity and how this set the scene and provided the model for the distinctiveness of Islamic education. Sami Hamarneh et al. (2017) refer to ways in which this tradition influenced conceptions of health care in early Islam, especially around the virtues proper to the healer, ones like kindness, mercy and compassion which would become synonymous with conceptions of teaching as well. In reference to the latter, Ammar al-Talbi (1993), says of Nasr al-Farabi (870-951CE):

... the whole activity of education, in al-Farabi's view, can be summed up as the acquisition of values, knowledge and practical skills by the individual, within a particular period and a particular culture. The goal of education is to lead the individual to perfection since the human being was created for this purpose, and the goal of humanity's existence in this world is to attain happiness, which is the highest perfection—the absolute good. (p. 356)

Al-Talbi (1993) cites al-Farabi's reference to the virtues that signal success in education as being both rational and ethical, virtues that must be instilled through balanced curriculum and pedagogy aimed at the individual's needs and dispositions, rather than through standardized means. For al-Farabi, education was for all citizens, appropriate to their talents and station. Al-Farabi's philosophy of the teacher role is one akin to that of the imam. 'Imam', in Arabic, connotes one who is well-regarded and whose example, or modelling, is followed. Hence, for al-Farabi, the teacher role is a divine one; the teacher stands before the student in the place of God. The teacher in Islam follows in the footsteps of the Prophet, the human being who, according to Islamic beliefs, stood most unswervingly in the place of God, whose instructions were most wise and who provided the supreme model for all Muslims to follow, including in his modelling of the fundamentals of education.

Reza Ali Nowrozi et al. (2013) show how Ali Ibn Sina (980-1037CE) shared al-Farabi's high-minded view of teaching and education. For Ibn Sina, teaching was best conceived of as a divine quest designed to bring the human to fulfilment according to God's plan. He laid emphasis on the moral nature of teaching and therefore the lofty duties imposed on the teacher to model the morality that lay at the heart of education's goals. Ibn Sina's ideas about teaching methods were so aligned, having not just pragmatic ends in mind but education's moral and spiritual ends as well.

Avner Gil'adi (1992) refers to Hamid al-Ghazali's (1058-1111CE) *Revival of Religious Sciences* as '… one of the most comprehensive and influential essays on ethics and education in medieval Islamic culture' (p. 45). Al-Ghazali, responsible for reformation if not initiation of a form of medieval Sufism, inserted an explicitly mystical element into his educational philosophy but, as with his general position that ungrounded knowledge is pointless, there was a persistent emphasis on education's practical application. It was mystical in that it is guided by divine ordinance, all worthy knowledge emanating from God and so the teacher-student relationship being principally about drawing the student into this fundamental understanding. At the same time, because God is not interested in knowledge that is not applied in practice, the same relationship must be centrally about providing the modelling necessary to ensure optimal student formation. In this regard, al-Ghazali's notion of modelling of virtue centered on the formation of character, instilling good behavior and teaching pupils how to avoid the kind of bad behavior that could result in their immortal loss (Attaran, 1987).

Al-Ghazali displayed a sensitivity to teaching worthy of the most avant-garde pedagogue (Gil'adi, 1992). He emphasized the need for students' imaginative and creative capacities to be stimulated, with memorization and rote learning largely rendered ineffective in drawing students into the ambience where optimal learning was likely to result. Hence, the relationship with the teacher was paramount because the teacher was the best source of stimulation. He encouraged teachers to be, above all, kind and encouraging and to be sparing in punishment (Orak, 2016). He wrote of the need for balance between the academic, the creative and the spiritual in the learning provided, noting especially the importance of music in instilling the disposition most likely to impel a student's imaginative capacity.

Similarly, Walid Ibn Rushd (1126-1198CE) shared much the same perspective on education as his fellow Muslim scholars (Fakhry, 2001). His particular emphasis on virtue formation, conceived of as a divine as well as a human venture, was for him the most important feature of Islamic education. He pondered on the need to develop the essential virtues of good character and civility in the young and, in the obverse, how to teach them best the means of avoiding those dispositions that might threaten such development. Fairly typical of his generation of Muslim scholar, Ibn Rushd always had an eye to the link between knowing and doing. It was not merely the conceptual aspects of good character that were important but their application in practice. For him, to know was to do, and so the principal importance of the teacher-student relationship was that the teacher not only provide the knowledge but model the practice as well. Ibn Rushd arguably moved Islamic education more closely towards Qur'anic conformity than his predecessors, even al-Ghazali, in

5

the sense that Qur'anic knowledge, especially as represented in Shari'a Law, was presented as the perfect way in which all the goals of education could be conceived of, and the essential virtues attained. In turn, these virtues were represented best in the Five Pillars.

Recent Developments in Western Education: An Internal Critique

The implicit critique of Western education by prominent Muslim educators, as seen above, offers cause for reflection on Western education's assumptions and priorities, especially since the birth of universal education and associated systems in the past century and a half. It also impels reflection on some of the internal critiques and debates that have characterized Western educational scholarship throughout the twentieth century and up until recent times.

Universal education in the West coincided with an extensive and intensive turn towards secularization in the nineteenth century, no doubt influencing the shape and form of systems of education at both school and post-school levels. The writings of John Henry Newman (1921, 1927) in England at the time provide some insight into ways in which the secularization imperative affected university education, including in the likes of Oxford University. There is a surfeit of evidence of similar influences in the ways that the public curriculum was shaped in school systems in Western domains (Lovat 2018). In a word, the public curriculum was dominated by those subjects that dealt with knowledge conforming to the empirical sciences, deemed to be hard knowledge, with the humanities in general relegated to the status of soft knowledge and a tendency for moral and religious knowledge to be delegated even further to the realm of the private domain. Progressively throughout the twentieth century, theology became less and less a feature of the public domain, surviving essentially through its attachment to the institutions of religion, mainly the various Christian churches. Similarly in schools, religious and moral education came to be seen increasingly as distinctive features of the church school, rather than constituting a major feature of public education in general. These historical realities no doubt account for much of the critique of Western education to be found in the likes al-Attas, detailed above (1979).

In spite of the general trends noted above, there have been persistent voices in the West that replicate the internal critique of Newman and the external implicit critique of Islamic scholars. John Dewey (1964), for instance, spoke against the exaggerated secularization thesis that emanated from the nineteenth-century, speaking of the overarching need for schooling to prioritize the cultivation of a mind that was directed towards reflectivity and a capacity for moral judiciousness on the part of students. Meanwhile Jurgen Habermas's (1972, 1974) theory of knowing illustrated well the limitations of the knowing resulting from the empirical sciences and the importance of the deeper knowing, including ethical understanding, that emanates from hermeneutical and critical reflection. Moreover, in later work, Habermas (1990, 2002) has pondered on the potential for moral, religious and theological knowing to offer distinctive insights that other knowing lacks, regardless of explicit institutional religious agendas.

The Deweyian and Habermasian critique illustrates the inherent weakness of educational assumptions conceived of merely in instrumentalist outcomes-based or competencies terms, not unlike the critique of Western education seen in the work of al-Attas and other Muslim scholars. It is a critique that has been vindicated in many ways by modern research into quality teaching, authentic pedagogy and various forms of moral education. In a variety of ways and across vastly different research regimes, it has been demonstrated that a holistic and moral approach to education is no mere option if the fullest effects of learning are to be achieved, including but not limited to academic learning.

The Carnegie Corporation's 1994 Task Force on Learning (Carnegie Corporation, 1996) in many ways impelled modern scholarship around the notion of quality teaching. It represented a turning-point in the dominant conceptions placed on the role of the school and the meaning of student achievement. It drew heavily on research uncovering flaws in earlier conceptions, such as those illustrated above, that had developed throughout the nineteenth and twentieth centuries' fairly uncritical elevation of the empirical sciences as representing the knowledge that counted most, if not exclusively. In this respect, the Task Force was crucial in the way it defined the range of learning skills that should be seen as constituting student achievement. By this, it began to blur the boundaries between what would normally be regarded as academic achievement and other core learning pertinent to education.

Beyond the more predictable aspects of intellectual development, the Task Force Report (Carnegie Corporation, 1996) introduced for the modern era notions of learning concerned with communication, empathy, reflection and self-management. Pointing to the inadequacy of surface learning, the report emphasized that effective learning unleashes within the learner the cognitive, affective and moral energies that engage, empower and effect learning of genuine depth. This revealed partially the reliance of Carnegie on new and emerging neuroscientific evidence that forced a revision of what was meant by cognition (see Bruer, 1999). Research insights from the works of Howard Gardner (1983), Robert Sternberg (2007), Daniel Goleman (1996, 2001, 2006) and Antonio Damasio (2003; Damasio & Damasio, 2007; Immordino-Yang & Damasio, 2007), each in their own way determined that cognition cannot be separated from other developmental factors, including those pertaining to emotion, sociality and morality. Hence, notions that pitted academic development against or even as separate from emotional, social and moral development in the way of the old taxonomies have effectively been discredited.

Since the time of the Carnegie Report, there has been a bevy of research and related practice designed to address the more holistic perspectives implicit in it. Work that furthered understanding of quality teaching and authentic pedagogy has dealt with elements of enhanced affectivity, sociality and morality. Fred Newmann and associates (1996) identified a range of teacher-related behaviors associated with strengthened student achievement. Newmann's work centred on identifying the "pedagogical dynamics" required for authentic pedagogy. These dynamics ranged from the instrumental (e.g. sound technique, updated professional development) to the more aesthetic and morally rich. For instance, "catering for diversity" was quite beyond more conventional notions of addressing individual differences. Newmann was referring to the centrality of the respectful and sensitive relationship between teacher and student, so ensuring an ambience where the student feels accepted, understood and valued. Such a conception clearly echoes one of the principal features of Islamic education, today and yesterday, as explicated above. Similarly, Newmann's concept of "school coherence" was of the school that is committed unswervingly to the good of the student, a morally-rich concept connoting dedication, responsibility, generosity and integrity on the part of all stakeholders, especially teachers, a notion also found in the Islamic literature noted above. This led naturally to the ultimate pedagogical dynamic of the "trustful, supportive ambience", deemed to be so indispensable that it would render all teaching ineffective if not attended to. The notion conforms well to Richard Peters' (1981) idea of education being an enterprise where something worthwhile is being intentionally transmitted in a morally acceptable manner and as a site where the "value condition" is indispensably allied to the "knowledge condition", a conjunction of conditions central to the essential features of Islamic education spelled out above.

Karen Osterman's (2010) work speaks further to this conjunction of learning conditions in her conception of the cognition/affect/sociality nexus. This nexus provides evidence of the enhanced learning capacity instilled by environments where students feel they belong and therefore experience strengthened emotional wellbeing. Osterman speaks not only to the need for the curriculum balanced by intellectual and more emotionally engaging work but explicitly to the integral connection between the support provided by the teacher-student relationship and the nature of the pedagogy provided by that teacher. It is the teacher whose pedagogy is characterized by the supportive relationship and balanced learning, as one integrated action, who is most likely to bring students to a new level of academic enhancement. Her work can be seen to instil in an integrated way the dominant features of Islamic education identified above.

In a similar way, Matthew Davidson, Vladimir Khmelkov and Thomas Lickona (2010) illustrate that "moral character" and "performance character" are essential to each other. They say of their "Smart and Good Schools Model of Character Education" that the model:

… focuses on performance character and moral character in an integrated way. The … approach seeks to maximize the power of moral and performance character by viewing character as needed for, and potentially developed from, every act of teaching and learning. (p. 428)

Meanwhile, work by James Arthur (2010; Arthur and Wilson, 2010), in a Templeton Foundation study in the UK, concluded that a concentration on moral character by the teacher who modelled the virtues and values entailed in it could transform the learning environment into one that maximized the potential for learning for all students. Brian Flay and Carol Allred (2010) speak to the notion of academic performance aligned with moral character as the "new basics" needed for successful living but that education systems persistently fail to draw these basics together. Their work shows that character development has clear ramifications for enhanced learning and that, equally, learning pursued in the right environment with the modelling teacher has positive flow on effects for character development. These two basics truly constitute a unity and, again, it is a unity reflected in the perspectives on Islamic education spelled out above.

Jacques Benninga's (Benninga et al., 2006) work provided as firm an empirical endorsement of the link between intellectual and moral development as exists anywhere in educational literature. This work traced the accumulated effects of enhanced performance at Californian basic skills test results when allied with the roll-out of a moral development program, finding that the latter had a clearly positive effect on skills development. Robert Crotty (2010) employed a Habermasian perspective to make sense of the improved academic focus that he saw so clearly demonstrated in the case studies he observed in the Australian Values Education Program, reporting on them patently arising from enhanced and explicit forms of moral/values education.

In many ways, the conceptions of education found in these recent reforms in Western education can be seen to align with the dominant features of Islamic education noted above, rather than with the narrower stereotype of Western education that al-Attas and other Muslim scholars have rightly regarded as oppositional to Islamic education.

The Australian Values Education Program:
A Case Study in Reform

As illustrated above, research insights and findings from the neurosciences, philosophy and pedagogy have coalesced in illustrating the importance of education being holistic in its focus, including in its provision of a balanced curriculum and the centrality of the teacher-student relationship, both central features of Islamic education. As also illustrated, such holistic perspectives are beginning to be seen in Western education regimes that have previously been marked by instrumentalist approaches. In Australia, where late twentieth century education was often characterized by its attention to instrumentalist competencies and outcomes (Mayer, 1992), the most senior political and bureaucratic forces spoke forcefully against this trend when they gathered in 1999 to set the agenda for educational objectives proper for the century to come in light of the most updated research findings available:

Australia's future depends upon each citizen having the necessary knowledge, understanding, skills and values for a productive and rewarding life in an educated, just and open society. High quality schooling is essential to achieving this vision ... Schooling provides a foundation for young Australians' intellectual, physical, social, moral, spiritual and aesthetic development. (MCEETYA, 1999, p. 1)

Furthermore, the same group met some years later to endorse further these directions:

Schools play a vital role in promoting the intellectual, physical, social, emotional, moral, spiritual and aesthetic development and wellbeing of young Australians. (MCEETYA, 2008, p. 4)

The curriculum will enable students to develop knowledge in the disciplines of English, mathematics, science, languages, humanities and the arts; to understand the spiritual, moral and aesthetic dimensions of life; and open up new ways of thinking. (MCEETYA, 2008, p. 13)

In a word, effective schooling connotes an environment that encourages, supports and nurtures the holistic development of its students. There is now an increasing store of evidence from research in moral/values education that the establishment of values-rich ambiences of learning, together with explicit discourse about values in ways that draw on students' deeper learning and reflectivity, has power to transform the patterns of student attitudes and behaviors, including around academic work, towards those more conducive to learning (cf. Noddings, 2002; Arthur, 2003; Rowe,

2004; Campbell et al., 2004; Benninga et al, 2006; Brock et al., 2008; Carr, 2006, 2007, 2010; Nucci & Narvaez, 2008; Lovat, 2010, 2017; Lovat & Clement, 2008a, 2008b, 2008c; Lovat & Toomey, 2009; Lovat et al., 2009, 2010a, 2010b, 2010c, 2011). Explicit approaches to moral and values education is increasingly being seen as an effective way in which a more holistic approach to learning can be achieved, resulting, among other things, in enhanced academic diligence. A persistent feature of such an approach is to be found in the strength of the teacher-student relationship and the balanced, more holistic curriculum, reflecting Islamic education's priorities.

Much of the kind of evidence cited above was captured in the research and practice of the projects emanating from the Australian Values Education Program (DEST, 2003, 2005, 2006; DEEWR, 2008; Lovat et al., 2009). Consistent with Newmann's thesis that the key to effective teaching is in the ambience of learning, project results pointed to the potential for the kind of environment and discourse germane to values education to bring transformational changes in the learning environment of the school and its classrooms, so influencing teacher-student relationships and improved academic diligence emanating from the more holistic approach to learning being taken.

Among much of the data from findings that signalled the practical implications of those neuroscientific insights that point to the circular effect between moral growth and holistic educational development, were the following from the researchers attached to each cluster of schools and responsible for verifying the findings:

Everyone in the classroom exchange, teachers and students alike, became more conscious of trying to be respectful, trying to do their best, and trying to give others a fair go (ie. practise fairness). We also found that by creating an environment where these values were constantly shaping classroom activity, teachers and students were happier, and school was calmer ... student learning was improving. (DEST, 2006, p. 120)

Starting from the premise that schooling educates for the whole child and must necessarily engage a student's heart, mind and actions, effective values education empowers student decision making ... students can be seen to move in stages from growing in knowledge and understanding ... to an increasing clarity and commitment ... and then concerted action in living those values in their personal and community lives. (DEEWR, 2008, p.11)

The inextricable link between an explicit moral focus and intellectual achievement was seen most clearly in the evaluation phase in the *Project to Test and Measure the Impact of Values Education on Student Effects and School Ambience* (Lovat et al., 2009). Among other features, this study focussed on the many claims made across

11

the years of the program about the importance of teacher-student relationships and a balanced approach to learning in instilling student achievement, the same two features that stand out in the summary of Islamic education noted above.

Changes impelled by an explicit values education approach included 'an improved environment' (Lovat, et al., 2009, p. 89), 'an increase in school cohesion', 'greater consistency across the staff in relationships with one another and with students', 'a clearer sense of purpose' (p. 106) and '... the creation of a safer and more caring school community.' (p. 10).

Findings portrayed plausible reasons why this improved school ambience might well lead to enhanced academic diligence. Greater efforts towards self-regulation and improved teacher-student relationships meant that less teaching time was being diverted to behavior management and more time could therefore be devoted to the core business of education. The teachers observed that these new found skills and behaviors, together with the more positive ambience created by it, resulted in students taking more control over routine tasks, so adding to their self-confidence and sense of competence; in turn, this appeared to lead to more independent learning and increased intrinsic motivation. They were also engaging at a greater intellectual depth (pp. 65, 100), taking more responsibility for their own learning and recognising the importance of respecting others' right to learn (p. 10) and were more likely to actively participate in decision-making (p. 15). In turn, changes in student attitude and application to school work led teachers to raise their own expectations for the students (p.100). Put together, and again reflecting on the central features of Islamic education noted above, it was the combination of enhanced teacher-student relationships and the more holistic and balanced approach to learning that worked together to strengthen academic achievement.

Further examples of this conjunction between enhanced teacher-student relations and the more balanced approach to learning impacting on student achievement are to be found in the following comments from teacher researchers:

... as schools give increasing curriculum and teaching emphasis to values education, students become more academically diligent, the school assumes a calmer, more peaceful ambience, better student-teacher relationships are forged, student and teacher wellbeing improves and parents are more engaged with the school. (p. 12)

... the effects of well-crafted values education programs extend to a transformation of student behaviour, teacher-student relationships ... (p. 16)

Teachers' comments suggested that improved relationships between students contributed to a more cooperative and productive learning environment. (p. 37)

The inherent connections between these various facets of behaviour, the positive ambience that results and improved academic focus were summarized in the report as follows:

... there was substantial quantitative and qualitative evidence suggesting that there were observable and measurable improvements in students' academic diligence, including increased attentiveness, a greater capacity to work independently as well as more cooperatively, greater care and effort being invested in schoolwork and students assuming more responsibility for their own learning as well as classroom 'chores'. (Lovat et al., 2009, p. 6)

CONCLUSION

In a day and age characterized by tension, suspicion and misunderstanding between Islamic and Western cultures, if not one of persistent supremacism on the part of the West towards Islam, consideration of an Islamic perspective on education, as conveyed in this paper, could be seen to have potential for enhanced respect and understanding by Western educators of the wisdom inherent in Islam. Judging by the internal critique of Western education's twentieth-century assumptions and priorities by Western educators themselves, it would seem that the critique of al-Attas that began this paper is justified. Furthermore, it would seem that the reforms represented by recent Western education's attempts around quality teaching, authentic pedagogy and forms of moral education, many of them impelled by updated neuroscientific insights, coincide with some of the central features of Islamic education found in today's and yesterday's literature. In this sense, Western education might well spend more time than is customary in considering the wisdom inherent in Islamic education, rather than persisting in the tradition of Western supremacism that tends to relegate Islamic education to one germane to a religious culture of no particular significance to Western education. In this way, a further source of wisdom would be more readily available to Western education, especially to those educators who themselves are critical of the narrow instrumentalism that has characterized it since the birth of the era of empirical science.

REFERENCES

Al-Attas, S. (1979). *Aims and objectives of Islamic education*. Jeddah: Hodder & Stoughton.

Al-Talbi, A. (1993). Al-Farabi (259-339 AH/872-950 AD). *Prospects: The Quarterly Review of Comparative Education, 23*(1/2), 353–372.

Al-Zeera, Z. (2001). *Wholeness and holiness in education: An Islamic perspective.* Herndon, VA: The International Institute of Islamic Thought.

Arthur, J. (2003). *Education with character: The moral economy of schooling.* London: Routledge. doi:10.4324/9780203220139

Arthur, J. (2010). Of good character: Exploration of virtues and values in 3-25 year-olds. Exeter, UK: Imprint Academic.

Arthur, J., & Wilson, K. (2010). New research directions in character and values education in the UK. In T. Lovat, R. Toomey & N. Clement (Eds.), International research handbook on values education and student wellbeing (pp. 339-358). Dordrecht, The Netherlands: Springer. doi:10.1007/978-90-481-8675-4_21

Attaran, M. (1987). *Great Muslim mentors' views about the upbringing of children.* Tehran: Ministry of Education Press.

Benninga, J., Berkowitz, M., Kuehn, P., & Smith, K. (2006). Character and academics: What good schools do. *Phi Delta Kappan, 87*(6), 448–452. doi:10.1177/003172170608700610

Brock, L. L., Nishida, T. K., Chiong, C., Grimm, K. J., & Rimm-Kaufman, S. E. (2008). Children's perceptions of the classroom environment and social and academic performance: A longitudinal analysis of the contribution of the Responsive Classroom approach. *Journal of School Psychology, 46*(2), 129–149. doi:10.1016/j.jsp.2007.02.004 PMID:19083354

Bruer, J. (1999). In search of . . . brain-based education. *Phi Delta Kappan, 80,* 648–657.

Campbell, R. J., Kyriakides, L., Muijs, R. D., & Robinson, W. (2004). Effective teaching and values: Some implications for research and teacher appraisal. *Oxford Review of Education, 30*(4), 451–465. doi:10.1080/0305498042000303955

Carnegie Corporation. (1996). *Years of promise: A comprehensive learning strategy for America's children.* Executive summary. Available at: http://www.carnegie.org/sub/pubs/execsum.html

Carr, D. (2006). Professional and personal values and virtues in education and teaching. *Oxford Review of Education, 32*(2), 171–183. doi:10.1080/03054980600645354

Carr, D. (2007). Character in teaching. *British Journal of Educational Studies*, *55*(4), 369–389. doi:10.1111/j.1467-8527.2007.00386.x

Carr, D. (2010). Personal and professional values in teaching. In T. Lovat, R. Toomey, & N. Clement (Eds.), *International research handbook on values education and student wellbeing* (pp. 63–74). Dordrecht, The Netherlands: Springer. doi:10.1007/978-90-481-8675-4_4

Crotty, R. (2010). Values education as an ethical dilemma about sociability. In T. Lovat, R. Toomey, & N. Clement (Eds.), International research handbook on values education and student wellbeing (pp. 631-644). Dordrecht, the Netherlands: Springer. doi:10.1007/978-90-481-8675-4_36

Damasio, A. R. (2003). *Looking for Spinoza: Joy, sorrow, and the feeling brain*. New York: Harcourt.

Damasio, H., & Damasio, A. (2007). Social conduct, neurobiology, and education. In M. M. Suárez-Orozco (Ed.), *Learning in the global era: International perspectives on globalization and education* (pp. 104–117). Berkeley, CA: The University of California Press and the Ross Institute.

Davidson, M., Khmelkov, V., & Lickona, T. (2010). The power of character: Needed for, and developed from, teaching and learning. In T. Lovat, R. Toomey & N. Clement (Eds.), International research handbook on values education and student wellbeing (pp. 427-454). Dordrecht, The Netherlands: Springer.

DEEWR. (2008). *At the heart of what we do: Values education at the centre of schooling*. Report of the Values Education Good Practice Schools Project – Stage 2. Melbourne: Curriculum Corporation. Available at: http://www.curriculum.edu.au/values/val_vegps2_final_report,26142.html

DEST. (2003). *Values education study* (Executive summary final report). Melbourne: Curriculum Corporation. Available at: http://www.curriculum.edu.au/verve/_resources/VES_Final_Report14Nov.pdf

DEST. (2005). *National framework for values education in Australian schools*. Canberra: Australian Government Department of Education, Science and Training. Available at: http://www.curriculum.edu.au/verve/_resources/Framework_PDF_version_for_the_web.pdf

DEST. (2006). *Implementing the national framework for values education in Australian schools: Report of the Values Education Good Practice Schools Project – Stage 1*. Melbourne: Curriculum Corporation. Available at: http://www.curriculum.edu.au/verve/_resources/VEGPS1_FINAL_REPORT_081106.pdf

Dewey, J. (1964). *John Dewey on education: Selected writings*. New York: Modern Library.

Fakhry, M. (2001). *Averroes: His life and influence*. London: One World Publications.

Faryadi, Q. (2015). An Islamic perspective of teaching philosophy: A personal justification. *Journal of Research & Method in Education*, 5(6), 49–60.

Flay, B., & Aldred, C. (2010). The positive action program: Improving academics, behaviour, and character by teaching comprehensive skills for successful learning and living. In T. Lovat, R. Toomey, & N. Clement (Eds.), *International research handbook on values education and student wellbeing* (pp. 471–502). Dordrecht, The Netherlands: Springer. doi:10.1007/978-90-481-8675-4_28

Gardner, H. (1983). *Frames of mind: The theory of multiple intelligences*. New York: Basic Books.

Ghuddah, A. (2010). *Prophet Muhammad, the teacher: And his teaching methodologies*. Dubai: Zam Zam Publishing.

Gil'adi, A. (2017). *Children of Islam*. Dordrecht, The Netherlands: Springer Nature.

Goleman, D. (1996). *Emotional intelligence: Why it can matter more than IQ*. New York: Bantam Books.

Goleman, D. (2001). *The emotionally intelligent workplace*. San Francisco: Jossey Bass.

Goleman, D. (2006). *Social intelligence: The new science of social relationships*. New York: Bantam Books.

Habermas, J. (1972). *Knowledge and human interests* (J. Shapiro, Trans.). London: Heinemann.

Habermas, J. (1974). *Theory and practice* (J. Viertal, Trans.). London: Heinmann.

Habermas, J. (1990). *Moral consciousness and communicative action* (C. Lenhardt & S. W. Nicholsen, Trans.). Cambridge, MA: Massachusetts Institute of Technology Press.

Halstead, M. (2004). An Islamic concept of education. *Comparative Education*, 40(4), 517–529. doi:10.1080/0305006042000284510

Hamarneh, S., Jochi, S., & Wuli, H. (2017). al-Tabari. In H. Selin (Ed.), Encyclopaedia of the history of science, technology, and medicine in non-Western cultures (pp. 930-931). Dordrecht, The Netherlands: Springer Nature. doi:10.1007/978-94-007-7747-7

Immordino-Yang, M. H., & Damasio, A. R. (2007). We feel, therefore we learn: The relevance of affect and social neuroscience to education. *Mind, Brain and Education: the Official Journal of the International Mind, Brain, and Education Society, 1*(1), 3–10. doi:10.1111/j.1751-228X.2007.00004.x

Lovat, T. (2010). Synergies and balance between values education and quality teaching. *Educational Philosophy and Theory, 42*(4), 489–500. doi:10.1111/j.1469-5812.2008.00469.x

Lovat, T. (2017). Values education as good practice pedagogy: Evidence from Australian empirical research. *Journal of Moral Education, 46*(1), 88–96. doi:10.1080/03057240.2016.1268110

Lovat, T. (2018). Spirituality in Australian education: A legacy of confusion, omission and obstruction. In M. de Souza & L. Halafoff (Eds.), *Re-enchanting education and spiritual wellbeing* (pp. 36–47). London: Routledge.

Lovat, T., & Clement, N. (2008a). The pedagogical imperative of values education. *Journal of Beliefs & Values, 29*(3), 273–285. doi:10.1080/13617670802465821

Lovat, T., & Clement, N. (2008b). Quality teaching and values education: Coalescing for effective learning. *Journal of Moral Education, 37*(1), 1–16. doi:10.1080/03057240701803643

Lovat, T., & Clement, N. (2008c). Values education: Bridging the religious and secular divide. *Journal of Religious Education, 56*, 40–49.

Lovat, T., Clement, N., Dally, K., & Toomey, R. (2010b). Values education as holistic development for all sectors: Researching for effective pedagogy. *Oxford Review of Education, 36*(6), 1–17. doi:10.1080/03054985.2010.501141

Lovat, T., Clement, N., Dally, K., & Toomey, R. (2010c). Addressing issues of religious difference through values education: An Islam instance. *Cambridge Journal of Education, 40*(3), 213–227. doi:10.1080/0305764X.2010.504599

Lovat, T., Dally, K., Clement, N., & Toomey, R. (2011). *Values pedagogy and student achievement: Contemporary research evidence.* Dordrecht, The Netherlands: Springer. doi:10.1007/978-94-007-1563-9

Lovat, T., & Toomey, R. (Eds.). (2009). *Values education and quality teaching: The double helix effect.* Dordrecht, Netherlands: Springer. doi:10.1007/978-1-4020-9962-5

Lovat, T., Toomey, R., & Clement, N. (Eds.). (2010a). *International research handbook on values education and student wellbeing*. Dordrecht, The Netherlands: Springer. doi:10.1007/978-90-481-8675-4

Lovat, T., Toomey, R., Dally, K., & Clement, N. (2009). *Project to test and measure the impact of values education on student effects and school ambience. Report for the Australian Government Department of Education, Employment and Workplace Relations by The University of Newcastle*. Canberra: DEEWR. Available at http://www.curriculum.edu.au/verve/_resources/Project_to_Test_and_Measure_the_Impact_of_Values_Education.pdf

Mayer, E. (Ed.). (n.d.). Key competencies: Report of the committee to advise the Australian Education Council and Ministers of Vocational Education, Employment and Training on employment-related key competencies for post-compulsory education and training. Canberra: AEC & MOVEET. Available at: file:///C:/Users/Tjl607/Downloads/scpp-00129-nat-1992.pdf

MCEETYA. (1999). *Adelaide declaration on national goals for schooling in the twenty-first century*. Canberra: Ministerial Council on Education, Employment, Training and Youth Affairs. Available at: http://www.curriculum.edu.au/mceetya/nationalgoals/

MCEETYA. (2008). *Melbourne declaration on educational goals for young Australians*. Canberra: Ministerial Council on Education, Employment, Training and Youth Affairs. Available at: http://www.curriculum.edu.au/verve/_resources/National_Declaration_on_the_Educational_Goals_for_Young_Australians.pdf

Moulton, J. (2009). Madrasah education: Negotiating belief and value differences in Islamic schools around the world. *Beliefs and Values*, *1*(1), 94–120. doi:10.1891/1942-0617.1.1.94

Nasr, S. (2010). *Islam in the modern world*. New York: Harper One.

Newman, J. H. (1921). *Apologia pro vita sua*. London: Everyman.

Newman, J. H. (1927). *The idea of a university defined and illustrated*. Chicago, IL: Loyola University Press.

Newmann, F., & ... (1996). *Authentic achievement: Restructuring schools for intellectual quality*. San Francisco: Jossey Bass.

Noddings, N. (2002). *Educating moral people: A caring alternative to character education*. New York: Teachers College Press.

Nowrozi, R., Nasrabadi, H., Heshi, K., & Mansoori, H. (2013). An introduction to Avicenna's thoughts on educational methods. *Journal of Education and Practice, 4*(9), 169–176.

Nucci, L., & Narvaez, D. (Eds.). (2008). *Handbook of moral and character education.* New York: Routledge. doi:10.4324/9780203931431

Orak, J. (2016, April). Education from the perspective of Islamic and western scientists (Case study: Ghazali and Plato). *The Turkish Online Journal of Design, Art and Communication,* 127-135.

Osterman, K. (2010). Teacher practice and students' sense of belonging. In T. Lovat, R. Toomey & N. Clement (Eds.), International research handbook on values education and student wellbeing (pp. 239-260). Dordrecht, The Netherlands: Springer.

Peters, R. S. (1981). *Moral development and moral education.* London: George Allen & Unwin.

Rowe, K. (2004). In good hands? The importance of teacher quality. *Educare News, 149,* 4–14.

Sokol, B., Hammond, S., & Berkowitz, M. (2010). The developmental contours of character. In T. Lovat, R. Toomey & N. Clement (Eds.), International research handbook on values education and student wellbeing (pp. 579-604). Dordrecht, The Netherlands: Springer. doi:10.1007/978-90-481-8675-4_33

Sternberg, R. (2007). *Wisdom, intelligence, and creativity synthesized.* New York: Cambridge University Press.

Sultana, Q. (2012). Philosophy of education: An Islamic perspective. *Philosophy and Progress, 51-52,* 10–36.

Zamiri, A. (1998). *History of education of Iran and Islam.* Shiraz, Iran: Sasan Press.

Chapter 2
Transmitting the Teachings of Islam in Contemporary Times:
Glimpses From Prophetic Approach

AbdulGafar Olawale Fahm

iD https://orcid.org/0000-0002-4904-793X

University of Ilorin, Nigeria

ABSTRACT

There is a growing body of literature that recognizes the importance of proper approach to transmission of learning. This is because an effective method teaching always goes a long way in helping to understanding what is being taught. Contemporary discourse on teaching style often stresses either a teacher-centered or student-centered approaches. This chapter takes a critical look at the Prophet Muhammad's methods of teaching Islam to the Companions (Sahaba). This study attempts to understand the intent of these methods used by the Prophet Muhammad and investigates their possible implications. Through historical and descriptive methods examines the primary sources in Islam – the Qur'ān and the life case of the Prophet Muḥammad as presented in his sayings and teachings (Ḥadīth). The study reveals that the prophetic approach, apart from being very effective, is also a very practical method that can be used in our contemporary times and provides a better understanding of the message of Islam and prophetic heritage.

DOI: 10.4018/978-1-5225-8528-2.ch002

INTRODUCTION

There have been quite a number of studies on the methods of teaching Islamic studies (Ahmad, 2001; Ashaari et al., 2012; Assegaf, Zakaria, & Sulaiman, 2012; Don et al., 2012; Göl, 2011; Sardar, 1983). An attempt was also made to determine the contributions of Arabic language in the study and the teaching of Islamic Studies in different higher institutions in the non-Arab world (Ahmad, 2001). In another study, the need for teachers in the discipline to reassess their methodology and approach due to the challenges exerted by globalization and modernity was identified as important (Ashaari et al., 2012). In order to do this, teachers must ensure the continuous relevance of the topics been addressed in class as well as endeavor to effectively respond to contemporary needs of the students in the modern world.

Furthermore, the idea of making *da'wah* a mainstream subject of Islamic Studies in higher institutions of learning has also been examined (Don et al., 2012). This is because the inclusion of *da'wah* is seen as a way of infusing in the student the desire and willingness to proselytize the religion. However, beyond proselytization of Islam, the successful utilization of educational technology for teaching Islamic Studies has also been highlighted (Göl, 2011). An increase availability of data and information in the 21st century through the sophisticated use of technological tools as necessitated the need to explore how educational technology can assist students to construct knowledge in the field of Islamic Studies.

This shows that there has been an attempt to use different methods in impacting the knowledge of Islamic Studies in terms of usage of technology, research-based teaching, and student-centered teaching, teacher-centered teaching, and all these forms can be said to have been combined by the Prophet in an incisive way in teaching his followers. It is against this backdrop that this study attempts to address Prophet Muhammad's method of impacting Islamic teaching on his companions with a view to identifying possible ways this can be implemented in teaching of Islamic studies in higher institutions. Through a look at the primary sources in Islam – the Qur'ān and the *Sunnah* as preserved in his sayings and teachings (Ḥadīth). This study examines these methods used by the Prophet and highlights their possible implications.

Defining Islamic Studies

Islam is the name of a religion whose first Prophet is Adam and last is Prophet Muhammad. It is believed to be the religion of every single genuine Prophet of God since the creation of humankind. Islam, in a technical sense, is a state of peace attained through surrender to God. Islamic Studies, on the other hand, is used to described an area of Theological Sciences which aims to control the social, political, economic, natural and physical aspects of life in service to God. It can also be seen as notions, issues, and advancements from and identified with Islam (Oloyede, 2004). Islamic Studies include all studies that are regarded as originating with Islam or developed and advanced under its influence, be they theological, literary, historical, philosophical or scientific (Siddiqi, 1961)

However, there are others who regard Islamic Studies not as a religious subject and in fact see it as having little to do with classical Islamic Studies as understood by Muslims for centuries. Rather, it is a study that investigates how the religion and culture of Islam influence specific societies and reflect philosophy, law, literature, art, and architecture. Also, it explores how Islam affects social, economic and political relations (Institute of African Studies, 2016). A more comprehensive definition of Islamic Studies holds that it is "the systemic study of Islam both as a religion (*al-din*) and as a civilization (*al-hadarah*) through the integration of the major disciplines of *Usul al-Din* (Islamic theology), *Shari'ah* (divine law), *Akhlaq* (ethics), with *dawah* (Islamic missionary work), Arabic language and its literature, Islamic history and civilization" (Manuty, 2011, p. 138).

There is also the view that two basic approaches exists in defining Islamic Studies; one narrows the definition and the second tends towards a broader definition. The reason for a narrow definition is to maintain quality and to make Islamic Studies distinct from humanities and social sciences. For broader definition, two reasons were also presented; the need to examine the evolution of modern Islam as well as the Islamic textual tradition and its social reality (Dien, 2007). Furthermore, in examining the definition of Islamic Studies, focus on what generally constitute religious sciences in Islam as a way of stating what is Islamic Studies within Islam. The reason for this approach is "to go beyond the discipline's 'Eurocentric' settings and reflect on the provision of the subject within its origins in Islam itself during its long history" (Khir, 2007, p. 257).

Basically, what can be gleaned from the above discussion on the definition of Islamic studies is that it is a disciplined defined based on the subject matter that is being addressed rather than a particular scholarly approach or tradition nor disciplinary approach.

Phases of Development in Islamic Studies

According to Martin, Empey, Arkoun, & Rippin (2016) the phases of the history of Islamic Studies can be divided into; theological beginnings, religious polemics 800-1100, crusade and Cluniac scholarship 1100-1500, reformation, 1500-1650, and discovery and enlightenment 1650-1900. However, it must be noted that the basis of their division is Islam as a topic in the West. Yet, one can still deduce from their analysis the evolution of Islamic Studies as a discipline of study.

Islamic studies can also be said to have emerged as a modern academic discipline primarily through its association with thought and mastery of Oriental Studies or Orientalism. At a point, there was a move from the investigation of the past to the investigation of present day Muslim social orders within particular local settings which eventually lead to Area Studies programmes (Nanji, 1997).

The field of Islamic Studies saw two further significant developments in the second half of the twentieth century. The first was related with the ascent of the purported logical investigation of the historical backdrop of religion that was in the end merged in endeavoring to oblige the investigation of Islam inside the train of religious studies. The second development came to fruition inside the limits of the sociologies when an ever increasing number of sociologists started to be keen on the investigation of "other" societies and people groups. Nonetheless, it is observable that the historical backdrop of Islamic Studies in the West uncovers that "there never was at any time in the past, a fixed paradigm that operated universally; the boundaries were constantly being revised" (Nanji, 1997, p. xvii).

Apart from the identified developmental stages described above, phases of development of Islamic studies can also be seen in countries such as the United States and Canada. The stages of development of the field experienced in the country are probably due to the varieties of scholars working within the broadly defined discipline of Islamic Studies. Among the academic backgrounds of Islamic studies scholars identified are; area studies background, religious studies background, social science background, humanities background and traditional Islamic education followed by a certain period of education in Western institution background (Hermansen, 1991).

Furthermore, a review of various works published from the early 1960s to late 80s demonstrated that the way Islam is understood by scholars is undergoing a process of change due to increased attention to the shaping function of definitions and concepts within the discipline of Islamic studies (Hermansen, 1991). This makes it a bit difficult for Islamic studies to be narrowly confined to strictly religious themes. In addition, this may be the result of the uniqueness of Islamic tradition and a way of unshrouding of the believe that textual studies of a religious tradition will invariably lead to purely religious themes.

Techniques in the Teaching of Islamic Studies

Different techniques have been identified in relation to the teaching of Islamic studies. For instance, the effective use of educational technology (ET) in order to help students of Islamic studies construct knowledge when taught (Göl, 2011). Another study noted that an effective use of ET and research-based teaching can help students to become critical thinkers while studying Islam (Asyafah, 2014; Göl, 2011).

Aqsha et al. (2011) examines the use of inductive and deductive approach in the teaching of Islamic studies. They observed that some Islamic studies teachers create a guide and instructional teaching so that they can achieve their teaching aims more quickly and more effectively. Furthermore, the use of sophisticated multimedia technologies in the teaching of Islamic studies was examined by Jusoh & Jusoff (2009). They pointed out that the use of multimedia in teaching and learning of Islamic studies enhances understanding and increase interest in the field (Jusoh & Jusoff, 2009). It also helps Islamic studies student in the knowledge requires to find the truth. Apart from guiding students towards the truth, it also simultaneously makes teaching and learning process enjoyable. In addition Zedan, Yusoff, & Mohamed (2015) found that Islamic Studies subject can be made interesting and entertaining through use of the multimedia tools. In Islam, the use of modern technology is encouraged as it helps towards the development of positive thinking, the ability to innovate and to trigger the drive for self-improvement (Lubis, Yunus, Lampoh, & Ishak, 2011).

Another technique in the teaching of Islamic studies that has been put forward is the teaching of Islamic studies supplemented with modern science teaching methods. The reason for supplementation with a modern scientific method is to aid the measurement of the success of an eclectic approach in the teaching of Islamic studies. That is student will have options to select a Major in Islamic studies and a minor in social sciences or another way (Ashaari et al., 2012). This has also led to a discussion on the improvement of the teaching of Islamic studies to address a problem base system of teaching method. Examples can be found in the approach of Imam Abu Hanifah (699-767M), Imam Ghazzali (1058–1111M) and Ibn Rushd (1126-1198M) among others, a situation one is faced with a contemporary problem and one has to find a solution. According to Ashaari et al. (2012) a practical example will be in the teaching of Hadith, for instance, the teaching of should not be theoretically and reading of the classical texts only but also supplemented with contemporary rational and critical thinking. In order to do so, students may be instructed to follow these steps: the student will be asked to understand the hadith without referring to the classical texts; he or she refer to classical text in order to understand the different method of understanding certain hadith; he or she compares his understanding of hadith with traditional ulama and find out similarities and differences; then read about its implications in different historical settings; finally, come to a conclusion and put it into the contemporary world (Ashaari et al., 2012). When student are only enjoined to read hadith only from the classical text without critically thinking about its implications in different historical condition, this can discourage productive and creative thinking and may not be able to implement their knowledge in a contemporary setting. That is why a supplement structure in the teaching of Islamic studies should be considered.

Another technique that has been proposed in the teaching of Islamic studies is the use of instructional materials (Sulaiman, 2013). Instructional materials enhance, facilitate and make teaching/learning easy, lively and memorable. They are also materials which the teacher uses in supplementing his teachings for better results. It can include the usage of chalkboard, charts, models, overhead projectors, films, television and computers in the teaching process. Hence, it is not just the' use of tools of technology alone but a systematic, integrated organization of machines (hard wares and soft wares) to solve problems in learning.

The Prophetic Methods

Prophet Muhammad is among the most emulated Prophets of Islam. This can be understood when one assesses properly the continuing influence he has among those who acknowledge him as the last Prophet. The role of Prophet Muhammad (S.A.W.) as educator and model, one who both instructed truth by mouth and showed truth in life is broadly brought about by Muslims as the perfect man. Hence, not exclusively did he go about as educator and model, however his instructing and case constitute a thorough and, from the point of view of numerous Muslims, an ideal code of thought and lead that will remain in effect until the end of time (Royster, 1978). This research identified the techniques used by Prophet Muhammad in teaching his companions about Islam and to encourage the usage of his techniques in teaching Islamic studies in schools. Some of the teaching methods as identified by Abu Ghuddah (2003) are examined below.

The Prophet reported to teach in such a way that he does not bore the listeners (Alshareef, 2007). It is said that when the Prophet would talk, a man tuning in to him, could tally the words on his fingers. The people could say that the Prophet said this, this, this, and this. This means that one would hear a saying from him once or twice, then, if someone is asked about it, one can easily say. In other words, when he would talk, he would not give a marathon address. In addition, the Prophet is also known to be moderate in his teachings. It is said that the Prophet would not always give lectures everyday in order not to bore the people rather he gave lectures occasionally (Alshareef, 2007). As a result, when the Prophey speaks it is always considered a special occasion. From this it can be deduced that in teaching Islamic studies effort should be made not to teach when the students have high tendency to be bored or not focus on what they are been taught.

Another method the Prophet often use when speaking is to talk at the intellectual level of the listener. An *hadith* which can be linked to this point, is the *hadith* of the Prophet when he informed Muadh bn Jabal, "Whoever says *la ilaaha illa Allah Muhammad ur RasulAllah* sincerely from his heart will enter paradise." Muadh said to Rasulullah, "Shouldn't I tell everyone?" The Prophet said, "No, because they will begin to lean, they will become lazy in their deen after that" (Alshareef, 2007). Also, from this point it can be stated that Islamic studies should be taught according to the intelletual capacity of the students.

Equally important is the use of questions and debate. This is called the Socratic method. There was a time the Prophet was said to have inquired from the Sahabahs, "What would be the situation of someone who has a river at his door and every day, five times a day he comes out and he takes a bath in that river? At the end of the day would he have any dirt on himself?" The companions replied, "There would be no dirt on him, O Prophet of Allah." So Rasulullah said, "Similarly there are the five salawat, cleansing the person in this way." So he asked them the question and they were able to make a meaningful conclusion (Alshareef, 2007). This method can also be used in teaching Islamic studies classes instead of the teacher just stating out the major lessons from the topic of the day, the teacher can ask in form of a question in order to aid the students in gaining a deeper understanding of the topic been learnt.

Also, among the method used by the Prophet in teaching the companions is the use of analogies. An example from the Prophet is the *hadith* of the lady who came and got some information about her mother who made a promise to do *Hajj* thereafter died. She asked the Prophet "Should I do Hajj on her behalf?" but the Prophet replied: "If your mother had any debts, would you pay them on her behalf?" The woman said, "Yes." Rasullah said: "The debt owed to Allah is more worthy of being fulfilled and paid off" (Alshareef, 2007). This shows incidence shows a very important lesson in the teaching method of the Prophet which is that in teaching Islamic studies teachers should attempt to use analogies more often to make points clearer to their students.

In like manner is the utilization of outlines or illustrations. The Prophet showed individuals using illustrations on the earth, or on the dust. For example, the Prophet once made a straight line through the sand and after that he made lines to one side and lines to one side, and afterward he mentioned verses relating with the *sabeel* (path) of Allah: "And do not follow the other paths as it will distract you and divide you from the path of Allah" (Alshareef, 2007). This is another important lesson for teacher of Islamic studies. The use of drawing and diagrams to illustrate a point is a good way of making a point clearer to the students.

The Prophet is also said to use gestures while talking. For example, the Prophet once raised his hand saying: "I and the person who deals with the orphans are in heaven, like this" and he joined his fingers (Alshareef, 2007). Another case is the point at which the Prophet was giving one of the companions exhortation, saying: "Be careful with this," (Alshareef, 2007) and he grabbed his tongue. The use of gesture is a very descriptive way of making lessons easy to remember for students and it will have a more lasting effect on the students.

Furthermore, the Prophet use of tangible shows or artifacts to teach. The Prophet would sporadically raise something up that was *haram* as a show to underscore it as *haram*. A case of this is the *hadith* of gold and silk for men. The Prophet raised the actual bits of gold and silk and said: "These are *haram* for the men of my *ummah* and *halāl* for the women of my ummah". Also, when the Prophet was talking about *ghulul* (stealing from the spoils of war), the Prophet as a matter of fact got the war spoils and he started disclosing to the Sahaabaa about the force of the *haram* of taking from the war spoils. He did this holding and remaining adjacent to the war spoils after the fight. So he did not simply make a reference to the war spoils; he really held it up (Alshareef, 2007). Teachers of Islamic studies can also emulate this method in the class on *halal* and *haram* in order to drive home the points of the topic.

Moreover, the Prophet answered questions before they are inquired. A case of this is the point at which the Prophet said: "The Shaytan will come to a person and say, 'Who created this, who created that?' until the Shaytan finally brings the person to the conclusion, 'Who created Allah?' Whoever has this happen to them should recite Surah Ikhlas and should spit three times to the left, dry spit, and say *'a'oodhubillah hi minash shaytan nirajeem*." Teachers of Islamic studies should also be able to predict the questions of the students before they are asked in order to cover as much area as possible on a particular topic. Further, on the same point, the Prophet at times answers with more than what is asked. This is because the Prophet often times pays consideration regarding the questioner's circumstance and endeavoring to perceive how this individual could profit significantly more. A case is the *hadith* about the people who went to the Prophet and got some information about making *wudu* from ocean water. Since they could not drink the ocean water, they were additionally feeling that it was not unadulterated (*tahir*). They needed to know how they should deal with a circumstance where they have drinking water, yet in the event that it is utilized for *wudu*, at that point there would be none left to drink when they are parched. So the Prophet stated: "The water is *tahoor*." (Alshareef, 2007) So one can make *wudu* with ocean water, in any case, the Prophet additionally started discussing fish, that the creatures that die from the water are *halaal* to eat. From this we can deduce that in teaching Islamic studies more explanations can be given beyond what the student asked especially when the context and the conditions of the question and the questioner are well known. In addition to this, is the *hadith* of a woman who asked the Prophet about *Hajj* for her infant. The Prophet inquired, "Who are you all?" The people replied, "We are so and so. Who are you?" The Prophet said, "I am *RasulAllah*." When he said that the lady raised her infant and said, "Is there *Hajj* for this baby?". The Prophet said, "And you will have the reward." In other words, the woman will be rewarded for the effort of taking the infant for *Hajj* (Alshareef, 2007).

From the above point it can be deduced another method of the Prophet which is to transform the inquiry into something that will be of more advantage, A case of this is where a man went to the Prophet and asked, the Prophet, "When is the hour?" The Prophet said, "What have you prepared for that final hour?" This is a redirection of the question to a more significant point. The questioner informed the Prophet, "I haven't prepared a lot of salah and I haven't prepared a lot of zakah (in addition to the *fard*), but I am preparing one thing – my love for Allah and His messenger." The Prophet said, "You will be with who you love" (Alshareef, 2007). This is another lesson to be learnt by teachers of Islamic Studies. They should endeavour to redirect their students' questions to a more significant lesson whenever the need arises. In addition to the point just mentioned is the *hadith* where the Prophet was asked, "What should the *muhrim* (someone in *ihram*) wear?" The Prophet addressed the inquiry by listing what the muhrim ought not wear (Alshareef, 2007).

Also, the Prophet allowed others to answer the questions. An example of this can be found in the *hadith* of a man who came to the Prophet and said that he had a dream that there were mists dribbling nectar and ghee and there was a rope that the Prophet had ascended. At that point the general population had come and one individual scaled the rope, and a few people were gathering a significant number of the droplets that were descending from the mists while others were not gathering that much. Prior to the Prophet replied with an understanding of the dream, Abu Bakr said, "O Prophet! Allow me to interpret it," and the Prophet allowed him to do so. So he disclosed to him that he was right on a few points and mixed up on others. Additionally, there are times where a man would go to the Prophet with a legitimate issue and he would ask a specific Sahabah to get up and make a judgment between them. That companion would state, "O Prophet of Allah, shall I judge between them while you are here, in our midst?" The Prophet would respond in the affirmative (Alshareef, 2007). Teachers of Islamic studies can also use this method to train their students in order for them to become more confident and well grounded in their field of learning.

Teachers of Islamic studies can also make use of the Prophet method of taking advantage of 'teaching moment'. An illustration is the *hadith* of the road kill. It occur during the time of the Prophet that there was, a dead goat with a distortion in its ear and the Prophet passed by it. Others were also passing by, and nobody was focusing on the dead creature, yet the Prophet said, "Look at this. Which one of you would buy this for such and such amount of money?" They said, "O Prophet, even if it were alive, no one would want to pay money for it. Because of its deformity, no one would care for it, and how much more so since it's dead." The Prophet then said, "Verily, the *dunya* is more worthless to Allah than this animal is to you. Just like you don't care about this, in the sight of Allah, this dunya is less worthy than this." So the Prophet used the occasion to teach what the dunya should mean to a

Muslim (Alshareef, 2007). Teachers of Islamic studies can make use of this method in order to not to make their classes monotonous. Another case is the hadith of the lady tossing her kid into the fire. This lady had lost her child who she was still nursing, for a drawn out stretch of time. So when the mother at last found the kid, she took the child and quickly began feeding the child. The Sahabahs were looking and were astonished at the gigantic love of this mother. Right then and there, the Prophet said, "Do you imagine that this woman would throw this child into the fire and burn it alive?" They said, "O Prophet of Allah, she would never do it so long as she is capable of protecting the child from that." The Prophet then said, "Indeed, Allah is more merciful to His slaves than this woman to her child" (Alshareef, 2007).

Notably, the Prophet also use oaths for emphasis. The Prophet would emphasize something by swearing by Allah. This happens in numerous *ahadith* and some *suwar* found in the Qur'an, for example, Surah Ash-Shams, *was shamsee wa-duhaahaa*; Surah Al-Lail, *wal layli ee-dha yagh-shaa*, and Surah ad-Dhuha, *wad duhaa*, among others. This means that teachers of Islamic studies can also use oath to drive home their points when teaching or in order to make their students pay attention to what they are been taught.

Likewise, the Prophet used repetition. In the event that there was something that required accentuation, the Prophet would repeat it three times. A companion of the Prophet Anas bn Malik said the Prophet would rehash something three times so individuals would comprehend what he was stating. A case of this is the *hadith* where the Prophet said: "Beware and destroyed from the ankles of the Hellfire" (Alshareef, 2007). It was said that the reason the Prophet repeated the words couple of times was that the Sahaba had ceased for *Salat-ul-Fajr*, and the Prophet was coming behind them. When he neared them he saw that as a result of the coldness of the night, they were not completely cleaning their feet and getting the water onto their lower legs when making wudu. The Prophet drew close to them, raised his voice, and said: "Beware and destroyed from the ankles of the Hellfire. Beware and destroyed from the ankles of the Hellfire. Beware and destroyed from the ankles of the Hellfire" (Alshareef, 2007). This shows that the use of repetition to draw attention of student can be a viable technique in the teaching of Islamic studies.

Equally important is the use of silence employed by the Prophet. It is said that the Prophet would call the audience by his name, making him focus, without noting or explaining to the audience why he is calling him. For instance, the *hadith* of Muadh where he is going with the Prophet and he said, "O Muadh," and Muadh said, "I am consistently here for you and constant in your assistance", and after that the Prophet stayed calm. They went on and after that the Prophet again said, "O Muadh," and then Muadh gave the same response and then the Prophet stayed calm. A little time passed and for a third time the Prophet said, "O Muadh," and Muadh said "I am consistently here for you and constant in your assistance" (Alshareef, 2007). This method can also be used by the teacher of Islamic studies when they notice there is or are students who are not paying attention in class. This can easily make the student concentrate more in class.

The Prophet at times also make physical contact when speaking as a method of getting his listeners attention. The Prophet would hold the hand or the shoulder of the individual to whom he was talking, to influence the individual to focus. An example is the *hadith* where the Prophet said "Be in this *dunya* as if you are a stranger or a passer by." The Prophet was holding the shoulders of the *sahabah* when he said this (Alshareef, 2007). Another case from the *hadith* is the point at which a kid came and solicited authorization from the Prophet to commit *zina*. The Prophet disclosed to him with questions, not answers. The Prophet clarified it with the goal that the kid arrived at the conclusions himself and toward the finish of the discourse the Prophet touched the kid's chest setting his hand close to the kid's heart and made *du'aa* for him. From these two episodes the importance of physical contact can be seen. Teachers of Islamic Studies can therefore use this method as a way of making sure the students pay attention in their classes.

The use of cliffhangers is another method of the Prophet. This entails the Prophet saying something and the audience members would not by any stretch of the imagination comprehend information disclosed. At that point he would pause and allow them to consider it, in this way expanding their want to learn it and tune in to his clarification (Alshareef, 2007). This method can also be adopted by Islamic studies teachers. It serves as a way of getting the attention of the students as well as making the students think about what is been said.

As a matter of fact, the Prophet adopted the use of stories of the past. This is a commonly used method that can also be seen in the Qur'an and the Sunnah. This shows that stories are an effective way through students in Islamic studies can be made to learn and not forget the topic they are been taught in class.

The Prophet at times also make effort to paying attention to focus groups. For example he would give careful consideration to ladies' instruction by reproving them and giving them counsel specifically. This, as well as give careful consideration to the youngsters. Additionally, the Prophet would go into the *souk* (market) addressing businessmen. The Prophet would pay special attention to specific groups who share same challenges or problem. In Islamic studies class, this method can also be adopted by focusing on specific group of people within the class when discussing a topic that they can easily relate with or that they might be really interested in. Furthermore, it is said that in the *Eid* sermon, the Prophet would give the *khutbah* and after that go before the ladies and give a discourse straightforwardly to them and for them. Also, there was a time the women complained to the Prophet that the men do not give them the opportunity to learn from him as much as they like and the Prophet resolve the situation by dedicating a specific day to them with the goal that he could teach them and they could uninhibitedly pose their inquiries (Alshareef, 2007).

Also, the Prophet used anger. An example from the Prophet about utilizing displeasure to instruct or make a point is the point at which the general population endeavored to do *shifaa'* for a lady who had stolen and have her pardoned from the punishment. The Prophet utilized outrage at that time to make the point that she cannot be pardoned (Alshareef, 2007). This shows that anger can also be an important tool that can come in handy when teaching students of Islamic Studies. Through anger the teacher can get the attention of the student and make them pay more attention in class.

CONCLUSION

This study, through a look at a primary source in Islam, the life example of the Prophet Muḥammad, has shown that there are many methods that could be adopted in making Islamic Studies more teacher-centered. In this paper we focused on the techniques used by the Prophet. It is believed that these methods offer a clearer understanding of the Prophet and thus lead to better way of teaching Islamic Studies.

In following the methods of the Prophet, one is able to reach a deeper understanding of the message and this helps in the transmission of Islamic knowledge. These methods of the Prophet are also important and required in educating Islamic Studies students, especially because of the saying of the Prophet that "If one person gets guided on your hands, it is better for you than a red she-camel" (Alshareef, 2007). This is to show the far-reaching effect of an appropriate technique in teaching generally and to Islamic Studies specifically. However, it is important to state here that, all of these techniques should not be adopted but alternated according to the demands of specific topics. There has to be a mix of these methods, since, the constant use one method could bore the students as well.

REFERENCES

Abu Ghuddah, A. (2003). *Prophet Muhammad–the teacher and his teaching methodologies*. Karachi: Zam Zam Publishers.

Ahmad, I. (2001). Teaching Islamic Studies in the Non-Arab World: With or Without Arabic? *Journal of Muslim Minority Affairs*, *21*(2), 273–285. doi:10.1080/1360200120092851

Alshareef, M. (2007). *Humanity's Teacher: 21 Teaching Techniques of the Prophet.* Retrieved August 31, 2017, from http://www.khutbah.com/en/ed_know/humanity_teacher.php

Aqsha, M., Melor, M., Tajul, M., & Mohd, N. (2011). The Perception and Method in Teaching and Learning Islamic Education. *International Journal of Education and Information Technologies*, *5*(1).

Ashaari, M. F., Ismail, Z., Puteh, A., Samsudin, M. A., Ismail, M., Kawangit, R., ... Ramzi, M. I. (2012). An Assessment of Teaching and Learning Methodology in Islamic Studies. *Procedia: Social and Behavioral Sciences*, *59*, 618–626. doi:10.1016/j.sbspro.2012.09.322

Assegaf, A. R., Zakaria, A. R., & Sulaiman, A. M. (2012). *The Closer Bridge towards Islamic Studies in Higher Education in Malaysia and Indonesia.* Creative Education; doi:10.4236/ce.2012.326149

Asyafah, A. (2014). Research based instruction in the teaching of islamic education. *SpringerPlus*, *3*(1), 755. doi:10.1186/2193-1801-3-755 PMID:25674481

Don, A. G., Muhamat Kawangit, R., Hamjah, S. H., Sham, M. F., Nasir, B., Asha'ari, M. F., & Abd Ghani, M. Z. (2012). Teaching Da'wah as Islamic studies (Teds) in higher learning institutions: Malaysian experience. *Advances in Natural and Applied Sciences, 6*. Retrieved from http://www.scopus.com/inward/record.url?eid=2-s2.0-84876710611&partnerID=40&md5=5505f41683251e6b765bec1531003443

Fears of Radicalism Constrains Scholars. (2007, February 9). *Times Higher Education Supplement.*

Göl, A. (2011). Constructing Knowledge: An Effective Use of Educational Technology for Teaching Islamic Studies in the UK. *Education and Information Technologies*, *17*(4), 399–416. doi:10.100710639-011-9165-9

Hermansen, M. K. (1991). The State of the Art of Islamic Studies in the United States and Canada. *Islamic Culture, 65*(1).

Institute of African Studies. (n.d.). *Islamic Studies.* Retrieved February 20, 2016, from http://www.ias.uni-bayreuth.de/en/subject_groups/h_islamic_studies/

Juhnke, G. A., Watts, R. E., Guerra, N. S., & Hsieh, P. (2009). Using Prayer as an Intervention with Clients who are Substance Abusing and Addicted who Self-Identify Personal Faith in God and Prayer as Recovery Resources. *Journal of Addictions & Offender Counseling*, *30*(1), 16–23. doi:10.1002/j.2161-1874.2009.tb00053.x

Jusoh & Jusoff. (2009). Using Multimedia in Teaching Islamic Studies. *Journal Media and Communication Studies, 1.*

Khir, B. M. S. (2007). Islamic Studies within Islam: Definition Approaches and Challenges of Modernity. *Journal of Beliefs & Values, 28*(3), 257–266. doi:10.1080/13617670701712430

Lubis, M. A., Yunus, M. M., Lampoh, A. A., & Ishak, N. M. (2011). The Use of ICT in Teaching Islamic Subjects in Brunei Darussalam. *International Journal of Education and Information Technologies, 1*(5).

Manuty, M. N. (2011). Islamic Studies Programs in Malaysia's Higher Learning Institutions: Responses to Contemporary Challenges of Modernity, Globalization and Post 9/11. In K. Bustamam-Ahmad & P. Jory (Eds.), *Islamic Studies and Islamic Education in Contemporary Southeast Asia.* Kuala Lumpur: Yayasan Ilmuwan.

Martin, R. C., Empey, H. J., Arkoun, M., & Rippin, A. (2016). Islamic Studies. In *The Oxford Encyclopedia of the Islamic World. Oxford Islamic Studies Online.* Retrieved from http://www.oxfordislamicstudies.com/article/opr/t236/e0395

Nanji, A. (1997). Mapping Islamic studies: Genealogy. *Continuity and Change, 38.*

Oloyede, I. O. (2004). The Place of Arabic and Islamic Studies in a Globalized Nation. *NATAIS Journal of the Nigeria Association of Teachers of Arabic and Islamic Studies, 7.*

Royster, J. E. (1978). Muhammad as Teacher and Exemplar. *The Muslim World, 68*(4), 235–258. doi:10.1111/j.1478-1913.1978.tb03359.x

Sardar, Z. (1983). The Future of Islamic Studies. *Islamic Culture, 57*(3).

Siddiqi, M. Z. (1961). Islamic Studies: Their Significance and Importance. *Islamic Culture, 35.*

Sulaiman, K. O. (2013). The Use of Instructional Materials for Effective Learning of Islamic Studies. *Jihāt Al-Islām, 6*(2).

Zedan, A. M., Yusoff, M. Y. Z. B. M., & Mohamed, M. R. (2015). An Innovative Teaching Method in Islamic Studies: The Use of PowerPoint in University of Malaya as Case Study. *Procedia: Social and Behavioral Sciences, 182,* 543–549. doi:10.1016/j.sbspro.2015.04.776

Chapter 3
Education Piety:
Special Reference to Abu Hamid al-Ghazali and Abdul Rahman Ibn Khaldun

Benaouda Bensaid
İstanbul Sabahattin Zaim University, Turkey

Salah Machouche
International Islamic University Malaysia, Malaysia

ABSTRACT

This chapter seeks to explore the crossroads between learning in Islam and spirituality, and also the methods according to which Muslim instructors shape students' experiences in a context of piety development. This study also examines questions pertaining to the concept of spirituality in education, methods pedagogic principles that further merge spiritual discipline with knowledge acquisition. The theoretical research draws on the textual analysis of early works of Muslim scholars, more specifically on Abdul Ibn Khaldun and Abu Hamid al-Ghazali, given their prominent positions in the history of Muslim education. This study shows that the Islamic learning has always taken students' spiritual growth for granted and has, despite differences of practices across Muslim regions, always maintained the refining of learners' spiritual character.

INTRODUCTION

Given that learning in Islam is intertwined with the holistic understanding of human nature, its origin, abilities, and faculties, and more importantly perhaps, with its spiritual consciousness and experience, it allocates weight to spirituality in all of

DOI: 10.4018/978-1-5225-8528-2.ch003

the branches of knowledge in such a way that it is fundamentally integrated with the Islamic worldview, purposes and higher ends of learning. Having said that, one should note that spirituality does not seek to substitute forms and methods of knowledge building; rather supports and sustains its health, growth and flourishing in milieus of reasoning and thinking. The instruction of spirituality however varies depending on the respective domains of learning inquiry, whether with respect to beliefs and religion, nature or human association (umr'an). Hence, the assessment of the spirituality of learning is held through a number of indexes including students' performance, cultivated discipline, quality of human conduct and moral performance, community engagement, community's interrelationships among community learners, and so forth.

This study investigates the influence of Muslim spirituality on learning. It draws on primary texts to gain insight in the converging areas of spirituality and learning as well as methods of assessment. This study also addresses other questions pertaining to the effective position of spirituality in Islamic learning including the following; how did early Muslim scholars conceptualized and managed the integration of spirituality into teaching curriculum; and further, how did they monitor and assess students' spiritual development while ensuring progress in education. Particularly, this chapter seeks to explore the experience of spiritual integration in learning in the work of the fourteenth Century notorious Muslim scholar, 'Abdul Rahman Ibn Khaldun. In this context, we will discuss spirituality according to Ibn Khaldun, its impact in both learning and personal development; the relationships associating spirituality with various branches of knowledge, in addition to the ways and means according to which instructors interwoven spirituality with learning and were able to assess spirituality in the learning space and on students' overall development. The research on the crossroads between education and spirituality is interesting in view of the fact that latter continues to play a central role in the historical development of Islamic learning. Reference to Ibn Khaldun highlights interestingly relevant themes such the position of belief and religion in the process of learning, as well as the impacts of interrelated concepts like human nature (*fitrah*), divine rules, and orders of thinking, moral values, and so forth.

Concept of Muslim Spirituality

The meaning of spirituality remains notoriously difficult to define with many opinions and (Wright, p.7). Swinton (2001) sees it as 'a personal and social process that refers to the ideas, concepts, attitudes and behaviours that derive from a person's, or a community's interpretation of their experiences of the spirit' (p.20)[1]. Elkins et al. define it as 'a way of being and experiencing that comes through awareness of a transcendental dimension and that is characterized by certain identifiable values in regard to self, others, nature, life and whatever one considers to be ultimate' (Elkins, Hedstrom, Hughes, Leaf, and Saunders, 4: 5-18).[2] For some others, spirituality in the field of learning and education is concerned with the realm of human life that is non-judgmental and integrated, and is about belonging, connectedness, meaning and purpose (Lantieri, 2001).

Some believe that "spirituality is a way of living, an attitude, a motivation, recurrent integration, and sustained conviction. It is a style, process and method by which one lives in light of the goal. It is an awakening which starts with looking within ourselves for self-discovery and continues on until one realizes that we are an integral part of the natural world"[3]. Others believes that "Spirituality is understood to be the determination that the mind produces, known as power of the will, to refine our human behaviours through our own positive thoughts, words and actions"[4]. These views however, are not very keen to consider faith; they do not view religion as part of the definition, and seek to restrict access to while placing their focus rather on human consciousness, personal experience, and beauty manifested in the natural environment as a principal axis of spirituality. Their attention to the divine (God) is thus marginalised or under some pretexts omitted altogether.

Yet, in spite of the fundamental differences surrounding the definition, role and position of spirituality in science and society, many researchers appreciate its relevance and significance in the broad areas of knowledge in general. In the field of health sciences for instance, nursing accommodates spirituality aid for the treatment of patients and their healthy recovery (Speck, 2007, p.16). A growing scholarship is advocating for spirituality to be recognized as an independent and well-defined science in areas of health care, nursing, business and management, and is increasingly seen as such (Giacalone & Jurkiewicz, p.3-28). With respect to the field of education, some define its main purpose as the development of the whole person and the respect all of needs of a human's innate nature (*fitrah*) including the spiritual, emotional, intellectual, physical, social, and aesthetic (Baba & Zayed 2015, p.52).

In Islam, however, spirituality has special meaning and character. The Qur'an makes reference to human nature using two words interchangeably; *ruh* (soul, breath, spirit) which appears on twenty-one occasions, and *nafs* (self) on more than two hundred sixty times. According to the Qur'an, humans do not have access to the domain of *ruh* and only have limited knowledge of it (Qur'an, 17: 85). In such context, spirituality may be defined as the very religion that regulates the relationship man and his Creator, himself, fellow humans, and with the surrounding environment. According to Nasr, the term *ruḥaniyyah* is the prevalent translation for spirituality; the term deriving from *al-ruh*, meaning spiritus. Nasr defined spirituality as the inner spiritual dimension of traditional religions dealing with the noumenal and which can only be experienced directly, and which extends beyond mental categories, but is not anti-intellectual (Nasr 2006: 209). This view finds support in Muslim spiritual tradition, which presupposes that neglect of the soul results in corruption of the inner being, and its eventual decline (Qur'an, 91: 9-10). For Nasr, Muslim spirituality is reflected in the presence of a relationship with Allah, affecting individual self-worth, a sense of meaning, and connectedness with others and nature (Nasr, 1997).

Spirituality may also be described as the state of heart (mind) and as a relationship with God, His signs, and with both animate and inanimate creatures. Spirituality denotes the human experience, whose essence and form are construed according to their obedience and submission to the divine, by way of certain beliefs, worship (rituals), social relations, and knowledge of the world. Spirituality capitalizes on one's inner purification; this involves observing the inner states of the self, known notoriously as the acts of the heart, and necessitates nourishing and preserving good manners and favourable states of the heart, exercising specific disciplines leading to the embodiment of virtuous habits (*riyadah mahmudah*), in addition to other additional requirements. Likewise, Islamic spirituality is not a subjectively self-centred experience that cannot be captured; it is rather a self-experience built on well-defined foundations and clear theoretical frame provided by the teachings of Islam. Spirituality may escape the parameters of broad generalizations and quantifying measurement emphasized in the conventional scientific methodology, there are however, other alternatives allowing for the objective explanation, expression, and transmission of its experience.

The composition of Islamic spirituality of belief, rituals, behaviour, knowledge of the world, and subjective experiences causes its relevance to science and its instruction not an impossible task. The measures which may be taken in the very beginning to make this integration process successful and indispensable to science is considering the field of instructed subject. The instructors should pay due attention to the connections established between spirituality and science with different learning contexts. With the multitude of science subjects, those inter-connections would vary from field to another and from subject to another. Moving towards that direction, Islamic spirituality is set to inculcate God's presence through appreciating the universe as a sign of divine creation, or as Sajjad noted:

"it must be such that faith is infused into the whole of his personality, creating in him an emotional attachment to Islam which enables him to follow the Qur'an and the Sunnah and be governed by the Islamic system of values" (Ashraf, 1979, p. 74).

Having said that, Muslim spirituality is not restricted to the fold of rituals and worship, nor is it contained in specific religious services. This is because worship is broad and allows for diverse contributions allowing one to address spirituality through natural sciences and vice versa. Pre-modern scientific discovery often joined between the organic unity of science and spiritual knowledge (Bakar, 2008, p. 61). Similarly, the review of spiritually driven science content in the field of education and instruction should not be viewed as a disguised escape or diverted from empirical objectivity, or a course causing disinterest in the study of the universe or exploitation of natural resources. On the contrary, the active presence of spirituality in the instruction of science assumes a profound position and role, further strengthening the spiritual credibility, validity, rational harmony, and contribution to shaping meaningful and constructive explanations and solutions. The questions and answers of spirituality, which are a complex interaction of beliefs, worldview, concept of life, values, tastes, and actions, are expected to generate active engagement and a strong motivation and commitment to understand nature and solve it mysteries, grasp the signs of the divine in the world, appreciate the divine blessing and bounties, and accordingly use and manage environmental resources wisely and responsibly.

Nature and Objectives of Islamic Learning

Islamic learning is set to be holistic drawing fundamentally from the divine revelation, echoing compatibility with the needs of *fitrah* of man (Qur'an, 30:30), purposive and moderate, establishing a caring attitude towards environment as advocated in the Qur'an. Zarnuji (d.1223) noted that the purpose of learning is consistently connected to the spiritual path. He noted, "Learning is striving for the good will of God, the future life, removing ignorance from himself and from the rest of ignorant, reviving of religion, the survival of Islam"[5]. In the first world conference on Islamic education held in City of Makkah in the year of 1977 with a participation of 313 scholars, attendees define Islamic education as follows: " Education should cater for the growth of man in all its aspects: spiritual, intellectual, imaginative, physical, scientific, linguistic, both individually and collectively and motivate all these aspects towards goodness and the attainment of perfection"[6]. This definition sees learning not as mere transfer of information rather a holistic planned program drawing from the divine revelation. The experience of learning is two folds; experience of skills and technical knowledge, and another of values embodied in religion.[7]

The above echo the Prophetic wisdom which goes as follows: "My Lord disciplined me and disciplined me well." In a different narration, Prophet Muhammad is reported to have said, "Three persons will get their reward double. [One is] a person who has a slave girl and he educates her properly and teacher her good manners properly [without violence] and then manumits and marries her. Such a person will get a double reward"[8]. On this occasion, Naqib al-Attas defines *adab* as "the discipline of body, mind, and soul, the discipline that assures the recognition and acknowledgement of one's proper place in relation to one's self, society, and community; the recognition of and acknowledgment one's proper place in relation, physical, intellectual and spiritual capacities and potentials."[9] The frame and functions of knowledge transcend the conventional material terms and boundaries, or as Kazmi noted, the function of knowledge to change the world is exactly what is subverted by reducing knowledge to a commodity. For him, knowledge is valued above all by its ability to facilitate the production of more and more commodities for our endless orgy of consumption[10].

Muslim scholars used different terms to express their appreciation of the rich content of learning, among those, are '*ta'lim*' (instruction) (Qur'an, 62: 2), *tarbiyah* (nurturing), *ta'dib* (discipline, inculcation of *adab*), *tadris* (teaching), *tawjih* (orientation), *irshad* (guidance) as used in the *Treatise for the Seekers of Guidance* (*Risalat al-Mustarshidin*) of al-Muhasibi, *tazkiyah* (purification) (Qur'an, 2: 151), *tanshi'ah* (bring-up), *ri'ayah* (caring protection), tahdhib (disciplining) as used in *Tahdhīb al-Akhlaq* by Ibn Miskawayh (d.1030), *Tahdhib al-Akhlaq* of al-Jahiz (d. 869), or Management of the affairs of young students, *Siyasat al-sibyan wa tadbirihim* by al-Qayrawānī (d.980), Spiritual education and training of Muhammad al-Anbari (d.1240) in (*Risalat fi-riyadah al-sibyan wa-ta'limihim wa-ta'dibihim*). In his work known as "*Ta'lim al-muta'alimin*" "Students' instruction", Zarnuji used the term "*ta'lim*", meaning cultivating and instructing. Following the discussion of the merits knowledge and virtue of pursuing paths of learning and sharing it, Ibn Jamā'ah (d. 1333) concluded that much of the excellence is restricted to the fulfilment of some of the following conditions. He states:

"Know, however, that everything we have said about the excellence of knowledge and the scholars applies only to scholars who practice what they know, who are reverent and God-fearing, who by their knowledge seek the face of God and proximity to Him in the gardens of Paradise. It does not apply to those who seek knowledge with evil intent, malicious designs, or worldly purposes such as fame, wealth, or vying in number of disciples and students"[11].

Islamic learning is intertwined with the revealed word '*Iqra*'' (read). According to Ibn Khaldun, instructing children the Qur'an is a symbol of Islam. He noted that different regions of the Muslim world adhere to this practice. He stated: "Muslims have, and practice, such instruction in all their cities, because it imbues hearts with a firm belief (in Islam) and its articles of faith, which are (derived) from the verses of the Qur'an and certain Prophetic traditions. The Qur'an has become the basis of instruction, the foundation for all habits that may be acquired later on"[12]. The word *iqra'* connotes different meanings including for instance, reading, reading a written thing, reciting with or without having script, proclaiming, conveying, calling, rehearsing, transmitting, delivering a message, collecting together, putting or arranging together part to part or portion to portion[13].

Early Arabic lexicons make reference to other linguistic meanings such as '*tafaqquh*' (understanding), '*dirasa*' (study), conception (*himl*), birth (*wilādah*), time (*waqt*), remembrance (*tadhakkur*), practice of ritual (*tannasuk*), and nearness (*dunuw*)[14]. Both the text and context of the Qur'an provided the main direction of the *iqra* activity, especially when made in fundamental reference to the name of the Lord (Qur'an, 96:1). The Islamic Revelation points to fundamental learning directions such as the need to drawing near the divine, devotion to Him, seeking His pleasure, and keeping remembrance of Him. It also introduces fundamental conceptual framework of learning characterised with reference to human nature, human thinking, human perception, accountability, motivation, purpose of life, sound thinking, thinking styles, in addition to core universal moral and ethical codes, social value system, and illustrations of vicegerenship leadership role man in the universe.

Madrasah is an auxiliary institution to Masjid, and has throughout the history of Islamic learning helped learning acquire its identity, shape and structure. According to Makdisi, Madrasa evolved through three subsequent stages, Masjid (*halaqa*: the nucleus format of learning), Masjid complex or Khan, and Madrassa[15]. It was initially established as a charitable trust under the law of *waqf (endowment)*. Madrassa can also be described as spiritually grounded institution, *pious endowment,* and endowment for piety generously established through acts of kindness and religious devotion[16]. Early notable Madrasas were established across different regions of the Muslim world like al-Qarawiyin in Morocco, Azhar in Egypt, al-Madrasah al-Nizamiyah al-Nizamiyah in Bagdad. The madrasa sought to achieve numerous objectives including spreading and supporting Sunni theology, understanding of the law, fighting against heretical and subversive tenets of the *Shi'ites*.[17] The development of Madrasas also points out to an actually serious business of the Muslim community allowing teachers and preachers advancing community religious knowledge whether in the field of Qur'anic memorization and comprehension, theology, jurisprudence, preaching and regulating personal and collective morality and ethics thorough sermon and fatwas, in addition to standing on guard for the community's orthodox in beliefs and spirituality.

In this context of the several tasks of madrasa, one should shed light on the endowment *waqf* system. Interestingly, most of *kuttab/katatib,* initiated for primary education, was set as philanthropic institutions having the Qur'an as its centre of in its curriculum.[18] In the beginning, students would learn and memorize the Qur'an, and thus learning by heart formed the starting point[19]. In Madrasa, learning was generally viewed as an activity of nobility as it seeks to nurture learners to become better Muslim individuals and vicegerents of God, especially with regards to the core belief that life success depends on fulfilling vicegerency (*khilafah*), and on the developing of *al-'abd* and *khalifah*. Islamic education appears to be specifically designed as fine tool to empower Muslims' knowledge and skills while ensuring developing the moral and spiritual personality of *al-'Abd* (servant of God) and *khalifah* (vicegerent).

Organization of learning in Madarsa is not necessarily uniform, as the founder has total freedom to choose specific courses[20]. However, the study of different methods of organization shows that there is a fine rationality behind the choices being made, which gives priority to spiritual development while also considering the emotional, intellectual, physical, moral, social, and other potentials.[21] Spiritual learning involves the study and practice of beliefs (*tawhid*), rules and laws (*aḥkām*), and morals (*akhlāq*). Qurayshi noted the following: "The teaching of the Qur'an was combined with instructions in more important religious precepts and usages, the proper response to Azan (call to prayer), ablution and prayer in Mosque congregation" [22].

At the madrasah, the legal values are well observed. For example, the individual obligation is given priority before the collective obligation. Also, the nobleness of the subject is also of significant importance. This makes learning and memorization of the Qur'an as the first choice made in Madrasas across the different regions of the Muslim world, with slight differences however, on placing the learning of Arabic as an auxiliary science[23]. Many traditional examples witnessed to this attention, like that of Imam al-Shafi'i (d. 820) who used to follow the following learning sequence from down prayer until noon hour: Qur'an, Hadith, revision, discussion, disputation and Arabic and its branches[24].

The institution of Madrasa provides students with conveniently interactive environment allowing for developing of positive relationships among themselves and with their teachers. Teachers are not regarded simply as agent of knowledge transmission, but more as, father, and discipliners (*murabbi*) facilitating students' growth and success. Good character and conduct of teachers are indispensable of effective learning and model influence. The author of *al-'iqd al-farid* (The Unique Necklace), Ibn 'Abd Rabbih, reported the advice of 'Amr bin 'Utbah to his child's instructor: "You should know that your reform [nurture] my child starting with your self-reform first. For them (students), good is what you do, and evil is that which you abandon"[25]. This explains why instructors are carefully selected, with close scrutiny of their good character, intellectual abilities, and professional skills. Muslim educationists provided a detailed list of the instructor's main tasks and responsibilities. 'Abul Barakat Badr al-Dīn al-Ghazī (d. 984 AH) makes reference to the following tasks list:

"He should after observing from the learner goodness (khayr) and reliability showing his maturity (rushd), discipline him gradually through prophetic manners, the pleased morals etiquettes, purification of the self through inculcating manners, fine and hidden behaviour (daqa'iq al-khafiyah). He should train himself the way of protection and maintenance in all his affairs; the inners and outer[26]. One of the many steps for teachers to take towards achieving this objective is to train learners

through words and acts of sincerity, truthfulness, good intention, and God-fearing all the times until death.[27]

Teachers are excepted explain to their students the ways according to which observing of those inner and outer manners improve their learning capabilities and achieving of happiness (*sa'ada*) and excellence. The spiritual exercise according to Abul Barakat shall open the door of knowledge before learners, widen his chest (*yansharih al-sadr*), gush from his heart sources of wisdom and intuitions, help gain blessings in his affairs/states and acts, be guided to rightness (*isabah*) of speech, acts, and judgments, increase his devotion with less attachment to life, help him adhere to permanent life and "reject" the temporary[28].

However, the learning and assessment of spirituality do not go without hurdles. The discipliner needs to look after students' personality development and fining of character alongside developing appropriate educational measures which take into account the learning program (subject), character of students, institutional rules and policies, and community social customs. The discipliner may for instance use "*the social life care*" to foster effective relationship with students while extending moral and spiritual care outside circles of learning, both direct and indirect observation (*muraqabah*) of learners' behaviour and of soft skills like altruistic intuitions and physiognomy (*firasah*). Engaging in communal religious activities is also used as a way to assess learners' spirituality as is the case of the five congregation prayer, fasting, performing night prayers, funeral prayers, circles of *dhikr* (God's remembrance).

Attention to time is of paramount importance in the domain of spirituality in learning. Often, educators would begin their classes just after the dawn prayer. Shafi'i (d. 204 AH/820) used to start his Qur'an classes right after dawn-prayer up until sunrise, and would continue on with the tradition of Prophet Muhammad followed by subjects of grammar, poetry and scientific methods.[29] Learning circles also remind learners of the divine; Teachers begin their lessons with prayers, praise of God and imploring His support, seeking the divine guidance, and would close with supplication for himself, teachers, scholars, parents, students and the community, and offering of prayers to the Prophet Muhammad[30]. According to the tradition, it is recommended to be in a state of physical purity with clean body and clothing, and is also preferable to dress up in white[31]. Some of the learning practices like use of wooden tablet for Qur'an memorization may be seen as an experience for understanding purity. As soon as the student masters memorization of the verses by heart, he is expected to clean his own wooden tablet with fine white clay. The tablet of the Qur'an should be handled with care. Throughout this learning experience, the student would be exposed repeatedly to the name of Allah, purification, consciousness of sin, and recording and erasing.

Views on Spiritual Learning

According to Muslim educationists, spiritual life leads to all life happiness and prosperity, and hence should be given utmost priority. In their scholarly works, they would generally draw on the hadith of the Prophet Muhammad on the need for purity of intentions to remind the reader of the critical position intention plays in the process of learning. However, in spite of their agreement on the need for purity in learning and scholarship, they appear to hold various views on how spirituality be instructed or incorporated in learning. In the following section, we shall present some of those views according to two prominent Muslim scholars, namely, Imam Abu Hamid al-Ghazali (d. 1111) and 'Abdul Rahman Ibn Khaldun (d. 1406).

Imam Abu Hamid al-Ghazali

The view of Ghazali on spirituality are often discussed with reference to modes of thinking, epistemological foundations of human knowledge, self-purification experience, withdrawal, renouncing of worldly life, self-purification, and criticism of the philosophical worldviews and modes of thinking. Less however, is devoted to the examination of the instruction of spirituality, especially with reference to science and scientific curriculum. The fruits of al-Ghazali's contribution to the field of spirituality are to be extended to this specific area where spirituality is intertwined with scientific instruction. The letter sent to al-Ghazali by his student asking him for guidance on identify which of the disciplines most deserves sacrifice, is useful in the future, and would bring solace after death[32]. Student's question highlights the need for spiritual cultivation. Perusing knowledge and being successful in that task does not by itself yield happiness in life. In responding, al-Ghazali reminded his disciple about honouring knowledge through practice in life. Al-Ghazali quoted the narrated dream about the mystic Sheikh Abu al-Qasim ibn Muhammad al-Junayd al-Baghdadi (d. 910) who was asked: "what good news?" He replied: "Explanation misses the mark and pointers come to nought. Nothing is of use [in the afterlife], but the prostrations we performed in the dead [mid] of night"[33]. Al-Ghazali cautions his student from bankruptcy of deeds, empty-handedness of the pure and righteous state of the soul. Stressing on spiritual states, al-Ghazali reminded his student about his motives of learning.

"O son! How many nights have you spent drilling yourself in knowledge and poring over books and denying yourself sleep? I do not know what is your motivation! If it is to gain worldly goods, to attract worldly ephemera, to acquire worldly appointment and compete with your peers and colleagues, then woe on you, and your judgment [the hereafter]: woe on you! But if your aim in this is to reinvigorate the prophet's

law (blessing and peace be upon him), to rectify your moral principles, and to break the domination of your (evil) soul, then blessings upon you" [34].

An overview of al-Ghazali's works ''*Ihya' 'ulum al-din*' (The Revival of the religious sciences), '*Ayyuha al-walad*' (Letter to a disciple), '*al-tafakkur fi-khalq Allah*' (Mediating Allah's creation), '*al-Munqidh min al-ḍalal*' (Deliverance from error), and '*Mīzān al-ʿamal*' (Criterion for *action*) showed that al-Ghazali approached spirituality as vital medicine for eternal life, unlike the medicine given by conventional physicians and which focus on treating the temporary body for temporary life. Spiritual medicine needs utmost attention and higher priority; this, renders learning it an obligation for those who understand the true meaning of life (*kulli dhī-lubb*)[35]. For al-Ghazali, spiritual medicine is not a field open for myths, irrationality, undetected subjectivity, unsubstantiated perceptions, which fall far from the reach of learning and examination. It is rather knowledge, faculties and skills which are to be learned, applied and instructed throughout different directions. The first direction is concerned with spiritual illnesses where the investigation of the causes, preparing of therapies, and alongside, the description of the implementation, represents core issues. The second pertains to acquisition and nurturing of excellent manners and morality. Al-Ghazali highlighted few important operations with regards to spiritual instruction: premise of ability of changing character through self-discipline (*riyada*), illustration of the ways of moral acquisition, methods of knowing the details of refining morality (*tahdhib*), ways of knowing the signs or symptoms of heart sickness, ways through which man rediscovers self-spiritual imperfections, evidences and ways of healing, signs of good character, ways of instruction and disciplining children at the early age, conditions of the will, and premises of purification (*mujahada*)[36].

As far as the etiquettes of children instruction the children, al-Ghazali draws attention to nurturing the perception of the hereafter in the heart and overtaking four major obstacles, namely, wealth (*mal*), reputation (*jah*), imitation (*taqlid*), and disobedience (*ma'siyah*)[37]. To sustain spiritual development, al-Ghazali suggests other preventive steps through which the disciple would develop a spiritual fire wall using four practices, namely, voluntary hunger (jūʿ/fasting), isolation (*khalwah*), silence (*ṣamt*), and night awakening (*sahar*)[38]. Al-Ghazali also enlisted a dozens of functions to be maintained in learning[39]. The first among which, is prioritizing the purification of the self from moral imperfections, reducing connections to the worldly material life, extensive planning of beneficial learning, learning of the ways leading to the most noble sciences, and striving for the highest objectives, closeness to God.[40]

The presence of spirituality in other works of al-Ghazali cannot be over-sighted. In his work "*al-tafakkur fi-khalq Allah*" (Meditating upon Allah's creation), for example, al-Ghazali provided an explanation of the meaning, forms, and processes of human thinking. He argues that the formation of innately spiritual states is a necessary step through which generating knowledge passes[41]. Spirituality in this context resembles a form of thinking on the signs of the Creator according to the outlook of *tawḥīd*. It may also be regarded as a form of activation of thinking and remembrance (*tafakkur and dhikr*) leading to understanding the creation of human, earth and what exists on it, and what is in between heaven and earth, and wonders of heavens. His conclusion was that those who think about all those wonderful creatures as manifestations of God's will, will be guided. In contrast, those who narrow down their thinking and reduce the existence of those wonderful creatures into material mechanical relations of causes and effect, they would suffer and deviate from the divine path.[42]

In this section, we need also to highlight the relevance of al-Ghazali's spiritual journey and experience as presented in his work "*al-Munqidh min al-Dalal*" (The Deliverance from error) to the spiritual learning and its epistemological context. The experience of al-Ghazali in this regard is interesting in the way he was able to extract his own spiritual practice and path which he did not acquire through imitation of some spiritual masters as is the general case with spiritual seekers, rather through choosing a hard path of rigorous investigation and examination of the four branches of knowledge, spiritual and intellectual claims made in theses filed. Those include: Muslim theologians, who allege that they are men of independent judgment and reasoning; the Batinites, who claim to be the unique possessors of *taʿlim* and the privileged recipients of knowledge acquired from the Infallible Imam; The Philosophers, who maintain that they are men of logic and apodictic demonstration, and the Sufis (mystics), who claim to be the familiars people with the Divine Presence and men of mystic vision and illumination.[43] Ghazali's years of mystical practice led him to final convictions that shaped the substance and direction of his entire life. Al-Ghazali found out that, unlike other groups, the Sufi consciousness and modes of thinking perfectly combine theoretical knowledge and practice. For him, the Sufi mode of life reflects a unique devotional way to follow: "*the way to God Most High, their mode of life is the best of all, their way the most direct of ways, and their ethic the purest.*"[44] It is not only about the practical life of this group but also their approach to knowledge and its goals. Al-Ghazali reported the aim of their knowledge as follows: "… is to lop off the obstacles present in the soul and to rid oneself of its reprehensible habits and vicious qualities in order to attain thereby a heart empty of all save God and adorned with the constant remembrance of God"[45].

The works of al-Ghazali show that spirituality is a fundamental ingredient of learning at all levels and feeds the acquisition of knowledge while engaging into practical life. Learning spirituality is an organized work corresponding the development of the children, path seekers, students, or adult learners. It is gradually initiated through the three major ways of creed, worship rituals, and morality. Spirituality here is not conceived as unchangeable aspect of human personality, rather, as a dimension reflects life dynamicity and is to be learned through rigorous methodology that takes in account all that compose the existence of man and his personality. Means and ways to spirituality also vary in their kinds and arrangements; they unite however around their fundamental objective, and leading to one common destination, that is, following the steps of Prophet Muhammad and drawing near to the Divine.

'Abdul Rahman Ibn Khaldun

Ibn Khaldun is largely known for his contribution to political thought, economics, education, and critic of historiography. Exploring the topic of spirituality in the works of Ibn Khaldun will show that his thought is deep nourished by Islamic spiritual consciousness. His early education, academic career, professions, perception of knowledge (epistemology), theory of human association, analysis of the rise and decline of civilization, pedagogy and educational theory, are all applied fields of spirituality. Therefore, the discussion of Ibn Khaldun's perspective on the subject would be useful to the understanding of the dynamics of belief in the context of complex changing life. The roots of spirituality in the thinking of Ibn Khaldun can be traced back to his family, early education, and more particularly, to the influence of his father and teachers.

"Ibn Khaldun's first and most influential teacher was his father, a man who shaped Ibn Khaldun's appreciation for Sufism and who inspired him to think independently. It was his father who would have encouraged the young the precocious Ibn Khaldun to go out in search of good teachers"[46].

His father's dedication to scholarly pursuit and aversion to all official positions represented significant starting point in his education career. In his autobiography[47] Ibn Khaldun describes his learning of the Qur'an under the guidance of Shaykh 'Abdullah Muhammad bin Sa'd Bural al-Ansarī[48]. Ibn Khaldun then describes the learning program while giving details about the life of his teacher of rational sciences (philosophy), known as Muhammad Ibn Ibrahim al-Abili (d.1356), and draws attention to some major works he studied by heart like fiqh, hadith, language, philosophy, poetry, and logics. Ibn Khaldun' exposure to various branches of knowledge led him to conclude that learning is not just about knowledge acquisition, but also about seeking the path of virtue, or as he noted: "Since my early age, I continued to strive to seek knowledge with eagerness to acquire virtues"[49].

Throughout his early education, Ibn Khaldun made space to spiritual thought and experience. In his (*Healing of the seeker and refinement of the matters*), he offers an interesting insight into the mystical learning and pedagogy, especially as to whether the seeker would need a guiding master in learning and practice of the *fiqh al-batin* or *tasawwuf* (mysticism). It appears that Ibn Khaldun's familiarity with the field of spirituality is visible through numerous intellectual areas such as his critic of the philosophers' false claim about attaining happiness; that is in fact the main concern of the discipline of spirituality. Ibn Khaldun's point is that philosophers assume "that happiness consists in the perception of existence with the help of such conclusions (if, at the same time, such perception is) combined with the improvement of the soul and the soul's acceptance of a virtuous character. Even if no religious law had been revealed (to help man to distinguish between virtue and vice), they think the (acquisition of virtue) possible by man because he is able to distinguish between vice and virtue in (his) actions by means of his intellect, his (ability to) speculate, and his natural inclination toward praiseworthy actions, his natural disinclination for blameworthy actions".[50]

Ibn Khaldun also explained that the philosopher's aspired certainty is not achievable. The abstract conceptions cannot be considered with certainty as so objects in the real world. Certainty in this case can be claimed through direct observation which is possible only in the sensational and tangible world. Ibn Khaldun criticizes the worldview and methods of logic demonstration of philosophers considering them as:

"The (opinion) the (philosophers) hold is wrong in all of its aspects. They refer all existentia to the first intellect and are satisfied with (the theory of the first intellect) in their progress toward the Necessary One (the Deity) which means that they disregard all of the degrees of the divine creation beyond the (first intellect). Existence, however, is too broad to (be explained by so narrow a view). "And He creates what you do not know." (Qur'an, 16: 8). The philosophers, who restrict themselves to affirming the intellect and neglect everything beyond it, are in a way comparable, to physicists [naturalists] who restrict themselves to affirming the body and who disregard (both) soul and intellect in the belief that there is nothing beyond the body in (God's) wise plan concerning (the world of) existence"[51].

Another interesting point is the spiritual environment Ibn Khaldun has had. His spiritual experience was not the result of mystical path or order. His works on mysticism, however, show that he had clear understanding of the phenomenon. In his Muqaddimah, he devoted an entire chapter to the discussion of mysticism in which he showed that not only was he writing about the intellectual history of Tasawwuf as a branch of knowledge and Muslim spiritual experience, but also stirring an interesting debate on the legitimacy and relevance of the Sufi methods to learning. Ibn Khaldun experienced a four years period of seclusion at the castle of Qal'at Ibn Salamāh (Algeria) in the mid of 1378, far from all official responsibilities, and that appears to have supplied him with an ideal environment of meditation and self-reflection. Ibn Khaldun reports the following: "I have stayed their four years avoiding myself all the occupations and I have started writing this book. I have completed writing the Prolegomena (al-Muqaddimah) in this wonderful and strange way, inspired to me in that retreat, ideas and meanings and expressions flowing on my mind till they became mature and its results are achieved."[52]

Spiritual experience is not, as advocated generally, necessarily framed within the matrix of seclusion, but may be the result of intense social relations and life. The result of Ibn Khaldun's spirituality can be seen throughout his professional life. His critic of the courts judges in Egypt and his decision to clean up some of the corruption occurring in the court of Egypt through impartial implementation of the rule of God, all must have been a result of a spiritual purity. In *al-Ta'rīf*, Ibn Khaldun reported the following: "I spoke out the truth for that, and I curbed the influence of the people of the lusts and ignorance". He added, "I assumed the charge of the honourable post and spared no effort to apply impartially the laws of God, undeterred either by influence or menace."[53] The other level of spirituality pertains to his perception of learning, knowledge and human thinking. He argues that humans are created different because of their divinely endowed intellectual abilities. The ability to think is used to find a way to earn sustenance, cooperate with fellow humans and building of society[54]. To stress those educational elements to help develop a balanced personality, Ibn Khaldun draws on the letter of Harun al-Rashid (d. 809) to Khalaf ibn al-Ahmar (d. 796) on how to educate his son Muhammad al-Amin (d. 813) in which he stressed on the importance of conceding the spiritual and moral dimensions of learning with an emphasis on teaching Qur'an recitation prior to any other subject. The instruction goes as follows:

"Teach him to read the Quran. Educate him in history. Let him narrate poems and teach him the Sunnah of the Prophet. Give him insight into the proper occasions for speech and how to begin a speech. Forbid him from excessive laughter except at the appropriate time. Accustom him to honour his relatives when they come to him and to give the military leaders places of honour when they come to his salon. Do not waste time without any knowledge that is useful to teach him. But to do so without vexing him with depression because it will kill his mind clarity. Do not be too soft later he will get to like leisure and become used to it. As much as possible, correct him kindly and gently" [55.]

Ibn Khaldun argued that learning must be explained within the framework that views human thinking through its broader scope. For him, God endowed man with various abilities to perceive the essence of things and their accidents which are subject to change and alteration. Those abilities however, can be organized in two groups: sensational abilities performed through the five senses and those which fall in the territory of power of thinking. In his words, "Living beings may obtain consciousness of things that are outside their essence through the external senses God has given them, that is, the senses of hearing, vision, smell, taste, and touch. Man has this advantage over the other beings that he may perceive things outside his essence through his ability to think, which is something beyond his senses".[56]

According to Ibn Khaldun, learning activity consists of three major cognitive periods: consciousness, ability of understanding, and skills. He sees the role of scientific instruction as a craft with the immediate objective of developing and acquiring skills. For him, this perception is supported by the fact that *"skill in a science, knowledge of its diverse aspects, and mastery of it are the result of a habit which enables its possessor to comprehend all the basic principles of that particular science, to become acquainted with its problems, and to evolve the details of it from its principles. As long as such a habit has not been obtained, skill in a particular discipline is not forthcoming"*.[57] Acknowledging existence of a period of consciousness that proceeds the immediate process of skills instruction should be used as evidence in supports of the role and presence of spirituality in learning.

Interestingly, Ibn Khaldun has crowned the acquisition of knowledge with purification of the soul. For him, human ability to think, is active according to three distinct levels: knowledge of values (knowledge of good and evil) develops what he called *the 'discerning intelligence'*, knowledge of nature, forms, accidents of things (objects) forges *'empirical intelligence'*, and theoretical knowledge builds *'speculative intelligence'*. These three forms of intelligence, as understood from the world of Ibn Khaldun, are not limited to mere acquisitions of information about the human world, but rather have greater value identified as "the possibility of reaching perfection of soul"[58].

Moreover, human personality is not subject to division because of its original make up as one single entity with various composites and abilities. For Ibn Khaldun, human perception is of two folds: perception of sciences and matters of knowledge (*'ulum and ma'arif*) and perception of the persisting innate states. Thus, learners are not a mere pot to which information or technical knowledge is to be poured in. This is because there is another critical side to be nurtured through generating positive and good spiritual feelings. For Ibn Khaldun, humans perceive both "sciences and matters of knowledge, and these may be certain, hypothetical, doubtful, or imaginary. Also, he can perceive "states" persisting in himself, such as joy and grief, anxiety and relaxation, satisfaction, anger, patience, gratefulness, and similar things". [59]

Another dimension to the story of Ibn Khaldun's perspective of spirituality with relation to learning is may be found in his critic of some pseudo-sciences on the basis their weak foundations and harms caused to spirituality and intellect, like astrology. "The sciences (of philosophy, astrology, and alchemy) occur in civilization. They are much cultivated in the cities. The harm they (can) do to religion is great. Therefore, it is necessary that we make it clear what they are about and that we reveal what the right attitude concerning them (should be)."[60] The argument of Ibn Khaldun against those types of knowledge are placed according to three different levels; the spiritual, cognitive, epistemological, and social. The word "religion" or "*al-din*" he used refers primarily to faith and spirituality. In the case of philosophical rebuttal, his first pretext is the corruption it causes to religious beliefs. Ibn Khaldun took his critic even to highest levels as shown in his disqualification of philosophy to achieve its supreme claimed objective namely, attainment of happiness. He states:

"It should be known that the (opinion) the (philosophers) hold is wrong in all its aspects. They refer all existentia to the first intellect and are satisfied with (the theory of the first intellect) in their progress toward the Necessary One (the Deity). This means that they disregard all the degrees of divine creation beyond the (first intellect). Existence, however, is too wide to (be explained by so narrow a view)"[61].

The above shows that Ibn Khaldun adopted a path similar to al-Ghazali through which he was able to underscore the importance of spirituality in learning. The experiences of both in the field of spirituality appears to be clearly variant, they however, share common understanding with regards to the human nature and needs. Ibn Khaldun addressed spirituality at different levels of human experience: emotional, cognitive, behavioural, and social. His novel disciplines of '*umran* (human association) also provided him another widow on the important position of spiritual learning from different angles. His main contribution is manifested through use of critical thinking in the domain of theory of knowledge to establish solid arguments on the significance of spirituality in the process of learning. He sees consciousness and self-innate states as pre-constituents of learning. Successful learning needs to meet the deep needs of humans and show them the way to eternal happiness.

INCORPORATING SPIRITUALITY INTO LEARNING

At the outset, one need to state that Islam rather holistically approaches the discussion of human cognitive and sensational abilities, seeing them an one unified entity of man. The Qur'an (30: 30) uses the term *al-fitrah* (human innate nature or predisposition) in the context of ordering humankind to follow the true religion. *Fitrah* embraces all creational ingredients pertaining to the human personality, physical, emotional, mental and behavioural. These interconnected elements work together under the auspice of the heart, or as Ghazali calls it, "The King" commanding other servant faculties. This view finds support in the Qur'an and the tradition of Prophet Muhammad. The term "*qalb*" (heart) appears 104 times in the Qur'an with three attributed cognitive functions: understanding (*ta'aqqul*), thinking deep (*tafaqquh*), and observing consequences (*tadabbur*). Prophet Muhammad said: "Beware! There is a piece of flesh in the body if it becomes good (reformed) the whole body becomes good but if it gets spoilt the whole body gets spoilt and that is the heart"[62]. Early Muslim education works shows that the work of integration is performed through use of various means and forms, taking into consideration the curriculum content (subjects of learning), the gradual stages of the of the child personality development.

The eve of spirituality in Islamic learning can be noted in the recommendation put forward by wealthy parents and rulers to the teacher (*mu'allim/mu'adib*). Integration does not start in the learning institution (*madrasa*), but with the parents' very decisions and choices. Parents' recommendations made for the private instructors showed that their prime objectives is to prepare their children for the afterlife in addition to knowledge and other skills would help them to encounter life challenges like language and calculus. This is found not only among ordinary people, but also those rich parents like merchants and rulers.

The history of Muslim learning show that branches of knowledge is subject to the Islamic worldview defining the concept of man, nature, origin, role in life, and destiny. Infusing spirituality into scientific instruction is made at two distinct levels; institutional, performed by the learning institution (*madrasa*) via delivery of programs, subjects, policies, and so on. The ideal key word that sums up the core objective of Islamic education is perhaps "the making of *al-khalifah*" "servant of God". There is yet another key concept of *ta'mir* of the making of *al-'umran*" or human association. The second critical task is set favourable conditions to facilitate fulfilment of the primary objectives. In the setting of the classroom however, the infusion of spirituality is carried out through the instructor' personality, the content of the subject matter, and method of delivery. The word "*aql al-mazid*" reflects learners' maturity fed through perceptions, spiritual states and skills. Therefore, acquiring knowledge in its "information format" should not be seen as the ultimate objective in Islam for it is a mean for deep change that renders learners' life pure approximation to God. Knowledge is set to generate sound and positive innate states which is called today knowledge embodiment, an understanding that one should practice what she learnt.[63]

However, The features and approaches of Islamic learning vary across regions and from Madrasa institution to another. However, the view of learning worldview, content, curriculum, instruction methodologies, textbooks, institution management, and regulations help provide typical pattern of Islamic education. For example, the priority given to the learning of the Qur'an shows that nurturing of child spirituality is regarded as fundamental learning objective. Parents see that early Quran memorization helps strengthen his spiritual and mortal immunity in later periods of development. In his *Qanun al-Ta'wil,* Ibn al-'Arabi describes his early learning experience as a merciful decree of the divine, when at the age of nine, his father assigned him to a Qur'an instructor to memorize the Qur'an and read it fluently.[64]

Given that textbooks serve the integration process of spirituality in learning, Muslim scholars have adopted several mediums for that sake. For example, they use effective introductions to remind learner on how the merits of spirituality in learning, like their comparison between the beauty of eternal life and the deception of worldly life. Textbooks were designed to help learners understand and believe that they should be servant of God. Textbook is to produce sophisticated learning features supported with the principle of unity of knowledge. Textbooks do not isolate different branches of knowledge from one and another, but rather bridge and connect them while also focus on specific streams of specialization. For instance, religious learning is not separated from other branches of knowledge pertaining to the study of natural world. Calculations (*hisab*) is thought early stage along the Qur'an and hadith. All branches of knowledge are to achieve the pleasure and satisfaction of the Creator.

Significant portion of learning regulations goes to instructors, their personal traits, character, knowledge and skills. Nawawi (d.1277), explains the requirements and manners of the instructor which he divided in two three categories[65]: self-character addressing the good manners to be inculcated by the instructor. In it, he highlighted the purity of intention and of seeking the pleasure of God as first requirement in addition to other inner and outer morals acts. The second category concerns the self-intellectual and professional development. According to this category, the instructor should make continuous and utmost effort to excel in reading, studying, commenting and criticizing, revising, and writing books without misestimating useful sources of knowledge. The last category relates to the art and methodology of delivery. He identifies thirty six rules and principles, among which, is to adopt gradual learning approach following prophetic styles (al-adab al-sunniyah), self-discipline with inner manners (riyadat al-nafs bil-adab wa-daqa'iq al-khafiya). The instructor in this category need to motivate learners through encouraging them about the virtues of knowledge and its reward keep his way of teaching lenient, away from harsh treatment or punishment. He should also equip his students with intellectual and methodological tools of learning to help them build arguments, understand and find the truth.

ASSESSMENT OF SPIRITUAL IN LEARNING

In broader sense, spiritual assessment is construed on the fundamental principle of *tawhid*, Prophethood, human nature, and the meaning and purpose of life. Madrasa institution provides a convenient field of teaching, learning and assessing. Life in madrasah and the routine interactions with instructors help develop a closer look at learners' spirituality. The most useful and direct assessment is held through observing the fulfilment of religious rituals in which the five obligatory prayers represent top priority. Students need to observe collective congregational prayers in Masjid. According to Ibn Khaldun, the informative knowledge of worship obligations need to be translated into grounded skills and habits in the soul which generates necessary knowledge and lead to happiness.[66] The three stations of learning can be articulated through keen observation and monitoring. Knowledge of the instructor about the child is not restricted to *madrasah* physical site. The instructor should investigate the child's conditions through consultation with parents and guardian of the child if he is an orphan, especially when the child's learning performance and behaviour are poor.[67]

The external influence can be traced through observing students' companionship and brotherhood. Prophet Muhammad is reported to have said: "A man is upon the religion of his best friend, so let one of you look at whom he befriends."[68] Al-Ghazali's advice is to seek friends with good thinking way, good conduct, not to be a sinners, or innovators not to be a worldly addicted person.[69] Companionship also refers to the studentship stage of the student where the later would manage to complete his basic course of law and begun graduate training by adhering to one particular scholar on a steady basis[70]. Moral habits present the big screen reflecting students' spiritual states. With knowledge and experience, the instructor can detect students' good behaviour like altruism, patience, truthfulness, thankfulness, humility, kindness, forgiveness, and so on and would discover evil deeds like greed, arrogance, and so forth.

CONCLUSION

For Islam, spirituality is not alien to learning or thinking, rather represents organic component of education and development. However, with the favourable stand of Islam on pairing spirituality with learning, the process of integration undergoes careful adjustments and adaptation, whether with respect to madrasah establishment, content selection, faculty appointment, use of strategies and techniques, and more importantly perhaps, the on-going spiritual training and role modelling in addition to monitoring and evaluation of students' spiritual growth. The integration of spirituality requires holistic approach in both the theoretical and practical fields of education alongside the creative strategies and techniques to effectively facilitate students' spiritual transitions and ascension however, in synchrony with community spiritual and moral practice. This research shows that, in the case of Islam, attention to spirituality in the education and learning carries with it many significant advantages; it revives the original definition of Islamic education, helps remedy the declining approach and delivery of current education in face of the aggressive secularism, and re-connect Muslim students with their worldview of *tawhid*.

REFERENCES

Abu Hamid, A.-G. (2005). *Ihya' ulum al-din: The Book of the purification of the self.* Beirut, Lebanon: Dar Ibn Hazm.

Al-Attas, S. M. N. (1979). Aims and objectives of Islamic education. Hodder and Stoughton.

Al-Qabisi, A. H. (1986). *Al-Risalah al-Mufassalah li-Ahwal al-Muta'alimin wa-Ahkam al-Mu'allimmin wa al-Muta'allimin.* Tunis: al-Sharikah al-Tunisiyyah li-Tawzi'.

Al-tafakkur fi khalq Allah (Ed.). (1995). *Maher al-Munjid.* Beirut: Dar al-Fikr al-Mu'asir.

Barakāt Badr al-Dīn al-Ghazī, A. (2009). *Al-Dduru al-Nadid fi adab al-mufid wal- mustafid. Annotated by Abu Ya'qub Nash'at Kamal Al-Misri.* Al-Jizah, Egypt: Maktabat al-Taw'iyah al-Islamiyah.

Bensaid, B., & Machouche, S.T. (1406). *Memorizing the Words of God: Special Reference to 'Abdul Rahman Ibn Khaldun'.*

Cheddadi, A. (Ed.). (2005). Al-muqaddimah. Morocco: Dār al-Funūn wa-al-'Ulūm wal-Adab.

Cook, J. (2010). Classical Foundations of Islamic Education. Brigham Young University Press.

Deliverance from Error. (1980). Boston: Twayne.

Dodge, B. (1961). *Al-Azhar: A millennium of Muslim Learning.* Washington, DC: The Middle East Institute.

Elkins, D. N., Hedstrom, J. L., Hughes, L. L., Leaf, J. A., & Saunders, C. (1988). Toward a Humanistic-Phenomenological Spirituality: Definition, Description and Measurement. *Journal of Humanistic Psychology*, *28*(4), 5–18. doi:10.1177/0022167888284002

Enan, M. A. (1961). *Ibn Khaldun: His life and work*. Lahore, Pakistan: Ashraf Press.

Fromherz, A. J. (2010). *Ibn Khaldun: Life and time*. Edinburg University Press.

Hashim, R., & Hattori, M. (2015). The decline of intellectualism in higher Islamic traditional studies: Reforming the curriculum. In Critical Issues and reform in Muslim higher education. IIUM Press.

Husain, S. S., & Ashraf, S. A. (1979). Crisis in Muslim Education. King 'Abdulaziz University.

Ibn 'Abd Rabbih, A. (1983). *Al-'Iqd al-farid*. Beirut, Lebanon: Dar al Kutub al- 'Ilmiyah.

Kazmi. (2006). Instructional Technology and Islamic Education: Intimation of Islamic Pedagogy. *Islamic Studies Journal*.

Khaldun. (1979). *Al-Ta'rif bi Ibn Khaldun wa-rihlatuhu gharban wa-sharqan*. Dar al- Kitab al-Lubnani li Tiba'ah wa al-Nashr.

Khaldūn, I. A. (1967). The Muqaddimah (F. Rosenthal, Trans.; N. J. Dawood, Ed.). Princeton University Press.

Mohamed, Y. (2015). The Duties of the Teacher *Al-Iṣfahānī's* Dharīʿa *as a Source of Inspiration for al-Ghazālī's* Mīzān al-ʿAmal. In G. Tamer (Ed.), *Islam and Rationality: The Impact of al-Ghazālī*. Leiden: Brill.

Nawawi, M. (1987). *Adab al-'alim wal muta'allim*. Tanta, Egypt: Maktabat al-Sahabah.

Omar, A. M. (2010). *Dictionary of Holy Qur'an* (2nd ed.). NOOR Foundation, International Inc.

Quraishi, M. A. (1983). *Some aspects of Muslim Education*. Universal Books.

Recommendations of the Fourth World conference on Islamic Education. (1983). Makka Al-Mukarrama, Umm al-Qura University.

Sabani, N. (2016). Understandings of Islamic pedagogy for personalised learning. The International Journal of Information and Learning Technology. doi:10.1108/ IJILT-01-2016-0003

Sibai, M. (1987). *Mosque libraries: An Historical Study*. London: Mansell Publishing Limited.

Suhnun, I. M. (1972). Adab al-Mu'allimin. Hasan Husni Abdul-Wahab.

Swinton, J. (2001). Spirituality and Mental Health Care: Rediscovering a 'Forgotten' Dimension. Jessica Kingsley Publishers.

Wane, N. N. (2011). Spirituality: A Philosophy and a Research Tool. In N. N. Wane, E. L. Manyimo, & E. J. Ritskes (Eds.), *Spirituality, Education & Society an Integrated Approach*. Sense Publishers. doi:10.1007/978-94-6091-603-8_5

Zarnuji. (1947). *The Instruction of the students: The Method of learning*. New York: King's Crown Press.

ENDNOTES

[1]   John Swinton. (2001), Spirituality and Mental Health Care: Rediscovering a 'Forgotten' Dimension. UK: Jessica Kingsley Publishers, p. 20.

[2]   Elkins, D.N., Hedstrom, J.L., Hughes, L.L., Leaf, J.A. and Saunders, C. (1988) 'Toward a Humanistic-Phenomenological Spirituality: Definition, Description and Measurement.' in *Journal of Humanistic Psychology* 28, 4, 5–18.

[3]   Njoki N. Wane. (2011). Spirituality: A Philosophy and a Research Tool, in Spirituality, Education & Society an Integrated Approach, Ed. Njoki N. Wane, Energy L. Manyimo and Eric J. Ritskes. The Netherlands: Sense Publishers, p. 76

[4]   Njoki. p. 78

[5]   Zarnuji. (1947). The Instruction of the students: The Method of learning. Trans. G. E. Von Grunebaum and Theodora M. Abel. New York: King's Crown Press, p.25.

[6]   Recommendations of the Fourth World conference on Islamic Education (1983). Kingdom of Saudi Arabia: Makka Al-Mukarrama, Umm al-Qura University, p.9.

[7]   Syed Sajjad Husain and Syed Ali Ashraf. (1979). Crisis in Muslim Education. King 'Abdulaziz University, Jeddah, p. 37.

[8]   Bukhari. Sahih al-Bukhari: Book of Fighting for the Cause of Allah (Jihad), Chapter: The Superiority of the People of the Scriptures (Jews and Christians) who embrace Islam.

[9]   Al-Attas, Syed M, N. (1979). Aims and objectives of Islamic education. Hodder and Stoughton, King Abdulaziz University, Jeddah, p.2.

10   Yedullah Kazmi. (2006). Instructional Technology and Islamic Education: Intimation of Islamic Pedagogy, In Islamic Studies Journal, vol. 45, no. 4, p. 543.

11   Bradley J. Cook. (2010), Classical Foundations of Islamic Education. Brigham Young University Press, Provo, Utah, p. 159.

12   Ibn Khaldun, *al-Muqaddimah*, p. 421.

13   'Abdul Mannân 'Omar. (2010). Dictionary of Holy Qur'an. USA: NOOR Foundation, International Inc., 2nd Edition, p.448.

14   William Lan, Arabic Lexicon.

15   Makdisi, George, p. 27.

16   Prophet Muhammad is reported to have said: "When a person dies, his deeds are cut off except for three: Continuing charity, knowledge that others benefited from, and a righteous son who supplicates for him" (Jami 'at-Tirmidhi, 1376, Book 15, hadith: 57).

17   Bayard Dodge. (1961). Al-Azhar: A millennium of Muslim Learning. Washington, D. C.: The Middle East Institute, p. 39.

18   Mansoor A. Quraishi. (1983). Some aspects of Muslim Education. Pakistan, Lahor: Universal Books, p. 13-14.

19   Sibai, Muhammad. (1987). Mosque libraries: An Historical Study. London and New York: Mansell Publishing Limited, p. 25.

20   Makdisi, p. 80.

21   Rosnani Hashim & Mina Hattori. (2015). The decline of intellectualism in higher Islamic traditional studies: Reforming the curriculum, In Critical Issues and reform in Muslim higher education. Malaysia, KL, IIUM Press, p. 116.

22   Quraishi, Mansoor. Some aspects of Muslim Education, p. 14.

23   See Ibn Khaldun's discussion of Islamic learning in Andalusia and Africa (Rosenthal, 1967, 422).

24   Makdisi, p. 81.

25   Ibn 'Abd Rabbih, Ahmad (1983). *Al-'Iqd al-farid*. Ed. Mufid M. Qamihah. Beirut, Lebanon:
Dar al Kutub al- 'Ilmiyah.

26   Abul Barakāt Badr al-Dīn al-Ghazī. (2009). Al-Dduru al-Nadid fi adab al-mufid wal-mustafid. Annotated by Abu Ya'qub Nash'at Kamal Al-Misri. Egypt, Al-Jizah: Maktabat al-Taw'iyah al-Islamiyah, p. 175.

27   Al-Ghazī, p. 175.

28   Al-Ghazī, p. 175.

29   Sibai, p. 28.

30   Sibai, p.28.

31   Al-Ghazī, p. 193.

32   Cook, Classical Foundations, p. 90.

33 Cook, p. 92.

34 Cook, p. 94.

35 Abu Hamid al-Ghazali. (2005). *Ihya' ulum al-din:* The Book of the purification of the self. Lebanon, Beirut: Dar Ibn Hazm, p. 929.

36 al-Ghazali, p. 929.

37 Al-Ghazali, p. 958.

38 Al-Ghazali, p.959.

39 *See:* Yasien Mohamed. (2015). "The Duties of the Teacher *Al-Iṣfahānī's* Dharīʿa *as a Source of Inspiration for al-Ghazālī's* Mīzān al-ʿAmal". In Georges Tamer (Editor), Islam and Rationality ; *The Impact of al-Ghazālī.* Leiden Boston, Brill, p. 186-206.

40 Al-Ghazali, p. 60.

41 Abu Hamid al-Ghazali. (1995). *Al-tafakkur fi khalq Allah*, Ed. Maher al-Munjid. Lebanon, Beirut: Dar al-Fikr al-Mu'asir, p. 41

42 Al-Ghazali, *Al-tafakur*, p. 143.

43 al-Ghazali, Abu Hamid. (1980). Deliverance from Error, Trans. Richard J. MᶜCarthy, S.J (Freedom and fulfilment). USA, Boston, Twayne.

44 Al-Ghazali, Deliverance.

45 Al-Ghazali, Deliverance.

46 Fromherz, Allen James. (2010). Ibn Khaldun: Life and time. UK: Edinburg University Press, p. 44.

47 Ibn Khaldun. Rihlat Ibn Khaldun sharqan wa gharban (*Acquainting Ibn Khaldun and his Journey in East and West*),

48 Ibn Khaldun. (1979). Al-Taʿrif bi Ibn Khaldun wa-rihlatuhu gharban wa-sharqan. Dar al-Kitab al-Lubnani li Tiba'ah wa al-Nashr, p. 17.

49 Ibn Khaldun, al-Taʿrif, p. 57.

50 Ibn Khaldun, al-Muqaddimah (Rosenthal), p. 400.

51 Ibn Khaldun, al-Muqaddimah, p. 401.

52 Ibn Khaldun, al-Taʿrif, p. 245-246.

53 Muhammad Abdullah Enan. (1961). Ibn Khaldun: His life and work. Pakistan, Lahore: Ashraf Press: p. 69-70.

54 Cheddadi, A. (Ed.). (2005). *Al-muqaddimah.* Morocco: Dār al-Funūn wa-al-ʿUlūm wa-al-Ādāb. vol. 3, p. 183

55 Ibn Khaldūn. A. (1967). *The muqaddimah* (F. Rosenthal, Trans., N. J. Dawood, Ed.). London, Bollingen Series, Princeton University Press, p. 426.

56 Ibn Khaldūn. A. (1967). *The Muqaddimah* (F. Rosenthal, Trans., N. J. Dawood, Ed.). London, Bollingen Series, Princeton University Press. p. 333.

57 Ibn Khaldun, al-Muqaddimah, p.340.

58   Cheddadi, Abdesselam. (1994), "Ibn Khaldun's Concept of Education in the Muqaddima". Paris, UNESCO: International Bureau of Education, vol. XXIV, no. 1/2, p. 7-19.

59   Ibn Khaldun, al-Muqaddimah, p.358.

60   Ibn Khaldun, al-Muqaddimah, p.398.

61   Ibn Khaldun, al-Muqaddimah (Rosenthal), p. 401.

62   Bukhari. Sahih al-Bukhari, vol. 1, Book 2, Hadith no. 49.

63   Noraisikin Sabani et al., (2016). "Understandings of Islamic pedagogy for personalised learning", In *The International Journal of Information and Learning Technology*, Vol. 33 No. 2, pp. 78-90.

64   Bensaid, B & Machouche S.T, "Memorizing the Words of God: Special Reference to 'Abdul Rahman Ibn Khaldun (d. 1406 A.D.), vol. no., p. 5.

65   Nawawi,Muhyiddin. (1987). *Adab al-'alim wal muta'allim*. Egypt, Tanta: Maktabat al-Sahabah, p. 29-43.

66   Ibn Khaldun, *al-Muqaddimah*, (Rosenthal) p. 352.

67   Al-Qabisi, Abul Hassan 'Ali. (1986). *Al-Risalah al-Mufassalah li-Ahwal al-Muta'alimin wa- Ahkam al-Mu'allimmin wa al-Muta'allimin*, Ed. Muhammad Khalid. Tunis: al-Sharikah al-Tunisiyyah li-Tawzi', p. 129.

68   Abu Dawud, Sunan Abu Dawud, 4833.

69   See Ihya' Ulum al-Din, Trans. Fazl-Ul-Karim (English), vol. 2, p. 98.

70   Makdisi, p. 128.

Chapter 4
Traditional Texts and Contemporary Teaching Techniques

Imran Mogra
Birmingham City University, UK

ABSTRACT

This chapter provides a synopsis of teaching techniques gleaned from traditional texts represented in Muslim canonical ḥadīth collections. To begin with, the life of Prophet Muḥammad is surveyed from a teacher's perspective. Thereafter, narratives which illuminate pedagogical strategies are analyzed to emphasize the need for teachers to have a repertoire of teaching methods. It is argued that the techniques derived from traditional texts are relevant as they resonate with contemporary educational ideas.

INTRODUCTION

Muslims believe that they are guided by the practice of the Messenger Muḥammad in various aspects of their life and work. It is therefore relevant to consider his practice in the context of teaching, learning and education. This chapter aims to surveys his life from a teacher's perspective and focuses on selected traditions which illuminate pedagogical strategies he used, demonstrating the need to take into account individual needs when teaching. Some of these methods are relevant as they resonate with contemporary educational ideas.

The article begins with a consideration of the meaning of *ḥadīth* and proceeds to present an overview of literature related to the life of Muḥammad to show the ways in which his life has been studied, indicating the significance of what he did and

DOI: 10.4018/978-1-5225-8528-2.ch004

taught. Thereafter several teaching methods are analysed and principles highlighted. The article concludes by highlighting the need for Muslim educators, in particular, to maintain such principles and incorporate these methods in their repertoire of teaching methods. For the purpose of this article it must be taken as read that the author considers Prophet Muḥammad to be a good teacher.

Ḥadīth literally means communication, conversation or something new. Technically, it stands for what can be attributed to Prophet Muḥammad of his deeds, sayings and tacit approvals (Mattson, 2013; Saud, 2013). *Sunnah* is the way of life of Prophet Muḥammad and *sunnah* means a recommended course of action. It also refers to the model behavior of Muḥammad (Azami, 1992; Burton, 1994). In common parlance, *ḥadīth* and *sunnah* are used interchangeably.

Muslim tradition also emanates both from Muḥammad, as developed and inspired by him, and from those around him. This became the basis for an ongoing tradition in which scriptures are interpreted and reinterpreted (Mattson, 2013). So the Prophet and the traditions he initiated and inspired offer complex insights into ways of teaching, learning, understanding and remembering the scriptures that are still beneficial for students today. Taking such an approach makes learning and teaching to be more contextualised, cumulative and personally integrated.

Background

The life of Muḥammad has fascinated and has been debated by both Muslim and non-Muslim researchers within various disciplines. Before considering his educational contribution it is valuable to acknowledge the range of subjects authored around his personality to illustrate his multifaceted contribution to human and cultural development. For instance, Guillaume (1955) and Lings (1991) utilised earliest sources to present his historical biography. Whereas, Watt (1961) depicted the socio-political environment during which Muḥammad emerged. Armstrong (1993) attempted to appreciate and understand Islam by focussing on him as a Prophet. She showed considerable insight and sensitivity and challenged previously held notions about Muḥammad by some Orientalists. Refutations of some of these allegations, related to his marriages, his integrity and use of violence are attempted by Haykal (1989). Mansoorpuri (1988), on the other hand, provided a scholarly analysis of his biographical narrative and Schimmel (1985) focussed on his unique position in the life of his followers.

Other works reflect and critique his various roles such as that of final messenger, commander and perfect model for humanity. Bauben (1996), in addition to sketching negative medieval images in the works of influential writers, also acquainted readers with the exemplary life of Muḥammad. In his book, *In Search of Muḥammad*, Bennett (1998) highlighted the significance of Muḥammad to Muslims based on the views of contemporary Muslims and historical texts. Reeves (2000) provided some reasons behind the distortion of Muḥammad's personality and his work is a contribution in promoting understanding both in plural societies and globally.

In the homilies of the contemporary intellectual Gülen (2000), readers access Muḥammad as a Prophet, sociologist, economist, preacher, father, husband and a true member of humanity. By focussing on aspects relating to education, Rahman (1980) surveyed his contributions and explained how Muḥammad was able to teach psychology, philosophy, the fundamental principles of morality and ethics. In addition, Jawad (1990) was able to argue for attributing to Muḥammad the reconciliation of the apparent contradiction between science and religion.

On a deeper level scholars have taken to specifics. Al-Hilaalee (1999), for instance, analysed and commented on the single '*ḥadīth of Gabriel*' identifying methodologies of teaching and the paths to follow when learning. In addition, Abu Guddah (1996), in his ground breaking work, highlighted precise teaching strategies, providing a basis for further endeavours in this important area of teaching and learning. Below, examples of some teaching methods are discussed in light of *ḥadīth* literature. Some scholars have expressed the need for such an endeavour for Muslim educators, in particular, so that they engage in thinking and constructing distinctive educational hermeneutics to discern pedagogic insights from their faith traditions. In addition to offering principles, values, and practices of education, he contends that it will avoid the confusion of what constitutes an Islamic pedagogy (Sahin, 2018). It will also avoid fossilization of pedagogy in a particular place or time (Memon, 2011).

MUḤAMMAD THE TEACHER

Teaching in Gradual Stages

Teaching requires pupils to be presented with simple aspects of a subject before venturing into the more complex and challenging ones so as to build secure foundations for their learning, understanding and development (Pritchard, 2017).

It is observed that Muḥammad, as a teacher, was mindful of the progressive nature of the revelation he received. It was a message that was both practical and theoretical and hence it had to be conveyed gradually taking into consideration his learners' needs, just as God had enjoined His laws gradually in their revelation and implementation (Mattson, 2013). This approach affords prioritisation by addressing immediate needs, allows understanding and relevance. It is also easier for retention. Significantly, it provides a sense of security for the learner to pose questions and construct meaning thereby developing confidence in the subject matter.

It is reported that the companions of Muḥammad used to learn ten verses of the Qur'ān from him. They would not go further until they knew what knowledge consisted therein, their meanings and how to act accordingly (Al-Tabarī, 1990). Knowledge and action when simplified for students, in its early stages, becomes easy and is motivational. Consequently, it usually manifests in an increased eagerness with profitable results. Conversely, when it is made difficult it is likely that students will either become disengaged or if they do connect, it is likely that it may be for a short period or without much enjoyment. Teaching incrementally assists in avoiding such pitfalls.

Teaching in Moderation

Another related method is to teach in moderation. Students benefit immensely when their learning does not make excessive intellectual and physical demands (Ewens, 2014). In this sense, a teacher is a facilitator and therefore has to ensure that moderation is exercised. This requires both the observation of aptitudes and contexts of lessons. 'Abdullah, a companion of Muḥammad, gave weekly religious talks. Someone requested daily preaching. To which 'Abdullah replied, "I am prevented from doing so as I hate to bore you. No doubt I take care of you in preaching by selecting a suitable time just as the Messenger used to do with us for fear of making us bored" (Al-Bukhārī, 1986:1:70). This clearly demonstrates that 'Abdullah learnt from his teacher Muḥammad to be fully aware of what he, as a teacher, was doing and of the conditions of his students. In other words, the Messenger despite being enthusiastic to teach his companions was mindful of their state of mind (Mahmud, 2010). This implies that a teacher should consider the quantity and quality of teaching. In addition, Muḥammad, on deputing any of his companions on a mission, would instruct: Give tidings (to the people); do not create (in their minds) aversion; show them leniency and do not be hard upon them' (Al-Qushayrī, 1971:4297). However, being lenient, does not imply that teachers should have no regard to rules. On the contrary, classrooms should have clear rules for behaviour and, not only should teachers take responsibility for promoting good behaviour, both within their classes and around the school, they should also have high expectations of behaviour from all their students.

Even though he was enthusiastic to teach he was mindful of the conditions and circumstances of his students to preclude boredom. He also searched for opportunities whereby he would provide advice to fresh minds. Indeed, he avoided teaching every day out of affection for his students so that their learning was based on love, curiosity and interest. In other words, a learning environment should promote self-motivation and independence, as the emotional and cognitive dimensions of learning are entwined (Dumont, Istance & Benavides, 2014).

Individual Differences

Muḥammad, it is noted, as an effective teacher, was particularly aware and catered for individual differences among his students. He would respond to each one according to his capacity and needs. He would safeguard the confidence of the beginners, waiting for their appropriate development, before introducing them to more complex concepts and ideas. He replied to questions according to their importance to the questioner taking care of their circumstances (Abu Guddah, 1996). These texts illuminate principles of taking into account the interest and background of learners in a classroom to increase motivation and differentiation.

Abu Hurayrah observed that a man came to the Messenger and asked, "O Messenger of God, can I embrace (my wife) while I am fasting?" He forbade him. Then came another person and asked, "can I embrace (my wife) while I am fasting?" He replied, "Yes" (Abu Guddah, 1996:85).

Those around were surprised. Thereupon the Messenger acknowledged their surprise and remarked I know why some of you are looking at each other; verily the old man can control himself.

The manner in which the Prophet differentiated through questioning and task is certainly evocative of teaching today as he encouraged learning through questions, stories, metaphors and analogies so that everyone understood his teachings. As a principle for teaching, this shows respect for diversity, experience, capabilities and ways of learning.

Muḥammad communicated effectively with his learners. He was skillful in debate, concise, clear in expression, lucid, made sound meaning and he was free from affectation (Al-Yaḥṣubī, 1991). Furthermore, there are indications in the above that it may be necessary at times to single out a group of students who possess a mature understanding of delicate and subtle pieces of knowledge. This would ensure that individual differences are respected as made explicit in other texts (Al-Bukhārī, 1986).

In elaborating the duties of a teacher, Al-Ghazālī, advocated that teachers should teach their students up to the power of their understanding. They should not teach them contents beyond the capacity of their understanding (Al-Ghazālī, 1993). For some students highly complex and difficult subject matters may prove to be demotivating when a learning environment should be enabling.

Dialogic Teaching

Alexander (2017) maintains that dialogic teaching has the potential to harnesses the power of talk for stimulating and extending children's thinking, and to advance their learning and understanding. To him, it is reciprocal and cumulative rather than the common question-answer-tell routines. Often the Messenger engaged in conversations, dialogues and interrogations with people of various backgrounds. Using a dialogic style awakens the attentiveness of students, invites reflection, motivates actions, creates a lasting impression and aids understanding. Abu Hurayrah heard the Messenger explaining, "If there was a river at the door of any one of you and you took a bath in it five times a day would you notice any dirt?" They said, "Not a trace of dirt would be left." The Messenger inspired by saying that is the example of the five prayers with which God removes evil deeds (Al-Bukhārī, 1986:1:506). Here the Messenger draws parallels between concrete and abstract concepts to enhance clarity in the mind of the students by encouraging visualisation.

In this example, his simple question directs students' perceptiveness to the reality of a genuine devotion. There is a delicate principle for motivation here. The characteristics of motivation should constitute emotional, practical and cognitive elements. In addition, if the above 'talk' is considered to be *reciprocal* and *supportive* and if the Messenger was seeking to move from interactions which are brief and random to those which are longer and more sustained (Alexander, 2017), then, this may be a way in which dialogic teaching was facilitated.

Analogies and Parables

Sometimes dialogues are insufficient for teachers and so another effective strategy for effective explaining is the use of examples, metaphors and analogies. Metaphors construct a model drawn from the realm of the world of senses to make abstract meaning understandable to the mind, by making the implicit meaning clear and by concretising abstract expressions (Doğan, 2002). Analogical deduction and inferences were applied by the Messenger for his teaching. When he noticed a narrow interpretation of a particular concept he was found to elaborate its meaning. When he stated an apparently contradictory good deed he followed his statement by a logical inference to remove the apparent contradiction from the minds of his students. He clarified vague ideas and made ambiguities apparent (Abu Guddah, 1996). Consequently, using such a technique enabled his students to emerge with a fresh and broad understanding and interpretation of matters related to and the application of the teachings of Islam at the same time recognizing its purpose and far-reaching consequences. Analogy encourages imagination and connection with what a learner already knows and it is particularly useful in understanding abstract concepts (Eaude, 2016).

It is reported that some poor people regretfully remarked: "Messenger of God, the rich have taken away (all the) reward. They observe prayer as we do, they keep the fasts as we keep them, and they give alms from their surplus riches." Upon this the Messenger said: "Has God not prescribed for you (a course) following which you can also give alms?" He then elaborated: "In every tasbih, (glorification of God), there is alms, in every takbir, (declaring the majesty of God), there is alms, in every ḥamd, (praise of God), there is alms, in every tahlil, (declaration that God is One), there is alms, enjoining good is an act of alms, forbidding evil is an act of alms, and in a man's sexual intercourse (with his wife) there is alms. They enquired: "Messenger of God is there reward for him who satisfies his sexual passion among us?" He said: "Tell me, if he were to devote it to something forbidden, would it not be a sin on his part? Similarly, if he were to devote it to something lawful he should have a reward." (Al-Qushayrī 1971:2198).

Here Muḥammad not only secured their involvement, but he weaved (Wragg & Brown, 1993) his students' views into the discussion and extended their thinking and ideas using familiar concepts and actions, to effectively explain how people can do good. As a teacher, he extended their thinking and included all in competing to do good according to their individual capacities. The use of examples and analogies need to be supplemented with exercises to ascertain their comprehension but also, where applicable, students should be presented with problems to solve to ensure they can apply their learning in their own context.

Sketching, Demonstrating and Digits

Illustrations, drawings and concept maps help to see the bigger picture of learning. Sometimes the Messenger relied, for clarification and certainty, upon sketches which he drew on the ground so that visual representations were made to present information and ideas thereby assisting those whose learning is enhanced through visual aids (Al-Bukhārī, 1986:8:427).

Demonstrations and signals are a commanding method of linking expressions and their meanings. In addition to sketches, explanations can be amplified through voice, actions and manipulating materials (Eaude, 2011). In using these teachers find provisions for involving learners physically to clarify and emphasise relevance of desired behaviours. Sahl reported that once the Messenger said, "I and the person supporting an orphan will be in Paradise like this, putting his index and middle fingers together" (Al-Bukhārī, 1986:8:34).

Here he encouraged physical associations by using his fingers to express ideas and emotions. In addition, to grab the students' attention and to assist them in remembering, Muḥammad used digits and thereafter clarified his point by enumerating each one. Once the Messenger announced that people take advantage of five conditions prior to five others: youth before old age, good health before illness, prosperity before poverty, spare time before becoming occupied and life before death (Al-Ḥākim, 1990).

Such techniques make it easy for students to seize the seriousness of the message and it assists in understanding the connotation by the application of opposites. The debate about whether didactic teaching or discovery learning is most effective is well known in the teaching profession (Turner-Bisset, 2001; Eaude, 2011; Ewens, 2014; Kyriacou, 2018). Muḥammad, depending on the circumstances, varied his styles and strategies so that on occasions he gave direct information and on others encouraged his students to explore. Hence effective teaching involves using both approaches.

In addition to learning through investigation, memorisation, repetition, understanding and action, writing was also encouraged and implemented as a learning tool. The Messenger had scribes for the Qur'ān, *ḥadīth*, letters, agreements and messages (Haykal, 1989; Mattson, 2013).

Demonstrations for Emphasis

To eliminate uncertainty it is sometimes essential to show an object physically. Such actions help to remember both the object and its related information.

'Ali reported that the Messenger held silk in his left hand and gold in his right hand. Then, he raised his hands with them and said, "These two (things) are unlawful for the males of my people and lawful for females" (Al-Qazwinī 1996:5:3595).

Making a verbal declaration would have sufficed. However, Muḥammad felt that a visual demonstration would have greater impact and eliminate any potential confusion or doubt. It has also been noted that experts in pedagogy agree that the exhibition of real life objects has higher retention value (Mahmud, 2010). The above methods show that the Messenger incorporated a range of stimuli into his teaching, demonstrating that teachers need a flexible repertoire of approach. As a principle it emphasises that people learn in different ways. Instead of considering these as isolated techniques, these examples evidence interconnectedness.

Delegation and Responsibility

One of the essential skills that teachers develop in their students is that of leadership and decision making. It is crucial for students to take responsibility for their own learning and for teachers to make available such opportunities to make them self-regulated learners (Dumont, Istance & Benavides, 2014). Occasionally, the Messenger was presented with personal cases and although these were personal he allowed his students to respond to these cases, showing perhaps both confidence in them and in their assessment.

A person came to the Messenger and declared that he had dreamt of a canopy from which butter and honey were trickling. He saw people collecting them in their hands in various quantities. In addition, he noticed a rope connecting the earth with the sky and he had observed that the Messenger was holding the rope and rising towards the Heaven. Then another person caught hold of the rope and rose towards Heaven. Then a third person caught hold of it, but it broke and it was rejoined for him and he also climbed up.

Having heard the dream, Abu Bakr requested if he would be allowed to interpret it. The Messenger, encouragingly, responded in affirmation. Thereupon, Abu Bakr interpreted. The canopy signifies the canopy of Islam. What trickles out of it as butter and honey is the Qur'ān and its sweetness and softness. What people collected in their palms implies the major portion of the Qur'ān or the small portion. And so far as the rope joining the sky with the earth is concerned, it is the Truth by which you stood (in the worldly life) and by which God would raise you (to Heaven). Then the person after you would take hold of it and he would also climb up with the help of it. Then another person would take hold of it and climb up with the help of it. Then another person would take hold of it and it would break; then it would be rejoined for him and he would climb up with the help of it. Messenger of God, asked Abu Bakr, "Tell me whether I have interpreted it correctly or I have made an error". The Messenger replied you have interpreted a part of it correctly and erred in a part of it". Thereafter Abu Bakr enquired: Messenger of God, tell me that part where I have committed an error." Thereupon the Messenger advised him not to take an oath (Al-Qushayrī, 1971:5643).

It is noteworthy from this account that the Messenger accepted the offer of Abu Bakr and took a constructive attitude toward his contribution. He also listened attentively to the entire interpretation. The eagerness of Abu Bakr to learn is also evident. This implies the need for a warm and positive relationship between teachers and their learners. Teachers should maintain good relationships with their students, whilst exercising appropriate authority, since positive relationships in a class play an important role in learning.

Assessment and Praise

Sometimes the Messenger would test his students. He would question them to sharpen their intelligence, reveal the essence of the matter, or assess their understanding. On receiving an appropriate response, he offered praise, verbally or physically. The following conversation may serve as an example of assessment and approval.

Ubayy reports that the Messenger enquired from him: "Do you know the verse from the Book of God, which, according to you, is the greatest?" I replied: "God and His Messenger know best." He repeated: "Do you know the verse from the Book of God, which, according to you, is the greatest?" I responded: "God, there is no god but He, the Living, the Eternal" [Qur'ān, 2:255]. Thereupon he struck me on my breast and praised: "May knowledge be pleasant for you…" (Al-Qushayrī 1971:1768).

The Messenger perhaps repeated the question to emphasise the information he was about to share or to get the full attention of his student so that he could realise its significance. Then he patted Ubayy as a way of congratulating him for his correct answer. Contemporary teachers know the role of praise as an incentive to motivate children to learn and the significance it has in promoting their self-esteem. Importantly, in addition to developing their intellectual capacities, teachers should create a safe and respectful classroom atmosphere where students can ask questions which address doubts that may have been raised about any issue under discussion. Providing opportunities of presenting doubts in question form is an effective way of satisfying curiosity and convincing students. In fact, it may be necessary to explain the matter more than once which the teacher should not hesitate to do so, such was the practice of the Messenger as well.

Jokes and Homour

Students often declare a desire for their teachers to have a sense of humour, to be polite, jolly, fair and patient (Burke & Grosvenor, 2003). The Messenger was observed to have applied cheerfulness in his interaction with children (Al-Bukhārī, 1986). He taught religious matters through amusement and tantalisation. However, the over use of humour and jokes may undermine authority and hence requires sensitive social awareness on the teacher's part (Kyriacou, 2018).

Controlled and good humour affords relaxation of the mind, strengthens relationships and refreshes the atmosphere in a class. Usually, a student is much happier when faced with a smile and cheerful countenance than a stern and a frown. Perpetual seriousness, in total absence of light-heartedness, is unwelcome to most students. When teachers convey to their students that they understand, share and value their perspective on a whole range of matters; academic, social and personal, it produces good rapport (Kyriacou, 2018). The Messenger although possessing extraordinary status, awe and character was conscious of maintaining an ordinary human face with his students so that his students felt free from anxiety which is conducive to learning.

Anas reported that the Messenger had the most sublime characters. Anas had a brother named Abu 'Umair. On one occasion, the Messenger came to their house and observed Abu Umair's sparrow had died. The Messenger amused in rhyme: "O Abu 'Umair, what has happened to nughair?" (Al-Qushayrī, 1971:5350).

Muslim scholars have extracted copious benefits from this text (Abu Guddah, 1996). The following may be relevant for learning and teaching. The teacher can have fun with their students. The use of an agnomen and of addressing a person by their diminutive so long as the person is not offended by mentioning it creates affection and a bond. A student may be provided with a pet for play and comfort in a classroom. The Messenger in this incident demonstrates his socializing with a child according to his intelligence and perceptions by inducing a rhyme in his question perhaps to console Umair's grief. Thus teachers need to be sensitive to the emotional needs of their children and ensure that they are comforted so that their learning is not affected by upsetting incidents. Significantly, they should attempt to show an interest in their hobbies and matters important to their students so that a trustworthy and humane bond is created.

Encouragement and Motivation

The Messenger motivated his students, towards the good he was promoting and warned against the consequence of the evil he was discouraging (Abu Guddah, 1996). He achieved this by utilising the promise of rewards and benefits and cautioning against its consequences and harms. For example, to encourage goodness, he promised that any person, who directs towards good, will receive the same reward as the doer (Al-Qushayrī, 1971). To discourage unacceptable behaviour, he announced that for a person to be called a liar it is sufficient for him/her convey everything he/she hears (Al-Sijistānī, 1984).

Such traditional texts are compelling when considered in light of behavior education. They provide ideas, in this case, for Muslim teachers in particular, to give good news using the favors of God. These can be used to reinforce positive responses to learning. For managing behavior a balanced approach is required. These traditions indicate the need to abstain from the exclusive use of threats and warnings, in their various forms, without combining them with good news and rewards. Furthermore, the *hadith* indicates the need for reconciling the hearts of students and avoiding adversities for them.

Personality

The Messenger announced that he was sent a teacher (Al-Qazwinī, 1996). He taught through a wide range of techniques; words, demonstrations, gestures, conduct and behaviour and utilised whatever methods he found to be sensitive, appropriate and effective for his students. One of the most effective means of achieving success in what he taught was his personality. His life and his personality were both a model and a technique too (Abu Guddah, 1996). In other words, not only did he model the actions that were expected from his students but the manner in which he taught those actions themselves became techniques for future teachers to use in their teaching as exhibited in the above texts. He had an approachable manner so that his pupils were not threatened by his presence - allowing an environment which was safe and secure where pupils were not afraid. Educators believe a calm, secure and safe learning atmosphere is conducive to good teaching and learning. The Messenger was an embodiment of love, affection and mercy which were certainly modelled in Muhammad's pedagogy (Ajem & Memon, 2011).

It has been suggested that whilst pedagogical principles and practices derived from the primary sources of Islam may be considered to be the best in teaching and learning (Mogra, 2010), for Muslims educators, this ought not to imply a rigidity and *ultima verba* for two main reasons. First, theologically, the subject matter of pedagogy is beyond the confines of faith (*'aqīdah*), which affords opportunities for experimentation, creativity and innovation based on the various disciplines such as psychology, sociology and anthropology, for example. Second, as evidenced from the above, the Messenger himself utilised a wide range of strategies with diverse students, both collectively and individually. It would, therefore, seem prudent to suggest that it is the adoption of flexibility that is in line with the Prophetic framework (*sunnah*) of pedagogy rather than a fixation on any ontologically and epistemologically informed practice, be it from Muslim traditions or otherwise. Thus, educators should treat pedagogies for what they are, i.e., means rather than ends. This flexibility safeguards variability of practice and diversity of interpretation (Memon, 2011). Upholding this kind of philosophical standpoint and practice is necessary to ensure that pedagogies are not essentialized from singular interpretations of the Qur'ān and Sunnah (Memon, 2011), for the pedagogy of the prophet-teacher took account of the diversity of races, ethnicities, socioeconomic positions, and genders which constituted his community (Al-Yaḥṣubī, 1991; Gülen, 2000).

CONCLUSION

It must be stressed that these teaching techniques from traditional texts of Muhammad have been mentioned as pointers and are not in any way decisive or conclusive.

Good teachers have many characteristics in common. They enjoy what they do and consider their role a significant one for the future of children in their care. They know their learners well so that they look forward to coming into their class. They understand what motivates their learners and have a repertoire of teaching methods.

They create a comfortable and non-threatening environment where children can be happy, creative and imaginative.

When the teacher aspect of the life of Muḥammad considered in light of professional values and practice for teachers, his high expectations of his students and his concern for his students' emotional, social, spiritual and academic development is evident. It seems that Muḥammad treated his students with respect, dignity and consideration and he was much concerned about his students to the extent that the Qur'ān had to comfort him. He communicated sensitively and effectively with the young and old, male and female, poor and rich, resident and travellers recognising their value and respecting their individuality.

Through his own lifestyle he demonstrated and promoted the positive values, attitudes and dispositions that were expected from his followers as outlined in the Qur'ān so that he was an ideal model. Muḥammad knew he was a temporal being and hence had to leave behind those who would continue his work and therefore prepared them to fulfil that role of learning and teaching. These methods are at least compatible or possibly evocative of some of the best insights of modern teaching methods, even though they may not have self-consciously developed as educational theories, but were born out of practice and expertise and within a remembered tradition focussing around the words of the Messenger. Further research is needed in terms of how these are conceptualised and operationalised among Muslims educators in different educational settings and geographical contexts.

This research received no specific grant from any funding agency in the public, commercial, or not-for-profit sectors.

REFERENCES

Abu Guddah, A. (1996). *Al-Rasūl al-Mu'allim wa asālibuhu fi al-t'alīm* [Prophet Muḥammad the Teacher]. Halab: Maktabah al-matbuāt al-Islamiyyah.

Ajem, R., & Memon, N. A. (2011). *Principles of Islamic Pedagogy, a Teacher's Manual. Islamic Teacher Education Program.* Toronto: Canada Razi Group.

Al-Bukhārī, M. I. (1986). *The Translation of the meaning of Sahīh Al-Bukhārī* (6th ed.). (M. M. Khan, Trans.). Lahore: Kāzi Publications.

Al-Ghazālī, A. H. (1993). *'Ihyā 'Ulūm-ud-Dīn* [The Revival of Religious Sciences] (F. Karim, Trans.). Karachi: Dārul Ishaat.

Al-Hākim, M. A. (1990). Mustadrak Al-Ḥākim. Beirut: Dar al-Kutub al-'Ilmiyyah.

Al-Hilaalee, S. (1999). *The Manners of the Scholar & Student of Knowledge.* Birmingham, UK: Salafi Publications.

Al-Qazwīnī, M. Y. (1996). *Sunan Ibn-i-Majah* (M. T. Ansari, Trans.). Lahore: Kazi Publications.

Al-Qushayrī, M. H. (1971). *Ŝahih Muslim* (A. H. Siddiqī, Trans.). Dār al Manār.

Al-Sijistānī, S. A. (1984). *Sunan Abū Dāwūd* (A. Hasan, Trans.). Lahore: Sh. Muḥammad Ashraf.

Al-Tabarī, M. J. (1990). *The Commentary on the Qur'ān.* Oxford, UK: Oxford University Press.

Al-Yaḥṣubī, `I. M. (1991). *Muḥammad the Messenger Ash-Shifa of Qadi `Iyad* (A.A. Bewley, Trans.). Granada: Madinah Press.

Alexander, R. J. (2017). *Towards Dialogic Teaching: rethinking classroom talk* (5th ed.). Dialogos.

Armstrong, K. (1993). *Muḥammad: A Western attempt to understand Islam.* London: Victor Gollancz Ltd.

Azami, M. M. (1992). *Studies in Hadith Methodology and Literature.* American Trust Publications.

Bauben, J. M. (1996). *Image of the Prophet Muḥammad in the West – A Study of Muir, Margoliouth and Watt.* Leicester, UK: The Islamic Foundation.

Bennett, C. (1998). *In Search of Muḥammad.* London: Cassell.

Burke, C., & Grosvenor, I. (2003). *The School I'd like.* London: RoutledgeFalmer. doi:10.4324/9780203439074

Burton, J. (1994). *An Introduction to the Hadith.* Edinburgh, UK: Edinburgh University Press.

Doğan, R. (2002). The Usage of the metaphor in the Prophet Muḥammad's (pbuh) ḥadīths as an educational method. *Muslim Educational Quarterly, 19*(3), 4–15.

Dumont, H., Istance, D., & Benavides, F. (2014). The nature of learning: An OCED stocktake. In A. Pollard (Ed.), *Readings for reflective teaching in schools* (pp. 102–105). London: Bloomsbury.

Eaude, T. (2011). *Thinking through pedagogy for Primary and Early Years.* Exeter, UK: Learning Matters.

Eaude, T. (2016). *New Perspective on Young Children's Moral Education: developing character through a virtue ethics approach*. London: Bloomsbury.

Ewens, T. (2014). *Reflective Primary Teaching*. Critical Publishing.

Guillaume, A. (1955). *The Life of Muḥammad: A Translation of Ibn Ishāq's Sīrat Rasūl Allāh*. Karachi: Oxford University Press.

Gülen, M. F. (2000). *Prophet Muḥammad: Aspects of his life*. The Fountain.

Haykal, M. H. (1989). *The Life of Muḥammad* (I. R. Al-Faruqi, Trans.). Karachi: Dārul Ishaat.

Jawad, H. (1990). Muḥammad the Educator: An Authentic Approach. *The Islamic Quarterly*, *34*(2), 115–122.

Kyriacou, C. (2018). *Essential Teaching Skills* (5th ed.). Oxford, UK: OUP.

Lings, M. (1991). *Muḥammad His Life Based on Earliest Sources* (2nd ed.). The Islamic Texts Society.

Mahmud, J. (2010). How the Messenger Taught his Students. Lahore: Al-Misbah.

Mansoorpuri, M. S. (1988). *Mercy for the Worlds* (A. J. Siddiqui, Trans.). Karachi: Dārul Ishaat.

Mattson, I. (2013). *The Story of the Qur'an: Its History and place in Muslim Life*. Oxford, UK: Wiley-Blackwell.

Memon, N. A. (2011). What Islamic school teachers want: Towards developing an Islamic teacher education programme. *British Journal of Religious Education*, *33*(3), 285–298. doi:10.1080/01416200.2011.595912

Mogra, I. (2010). Teachers and teaching: A contemporary Muslim understanding. *Religious Education (Chicago, Ill.)*, *105*(3), 317–329. doi:10.1080/00344081003772089

Pritchard, A. (2017). *Ways of Learning* (4th ed.). Abingdon, UK: Routledge. doi:10.4324/9781315460611

Rahman, A. (1980). *Muḥammad the Educator of Mankind*. London: The Muslims Schools Trust.

Reeves, M. (2000). *Muḥammad in Europe: A Thousand Years of Western Myth-making*. New York: New York University Press.

Sahin, A. (2018). Critical issues in Islamic education studies: Rethinking Islamic and Western liberal secular values of education. *Religions, 9*(11), 335. doi:10.3390/rel9110335

Saud, L. (2013). Islamic Beliefs: The Development of Islamic Ideas. In A. B. McCloud, S. W. Hibbard, & L. Saud (Eds.), *An Introduction to Islam in the 21st Century* (pp. 51–80). Oxford, UK: Wiley-Blackwell.

Schimmel, A. (1985). *And Muḥammad is His Messenger: The veneration of the Prophet on Islamic Piety*. Chapel Hill, NC: The University of North Carolina Press.

Turner-Bisset, R. (2001). *Expert Teaching*. London: David Foulton.

Watt, W. M. (1961). *Muḥammad: Prophet and Statesman*. Oxford, UK: Oxford University Press.

Wragg, T., & Brown, G. (1993). *Explaining*. London: Routledge. doi:10.4324/9780203308479

Chapter 5
Transformational Islamic Leadership:
A Case Study From Singapore

Diwi Abbas
Nanyang Technological University, Singapore

Charlene Tan
 https://orcid.org/0000-0002-5711-3749
Nanyang Technological University, Singapore

ABSTRACT

This chapter focuses on transformational Islamic leadership based on a case study of a madrasah in Singapore. The research findings underscore the significance of an Islamic leader in articulating and promoting a shared vision, demonstrating exemplary behavior, working towards group goals, rendering individual support, providing intellectual stimulation, and setting high expectations. A major implication is that Islamic leadership contributes to the existing literature on transformational leadership by highlighting the religious motivation, principles, and values for madrasah leaders.

INTRODUCTION

The changing and challenging settings within schools, in society and across the globe require educational leadership to be adaptable, dynamic and innovative. Educational leaders must re-fashion themselves as the bridge between the school community and the society, serving as creators of visions for their schools. It is incumbent that

DOI: 10.4018/978-1-5225-8528-2.ch005

they understand where their school "fits into the bigger picture" for the present and into the future (Myint & Salleh, 2009, p. 125). Among the leadership theories, transformation leadership has been the focus since the 1990s (Bass, 1997; Bass & Avolio, 1994; Burn, 1978; Leithwood & Jantzi, 2000; Tichy, & Devanna, 1986). Essentially, transformational leadership disfavours direct control, supervision, and instruction, preferring instead the enhancement of an organisation's capacity to determine its purposes and support changes in teaching and learning (Hallinger, 2003). Despite an impressive body of literature on transformational leadership, there is limited research on the application and relevance of transformational leadership in Islamic educational contexts. This chapter aims to fill the gap by examining the leadership philosophy and practices in a madrasah in Singapore. The first part of the chapter introduces the theory of transformational leadership and leadership in Islam. The next section reports the research study in terms of the methodology, key findings and implications.

Transformational Leadership and Leadership in Islam

Transformational Leadership

Burns (1978), in his book titled *Leadership*, contrasts transforming leadership with transactional leadership. Transforming leaders appeal to the moral vision and values of their followers so as to motivate them to reform organisations and institutions. Transactional leadership, in contrast, motivates followers by appealing to their self-interest and exchanging benefits. Yukl (2006) points out that the underlying influence processes for transactional and transformational leadership "can be inferred from the description of the behaviour and effects on follower motivation" (p. 266). Transactional leadership concentrates on motivating followers by exchanging rewards for performance of job expectations. Such a leadership style is a fundamental leadership practice in which a leader identifies roles, expectations, and performance parameters, and guides followers to desired results. In contrast, a transformational leader interacts with followers in ways that stimulate their thinking, inspire their performance, and result in performance beyond expectations.

Bass and Avolio (1994) developed a Full-Range Leadership Model that suggests that transformational and transactional leadership behaviours, when displayed at appropriate conditions and environment, would increase the effectiveness of an organisation tremendously, resulting in transformation through higher-order change. Leithwood and Janzi (1996) carried on the work of Burns and Bass on transformational leadership by adapting it to the school setting. They believe that the transformation leader portrays six behaviours that characterise transformation leadership. The behaviours are as follows:

1. Providing and articulating a vision: behaviour on the part of the leader aimed at identifying new opportunities for his or her school and developing, articulating, and inspiring others with his or her vision of the future;

2. Providing an appropriate model: behaviour on the part of the leader that sets an example for staff members to follow consistent with the values the leader espouses;

3. Fostering and acceptance of group goals: behaviour on the part of the leader aimed at promoting cooperation among staff members and assisting them to work together toward common goals;

4. Providing individual support: behaviour on the part of the leader that challenges staff members and concern about their feelings and needs;

5. Providing intellectual stimulation: behaviour on the part of the leader that challenges staff members to re-examine some assumptions about their work and rethink how it can be performed;

6. High expectations: behaviour that demonstrates the leader's expectations for excellence, quality, and high performance on the part of the staff.

Leadership in Islam

Leadership in Islam refers to "a social process in which the leader seeks to achieve certain organisational goals by garnering the support from relevant stakeholders – primarily followers – while fully complying to Islamic teachings and principles" (Shams-ur-Rehman, 2008, p. 28). Researchers such as Adnan (2006), Saeeda (2006), Tan (2014) and Tan and Abbas (2009, 2012, 2017) have maintained that a dominant feature of leadership in Islam, voiced strongly in the recent literature on leadership, is an emphasis on moral and ethical values for leaders and teachers. Islam is fundamentally an ethical religion, placing utmost emphasis on ethics and the moral character of its adherents. Scholars of Islamic leadership are in agreement about the sources which Islamic leadership principles are derived primarily from (Beekun & Badawi 1999; Hisham 1992; Jusoh, 2009; Juma'at, 1990; Mahmud, 2004; Muhamad., Mohd. & Suyurno, 2008; Muhammadi, bin Hj Marzuki, & Mohd, 2015; Saeeda, 2010; Shams-ur-Rehman 2008; Veithzal, 2009). The key sources are as follows: Quran is the primary resource for Muslims to derive leadership principles; Prophet Muhammad (*pbuh*) is believed by Muslims to be the model par excellence for leadership; The Wise Caliphs who became the leaders for the Muslims after the death of the Prophet, namely Abu Bakar, Umar, Uthman and Ali, followed the teachings of the Quran and the Prophet Muhammad (*pbuh*); and Pious Followers – besides the wise Caliphs, there are many more leaders and individuals believed by Muslims to possess great wisdom who practised the principles of Islam and followed the teachings of the Prophet Muhammad.

Research Study

The research objective is to identify the values, principles and behaviour of madrasah leaders in Singapore. A brief introduction to madaris in Singapore is in order here (for details, see Aljunied, & Dayang, 2005; Tan, 2009; Tan & Abbas, 2012, 2017). Among the oldest educational institutions established in Singapore are the Islamic schools or better known as madrasah. The number of madaris grew after the World War, and is said to be in the range of 69 madaris in 1950s and 1960s (Sa'eda, 2009). However, with Singapore's independence and the emergence of public schools for all Singaporeans, the number of madaris diminished in number, though not in stature, in the eyes of the Muslim community. In the 1980s, full-time madaris had shrunk to only six. There are at present about 4,000 students studying in the 6 full time madrasah. Each madrasah has its own Management Committee (MMC) that is registered under the Education Act. The madrasah also fall within the Education Act under the Ministry of Education where they are considered as private schools. In was only in 1993 that all the 6 madrasah agreed upon a common syllabus and textbooks for primary school level prepared by MUIS (the Islamic Religious Council of Singapore). They also agreed to have a common examination for religious subjects at the end of 10 years of education called Peperiksaan Sijil Thanawi Empat (PSTE) [Examination Certificate for Secondary Four] administered by MUIS. (Abdullah, 2007).

The madaris in Singapore had undergone various transformations and evolutions in terms of its curricula and subjects based on various external and internal factors. In terms of curricula and syllabi, essentially each madrasah designed and decided on its own aims and objectives. The subjects offered by the madaris include religious subjects such as Tawhid (monotheism), Fiqh (Jurisprudence), Tafsir (Quranic Exegesis), Hadith (Prophetic sayings), Seerah (Biographical Life of the Prophet) and the teaching of Arabic language which is the Quranic language, and academic subjects such as English, Malay, Mathematics, Science, Geography and History. The distribution of periods for each subjects differ among the madaris, based on their own emphasis and focus. In terms of examinations, the madaris prepared their students for national examinations such as the Primary School Leaving Examination (PSLE) and as examinations for the religious subjects such as the PSTE.

Set in the broader context of leadership from an Islamic perspective, this research links the leadership role of the madrasah leader to transformational leadership. Guided by the purpose of the study, the research question underlying the investigation in this study is: To what degree do the leadership values, principles and behaviours of the madrasah leaders exhibit transformational leadership? This study used a qualitative ethnographic qualitative approach based on a case study of a madrasah, known as Madrasah X in this chapter. Madrasah X has been selected for our research as it offers an interesting and pertinent example of leadership change, having gone through about twelve different principals and leaders. Madrasah X was the least known madrasah in the 90's, and it went through a total transformation over the years. Currently, Madrasah X is among the top performing madaris owing to its good reputation in the Muslim community. Madrasah X was highly visible in the media, in the mainstream press, the Malay and English daily, and it was even once featured in an international coverage by a western media. The students of Madrasah X was under the spotlight for their impressive performances in national examinations, national competitions, innovative programmes, inter-school programmes with other national schools.

Data from in-depth interviews, school observations, interviews and artefacts were analysed using qualitative research methods. Interviews were conducted with the staff members, students, parents and other stakeholders. Two leaders were the subjects for this study: Leader A and Leader B. Leader A was originally the main subject for the study as he served as the Executive Director of the madrasah which functionally made him its highest authority figure. After the initial interviews with Leader A, it was made known to the researcher that Leader B had been employed as the madrasah's Vice-Principal and was asked to understudy Leader A for a certain period of time before he would eventually take over as principal. A total number of 22 staff members (including teachers, Subject Heads, Heads of Department, Vice-Principals and support staff, 24 students [primary and secondary students], 13 parents and 9 stakeholders [vendors, religious teachers]) were interviewed. It was explained to them that the primary objective of this study was to capture their observation on the two leaders and their leadership behaviour.

The observations entailed interactions between the leaders and various groups of people within the madrasah compound for a period of six months. The interview process, the observation protocol, and requests for access for artefacts and documents were carefully communicated to the two subjects. Upon their agreement and the boundaries clearly stated, the researcher ensured proper informed consent document were issued and signed by all parties involved. Ethical issues pertaining to anonymity, confidentiality, freedom from harm and the right to refuse to participate or to cancel participation. After selecting teachers, support staff, students, parents of students and other stakeholders, informed consent was sought prior to each interview. The ethnographic methods used for data collection were: observation, interviews and artefacts and document analysis. All research data were recorded, transcribed, coded and analysed and the process began from the time the researcher was attached to the madrasah.

Key Findings and Discussion

This section represents a summary of the respondents' perceptions and the researcher's observations of the Islamic leadership values, principles and behaviour of the madrasah leaders. The explanations and clarifications by the two leaders of their leadership behaviour were also captured to shed some light over the way they behaved.

Providing and Articulating a Vision

There seems to be a consensus among the different groups in the madrasah that the leaders articulate a clear vision for the madrasah. The two leaders, especially Leader A, clearly indicated the need to be clear about the future direction of the madrasah; they were fully cognisant that the madrasah community, stakeholders, parents, MUIS, the general Muslim community and even the government show a keen interest in the performance and direction of all the madrasahs in Singapore, including Madrasah X. Leader B explained the society's expectation in his remark below:

"_____ (Madrasah Leader A) is able to ensure that [the] madrasah is able to withstand societal's expectations. Because of the societal's expectations which are very, very strong, he believes that whatever is done, is done with the best interest of the madrasah and InsyaAllah (God willing) we can.....now I see his dilemma, there are many other bigger stresses that we have to handle..." [Madrasah Leader B]

There were repeated mentions by staff and teachers from Madrasah X of the clear vision articulated by the leaders, especially by Leader A. The following comments by the teachers alluded to this fact:

"For _____ (Madrasah Leader A) when he led the meeting, he was very clear as to the direction that the madrasah should be going. So, the decision was kind of precise and he would work out everything that we need to work on. When he tells us what we need to do, it is quite clear. So, that in a way allows us to also get on with our work better." [Madrasah Teacher 15]

Consulting

Another transformational leadership behaviour demonstrated by the leaders in Madrasah X is the leadership of consulting. The qualitative data analysis found this particular behaviour of the leader as the most significant as this was mentioned by many respondents including the leaders. Leader A asserted to the researcher that consulting is a leader behaviour which he considered as highly important and an integral part of leadership in a madrasah environment. He clarified that the madrasah's mission and vision documented in the Staff Handbook and in the Pupil Development and *Tarbiyah* Department (PDT) Manual was constructed from the ground. Teachers and staff were given numerous opportunities to be involved, voice opinions and alter current practices through discussion and consultation. This culture was in operation from the day that he took over the management of the school. Leader A explained that the madrasah, as a unit,

"continue to learn, adjust, adapt, but it is still based on the values that we chose for ourselves, which went through a very thorough and tedious process that took one year plus via discussion, focus groups, training because I believe it has to start from there." [Leader A]

Consulting is aligned with the concept of *shura* (mutual consultation). *Shura* (mutual consultation) is a concept that is introduced in the Quran (Mustafa, 1999), which is simply defined as a communication process that requires discussion, exchanges of thoughts and opinions, collation and collections of data and facts, exchanges of related information and ideas from multiple perspectives. The conclusion and the best solution arose from the discussions could be made as the chosen solution. The madrasah's staff handbook termed *shura* (mutual consultation) as 'jammah-centric' and operationalised it as 'leadership and followership consultative'. The staff understood the significance of consultation as it was clearly instituted in the madrasah and claimed to be a mechanism vigilantly espoused by the madrasah, including the management. The *Shura* (mutual consultation) was clearly instituted in the Pupil Development and Tarbiyah Department (PDT) manual that explains the exact processes and procedures in conducting *shura* (mutual consultation) in Madrasah X. The respondents believed that this *shura* (mutual consultation) was very much alive and active in Madrasah X. A staff member recounted that Leader A had allowed the decision made by the Council to stand even though he had strong objection of its final decision.

"Oh for me, he believes in shura (mutual consultation). I think that is his strength. Many times he disagreed with us (laugh), like the caning incident last year, but because of the shura (mutual consultation) concept, he goes with it, but he was not there when we caned the student." [Madrasah Teacher 4]

Supporting and Motivating

The leaders were deemed to show a supporting behaviour. In particular, most respondents agreed that Leader B treated the staff with much empathy and understanding. Hence, the staff recognised the fact that the leaders were able to understand the staff's problems and struggles.

"_____ [Leader B], he's people to people kind of person, he's able to handle even the most challenging parents, in a way that he's able to soothe, but at the same time meet their needs." [Madrasah Teacher 16]

As the madrasah is privately funded and ample financial resources were not at their disposal, both principals motivate the staff with non-monetary rewards. Leader A looked at other non-material means to motivate his staff:

"It's so easy to make them feel good about what they do lah. You make a point to always give praises lah. And teachers like it when their opinions are being considered, when their work is being appreciated, when their views are being implemented. These are more important things as a sense of motivation, rather just monetary reward." [Madrasah Leader A]

The praises, recognition, acknowledgement of the hard work of the teachers are important to teachers and these were mentioned by the respondents. The motivating behaviour was very much appreciated by the staff as commented below:

Mr _____ (Madrasah Leader A) replied to me that I am a very senior teacher, with years of valuable experience and he needs to learn a lot from me. That was his reply to me. I saved that email to this day." [Madrasah Teacher 1]

Leader A made a very conscious effort to 'catch the staff when they are doing something good' and would make it a point to commend the staff behaviour in their emails to the staff, either directly to the staff concerned or as a mass email to all staff.

Another component used by the leaders of Madrasah X in motivating their staff and teachers are by rallying them towards the shared conviction in the intrinsic motivation of serving Allah by serving the madrasah. Rewards of the hereafter and the service towards Allah provide compelling goal and purpose for staff to push forward to work hard to be worthy of such intrinsic rewards. Such emotional appeals to the staff's faith and conviction connected to some staff and gained their support and commitment to the madrasah vision.

Exemplary Behaviour

Providing an appropriate model is another behaviour portrayed by a transformational leader. The policy of the madrasah was set and established by the madrasah community after numerous retreats and these were reviewed yearly. One of the fundamental values that was impressed upon the madrasah community, permeating throughout the madrasah community is the concept of *'salam-kalam-khadam'* (spreading greetings, spreading good word, spreading the spirit of service). The policy is based on the Quranic foundation about the importance of spreading *salam* (greetings) among Muslim brothers and sisters assists in cementing brotherly love amongst Muslims, as mentioned in the Prophetic traditions which says that spreading *salam* (greetings) is one sure way of loving other Muslim brethren which is a condition for one to be granted paradise.

During the observation sessions, Leader A on several occasions, had given *'salam'* (greet) to students before and after assembly, as well as before and after congregational prayers which were performed at the mosques, and to some parents. Leader B was also perceived by the respondents to be a role model for the *Salam-Kalam-Khadam* Model (spreading greetings, spreading good word, spreading the spirit of service). He was cited as always being the first to offer Islamic greetings to staff. A student [Madrasah Student 3] comment remarked that he considered Leader B as a patient man and he had observed that he would say *'Assalamualaikum'* (May peace be upon you) to students and would enquire about our well-beings.

Both the leaders in the madrasah are not just school administrators but also religious leaders. Leader A of the madrasah attributed his use of the leadership principles to his faith (Islam, Qur'an, and the Prophet's Muhammad's life), and his readings on leadership principles and leadership theories. Leader B reported that the Prophet Muhammad has a strong impact on his leadership practices, behavior, approaches and principles. Leader A listed performing special prayers to seek assistance whenever he faces difficult staff or challenges. He stressed that he would maintain *ukhuwwah* (brotherhood) despite having differences of opinions with his staff and others. Leader A also set the values for the madrasah after much deliberation with the staff by highlighting the calling of Muslims as *khalifah fil ardh* (vicegerents on earth).

Ihsan (Compassion)

One particular Islamic principle that surfaced from the data is the value of *ihsan* (compassion) which is described as an act of kindness that is meant to benefit others. It also entails doing good, forgiving and helping a person in times of need without expecting anything in return. There were numerous accounts of the second chances given to many teachers and students. One staff [Madrasah Teacher 18] observed that the leaders were cautious in using the 'stick' and showed more leniency towards the staff. The staff linked such behaviour to the value of *ihsan* (compassion) which is the values of Madrasah X. It is evident, according to this particular respondent, that the leaders' approach is continuing giving chances after chances for the staff to improve on their mistakes. Another teacher made the following comment:

"For example, the late coming of teachers. Sometimes it can be quite straightforward, but because of the 'ihsan' (compassion) factor, giving the stick is quite rare. At most, they would meet and talk, not reprimanding them. I mean, in terms of human relations in Madrasah X, it's always been about giving that person respect." [Madrasah Teacher 10]

High Expectations

In times of change, there was bound to be more work involved as the staff began to undertake the necessary steps to embrace the changes. The leaders of the madrasah placed high expectations on their staff and encouraged staff to strive for excellence, quality, and high performance. One of the strategies in ensuring that the quality and high performance was checked through quality finished products, through submission of reports to the management. Madrasah Teacher 19 shared how detailed the leaders are, especially Leader A, in ensuring that the schedule is met, and that the quality is maintained. Another teacher, Madrasah Teacher 13, was of the opinion that the high standards had been set by the leaders had contributed to the staff being more "open-minded to try new things, new initiatives, new programmes by MUIS. The teacher believed that as time went on, the staff at Madrasah X took the challenge of new programmes being offered to them, reviewing them, looking into their weaknesses and fine-tune those that were necessary. This positive attitude towards looking at something new was rather refreshing and the leaders of Madrasah X were strong figures that move the staff in this direction of accepting change. Another teacher also concurred that the high standards set by the leaders, did successfully permeated to the whole madrasah and the staff came on board, albeit some ever so slowly. He remarked:

"I think he is always on top of things, monitoring everything, to look at those things that need to be changed, or those things that need to be further improved, even though it may be difficult for the teachers to do it, as the madrasah teachers may be used to dealing with changes very slowly and gradually, but eventually these teachers eventually realised that things do need to change. [Madrasah Teacher 20]

Leader A explained that he demanded high standards and excellent results from his staff as it is expected from us, according to the values that they hold. He made the following comment:

"Of course you need to get excellent results. My values are basically reflected in the values, First choice, God-conscious, people-centred and excellence driven. These are my main preoccupations. Making sure that these are really alive, through the systems, through the policies, through the curriculum, through the behaviour and through the results that we show lah eventually. Because when you empower them with that, then when it is done, you can just walk away and you know that the legacy will continue." [Madrasah Leader A]

In sum, the research findings suggest that a transformational leadership style has been adopted by the leaders of the madrasah. All the four components of transformational leadership – individual consideration, intellectual stimulation, inspirational motivation, and idealised influence - are exhibited by the leaders of the madrassah. Many respondents hailed Leader A as visionary who was capable of constituting clarity in the implementation process towards his vision; they describe him as visionary, progressive, a thinker and innovator. In terms of the transformational leadership behaviour of consulting, it is evident that there is a clear process and procedure of the *shura* (mutual consultation) platform in Madrasah X. This was testified by many respondents that *shura* (mutual consultation) was implemented and accepted as the common vocabulary amongst staff. The research findings also shown that the madrasah leaders diligently worked on engaging their teachers and staff and prodding them to venture outside of their comfort zone. Special grants were allocated to support creative programmes proposed by the teachers. Many avenues and platforms were introduced to stimulate teachers to think creatively and not be constrained to suggest innovative suggestions in dealing with new set of ideas, changes and environment. Many respondents indicated that they feel supported by their leaders as they break free from their comfort zone and as they venture to try novel approaches and develop creative ways of dealing and addressing challenges and issues faced at Madrasah X.

Our research findings have underscored the significance of an Islamic leader in articulating and promoting a shared vision, demonstrating exemplary behaviour, working towards group goals, rendering individual support, providing intellectual stimulation, and setting high expectations (Leithwood & Janzi, 1996). A transformational leader is one who talks optimistically with enthusiasm and provides encouragement and meaning for what need to be done (Bass, 2006). Such a leader expends efforts to challenge their staff intellectually, to persuade them to question and re-examine their assumptions and the present circumstances and to strive towards innovative and creative solutions to problems (Bass, 2006). It is equally vital that the leader create a safe and open environment that is conducive to the creation and sharing of knowledge, in order to encourage a continuous flow of ideas from the staff.

Implications

There are three major implications arising from our study for transformational Islamic leadership. The first is that our case study had indicated that the values and behaviour that had been surfaced by the respondents are those that are based on Islamic moral principles and values. Exemplary behaviour such as patience, unity, humility, and gentleness would be valued by all. In particular, the virtue of *ihsan* (compassion) is an integral value in Islam; Beekun and Badawi (1999) listed *ihsan* (compassion) as one of the layers of the moral character and personality of a leader. It is evident through the repeated mentions of the term *ihsan* (compassion) in the interviews with the respondents, through observations of interactions between the leaders and the staff, teachers and students, that the value is very much alive and clearly manifested in the daily running of Madrasah X. According to Beekun and Badawi (1999), the process of leading an Islamic organisation involves developing followers through *tazkiyyah* (growth), which is similar to the process of intellectual stimulation factor of transformational leadership. In leading an Islamic organisations, leaders must reach out to all individuals as every person needs to hear the message of Islam; they must seek the verbal commitment of their staff; they must expect gradual growth from staff, they must understand the staff's capacity and capability and allocate tasks accordingly; and most importantly, the leaders must exhibit patience and tolerance with followers' fluctuating moods when dealing with ups and downs of new initiatives and ventures.

The second implication is that the transformational leadership practice of consulting is in tandem with the concept and benefits of *shura* (mutual consultation) for Islamic leaders. The behaviour of consulting one another before any decision is made as a group, is akin to another transformational leadership behaviour of fostering and acceptance of group goals (Leithwood & Janzi, 1996). In fact, the *shura* (mutual consultation) goes beyond accepting of group goals as the *shura* (mutual consultation) process ensures that staff would be included and would be actively engaged in the decision making process for the group. In essence, *shura* is a collaborative structure combines the two transformational leadership behaviour of consulting and fostering and acceptance of group goals. Such collaborative structures would enhance and lead towards teachers' conviction that their voices are important to the organisation and they would be involved in shaping and framing the context, policies and programmes that are implemented in the organisation.

One of the benefits of *shura* (mutual consultation) for an organisation is in getting cooperation and a solid support from its members. Ignoring *shura* (mutual consultation) may invite negative implications such as expansion of conflicts and crises in an organisation which may bring about disagreement and discord amongst them. Fullan (2001) contends that leaders of change should welcome people who resist change as they may provide a rich resource of ideas or counter-ideas to the changes that were to be implemented. Therefore, in Fullan's framework, *ikhtilaf* (disagreement) should not be frowned upon, dismissed and those who have *ikhtilaf* (disagreement) should be included in the discussion sessions, as the leaders should see discussions with the resisters as opportunities and platforms to learn more about the changes that the as the resisters tend to be able to see more complexities in the change situation. Mustaffa (1996) listed several ethical principles in the area of managing differences in opinions in Islam which includes possessing a positive attitude towards differences of opinions, multiple perspectives and viewpoints; having good opinions of others and avoiding opinionated attitudes and outlooks; communicate effectively and respectfully and deliberate ideas and thoughts thoroughly and deliberately; God-consciousness (*taqwa*) and brotherhood (*ukhuwwah*) are the primary pillars and guiding principles in managing all exchanges and differences of opinions, display utmost respect towards each other; and tolerate and make allowance to mistaken views and opinions.

The third major implication is that Islamic leadership contributes to the existing literature on transformational leadership by foregrounding the religious motivation for the leaders. Rather than a secular version of transformational leadership, transformational Islamic leadership is grounded in Islamic teachings. Education in Islam involves acquiring intellectual knowledge and spiritual knowledge. Ashraf (1993) argues that "[a]cquiring knowledge in Islam is not meant to be an end unto itself, but only a means to stimulate a more elevated moral and spiritual consciousness leading to faith and righteous action" (p. 23). It is detrimental to weigh reason more favourably than spirituality as this stunt the holistic growth and development of a man. Separating the spiritual development of the human being from the rational, temporal aspects of the same person, says one prominent Islamic educationalist, "is the main cause for the disintegration of the human personality" (Ashraf, 1993: 2). As demonstrated in our case study, both Leader A and Leader B reported that Islam influenced their behaviour and practices, and they both provided many examples from the Islamic faith that supported their practices. Leader A chose *khalifah fil ardh* (vicegerents on earth) as relatable to all in the madrasah community. This is very much enshrined in the Quran and portrayed throughout Islamic history.

CONCLUSION

This research study has provided an investigation of the leadership behaviour of Islamic leaders in a madrasah using the conceptual framework of transformational leadership. Since there is no previous research on Islamic school leadership in Singapore, this study has added to the knowledge base about leadership in an Islamic school in Singapore. The findings had identified a unique connection between transformational leadership behaviour and Islamic leadership principles. Consulting behaviour is closely aligned to concept and process of *shura* (mutual consultation) which is an integral component of Islamic leadership. Therefore, consulting as a leadership behaviour has its basis in Islam which would render it more appealing as a behaviour for Islamic leaders. Providing an appropriate model that sets an example for staff members is likewise consistent with how high Islam value its followers emulating the behaviour of the Prophet Muhammad as they then serve as role model for their own followers. Fostering a vision for the group is another transformational behaviour that is displayed in this study. However, in Islamic leadership, the leader needs to ponder and be more scrupulous in crafting the vision and ensure that it follows the Islamic worldview to garner full support from the followers.

As for future research, two recommendations are suggested to expand our knowledge of the Muslim leadership in a madrasah. First, more studies on Islamic leadership are needed to enhance the existing report. Future studies could examine leaders' values, principles and behaviour from other madaris in Singapore and other parts of the world. In addition, more studies on Islamic leadership should be conducted not only in educational arena, but in government and business community. The different environment, values and other mediating factors could be investigated on its impact on Islamic leadership. There could also be more research studies that examine the relationship between transformational leadership and demographic characteristics of teachers in Islamic schools. How teacher gender, ethnic background, years of experience, and ethnicity interact with principals' demographic characteristics to influence teacher perceptions might be considered in future research.

In conclusion, the findings of this study have shed light to those leadership behaviours that assist a smooth implementation of the changes and educational reforms in a madrasah environment. This study provides an opportunity for madrasah leaders to reflect on how others see them vis-as-vis how they see themselves, to unearth and discern their own leadership behaviour, and to provide better leadership in Islamic institutions. The findings from the study serve to inform policymakers of the complexity of the roles of the leader in a madrasah environment. The study hopes to foster better understanding and stimulate more dialogues between the policymakers and the madrasah leader and the madrasah community in general to further and enhance the relationship between them.

REFERENCES

Abdullah, O. (2007). *The role of madrasah education in Singapore: A study on the philosophy and practice of madrasah education in a secular state and plural society* (Unpublished masters dissertation). International Institute of Islamic Thought and Civilization (ISTAC), Kuala Lumpur.

Adnan, A. (2006). *A study of Islamic leadership theory and practice in K-12 Islamic schools in Michigan* (Unpublished doctoral dissertation). Brigham Young University.

Aljunied, S. M. K., & Dayang, I. H. (2005). Estranged from the ideal past: Historical evolution of madrassahs in Singapore. *Journal of Muslim Minority Affairs, 25*(2), 249–260. doi:10.1080/13602000500350694

Bass, B. M. (1998). *Transformational leadership: Industrial, military, and educational impact*. Mahwah, NJ: Erlbaum.

Bass, B. M., & Avolio, B. J. (Eds.). (1994). *Improving organisational effectiveness through transformational leadership*. Thousand Oaks, CA: Sage Publications.

Beekun, R. I., & Badawi, J. (1999). *Leadership: An Islamic perspective*. Amana Publications.

Burns, J. M. (1978). *Leadership*. New York: Harper & Row.

Fullan, M. (2001). *Leading in a culture of change*. Jossey Bass.

Hallinger, P. (2003). *Reshaping the landscape of school leadership development: A global perspective*. Portland, OR: Swets & Zeitlinger.

Hashim, R. (1997). The construction of an Islamic-based teacher education programme. *Muslim Education Quarterly, 14*(2), 57–68.

Juma'at, M. (1990). *Principal and teacher perceptions of the principal's instructional leadership role in primary schools* (Unpublished masters dissertation). National Institute of Education, Nanyang Technological University, Singapore.

Jusoh, K. A. (2009). *Siri Kepimpinan: Evolusi Kepimpinan 1, Tinjauan Teori-Teori Terpilih* [Leadership Series: The evolution of leadership, a study on selected theories]. Kuala Lumpur: Kasturi Jingga Corporation Sdn Bhd, 75.

Leithwood, K., & Jantzi, D. (2000). *Making schools smarter: A system for monitoring school and district progress*. Thousand Oaks, CA: Corwin Press.

Mustaffa. (1996). *Leadership dynamism: Instilling vision for the future century*. Kuala Lumpur: TerajuDinamikSdn.

Myint, S. K., & Salleh, I. M. (2009). *Transformative leadership and educational excellence*. Rotterdam: Sense Publishers.

Othman, M. S. B. A. (2004). Characteristics of Islamic management: principles and implementation. Brunei: Civil Service Institute.

Shams-ur-Rehman, T. (2008). Merging spirituality and religion: Developing an Islamic leadership theory. *IIUM Journal of Economics and Management, 16*(1), 15–46.

Tan, C. (2009). The reform agenda for madrasah education in Singapore. *Diaspora, Indigenous, and Minority Education, 3*(2), 67–80. doi:10.1080/15595690902762068

Tan, C. (Ed.). (2014). *Reforms in Islamic education: International perspectives*. London: Bloomsbury. doi:10.5040/9781472593252

Tan, C., & Abbas, D. B. (2009). The 'Teach Less, Learn More' initiative in Singapore: New pedagogies for Islamic religious schools? *KEDI Journal of Educational Policy, 6*(1), 25–39.

Tan, C., & Abbas, D. B. (2012). Madrasahs and the state: Which worldview? In J. Tan (Ed.), *Education in Singapore at the beginning of the 2010s* (pp. 89–99). Singapore: Prentice Hall.

Tan, C., & Abbas, D. B. (2017). Reform in Madrasah education: The Singapore experience. In M. Abu Bakar (Ed.), *Rethinking madrasah education in the globalised world* (pp. 195–209). New York: Routledge.

Tichy, N. M., & Devanna, M. A. (1986). *The transformational leader*. New York: Wiley.

Veithzal, R. D. A. A. (2009). *Islamic leadership: Membangun superleadership melalui kecerdasan spiritual* [Islamic leadership: Super leadership through spiritual intelligences]. Jakarta: PT Bumi Aksara.

Yukl, G. (2006). *Leadership in organisations* (6th ed.). Pearson Education.

Chapter 6
Development of Curriculum Keaswajaan (Nahdlatul 'Ulama) in Character Formation:
Moral Study on Islamic Education

Afiful Ikhwan
 https://orcid.org/0000-0002-6412-3830
Universitas Muhammadiyah Ponorogo, Indonesia

Ju'subaidi Ju'subaidi
Institut Agama Islam Negeri (IAIN) Ponorogo, Indonesia

Elfi Mu'awanah
Institut Agama Islam Negeri (IAIN) Tulungagung, Indonesia

Ali Rohmad
Institut Agama Islam Negeri (IAIN) Tulungagung, Indonesia

ABSTRACT

The curriculum is one component that has a strategic role in the formation of graduate character. Educational institutions have the authority to develop their curriculum in accordance with the development of society (social needs), the world of work (industrial needs), the development of science and profession (professional needs), as well as the specificity and superiority of educational institutions (core character building). The curriculum of college peculiarities developed as a course of personality character forming of learners. The course of keaswajaan (Nahdlatul 'Ulama / ke-NU-an) is a study material that aims to build a normative framework and Islamic charity according to the vision and mission of each college. This chapter aims to analyze and find the concept of character values in the curriculum of keaswajaan.

DOI: 10.4018/978-1-5225-8528-2.ch006

INTRODUCTION

The curriculum is a teaching and learning design program guided by educators and students. The curriculum is one component that has a strategic role in the education system (Rusman, 2009). From a very strategic and fundamental role in the running of good education the curriculum has a role in achieving goals because whether or not a curriculum can be seen from the process and the results of the achievements that have been taken (Lansu, Boon, Sloep, & van Dam-Mieras, 2013). Through national curriculum planning and development it has been and is always carried out by the government, including at the tertiary level as in this text the most important is how to realize and adjust the curriculum with learning activities.

In connection with the mandate to develop the curriculum, the conditions in the field show that there is a variety of abilities that universities have in developing the curriculum. There are universities that have been able to develop their curricula, and some have not been able to develop their curricula, this is due to competitiveness and human resources that are not upgraded, what else are universities under the auspices of the organization, most of its human resources are concurrent with other institutions this is one of the inhibiting factors of concentration in developing curriculum to improve the quality of Islamic education characterized in Islamic universities.

As stated in Government Regulation No. 17 of 2010 Article 97 states that "Higher education curriculum is developed and implemented based on competency (KBK)" (Pemerintah, 2010). This statement has reaffirmed Kepmendiknas No. 232 / U / 2000 concerning Guidelines for Preparation of Higher Education Curriculum and Assessment of Learning Outcomes of Students, as well as Kepmendiknas No. 045 / U / 2002 concerning Higher Education Core Curriculum.

Furthermore, with the enactment of Law Number 32 of 2004, the Regional Autonomy Government reminds of the possibilities of developing an area in a conducive atmosphere and in democratic insights which include the management and development of education. With the change in education management from a centralistic (central) nature, it turns into decentralized (regional). Tilaar emphasized that the policy of implementing national education that needs to be reconstructed in the context of regional autonomy or scientific autonomy related to improving the quality of education is through a national consensus between the government and all levels of society (Sidi, 2000).

The curriculum developed in the discussion of this manuscript focuses on the subject matter of the arts is a group of study materials and courses that aim to shape the attitudes and behavior of students (students), who are faithful and devoted to God Almighty and noble character, have a strong personality, and are independent and have social and national responsibilities. This group of courses has a content that determines the material of student identity, both related to him as a believer or an Indonesian, to be able to develop that personality, the methodological aspects of this subject group are not only built on the normative, speculative or intuitive paradigm rather, it is a compulsory subject that is built on the basis of the amali paradigm in Islam.

The application of compulsory subjects for the formation of the character of Islamic education, which is one of the bases in curriculum development in educational institutions under the auspices of Islamic organizations, is inseparable from the purpose of character building (students) after graduation truly has their own characteristics each of which has one goal, namely to improve the quality of its graduates in developing Islamic education as it is packaged into a tool called the curriculum, and also in line with the objectives of national education, namely to improve the quality of Islamic education achieved accurately (Direktorat Pendidikan Tinggi Agama Islam (Ditpertais) STAIN Kudus, 2014).

As with Lickona's theory, which views the character as having three interrelated elements, namely moral knowing, moral feeling, and moral action (Lickona, 2013), which form learners in accordance with the material of the eye. compulsory lecture forming personality personality at the Nadlatul 'Ulama (NU) campus. Lickona's thinking strives to be able to be used to shape the character of students in accordance with their respective characteristics in the location of research that researchers associate their sources from the Qur'an and Hadith.

As a higher education institution in the development process that must be oriented towards future (future oreiented university), it means that universities, institutes or high schools must prepare competitive graduates in facing global challenges and be able to carry out the duties and responsibilities for a heavier future, because participants students will not live in the same climate as the present and the future, therefore higher education must be able to capture competitive changes along with the rapid development of science with its distinctive autonomy.

The purpose of the discussion of this manuscript is to analyze and find the concept of character values in the religious curriculum developed in universities under the auspices of the Nahdlatul 'Ulama (NU) Islamic organization. The benefits of this manuscript discussion provide a broad perspective on the management of curriculum development in non-profit institutions, namely educational institutions, both educational institutions in the form of schools, madrasas or pesanteren and also good education at the primary, secondary and tertiary levels and also expected to be useful for concept formulation the management of curriculum development is to shape character in public schools (which adopt Islamic Education), in madrasas, or in Islamic boarding schools and also in education at the primary, secondary and tertiary levels.

Curriculum Development in an Islamic Perspective

According to the popular scientific management dictionary meaning management of business, management, management of effective use of resources to achieve the desired goals (Pius Partanto & Dahlan Albari, 2001). Etymologically, said management comes from the word managio which means management or managiare, which is training in managing steps, or it can also mean getting done through other people (Ikhwan, 2013). There is also another opinion that in terms of terms, management comes from managing. This word, comes from Italy; managgiare which literally means handling or training a horse, meaning it means leading, guiding, or regulating. So from the origin of this word, management can be interpreted as managing, controlling, leading or guiding (Mulyono, 2008).

According to management experts is the process of utilizing people or other sources to achieve organizational goals effectively and efficiently (Muhammad Eliyasin & Nanik Nurhayati, 2012). Nanang Fattah gives a restriction on the term management that management is a process of planning, organizing, leading, and controlling the organization's efforts in all its aspects so that organizational goals are achieved effectively and efficiently (Fattah, 2001).

Meanwhile, according to Malayu Hasibuan, it provides a definition that management as a science and art regulates the process of utilizing other resources effectively and efficiently to achieve certain goals (Hasibuan, 2008). Oemar Hamalik limits the definition of management as a social process with regard to the overall human endeavor with the help of other human beings and other sources, using efficient and effective methods to achieve previously determined goals (Hamalik, 2010).

From the various definitions above, it can be concluded that management is a science or art that regulates the process of utilizing human resources and other sources that support the achievement of goals effectively and efficiently. From this understanding can be raised a form of understanding that in management there is a process which is a form of ability or skill to obtain results in order to achieve goals through organizational activities. This process includes the initial stages of planning, organizing, guiding, controlling and evaluating to achieving goals.

Furthermore, relating to the characters in the world of management, character has the meaning of quality, degree, level (Pius Partanto & Dahlan Albari, 2001). In English, quality is termed "quality" (Salim, 1987). Whereas in Arabic it is called the term "juudah" (Ali, 2003). In terms of the term the character has a fairly diverse understanding, contains many interpretations and contradictions. This is because there is no standard measure of the character itself. So it is difficult to get a similar answer, whether something is of a quality character or not.

However, there are general criteria that have been agreed that something is said to have character, surely when it is of good value or has good meaning. Essentially the term quality indicates to something the size of an assessment or award given or imposed to the goods and or their performance (Aan Komariah dan Cepi Triatna, 2008).

According to B. Suryobroto, the concept of character / quality implies the meaning of the degree of excellence of a product (work / effort) in the form of goods and services, both tangible and intangible (Suryobroto, 2004). From some of the above meanings, quality has the meaning of size, content, provisions and assessment of the quality of goods and services (products) which have absolute and relative properties. In absolute terms, character is a high standard and cannot be excelled. Usually referred to as good, superior, beautiful, good, expensive, luxurious, etc (Sallis, 2012). When linked to the educational context, the concept of the character of education is elite, because there are only a few institutions that can provide educational experiences with high character to students who are poured directly into each line of activity with curriculum tools.

As explained above, in management there are several capabilities that must be possessed by the leadership. By using the foundation in Islam (Al-Qur'an, Al-Hadist and the words of the Companions) these abilities have actually been advocated and given an example by the Prophet, this means that competence has been regulated and considered in the concept of Islamic teaching, namely:

1.   Understanding of Insights or Educational Platform

"From An-Nas (May Allah bless to him) he said: Rasulah SAW has said" Searching for knowledge is obligatory to all Muslims. And getting knowledge is not an expert such as swarming pigs with gems, pearls and gold ". (Ibn Majah) (Lembaga Ilmu Dakwah & Publikasi Sarana Keagamaan, 2011).

2.   Understanding of students

"Indeed, for the sake of my father and mother, I have never seen a teacher before (Rasullah) or after him who better teaches from him. And for Allah's sake, he never hates me, never hits me or denounces me. He says" Surely this prayer not worthy of him in the slightest words of man. Only he is a Tasbih, a Takbir and a Qiratul Qur'an. "(Muslim) (Al-Bani, 2008).

3.   Curriculum Development

"Ali ibn Abi Talib said: Teach your children then they were created for an age that is not your age" (Muslim) (Al-Bani, 2008).

4.   Learning Design

"O ye who believe, fear Allah and let every one of you pay attention to what He has done for tomorrow (the Hereafter); and fear Allah, Verily Allah knows what you do" (Al-Hasr: 18) (Taufiq, n.d.).

5.   Exemplary Learning Implementation

"Call (men) to the path of your Lord with good wisdom and teaching and debate with them in a good way. Verily your Lord is the one who knows more about who is lost from His way and who knows more about those who get guidance "(an-Nahl: 125) (Taufiq, n.d.).

6.   Utilization of Learning Technology

"Who teaches (humans) by using a pen" (Al-'Alaq: 4) (Taufiq, n.d.)

7.   Evaluation

"Gabriel's condition always tests the Prophet Muhammad. Indeed the condition of the Prophet is the most generous person among humans especially when the month of Ramadan when the Angel Gabriel met him. Gabriel met the Prophet in every night in the month of Ramadan. Then the Prophet read the Qur'an when Gabriel met with him the Prophet is the most generous person with kindness like the wind that blows. (Mutafaqun 'Alaihi) (Lembaga Ilmu Dakwah & Publikasi Sarana Keagamaan, 2011).

The management process includes four stages in the form of planning, organizing, guiding, actuating, controlling and evaluating, as in the Qur'an also explained.

Character Values in Indonesia

The values developed in cultural education and national character are identified from the following sources (Andriani, 2015):

1.   Religion: Indonesian people are religious communities. Therefore, the lives of individuals, communities and nations are always based on the teachings of religion and belief. Politically, state life is based on values that come from religion. On the basis of these considerations, the values of cultural education and national character must be based on values and rules that come from religion.

2. Pancasila: the unitary state of the Republic of Indonesia is upheld on the principles of national and state life called Pancasila. Pancasila is found in the Preamble of the 1945 Constitution and further elaborated in the articles contained in the 1945 Constitution. This means that the values contained in Pancasila become values that govern political, legal, economic, social, cultural and artistic life. Cultural education and national character aims to prepare students to become better citizens, namely citizens who have the ability, will, and apply the values of Pancasila in their lives as citizens.

3. Culture: as a truth that there is no human being who lives in a society that is not based on cultural values that are recognized by the community. These cultural values are used as a basis for giving meaning to a concept and meaning in communication between members of the community. Such important cultural positions in people's lives require that culture be a source of value in cultural education and national character.

4. National Education Objectives: as a formulation of quality that must be possessed by every Indonesian citizen, developed by various education units at various levels and pathways. The purpose of national education contains various human values that must be owned by Indonesian citizens. Therefore, the aim of national education is the most operational source in the development of cultural education and national character.

Character education is understood as an effort to instill intelligence in thinking, appreciation in the form of attitudes, and experiences in the form of behavior in accordance with the noble values that become his identity. The naming of character education cannot just transfer knowledge or train a certain skill. Character education needs processes, exemplary examples, habituation or civilization in the environment of students in a school/ madrasah environment, family, community environment, or the mass media environment.

The values for the nation's cultural and character education are eighteen, as shown in the table below (Andriani, 2015):

VALUE AND CHARACTER EDUCATION APPROACH

1. Approach Definition

The approach is generally defined as our starting point or point of view of the learning process, which refers to the view of the occurrence of a process that is still very general, in which it accommodates, inspires, strengthens, and bases learning methods with certain theoretical coverage.

Table 1. Values of Cultural Education and Character of Indonesian Nation

No	Value	Description
1	Religious	Attitudes and behaviors that are obedient in carrying out the teachings of their religion, tolerant of the implementation of other religious services, and live in harmony with other religious followers.
2	Honest	Behavior based on the effort to make himself a person who can always be trusted in words, actions, and work
3	Tolerance	Attitudes and actions that respect different religions, ethnicities, ethnicities, opinions, attitudes and actions of others.
4	Discipline	Actions that show orderly behavior and comply with various rules and regulations.
5	Hard Work	Behavior that shows genuine effort in overcoming various obstacles to learning and assignments, as well as completing tasks as well as possible.
6	Creative	Thinking and doing something to produce new ways or results from something that you already have.
7	Mandiri	Attitudes and behaviors that are not easily dependent on others in completing tasks.
8	Democratic	Ways to think, act and act that assesses the rights and obligations of himself and others.
9	Curiosity	Attitudes and actions that always strive to know more deeply and broadly from something they learn, see, and hear.
10	The spirit of nationality	The way of thinking, acting and being mindful that places the interests of the nation and the state above their self and group interests.
11	Homeland Love	How to think, behave and act that shows loyalty, care and high appreciation for the language, physical environment, social, cultural, economic and political nation.
12	Appreciating Achievements	Attitudes and actions that encourage him to produce something that is useful for the community, and recognize, and respect the success of others.
13	Friendly/ Communicative	Actions that show pleasure in talking, associating, and working with others.
14	Love of Peace	Attitudes, words, and actions that cause others to feel happy and safe for their presence.
15	Love to Read	Habits provide time to read various readings that give virtue to him.
16	Care for the Environment	Attitudes and actions that always try to prevent damage to the surrounding natural environment, and develop efforts to repair the natural damage that has already occurred.
17	Social Care	Attitudes and actions that always want to provide assistance to other people and communities in need.
18	Responsibility	A person's attitude and behavior to carry out his duties and obligations, which he should do, to himself, the community, the environment (natural, social and cultural), the state and God Almighty.

Language, approach means process, action, and approach. With this understanding, the approach in the context of education can be interpreted as a process, act, and approach to and facilitate the implementation of education.

The approach according to T. Raka Joni quoted by Soli Abimanyu and Sulo Lipu La Sulo is interpreted as a common way of looking at problems or objects of study. So, the approach is used when it comes to common ways and or assumptions in addressing a problem in the direction of the solution. For example, the system approach led to the perceived linkage between a number of elements considered to have systemic relations.

In general, the approach to learning is viewed in terms of the process divided into two, namely; a teacher-oriented / educational institution approach (traditionat teacher/ institution centered approach) and student-centered approach (Andriani, 2015).

a.   *Traditionat Teacher/Institution Centered Approach*

A teacher-oriented / educational institution approach is a conventional learning system where almost all learning activities are controlled by teachers and staff of educational institutions (schools) (Desai & Johnson, 2014). The teacher communicates his knowledge to students based on the demands of the syllabus. Characteristics of a teacher-oriented approach that the teaching and learning process or communication process takes place in the classroom with face-to-face lecture methods scheduled by the school. During the learning process, students only receive what is conveyed by the teacher and are only given the opportunity to ask questions (Andriani, 2015).

b.   *Student Centered Approach*

Learning approach oriented to students is a learning system that shows the dominance of students during learning activities and the teacher is only as a facilitator, mentor and leader. Learning characteristics with a student-oriented approach that learning activities vary by using a variety of learning resources, methods, media, and strategies alternately so that during the learning process students participate actively both individually and in groups (Andriani, 2015).

2. Value and Character Education Approach According to Experts

Thomas Lickona in his book Educating for Character: How Our Schools Can Teach Respect and Responsibility exemplifies the moral crisis that occurs, in this case in America, starting with the outbreak of individualism that emphasizes personal interests and has given rise to an attitude of selfishness as a lifestyle. The nature of individualism tends to be selfish and then develops into a lot of deviations in values and characters, in this example Lickona shows 10 indications, such as violence and acts of anarchy, theft, fraudulent acts, neglect of applicable rules, brawl between students, intolerance, language use that is not good, premature sexual maturity and irregularities, and self-destructive attitudes (Dalmeri, 2014).

In 1987, this kind of moral setback was felt by many countries who joined in a conference on moral education. As a conclusion, at the conference, paralysis in the value field tended to focus on the problems that occurred several years ago regarding the teaching of values. That is, the education system must again be used as a media that can help these downturns.

In the same language, Asep Saeful Hidayat said that the quality of the learning process is the object of the first accusation against the low character of students. Learning designer experts place a step in analyzing student characteristics before the selection step and developing learning strategies. This implies that whatever learning theory is developed and whatever strategy or approach chosen for learning needs must be based on character values (Dalmeri, 2014).

In this case, through 11 Principles of Character Education Thomas Lickona proposed principles in character education, one of which was the use of a comprehensive, intentional and proactive approach to character building. In his explanation related to the purpose of a comprehensive, intentional and proactive approach here, Lickona further wrote:

"Schools committed to character development look at themselves through a character lens to assess how virtually everything that goes on in school affects the character of students. A comprehensive approach uses all aspects of schooling as opportunities for character development. This includes the formal academic curriculum and extracurricular activities, as well as what is sometimes called the hidden or informal curriculum (e.g., how school procedures reflect core values, how adults model good character, how the instructional process respects students, how student diversity is addressed, and how the discipline policy encourages student reflection and growth)" *(Lickona, 2010).*

Which means that in this approach schools as education providers must see that almost everything in the school environment will influence the formation of students' character so that all aspects in it are used as opportunities for character development, both in formal academic curricula and extra-curricular activities. Character values in the learning process are also deliberately included and carefully designed as an integral part of learning.

Different Thomas Lickona, Superka in more detail provides 5 approaches that can be used in values and character education. This approach is an inculcation approach, a cognitive moral development approach, a value analysis approach, a value clarification approach, and an action learning approach (Dalmeri, 2014). Each approach proposed by Douglas P. Superka can be explained as follows:

a.   Inculcation Approach

The investment approach (inculcation approach) is an approach that emphasizes the planting of social values in students. The purpose of the value planting approach is to instill certain desired values. According to this approach, values are seen as standards or rules of behavior originating from society and culture. Assessing is considered as the identification of processes and socialization where someone, sometimes unconsciously, takes the standards or norms of other people, groups, or communities and combines them into their own value system (Superka, 1976).

In this view the task of value education is to instill values so that people must place themselves efficiently according to the roles determined by society. Furthermore, this value planting approach is often assumed to be a negative approach. But this approach is often used by many people, including the clergy (Zakaria, 2000).

As an example of this approach, Superka suggests that a teacher, for example, might react very deeply and violently to a student who has just said racial insults to other students in the class (Superka, 1976).

This can be an example of a short but emotional form of education on the crime of racism or a simple expression of disappointment in student behavior. However, the teacher in this position is doing what is called implanting. Perhaps this is because he believes that the eternal values of human dignity and respect for individuals are very important for the survival of a democratic society. This reflects the widespread belief that, in order to ensure the continuity of culture, certain basic values must be instilled in its members.

The method often used in the learning process according to this approach includes: exemplary, positive and negative reinforcement, simulation, role playing, and so on (Dalmeri, 2014). Of the several methods above, according to Superka, what is often used and effective is the strengthening method. This process may involve positive reinforcement, as the teacher praises students for behaving according to certain values. while the negative reinforcement can be done by the teacher by, for example, punishing students who behave contrary to certain desired values. In many ways reinforcement often only smiles or, sullen will tend to strengthen certain values. But reinforcement is still applied consciously and systematically.

Another method that can be used is the exemplary method, which in Superka language is called the modeling method, in which certain people are used as models of desired values where the teacher expects students to adopt these values (Superka, 1976).

However, as an approach to the education process, the value-planting approach has advantages and disadvantages. These advantages and disadvantages include (Zakaria, 2000): (a) surplus: this approach is widely used in various societies and adherents of religion have a strong tendency to use this approach in the implementation of religious education programs. (b) minus: this approach is considered indoctrinal, not in accordance with the development of democratic life and this approach is considered to ignore the right of children to choose their own values freely.

b.   Cognitive Moral Development Approach

This approach is often referred to as a cognitive development approach because its characteristics emphasize cognitive and developmental aspects. This approach is an attempt to stimulate students to develop more complex moral reasoning patterns through successive and sequential stages. The sequential stages here are defined as the stages of development of thinking in making moral judgments, from the lower levels to the higher levels.

This cognitive moral development approach is based on moral development theory. In the theory put forward by Kolhberg, that human cognitive development is divided into three levels, namely:

i.   Pre-Conventional Level

At this level rules contain moral measures made based on authority. Children do not violate moral rules for fear of threats or punishment from authorities.

This level is divided into two stages. First, the stage of orientation towards compliance and punishment. At this stage the child only knows that the rules are determined by the existence of power that cannot be contested. The child must obey, or if not, will be punished. Second, the relativistic stage of hedonism. At this stage the child is no longer absolutely dependent on the rules that are outside of himself that are determined by others who have authority. Children begin to realize that each incident has several aspects that depend on one's needs (relativism) and pleasure (hedonism) (Kurnia, 2008).

ii.   Conventional Level

At this level the child obeys the rules that are made together to be accepted in his group. Attitude is defined not only in conformity with social order, but also loyalty. As a result, individuals actively maintain, support and identify with people or groups within it.

This level also consists of two stages. First, the orientation phase regarding good children. At this stage the child begins to show the orientation of actions that can be considered good or not good by others or the community. Something is said to be good and true if the attitude and behavior can be accepted by other people or society. Second, the stage of maintaining social norms and authority. At this stage the child shows good and right actions not only to be accepted by the surrounding community, but also aims to be able to maintain the existing social rules and norms as a moral obligation and responsibility to implement the existing rules.

iii.   Post-Conventional Level

At this level the child obeys the rules to avoid the punishment of his conscience. At this level there is a clear attempt to achieve a personal definition of moral values to determine principles that have validity and separate applications from group authority and separate from individual identification with the group.

This level also consists of two stages. First, the orientation phase towards the agreement between himself and the social environment. At this stage there is a reciprocal relationship between himself and the social and community environment. Someone obeys the rules as an obligation and responsibility in maintaining the harmony of community life. Second, the universal stage. At this stage, in addition to the existence of subjective personal norms, there are also ethical norms (good / bad, right / wrong) that are universal as sources of determining something related to morality.

A brief cognitive development approach can be used in the process of education in schools, because this approach emphasizes the developmental aspects of thinking skills. Therefore, this approach pays full attention to moral issues and resolves problems related to the contradiction of certain values in society by paying attention to the levels and stages mentioned. Its use can turn on the classroom atmosphere.

The method that can be used in this cognitive development approach is to present the value of factual stories which are then discussed in small groups. Through short reading or film, students are presented with stories that involve one or more characters who are faced with a moral dilemma. Students are asked to state what must be done by the person in the story and by giving reasons for the answer, and then discuss it with others.

Kohlberg's research shows that exposing students to a higher level of reasoning through group discussion stimulates them to reach the next stage of moral development. Kohlberg's theory is considered to be most consistent with scientific theory, sensitive to distinguishing ability in making moral judgments, supporting moral development, and exceeding various other theories based on the results of empirical research.

According to Galbraith and Jones, there are three important variables in group discussion related to moral issues in order to run effectively, and thus, there is an increase in moral development in students. The three variables are:

- Stories that present real conflict to a person who is the main character, including a number of moral issues that need to be considered, and issues / problems that result in differences of opinion between students about the appropriate response to these situations.
- A leader who can help focus the discussion on moral reasoning.
- Classroom climate that encourages students to express their moral reasoning freely.

However, as an approach to the educational process, cognitive moral development approaches have advantages and disadvantages. These advantages and disadvantages include:

Surplus of Cognitive Moral Development Approaches

- The cognitive development approach is easy to use in the process of education in schools, because this approach emphasizes the developmental aspects of thinking skills.
- Because this approach pays full attention to moral issues and resolves problems related to certain values in the community, the use of this approach is interesting.
- Its use can turn on the classroom atmosphere.

Minus of Cognitive Moral Development Approaches

- This approach displays the biases of western culture. Among other things, it highly upholds personal freedom based on liberal philosophy.
- This approach also does not attach importance to the criteria of right wrong for an action. What is important is the reason stated or moral considerations.

c. Values Analysis Approach

Value analysis approach emphasizes the development of students' ability to think logically, by analyzing problems related to social values. When compared with the cognitive development approach, one of the differences between the two is the value analysis approach emphasizes more on the discussion of problems that contain social values. The cognitive development approach emphasizes individual moral dilemmas. In contrast to the moral development approach, value analysis concentrates primarily on social value issues rather than personal moral dilemmas. Therefore, the analytical approach provides an understanding of aspects of moral values that can be applied to social life.

There are two main goals of moral education according to this approach. First, it helps students to use logical thinking skills and scientific findings in analyzing social problems, which are related to certain moral values. Second, helping students to use rational and analytic thinking processes, in connecting to formulate concepts about their values.

The philosophical basis of the analytical approach is a combination of rationalist and empirical views of human nature. Assessing is a cognitive process of determining and justifying facts. Thus, the valuing process can and should be carried out based on facts and reasons, and the consideration is not of conscience, but with logic rules and procedures.

The method most often used in an analytical approach to assess an action is a group learning method based on social value problems and issues, library study and field research, and rational class discussion. The stages of intellectual operations that are often used in value analysis include stating the problem, questioning and strengthening the relevance of the report, applying the same case to fulfill the requirements and correcting the position of values, showing logical and empirical inconsistencies in the argument, and testing evidence.

However, as an approach to the educational process, the value analysis approach has advantages and disadvantages. These advantages and disadvantages include: (a) surplus: easy to apply in classrooms, because of its emphasis on developing cognitive abilities and this approach offers systematic steps in the implementation of the moral learning process. (b) minus: this approach strongly emphasizes cognitive aspects, and instead ignores the affective and behavioral aspects and this approach is the same as the cognitive development approach and the value clarification approach, very heavy giving emphasis to the process, less concerned with the value.

d. Values Clarification Approach

A value clarification approach (emphasis clarification approach) emphasizes efforts to help students in assessing their own feelings and actions, and increase their awareness of their own values by thinking rationally and also using emotional awareness together.

The value education objectives according to this approach are three, namely: First, helping students to realize and identify their own values and the values of others. Second, helping students so that they are able to communicate openly and honestly with others, related to values that can be actualized in their own lives. Third, help students, so that they are able to use together the ability to think rationally and emotional awareness, to understand their own feelings, values, and patterns of behavior.

So, the value classification approach can provide more objective insight for students in living their social life in accordance with the moral values that apply to shape their character.

The clarification approach is a more complex approach than other values education approaches so that sometimes uses various methods. This method includes small group discussions and large group discussions, individual and group work, listening to songs and artwork, games and simulations, as well as personal journals and interviews. These methods are designed to stimulate students to reflect on their thoughts, feelings, actions, and values.

However, as an approach to the education process, the value clarification approach has advantages and disadvantages. These advantages and disadvantages include: (a) surplus: this approach gives high appreciation to students as individuals who have the right to choose, respect, and act based on their own values and the teaching method is also very flexible, as long as it is seen in accordance with the formulation of the assessment process and four specified guidelines. (b) minus: this approach also displays the biases of western culture, in this approach, the criteria for right and wrong are very relative, because they attach great importance to individual values and value education according to this approach does not have a specific purpose with regard to value. Because, for adherents of this approach, determining a number of values for students is unnatural and unethical.

e. Action Learning Approach

The action learning approach (action learning approach) emphasizes efforts to provide opportunities for students to perform moral actions, both individually and collectively in a group.

There are two main objectives of moral education based on this approach. First, giving students the opportunity to do moral actions, both individually and collectively, based on their own values. Second, encourage students to see themselves as individual beings and social beings in association with others, who do not have complete freedom, but as citizens of a society, who must take part in a democratic process.

The teaching methods used in the value analysis and value clarification approaches are also used in this approach.

However, as an approach to the education process, learning approaches do have advantages and disadvantages. These advantages and disadvantages include: (a) surplus: the programs provided and provide opportunities for students to actively participate in democratic life where opportunities like this, get less attention in various other approaches. (b) minus: difficult to do. According to him, some of the programs developed by Newmann can be used, but overall it is difficult to implement.

Concept of Character Values in the *Keaswajaan* (Nahdlatul 'Ulama) Curriculum

1. Moderate Values (Tawassuth)

Khairul umuri aw sathuha (moderate is the best of deeds). Tawassuth can be interpreted as standing in the middle, moderate, not extreme, but has a steadfast attitude and stand in the face of a dilemmatic position between liberals and conservatives, right and left, Jabariyah and Qadariah, by considering the benefit of the people in the corridors of the guidance of the Qur'an and Sunnah .

Being tawassuth in the field of aqidah is on the one hand not trapped in blind and too liberal rationality (thus excluding the Qur'an and the sunnah of the messenger), on the other hand still puts the mind to think and interpret the Qur'an and al-Sunnah in accordance with conditions.

Tawassuth's jurisprudence or Islamic law is a set of legal concepts that are based on the Qur'an and sunnah, but its understanding is not just relying on tradition, nor on rationality of reason alone. Tawassuth's Sufism is a divine spirituality that rejects the concept of achieving haqiqah (the nature of God) by leaving the Shari'ah or vice versa. Tawassuth's Sufism makes taqwa (shari'ah) the main road to nature (Dewan Redaksi Ensiklopedia Islam, 1997).

2. Tolerance Values (Tasamuh)

Tasammuh is tolerant, an attitude pattern that respects differences, does not impose a will and feels right on its own. Values that govern how we must behave in daily life, especially in religious and community life. Let everything be particular, it doesn't have to be uniform with us. The direction of this tolerance is awareness of pluralism or diversity, whether in religion, culture, belief, and every dimension of life that should complement each other. As the concept of *bhinneka tunggal ika* (different but still one) and the verse of Al-Quran which reads *"lakum dinukum wal-yadin"* (for you your religion, for me my religion) with this difference we get mercy, our lives are more varied.

In the current flow of philosophy, it is time to sweep (sweep) and break down the metaphysics of presence (a single concept whose truth is one). A concept that imposes its truth on others, without accepting differences and rejecting other truths.

3. Balance Values (Tawazun)

Tawazun means a balance in the pattern of relationships or relations, both those that are between individuals, between social structures, between the State and its people, as well as between humans and nature. Balance here is a form of relationship that is not biased (benefiting certain parties and harming others). However, each party is able to place itself in accordance with its function without disrupting the function of the other party. The expected outcome is the creation of a dynamic life.

In the social domain that is emphasized is egalitarianism (equality of degree) of all humanity. No one feels more than others, the only difference is the level of piety. There is no domination and exploitation of someone to other people, including men to women.

In the political sphere, tawazun requires a balance between the position of the State (rulers) and the people. The ruler must not act arbitrarily, close the taps of democracy, and oppress his people. Whereas the people must always comply with all regulations aimed at common interests, but also always control and supervise the running of the government.

In the economic sphere, tawazun requires the development of a balanced economic system between the position of the State, the market and the community. The function of the State is as a regulator of financial circulation, capital turnover, the making of signs or rules for playing together and controlling their implementation. The task of the market is to distribute products that position consumers and producers in a balanced manner, without any party being bullied. The function of society (especially consumers) on the one hand is to create a conducive economic environment in which there is no monopoly; and on the other hand controls the work of the state and the market.

4. Justice Values (Ta'adul)

The purpose of ta'adul is justice, which is an integral pattern of tawassuth, tasamuh, and tawazun. With balance, tolerance and moderation, it will lead to a value of justice which is the universal teaching of Aswaja. Every thought, attitude and relationship must always be aligned with this value. The meaning of justice that is meant here is social justice. That is the truth value that regulates the totality of political, economic, cultural, educational, and so on. History proves how the Prophet Muhammad was able to make it happen in Medina society. So also Umar bin Khattab who has laid the foundation for a great Islamic civilization. Actually these four values are the methods of thinking and patterns of social change of the Prophet and his companions.

Concept of the Development of *Keaswajaan* (Nahdlatul 'Ulama) Curriculum

First, the curriculum in each Study Program in the Nahdlatul 'Ulama Education Institution has a concept of around 30% which is developed on the emphasis on its originality, such as in the subject matter of the arts itself by using the development concept design of the curriculum subject matter (curriculum that presents courses separately from each other), like PAI material, a lot. Islamic civilization, kalam science, fiqh science, perbasi mazhab, qiraatul qutub, and the method of da'wah, it is all contained in the basic competency and syllabus indicators and SAP by each lecturer with integrated (Ikhwan, 2014) among them and strengthens the values of their creativity in each subject besides the subject of religion, and It is all through good planning, organizing, actuiting and evaluating, including lecture material, all of which are as stated in the Syllabus and Lecture Program Unit (SAP) in any subject that emphasizes aswaja.

Secondly, the development of the curriculum in all the study programs at the Nahdlatul 'Ulama Education Institute is more in the concept of the Shafi'i school of thought, as well as the NU's general understanding. This is to reflect an institution or institution with the concept of ahlus'sunnah waljama'ah in accordance with the name of the course and creating a Private Islamic Religion Higher Education (PTAIS) which is different from other institutions, while the conceptual values are tawasuth (moderate, attitude middle, middle, not extreme left or extreme right), tasamuh (tolerance), tawazun (balanced in all things, including the use of theorem 'aqli and dalil naqli), tasawuf (purifying the soul), and amar ma'ruf nahi munkar .

Third, the concept of developing (Ikhwan, 2017) a local content curriculum focuses more on this emphasis on Islamic understanding than on other scientific disciplines, this assumption is because the Nahdlatul 'Ulama Educational Institution is an Islamic higher education institution which is also under Nahdlatul' Ulama.

Fourth, in order to truly fit the curriculum concept of the organization with the vision of the umbrella organization, NU, the Nahdlatul 'Ulama Education Institute requires all lecturers and registered staff to be members of NU with proof of KARTANU (NU Member Card), as well as the recruitment of Lecturer Educators and The Education Personnel, it was stated expressly that it did not mean discrimination, but according to the vision and mission set forth in the AD / ART before this campus was established and also so that the formation and development of the curriculum in the Nahdlatul 'Ulama Educational Institution did not come out of the character of its originality.

Fifth, the concept of the Islamic curriculum starts from the goals of NU, starting from the teachings, history, thoughts and characters, namely: instilling principles of religiousness towards students in acting and behaving whose basic principles include ahlussunnah wal jama'ah, tasawuf (purifying the soul), tawazun (balanced between worldly and ukhrawi), moderate (middle way), not radical or extreme.

Sixth, the concept of developing a curriculum worthy of the scholarship in the Nahdlatul Educational Institution 'This scholarship is conditional and flexible, it always develops through the results of the NU conference, so the core concept of religiousness is used in all NU universities including the Nahdlatul' Ulama Educational Institution.

Seventh, the concepts of intra curricular and extra curricular that are interrelated and mutually supportive are also integrated (Othman, Hussien, Ahmad, Rashid, & Badzis, 2017), such as the NU Youth (IPNU), Fatayat, Banser, Indonesian Islamic Students Movement (PMII), Pencak Silat Pagar Nusa (PN), etc.

Development of *Keaswajaan* (Nahdlatul 'Ulama) Curriculum

First, the implementation of religious values at all levels of education whose educational institutions are under the auspices of NU characterized by the character of religion to be relevant by following the development of science and technology.

Secondly, the implementation of religious values at all levels of education whose educational institutions are under the auspices of NU characterized by religious character become relevant by aligning socio-cultural conditions such as: students' psychological development related to intelligence, environmental influences, absorption of graduates by the workforce are factors that influence the implementation of religious values.

Third, the implementation of religious values at all levels of education whose educational institutions are under the auspices of NU characterized and characterized by being relevant to adjusting environmental conditions (stakeholders) such as: the influence of environmental culture, the influence of globalization, political influence, demands of the community, etc. it is all in harmony with current developments (contemporary). NU 20 years ago must be different from NU at this time, because if the development of the curriculum of religious values is not able to analyze the development of the three then the existence of the curriculum as an artery in education is not relevant to be actualized.

Fourth, the implementation of religious values is also a demand of the Higher Education Data Base (PD-Dikti), all of the lecturers' track records are clear and detailed in it: educational history, research records and community service whether or not based on religion, so the community can also knowing and taking part in supervising and overseeing the development of the campus, is it really in accordance with the vision and mission of the Nahdlatul Education Institute? Islamic campus scholars who are under the auspices of the NU Islamic organization.

Fifth, the development of science and technology is a major factor in the management of curriculum development in implementing religious values, so that it can be achieved in accordance with the vision and mission of the NU Islamic organizations and Islamic organizations, according to the expectations of the people who have recently been busy with Islamic issues. hard-line.

Sixth, the implementation of the development of a curriculum worthy of the arts at the Nahdlatul 'Ulama Education Institute is to see the market needs or satisfaction of the NU community consumers, the influence of Islamic culture, the demands of the Islamic community at large by referring and always adopting the latest books on aswajaan, browsing the internet (Web PB NU) and discussions with NU figures.

Seventh, the implementation of religious values in curriculum development in character building through four stages; (a) planning; by adhering to the vision and mission of the educational institution foundation and NU, as the results of the 33rd NU Congress in Jombang, then the "Islam Nusantara" program, a five-year curriculum workshop presents curriculum experts with recommendations from PC NU Kabupeten or NU Provincial PW, inviting the head of the school or madrasah NU, Ma'arif, Diponegoro and under the auspices of other NU foundations, the preparation of the Syllabus and the Lecture Program Unit (SAP) in every 30% Islamic course, the making of dictates to all permanent lecturers, writing a reference book about the religion to hold mandatory learners, plan research and service about Islam Nusantara, Islam Aswaja, Traditional Islam through its publication unit in the form of journals, research results, books, articles on the NU website and the Nahdlatul 'Ulama Education Institute. (b) organizing; form Team Work Sie. Division of Higher Education NU Branch Management, Chairperson of Educational Institution Foundation, Head of Educational Institution as director, Deputy Head as responsible for academic field which is broken down by accountability to the head of department, then goes down to chairmen of study programs who determine scheduling of Islamic and Islamic subjects., the quality assurance center (PJM) of the institution as a control of the curriculum development process and community research and development center (P3M) supporting lecturers' activities in the field of research, the writing of the religious textbooks, community service about the arts and lecturers as the implementers of the curriculum and the Academic staff especially the programming part courses, (c) implementation (actuiting); (1) during OSPEK (Campus Introduction Orientation) there are Islamic religious material, (2) general stage, (3) students are distributed in the handbook of students' code of ethics, (4) integrating the character values of the students in each step and activities adapted to the objectives to be achieved, not only in the course (intra curricular), apart from such extracurricular activities: Indonesian Islamic Student Movement (PMII), Nahdlatul 'Ulama Youth Association (IPNU), Fatayat (for female students), Pencak Pagar Nusa Silat, (5) halaqah (study) or monthly seminars about the authenticity of lecturers to students outside lectures by reviewing the yellow book of lecturers from the lecturer on schedule, (6) lectures by emphasizing honesty, healthy competition, and always inviting to do something by starting with yourself. So that in the end these things will become a culture that has an impact on the reality of the implementation of character formation with tawasuth values (moderate, middle, moderate, not extreme left or extreme right), tasamuh (tolerance), tawazun (balanced in all matters, including the use of theorem 'aqli and the proposition of naqli), Sufism (sanctifying the soul), and amar ma'ruf nahi munkar (7) integration in each of the subjects of silence by referring to the subject of scholarship and (d) assessment (evaluating) ; (1) input from the community (stakeholders) through an umbrella organization (educational institution foundation), (2) the lecturer controls and assesses whether there is an addition to the current Aswaja issue from the results of the application of courses in the classroom, related to NU, ISIS, etc. if deemed necessary the addition or reduction will be delivered when the five-year curriculum workshop will come at the same time for the preparation of re-accreditation, (3) through the Midterm Examination (UTS) and the Final Semester Examination (UAS), (4) analyzing the results of the lecturers' assessment conducted by students at the end of each semester from the Center for Quality Assurance (PJM) with a minimum standard score of sixty-five (65).

RECOMMENDATIONS AND FUTURE DIRECTION

The author hopes this article can contribute to the Educational Institution. Based on the findings about the curriculum development strategy and its influence on the quality of education, the researchers then presented the following suggestions:

The central government (Sidiq & Ikhwan, 2018) as the protector of educational institutions is time to pay more attention to the existence of private educational institutions that are under the auspices of Islamic organizations and educators, so that they are motivated and willing to work as well as possible for the advancement of Islamic education.

Publish the "success" achieved by private education institutions in changing the conditions of their institutions, to be exemplified or adopted by leaders of other Islamic institutions or other parties who have an interest in advancing their organization, so that private education institutions are considered advanced and able to compete with public education institutions or general who is more senior and big.

For other researchers who are interested in conducting research on the Management of Curriculum Development in the Characterization of Character Building, there are still many gaps or problems that can be examined. This is one way to participate in improving private education institutions that have been considered left behind.

This study contains a number of limitations, so it is important to conduct further research, especially on Curriculum Development Management in the Formation of Student Character from other fields such as quality assurance performance, or about the competence of human resources (HR) such as the achievements of lecturers and students, because these fields determine the improvement of education quality.

CONCLUSION

Formation of the character of the character with a programmed and non-programmed integration pattern between the curriculum that has been established (programmed) by educational institutions and daily behavior (non-program). (1) Moral Knowing (knowledgeable character); moral awareness, understanding the belief based on the Qur'an and al-Hadith, moral values can distinguish between good/ Islamic character and bad, perspective-taking gives a view to other people's character, moral reasoning adjusts to the conditions and situations of science and technology, social and stakeholder, decision making makes decisions in dealing with character problems at any time after situations and conditions, self-knowledge knows itself by referring to the Qur'an and al-Sunnah. (2) Moral Feeling (feeling character); conscience, learning self-esteem with conscience, Lecturer self-esteem gives a task to do for self-esteem, responsibility, honesty, and kindness in accordance with the values of religion, empathy or tolerance among fellow human beings, loving the good love in the goodness of the key to the character of beauty, self-control controls itself to curb pleasure beyond the limits of the teachings of religious values, humility humility correct weaknesses or lacks/ evaluates themselves on the basis of self-reliance. (3) Moral Action (character action), competence can overcome conflict by listening, communicating and deciding together the problem solving for benefit, Will mobilizes moral energy about what is being thought and what must be done does not come out of the values of religion, one heart with what is done and what has been known after studying the beauty, the habit of cultivating being good and right according to the values of religion. Cognitive (intelligence), affective (behavioral) and psychomotor (skill) learners appear to be in accordance with NU's vision and mission. The implementation of the curriculum is influenced internally and externally; internal curriculum of religious subjects that interact with other subjects both compulsory and optional, such as courses on Islamic religious education, history of Islamic civilization, science of kalam, science of fiqh, ulumul qur'an, ulumul hadith, comparison of mazhab, qira'atul qutub and the method of da'wah. Whereas the external ones; (1) in the Nahdlatul 'Ulama Education Institute PMII, IKA-PMII, IPNU, Fatayat, and the Center for Philosophy and Theology Studies (PKFT).

REFERENCES

Aan Komariah dan Cepi Triatna. (2008). Visionary Leadership: Menuju Sekolah Efektif terj. Ahmad Ali Riadi & Fahrurozi. Jakarta: Bumi Aksara.

Al-Bani, M. N. (2008). *Ringkasan Shahih Muslim, terj., Elly Lathifah*. Jakarta: Gema Insani.

Ali, A. (2003). *Kamus Inggris-Indonesia-Arab*. Yogyakarta: Mukti Karya Grafika.

Andriani, R. (2015). Nilai-Nilai Pendidikan Budaya dan Karakter Bangsa. Retrieved from http://www.membumikanpendidikan.com/2015/03/nilai-nilai-pendidikan-budaya-dan.html

Dalmeri. (2014). Pendidikan Untuk Pengembangan Karakter, Telaah terhadap Gagasan Thomas Lickona dalam Educating for Character. Jurnal Al-Ulum IAIN Sultan Amai Gorontalo, 14(14), 278.

Desai, M. S., & Johnson, R. A. (2014). Integrated systems oriented student-centric learning environment: A framework for curriculum development. *Campus-Wide Information Systems, 31*(1), 24–45. doi:10.1108/CWIS-01-2013-0002

Dewan Redaksi Ensiklopedia Islam. (1997). Ensiklopedia Islam Cet. IV. Jakarta: PT. Ichtiar Baru Van Hoeve,.

Direktorat Pendidikan Tinggi Agama Islam (Ditpertais) STAIN Kudus. (2014). Kurikulum Berbasis Kompetensi. Retrieved from http://www.ditpertais.net/stainkudus/kdsprodi03.htm

Fattah, N. (2001). *Landasan Manajemen Pendidikan*. Bandung: Remaja Rodaskarya.

Hamalik, O. (2010). *Manajemen Pengembangan Kurikulum*. Bandung: Remaja Rodaskarya.

Hasibuan, M. (2008). *Manajemen Sumber Daya Manusia*. Jakarta: Bumi Aksara.

Ikhwan, A. (2013). Pengembangan Kurikulum Pendidikan Agama Islam (PAI). Malang: Insan Cita Press dan STAIM Tulungagung. Retrieved from https://scholar.google.co.id/scholar?hl=id&as_sdt=0,5&cluster=10168247928958272298

Ikhwan, A. (2014). Integrasi Pendidikan Islami (Nilai-Nilai Islami dalam Pembelajaran). Ta'allum: Jurnal Pendidikan Islam, 2(2), 184. Retrieved from http://ejournal.iain-tulungagung.ac.id/index.php/taalum/article/view/574

Ikhwan, A. (2017). Development Of Quality Management Islamic Education In Islamic Boarding School (Case Study Madrasah Aliyah Ash Sholihin). Al-Hayat. *Journal of Islamic Education*, *1*(1), 117. Retrieved from http://alhayat.or.id/index.php/alhayat/article/view/7

Kurnia, I. (2008). *Perkembangan Belajar Peserta Didik*. Jakarta: Direktorat Jenderal Pendidikan Tinggi Departemen Pendidikan Nasional.

Lansu, A., Boon, J., Sloep, P. B., & van Dam-Mieras, R. (2013). Changing professional demands in sustainable regional development: A curriculum design process to meet transboundary competence. *Journal of Cleaner Production*, *49*, 123–133. doi:10.1016/j.jclepro.2012.10.019

Lembaga Ilmu Dakwah & Publikasi Sarana Keagamaan. (2011). Kitab Hadits 9 Imam. Jakarta Timur: Lidwa Pusaka i-Software.

Lickona, T. (2010). 11 Principles of Character Education. Retrieved from http://www.character.org/uploads/PDFs/ElevenPrinciples_new2010.pdf

Lickona, T. (2013). *Educating for Character, Mendidik Untuk Membentuk Karakter, terjemahan Juma Abdu Wamaungo*. Jakarta: Bumi Aksara.

Muhammad Eliyasin & Nanik Nurhayati. (2012). *Manajemen Pendidikan Islam*. Yogyakarta: Aditya Media Publishing.

Mulyono. (2008). Manajemen Administrasi dan Organisasi Pendidikan. Yogyakarta: Ar-Ruzz Media.

Othman, A., Hussien, S., Ahmad, I. S., Rashid, A. A., & Badzis, M. (2017). Islamic integrated education system model in the Malay archipelago: Implications for educational leadership. Intellectual Discourse, 25(1), 203–226. Retrieved from http://search.ebscohost.com/login.aspx?direct=true&db=lxh&AN=123963599&site=ehost-live

Pemerintah, P. (2010). PP Nomor 17 Tahun 2010 Paragraf 11 Pasal 97 tentang Kurikulum. *Pub.*, *L*(97), 33.

Pius Partanto & Dahlan Albari. (2001). *Kamus Ilmiah Populer*. Surabaya: Arloka.

Rusman. (2009). Manajemen Kurikulum. Jakarta: Rajawali Press.

Salim, P. (1987). *The Contemporary English Indonesian Dictionary*. Jakarta: Modern English Press.

Sallis, E. (2012). *Total Quality Management in Education*. Yogyakarta: Ircisod.

Sidi, I. D. (2000). *Kebijakan Penyelenggaraan Otonomi Daerah Bidang Pendidikan (makalah)*. Bandung: UPI.

Sidiq, U., & Ikhwan, A. (2018). Local Government Policy Regarding Mandatory Students Diniyah Takmiliyah in Indramayu Regency. KARSA: Journal of Social and Islamic Culture. doi:10.19105/karsa.v26i1.1444

Superka, D. P. (1976). *Values Education Sourcebook, Conceptual Approach, Material Analyses, and an Annotated Bibliography*. Social Science Eucation Consortium Inc.

Suryobroto, B. (2004). *Manajemen Pendidikan di Sekolah*. Jakarta: Rieneka Cipta.

Taufiq, M. (n.d.). Al-Qur'an dan Terjemah; Al-Qur'an In Word. *Software Quran In Word*.

Zakaria, T. R. (2000). Pendekatan Pendekatan Pendidikan Nilai dan Implementasi dalam Pendidikan Budi Pekerti. *Jurnal Pendidikan Dan Kebudayaan, 26*(2), 479–495.

Chapter 7
Islamic Educational Values in Life–Cycle Rituals:
An Ethnographic Study in Kluet Timur Community, Aceh, Indonesia

Abdul Manan

iD https://orcid.org/0000-0003-3299-0662
The State Islamic University of Ar-Raniry Banda Aceh, Indonesia

ABSTRACT

This study discusses the series of life cycle rituals the people of Kluet Timur, South Aceh implement. The study focuses on five main rituals—the rituals of pregnancy, giving birth, circumcision, marriage, and death. Islamic educational values contained in each ritual are also described. To collect this data, this qualitative study applied observation and interview methodologies. The values of customary education, Tawheed, health, and correct decision making can be found in the rituals of pregnancy and childbirth. The values of responsibility and health appear in the ritual of circumcision. The people of Kluet Timur develop the values of deliberation, consensus, and togetherness in the ritual of marriage. The values of solidarity and cooperation are reflected in the implementation of the death ritual.

BACKGROUND

Tanoh Kluet is one of the areas in South Aceh, consisting of four sub-districts, namely, North Kluet, South Kluet, Kluet Timur, and Central Kluet. The Acehnese, Aneuk Jamee, and Kluet ethnic groups inhabit the four sub-districts. As a society

DOI: 10.4018/978-1-5225-8528-2.ch007

that profoundly upholds local cultural values, Kluet people still maintain the use of Kluet language and traditional rituals. The local people perform rituals that include the life and death rituals whose aim is to retain the religious, cultural, and educational values of their ethnic group. In fact, this developing tradition strongly agrees with the teachings of religion, evident in the *hadih maja*[1] (Acehnese proverb), '*hukom ngen adat lagee zat, ngon sipheuet*' ("Law and custom is like a substance and its inseparable nature"). The differences in culture and customs in several regions of Aceh are supported by Act No. 44 of 1999, concerning the Implementation of the Privileges of the Special Province of Aceh. Regions in Aceh are permitted to implement various policies in an effort to empower, preserve, and develop customs and traditional institutions in their territories if they comply with Islamic law. In addition, Act No. 11 of 2006 concretely underlies the implementation of customs in Aceh.

This study discusses the series of traditional rituals, including those of the life cycle and death, which the people of Kluet Timur still carry out. The area is considered to represent the originality of the Kluet community culture, reflected in each stage of the birth-to-death ceremonies. This study also aims to display the Islamic educational values of life-cycle rituals of the Kluet community.

LIFE-CYCLE RITUALS OF THE KLUET TIMUR COMMUNITY

As a one of the sequences in life which happen within a community, life-cycle rituals occur in the form of either ceremonial or custom festivals. From the perspective of the religious dimension, those practices always aim to be closer to God (Muhammad, 2007, pp. 1-2). Indonesia, a country consisting of numerous tribes, has its special customs in the deployment of life-cycle rituals. The tradition of the Balinese, for instance, appears in the form of values, norms, ethics, beliefs, customs, customary laws, and other distinctive rules (Sirtha, 2013). Likewise, the customary values of the Sundanese also do the same thing, reflecting on Islam (Maulana, 2013). Meanwhile, acculturations of the local culture also contribute to the foundation of the new tradition. For example, the people of Pidie, Aceh, execute the ritual of *rah ulei* (washing the head with water) in the cemetery of *ulama* (Islamic scholar) (Arifin & Khambali, 2016). Therefore, the customary tradition to which the community commits cannot circumvent containing the theological, sociological, political, family, and educational values. The last-mentioned values, the focus of this study, attempt to discover the concepts of education contained and believed among the people of Kluet Timur, Aceh. This aligns with what Manan has conceptualized—that the life-cycle ritual is essential to unearthing existing information or social relationships (Manan, 2015). One could obtain ritual information based on the theory and direct practice of the subject customary activities.

METHODOLOGIES

This study uses the framework of a qualitative approach. The researchers collected data by using observation and interviews. The observation was of the activity of the people of Kluet Tmur before, during, and after rituals mentioned. Meanwhile, people in selected samples participated in the interviews, chosen using purposive sampling (Krathwohl, 1993, p. 12). The samples involved were village legal officials and other figures, and related parties in the local village of Kluet Timur. The interview, which was in the form of an open-ended interview, was applied as "prepared" and "unprepared" to match the activity of the samples (Sugiono, 2005, pp. 73-74). The data were then analyzed in appropriate applications of qualitative data analysis, including data reduction, data display, and conclusion drawing (Moleong, 2000, pp. 103-104).

THE RITUAL OF PREGNANCY

Two rituals are performed during the pregnancy of a woman in the Kluet community, namely the ritual of *'bha boh kayee'* (carrying fruits) and the ritual of *'mee bue'* (delivering rice). The former ritual is prepared by *'mak tuan'* (the mother of the groom) with her sisters at the three-month point of the pregnancy of *dara baro* (the new bride). The latter ritual is carried out at four to five months into the bride's pregnancy (Rasyidah, 2012). The capacity of the *'mee bue'* ritual in this case depends on the individual's financial ability to carry it out.

In addition, abstinences are also observed by *dara baro* in order to maintain her smooth delivery process. On the one hand, the Javanese people in Deli Serdang believe that the abstinences for pregnant women only occur for a month of pregnancy or in the first period of pregnancy (Dermawan, 2013). On the other hand, in Aceh, the abstinences upon them are in force for more than one month of pregnancy. In this case, the family of the *dara baro* maintains extra-strict supervision of their child's activities. Those abstinences include food and behavior restrictions. According to traditional midwives and one of the residents of Kluet Timur, vegetables such as jackfruit, breadfruit, spinach, kale, and pumpkin are thought to affect the presence of a fetus conceived by a pregnant woman, due to their role in producing gas in the body. Pregnant women are also prohibited from going out during *maghrib* (dusk) since *maghrib* time is the time when a *syaitan* (evil spirit) wanders around, sitting or standing at the door of the house, because it can complicate the labor process, or leaving the house at night to prevent her family from being slandered and disgraced.

Similar to the women, the husbands whose wives are pregnant also face some restrictions. From the Kluet community's standpoint, they are prohibited from hurting or killing animals. If these restrictions are not respected, the Kluet community believes that their wives' labor will have trouble, such as breech. They are also forbidden to denounce or demonstrate the behavior of people with disabilities both physical and mental. They believe these abstinences can keep their children from being individuals who enjoy making fun of others, as well as avoiding their children getting a *tungkik* (ear infection).

THE RITUAL OF GIVING BIRTH

Once, the Kluet community requested a *rubiah's* (traditional midwife) assistance with the process of giving birth and bathing female corpses. Even though the role has now been replaced by the village midwife, who is paid by the government program, some Kluet community members still use *rubiah* service. However, obstetricians also become an alternative, specifically for pregnant women who have problems with their uterus.

The Kluet community conducts several birth rituals. The first ritual is to cut the umbilical cord. The umbilical cord and placenta are then collected together and buried around the house, marking the site by planting coconut trees on it. Therefore, most Kluet people have coconut trees of the same age as they are.

Furthermore, after the baby is born, the *bang* and *qamat* (call to prayer and *iqamah*) are echoed by the baby's father, his guardian, or a *teungku* (religious leader), who attend the procession. Normally, the Acehnese people only voice the call to prayer to the baby boy, and the *iqamah* to the baby girl. On the contrary, the Kluet community always echoes *bang* and *qamat* to newborn babies, both male and female. This ritual is intended to make the baby become a person who always believes in Allah the Almighty and the Prophet Muhammad (peace be upon him).

The baby is then given a name (*mere gere*) by his parents or the *teungku kampong* (village religious leader). The *teungku* directs the naming process in accordance with the context of Islamic teachings. In general, the ritual is followed by reading the *surah* of Yasin and prayers recited by the *teungku* for the welfare of newborn babies.

The next birth ritual is *turun bo lawe* (introducing the newly born baby to the public). This ritual is performed on the 40th day following his/her birth. The midwife who handles the delivery process carries the baby to the mosque, followed by the baby's parents and grandparents. The baby is bathed using water from the mosque's well or water that has been prepared from the place of ablution of the mosque. By performing the ritual *turun bo lawe*, both the babies and their mothers can leave the house, as they are free from abstinence.

THE RITUAL OF CIRCUMCISION

In general, the people of Aceh perform the ritual of the circumcision on every adolescent boy (9 to 13 years). Two factors influence this ritual, namely, the physical condition of the child and the economic state of the child's parents. In the Kluet area, this ritual is called *peusunat*, and its implementation is quite similar to that performed by the Acehnese people. However, several processes are crucial for them.

The first implemented process is the decision-making and its notification, which takes place in one family. Usually this discussion involves *niniak mamak* (a brother or a sister of the mother of the child). If the discussion about the third debt[2] is agreed upon, then a celebration will be held. Later, all big families, both the distant and the close relatives, will be invited.

Then, *nendok wari* is performed in the next *peusunat* process. *Nendok wari* is a discussion to determine the *peusunat* day, which involves the family of the child, and local custom figures and legal figures. The level of seriousness of the family in carrying out this celebration is seen in the sending of a mouthpiece[3] to the aforementioned figures, as well as the local youths attending the ritual. For men, families usually give cigarettes during *nendok wari*, while betel nuts, betel, tobacco, and lime are provided for women. If the day has been settled, the women will prepare *ncinar*[4] and pick vegetables in the fields. Meanwhile, the men will look for firewood in the mountains, prepare cooking places, and place kitchen utensils. In addition, there are those who decorate the location of the party. In this case, the nuances of togetherness and cooperation are sensed in the activity.

The *peusunat* feast is generally held when the harvest season comes. The Kluet Timur community, the majority of whom are farmers, have prepared rice, the main part of the feast. For them, side dishes are complementary. Moreover, the people of Kluet Timur favor vegetables more than fish and meat. However, some types of endemic fish that are easily obtained in the Kluet River in certain seasons are also sometimes processed as a dish. Relatives and neighbors usually compete with each other to donate side dishes and their equipment to the host.

Furthermore, the child will have henna applied (*Lawasonia enermis*), known as *mekacar*,[5] on the night of *mureh beras*, the night before the celebration. The next day, the function called *namat* and *nyolong anak senat* occurs. *Namat* is a recitation of *khatam Al-Quran* (the prayer recited after completing the whole surah in the Qur'an) for the circumcised child. Whereas *nyolong anak senat* means leading the child to be taken to a mosque, river, or bathing place, the process is actually a task of the *pemamoan* (guardian of the child). However, the *pemamoan* sometimes delegates it to the *perimpean* (the grandfather or grandmother of the child to be circumcised) by giving them wages.[6] The next process is the *mpanger*. In this process, the child is cleaned and bathed using water mixed with kaffir lime by the people who have been previously appointed.

Meanwhile, other family members carry out the *nyerah* procession from the location of the celebration to the *mudim* (circumcision agent), or the doctor who will circumcise the child. This procession is also attended by *khatib, bileu* (bilal), and young people of the village. All the processes related to the circumcision and its accountability are then delegated to the *mudim*.

The next process is to bring the child home to be circumcised by the *mudim*. When the process takes place, the community will cheer to suppress the sound of the child's crying and his mother's anxiety. The child sleeps in the mattress that has been prepared for three days. Before recovering from the injury to his genitals, the child is guarded by his *perimpean* and young people of the village, who had been asked previously to be ready.

After the circumcision is completed, the *mido ijin* process is carried out. In this process, the guardians, *pemamoan, niniak mamak*, the local custom and law officials, and the local youths reunite. They discuss all the deficiencies that occurred during the event, which are their joint responsibility.

Meanwhile, the child who has been circumcised must wait two or three days for the wounds of his genitals to dry. When the bandage is taken off the wound, the family prepares special dishes called *tremandi*. This dish is made from sticky rice flour mixed with clean water. Then, the mixture is made in an oval form to the size of a thumb and squeezed in the center before it is put into boiling coconut milk. This dish is served in a plate or a bowl to the guests. This *tremandi* means that all the *sunat rasul* (circumcision) processions have been completed. The presentation also symbolizes that the child is allowed to do the *ridi* (bathing).

The Kluet community also carries out the circumcision for girls. The difference between circumcision for girls and for boys lies in the time of the implementation, duration, process, and location. The process was not carried out specifically, but was held at the same time as other festivals, such as marriage or circumcision. In addition, the duration of female circumcision is relatively shorter. The process of circumcising girls is handled by female circumcision agents. The location of the circumcision is different from that of boys. In the process, girls are given trinkets to look more beautiful.

THE RITUAL OF MARRIAGE

The Kluet Timur community also has a series of processions in performing marriage rituals. The first ritual is called *kusik di tepian*. The activity is an assessment that involves one member from the man's side, such as the grandfather (*muan*), and a member from the woman's side, such as the uncle (*mamo*). Initially, the dialogue takes place at the banks of the *Krueng Kluet* (Kluet river) while fishing. As time has gone by, *kusik di tepian* has come to be done at homes, markets, or other places.

Furthermore, the results of this *kusik di tepian*'s meeting are delivered at the *kusik di halaman*. This second phase is usually carried out at the woman's home and attended by several family members from both parties, including *niniak mamak* and the parents of the woman.

The third process of the ritual is *kusik di batang ruang/nyusuk*. This procession is attended by trustees (guardians) and *pemamoan* from the man's party who visit the woman's house. This *nyusuk* phase also involves the village officials, customs and legal officials such as the *geuchik* (village chief), village secretary, village religious leader, and the leaders of village customs and law. At this stage, the discussion is mainly to settle the amount of the *mahar* (dowry).[7] After the agreement is obtained, the *meutunangan* (engagement) event is held, attended by trustees and *pemamoan* from both parties, including the village religious leader, village officials, and other relatives. Generally, the event is held in the morning at the bride's house. During the event, the two parties talk to each other and respond in rhymes. The host completes this *meutunangan* event with a set of traditional materials such as *cerano* (cerana), while the *niniak mamak* or *pemamoan* from the bridegroom party carries the *bate meukato*.

The presence of the bridegroom's entourage at the bride's house for the engagement is called *mobokon tando* or *kalang batang*. Before going to the bride's house, the *mobokon tando* event begins with the arrival of the *pemamoan* and the guardians to the house of the leader of village custom and law, to state the purpose of the event. As is the tradition of the Kluet Timur community, several important things are included as symbols to show their good intention. In this case, a *cerana* (metal container) is filled with betel leaves, gambier, areca nut, whiting, cloves (if any), and galangal that used to meet that purpose. Then, they go to the bride's house after agreeing to the following engagement conditions:

1. The engagement is carried out by the *niniak mamak* of both parties;
2. The parents/guardians are obliged to involve the *niniak mamak* in the meeting program, while the *geuchik* (village head) acts as the monitor and the regulator of the event;

3.   The geuchik must be involved in the meeting. If he is not included, the two parties will be penalized twice the amount of the dowry;

4.   The highest amount of dowry is 8 *mayams* and the lowest is 2 *mayams*;

5.   No *'uang hangus'* (preparatory money or unexpected funds used for an event) is included or allowed to be charged in this festivity.

For the people of Kluet Timur, *meutunangan* (the engagement) is not obligatory before the wedding. However, the event is sometimes carried out, depending on the decision of the bride and groom's party. After agreeing on the *mureh beras* (wedding procession), the two families gather at the venue of the feast. They decorate the house, cook rice and side dishes, wash dishes, build kitchens for cooking, and take firewood. Meanwhile, the *perimpean*[8] performs *mekacar*[9] rituals for the prospective bride. Once, the ritual took place four nights in a row until the night of *mureh beras*. Today, the ceremony is done on the night of *mureh beras* only.

Literally, *mureh beras* means washing/cleaning the rice. The name represents the process conducted by the *niniak mamak*, which involves carrying the sticky rice, turmeric water, *ampi* (the container for the ritual offering), and other ingredients to a river or a mosque. The purpose of the procession is to signify that the festivity had begun. The Kluet Timur community also believes that *mureh beras* aims to present the bridegroom and the bride to a wide audience on a beautifully decorated wedding dais, so guests in attendance can directly congratulate both of them.

After the *mureh beras* has been completed, the host invites the external parties (village officials, custom and legal officials, as well as young people of the village) and internal parties (*niniak mamak, pemamoan*, guardians, and other family members) to gather and talk in their homes. The meeting is intended to say farewell to all parties who had been involved in the series of pre-festive activities. Then, the event closes by reading the prayer of salvation.

THE RITUAL OF DEATH

Death is the unavoidable phase of every life. The people of Kluet Timur conduct all the rituals related to death, based on the teachings of Islam, which are mentioned in verse 3 of Al-Maidah, and as practiced by the Prophet Muhammad (peace be upon him). The *pedirum, tukam,* and *fardhu kifayah* (a collective compulsory ritual in Islam) are several processions that the Kluet people do as part of death rituals.

Pedirum is a notification of death to the community. Four ways of carrying out this activity occur. First, the news of the disaster is spread from mouth to mouth, to family, friends, and neighbors when they meet. Second, the *pedirum* is done by hitting the drum in the mosque. If the drum is hit four times, the physical condition of the deceased person is still perfect, while if the drum is hit three times, it indicates that the physical condition of the deceased is no longer perfect, such as the babies who die prematurely. Third, the *pedirum* is carried out by utilizing electronic devices in the form of microphones and loudspeakers. In this case, the mosque management team acts as the mediator to deliver the news of death to the surrounding community after receiving a report from one of the family members of the deceased. Fourth, mobile phones or similar devices are also used to inform of the death, since they are popular as communication media. Recipients of this death message usually leave their work in order to mourn at the funeral home. This is done as a form of condolence and motivation for the families left behind. In the meantime, the local youths work together to dig the grave, the place for the dead to be buried.

The presence of the people in the community at the former house of the deceased is called *tukam*. As mentioned above, the purpose of their presence after getting the news of the death of one of the *pedirums* is to support the mourning family as a manifestation of their empathy. In fact, it is considered very noble to motivate the mourning family (homeowners and abandoned family members). Local custom and law officials also attend the funeral home in order to regulate the ritual of *fardhu kifayah*.

As a fundamental part of Islamic teachings, the ritual of *fardhu kifayah* conducted by the people of Kluet Timur involves four main processes, namely bathing, shrouding, praying, and burying the body. The local village legal officers guide the process of bathing the corpse, involving their sons or brothers if the body is a male. Conversely, the daughters or sisters are involved for a female body. The oldest son sits at the corpse's head. Then, another young family member sits next to the body and the leg. The same thing applies to female family members. The bath is usually done behind the house, in the living room or the kitchen. All preparations for bathing the corpse are previously prepared, including water and aromatic fragrances. Technically, the legal officials pour water all over the corpse and rub all the body parts clean. Family members involved in bathing the corpse follow the instructions given by the legal officials. They use soap to clean the bodies. In a hollow body part, they use gloves or cloth that has been provided. They also slowly knead the abdomen to remove the impurities. Then, the corpse is bathed by using *limau mungkur* (kaffir lime) juice. This process is called *mpanger*. Finally, the corpse is bathed in plain water and taken to the ablution by the legal officials.

The second process is shrouding the corpse. This procession is carried out and guided by the legal officials of the local village. Previously, every cavity of the corpse' body had been covered with cotton. The arms of the corpse had also been placed to the chest like people who were praying. Three-layer shroud wraps that have been given floral fragrances, leaves, or other fresh scents have been provided by the village people, by collecting money jointly. The collection of money is usually managed by the same officials, such as *imum chik* (a village religious leader). It is intended that if one of the residents dies, the family does not need to look for the shroud. If the mourning family happens to be rich, the layer of shroud is permitted to be added in accordance with the provisions of religious teachings and the agreement of community customs. This is usually done by villagers who bring home the shroud after returning from pilgrimage. The shroud itself has been purified with *zamzam* water.

After the shrouding is done, the corpse is then lifted and placed into a *keranda* (bier), which is headed to the nearest mosque or *meunasah* (a smaller size mosque) to be prayed for. Before doing so, the host or *keuchik*, the village chief) delivers the last words to the attendants. The words are mostly about the character of the dead and the debts left by him. Apology for the mistakes made by the deceased during his life is also conveyed. On the way to the mosque, the groups chant a *selawat* (Islamic invocation) upon the Prophet Muhammad P.B.U.H. As soon as they arrive at the mosque, the dead body is placed before the pilgrims, who stand in line and have odd *saf* (praying rows). The prayer is led by the sons of the deceased as suggested by the Prophet.

The last process of *fardhu kifayah* is burying the dead. The people of Kluet Timur normally bury the dead in the cemetery provided by the local village. In that area, the dead body is elevated from *keranda* by some individuals, while three or four people are already waiting to carry the corpse. They then put it down slowly into the burial hole. The body of the dead is positioned facing the Qiblah. The shroud bonds of the dead are also removed one by one, one of which is placed at the feet of the dead. When those processes are completed, the burial hole is filled and formed into a soil mound. A jatropha is embedded on the mound near the head and the feet of the dead body. On the seventh day of the death, an oval rounded stone, which has *burek* (black speckle) colors, is placed near the *jatropha*.

The Acehnese people usually arrange the *kenduri* (feast) of the death. Although it is not an obligation in Islam, this tradition has been passed down through generations. Consequently, in the view of Acehnese people, it is a taboo when *kenduri* death is not implemented. For the people of Kluet Timur, it is carried out based on the economy of the host. Some people apply it for seven nights in a row. Some hold it on the odd nights only, which are counted from the first day of the death—for example, the first, the third, the fifth, and the seventh night. However, the *kenduri* of the death is fundamentally aimed at praying for the deceased. In addition, the ritual aims to entertain the family left by the deceased, so they can stand against the grief and mental deterioration. Therefore, the people of Kluet Timur sincerely bring contributions to the host of the ritual, like donated cakes, rice, sugar, or money. Those are given on the nights of the ritual and have been set up in discussion with the local village.

THE RITUAL OF PREGNANCY AND GIVING BIRTH

Islamic educational values are reflected in the life-cycle rituals performed by the people of Kluet Timur, in the rituals of circumcision, pregnancy, marriage, and death. In the ritual of pregnancy for instance, they relate to the introduction of basic reality in social life or the basics of religious teachings, particularly the Tawheed values. One example is the suggestion given to pregnant women to recite the verses of Quran in order to establish the aforementioned value for the newborn. Then, in the ritual of giving birth, the value of Islam is contained in the handling process after giving birth. The newborn is chanted with *azan* and *iqamah* by the midwife who is handling the process, or even by the baby's father. This is in accordance with the suggestions in Islam, which expect the children to always obey and commit to the command of Allah, the Almighty, during their lifetime. Moreover, the process of *mere gere* (giving name to the newborn, performed by the parents or the local *teungku*) also reflects the educational value from Islamic teachings. The name given to the baby is typically contained in and associated with the prayers the baby's parents request. The traditions mentioned are expected to result in Tawheed children who have good personality, politeness in communication, healthy body and spirit, and cleverness in doing anything (Samad, 2015).

Furthermore, the social relations of the local community are also strengthened with the deployment of the *bo lawe* tradition (in Southwest Aceh, called *peutron aneuk*—stepping the baby's feet to the ground) (Ervina, 2017). The relationships can be seen from the teamwork among the people involved. As a result, *silaturahmi* (friendship), the spirit of cooperation and the reciprocal relationships between each other are increased.

In Indonesia, many pregnant women still consider pregnancy as a normal, natural, and unexceptional matter. Such an assumption indirectly makes them fail to realize the importance of pregnancy examination in order to detect the high risk of giving birth (Apriliawati. 2011, pp. 116-117). In fact, nutritious foods also affect their health. Abstinences related to the pregnancy appeared within the communities in particular areas of Indonesia. The pregnant women are prohibited from consuming eggs, which may lead to difficulties in childbirth. They also are banned from eating meat, which may cause excessive bleeding. Those abstinences lead to the lack of nutritious food for the health of the pregnant women and their babies. In addition, other beliefs bring adverse effects to health—i.e., that pregnant women should decrease their food consumption in the eighth and ninth months of pregnancy. For instance, they are not allowed to eat foods served on a large plate; they are banned from sitting in front of the home's door; they are forbidden to go out of their home at dusk and in the evening. The abstinences mentioned, which become local tradition, should not be violated. Besides, the pregnant women must keep their baby healthy. Therefore, they are not permitted to do heavy work that can lead to disorders of the fetus.

On the process of giving birth, traditional midwives (called *ma blien* in Acehnese) are the dominant alternative to facilitate that process, particularly in rural areas. The selection is based on several factors such as the distance, cost, and ergonomics. Even though they have already undergone the labor training, they still carry out the traditional practices. However, the existence of traditional midwives in Aceh cannot be separated from the local traditions, specifically for the process of pre- and post-childbirth, which is extremely risky (Fuadi, 2018). Medically, the classic causes of maternal deaths in childbirth are bleeding, infection, and eclampsia (disorientation or seizures in pregnancy). Such conditions cannot be addressed if decision-making does not occur as soon as possible. Responding and decision-making become vital and should consider the factors mentioned above. Hence, the Islamic educational value apparent in this case is the appropriateness of the decision-making to bring the pregnant women to the right place, either the hospital or the clinic of the traditional midwives. In Riau, one of provinces in Sumatra, intervention of the husband or parents/parents-in-law contributes greatly to determining decisions, beliefs, myths, and taboos concerning pregnant women (Kartikowati & Hidir, 2015).

After labor is complete, other abstinences and items to be avoided by pregnant women and their babies reappear. For instance, pregnant women are urged to eat certain foods to increase breast milk, to have massage on their stomach in order to return it to its original position, to put certain ingredients and herbs in their vagina for cleaning the blood and fluids from childbirth, and to drink medicinal tonic to strengthen the resistance of their body. Hence, the process of pregnancy and giving birth occurring among the people of Kluet Timur contains Islamic educational values of custom, Tawheed, health, and appropriate decision-making.

THE RITUAL OF CIRCUMCISION

The people of Kluet Timur believe that the transition of children into adulthood is a crucial period. They are expected to have a sense of responsibility toward themselves, their families, and their communities. *Peusunat* (circumcision) is regarded as a statement that a boy has left his childhood to embrace his maturity.

The value of health is also reflected in the *peusunat* ritual. Circumcision can keep the genital from pubic inflammation or disease. It also provides immunity against urinary irritation, prevents occurrences of sexually transmitted infections like Herpes, Chlamydia, Gonorrhea, and uterine cancer (for women), and restrains malignant cancer occurring in the genitals (Tim Riset Penerbit Al-Qira'ah, 2010). Besides being able to recognize his genital function, a circumcised boy also has implemented the manifestation of Islamic sharia. *Peusunat* teaches cleanliness, beauty, and protection in the desire of a circumcised boy.

By employing *peusunat*, a boy is already considered to have entered puberty, so he must perform the obligatory prayers, Ramadan fasting, and other suggested practices taught in Islam. In addition, organizing a ritual of *peusunat* is an action to conserve and uphold the preservation of the local customs. The cultural values are not only transferred to the boy, but also directed to the boy's family and the ritual attendants. Additionally, discussing the matters of *peusunat* ritual contribute to Islamic educational values.

Therefore, regarding the *peusunat* ritual, the people of Kluet Timur who help and participate in the event have indirectly implemented the social values. The implementation of *peusunat* was first performed by the Prophet Abraham. It is the most religious practice recommended in Islam (Asy-Syarbini, 1995, p. 540). However, various procedures for its implementation have existed in each area of Aceh, including Kluet Timur. As mentioned earlier, the local people have their own respective roles in the *peusunat* ritual. Everybody involved in the ritual works for one goal. Their social values are reflected in their cooperation. They do not expect rewards and wages for their involvement. As a result, that situation strengthens the familiarity among participating individuals.

THE RITUAL OF MARRIAGE

The ritual of marriage is an essential effort for the formation of a new family. A variety of special stages are observed in carrying out the ritual, including selecting an appropriate partner for life and the consent of both parties around the bride and groom. These are done for the sake of getting blessings from Allah, the Almighty, and performing the Sunnah of the Prophet Muhammad P.B.U.H. Besides, the ritual is employed to obtain legal recognition from the community. This also applies to the people of Kluet Timur. They carry out the ritual of marriage in three phases, namely, before, during, and after the ritual of marriage. However, as time has gone by, the phases are abandoned because they require substantial time for their implementation. Therefore, in order to preserve the cultural sustainability of Kluet Timur, the awareness of the social values contained in the ritual of marriage is redeveloped by the local people. They want to implant such awareness into the younger generation's perspective.

The values of cooperation and conciliatory consensus are also contained in the ritual of marriage. The people of Kluet Timur usually discuss every problem, either the minor problems happening in the family or the major ones in the village. In the ritual of marriage, its procedures are of great concern. This can be seen in the process of *nendok wari*, arranged in the context of family and the context of community. The result becomes a reference for the implementation of the ritual.

The sense of togetherness shown by the people of Kluet Timur also occurs right in the process of marriage, for instance, in decorating the dais, looking for the firewood, making the cooking kitchen, and preparing the food and cooking utensils. Those activities reflect the mutual values within the community (Manan, 2014). The existence of those values is supposed to be kept and maintained, in order to conserve the Kluet Timur community's identity. Consequently, a sense of empathy, sympathy, and familiarity is established among the individuals.

THE RITUAL OF DEATH

The ritual of death cannot be parted from human life, according to the ancestral values and traditions embodied in them. The gathering of residents or relatives, who attend the ritual of death, symbolizes the solidarity of values among them. Yet, current globalization erodes those values, and that has also happened among the people of Kluet Timur. It is not completely abandoned, and a sense of concern for one of the neighbors who has died remains apparent. They still have a willingness to attend the funeral home to give donations in the form of food or money. They also come to wait upon the family left by the deceased. Even the people of Kluet Timur prepare the needs of *fardhu kifayah* for the dead, including the rituals of bathing, shrouding, praying, and burying. This is no different from the ritual of death in the Southeast Aceh, which also contains religious and social values (Yun, 2017).

Social values and cooperation are also clearly seen after those parts of the death ritual are implemented. The people of Kluet Timur believe that a death is a natural process of displacement between the uterus, the world and the hereafter. Accordingly, they share mutual help for the families of the dead by participating in the implementation of the death *kenduri*, including reciting *tahlilan* or *talkin* for the deceased (Manan, 2016). A similar ritual also occurs in Gorontalo, South Sulawesi called the *hileyiya* tradition (Darwis, 2015). Both death rituals in Aceh and Gorontalo have the same purpose, i.e., to remember the dead and to beg for forgiveness from Allah, the Almighty. In each stage of the ritual, the people involved indirectly develop the value of fraternity among them. Such a sense of tolerance becomes a unique aspect of the death ritual performed.

CONCLUSION

There are Islamic educational values in the life-cycle rituals that the people in Kluet Timur observe. In the ritual of pregnancy, pregnant women are taught to inculcate the values of Tawheed and Islamic education in their baby. The value of health can also be seen in how they take care of the baby and how to determine the decisions to address a problem that may appear before and after giving birth. The values of responsibility and health in the children who get to be adults are also developed in the *peusunat* ritual. In the ritual of marriage, the people of Kluet Timur together contribute to the event. As a result, they tacitly share deliberations, consensus, and togetherness. Meanwhile, the values of solidarity and cooperation can be noticed clearly in the death rituals, based on the local people's belief that they are definitely going to need the help in advance of needing it. Therefore, the above-mentioned rituals become a unique tradition to be conserved.

REFERENCES

Apriliawati, R. (2011). *Panduan Pintar Ibu Hamil. Cet. Ke-1*. Yogyakarta: Moncer Publisher.

Arifin, M., & Khambali, K. B. M. (2016). Islam dan akulturasi budaya lokal di Aceh (Studi terhadap ritual *rah ulei* di kuburan dalam masyarakat Pidie Aceh). *Jurnal Ilmiah Islam Futura*, *15*(2), 251–284. doi:10.22373/jiif.v15i2.545

Asy-Syarbini, M. A. (1995). *Mughni Al Muhtaj Ila Ma'rifat Al Ma'ani Al Fadhul Minhaj, Juz V.* Baerut: Dar Al Kutub Al Ilmiyah.

Darwis, R. (2015). Tradition of Hileyiya: The interaction between religion and traditions in Gorontalo in sociology of Islamic law perspective. *Analisa: Journal of Social Science and Religion*, *22*(1), 57–68.

Dermawan, Y. G. (2013). *Tabu dan Mitos Seputar Wanita Hamil Pada Etnik Jawa di Desa Bakaran Batu Kabupaten Deli Serdang* (Unpublished undergraduate thesis). UNIMED.

Ervina, I. (2017). *Ritual Peutron Aneuk dan Dampaknya Terhadap Kehidupan Masyarakat di Gampong Tokoh Kecamatan Manggeng Kabupaten Aceh Barat Daya* (Unpublished Undergraduate Thesis). UIN Ar-Raniry.

Fuadi, T. M. (2018). Mengkontruksi kearifan lokal dalam pengobatan tradisional reproduksi oleh dukun bayi di Aceh. *Prosiding Biotik*, *2*(1), 279–283.

Kartikowati, S., & Hidir, A. (2015). Sistem kepercayaan di kalangan ibu hamil dalam masyarakat Melayu. *Jurnal Parallela, 1*(2), 159–167.

Krathwohl, D. (1993). *Methods of Educational and Social Science Research.* New York: Longman.

Manan, A. (2014). The ritual of marriage (An ethnographic study in West Labuhan Haji, South Aceh). *Jurnal Ilmiah Peuradeun-International Multidiciplinary Journal, 2*(2), 17–44.

Manan, A. (2015). *The ritual calendar of South Aceh, Indonesia.* Wissenschaftliche Schriften der WWU Münster, Reihe X, Band 22, MV-Verlag-Germany.

Manan, A. (2016). The ritual of death in Aceh: an ethnographic study in Blangporoh village, West Labuhan Haji, South Aceh, Indonesia. In Parts and Whole. Muenster: Lit Verlag.

Maulana, M. M. (2013). Upacara daur hidup dalam pernikahan adat Sunda. *Refleksi, 13*(5), 623–640.

Moleong, J. L. (2000). *Metode Penelitian Kualitatif.* Bandung: Remaja Rosdakarya.

Muhammad, N. (2007). *Antropologi Agama.* Banda Aceh: Ar-Raniry Press.

Rasyidah, R. (2012). Konstruksi makna budaya Islam pada masyarakat Aceh. *IBDA: Jurnal Kajian Islam dan Budaya, 10*(2), 218-230.

Samad, S. A. A. (2015). Pengaruh agama dalam tradisi mendidik anak di Aceh: Telaah terhadap masa sebelum dan pasca kelahiran. *Gender Equality: International Journal of Child and Gender Studies, 1*(1), 111–124.

Sirtha, N. (2013, February 27). Menggali kearifan lokal untuk Ajeg Bali. *Bali Post.* Retrieved from http://www.balipos.co.id/baca/20130227/meggali-kearifan-lokal-untuk-ajeg-bali.html

Sugiono, S. (2005). *Memahami Penelitian Kualitatif.* Bandung: Alfabeta.

Tim Riset Penerbit Al-Qira'ah. (2010). Khitan dalam Perspektif Syari'at dan Kesehatan. Jakarta Timur: Pustaka Al-Kautsar.

Yun, Y. S. (2017). *Ritual Kematian di Aceh Barat Daya (Studi Etnografi di Gampong Kampung Tengah Kecamatan Kuala Batee)* (Unpublished Undergraduate Thesis). UIN Ar-Raniry.

ENDNOTES

[1]   Hadih maja is one of the oral poems or literary works containing messages or satire.

[2]   The people of Kluet Timur acknowledge several debts that should be paid by the parents. The third debt means organizing the ritual of circumcision for their boy.

[3]   A mouthpiece is one or several people who are assigned to deliver the message related to the celebration or to invite friends to be present at the event later. Nowadays, this mouthpiece is in the form of an invitation card that has been printed neatly.

[4]   Rice drying is the process of grinding the rice through the rice-grinding machines, performed in order to produce rice for the use on the *peusunat* day.

[5]   *Mekacar* is applying the henna that has been finely ground. It is smeared on the fingers, toes, and around the soles of feet of the child to be circumcised.

[6]   The wages in question can be in the form of a packet of cigarettes or depend on the request of the importers. Usually they do not ask for things that are impossible to give.

[7]   The amount of *mahar* (dowry) in Kluet community has been stated since 1978. The highest amount of which is 8 *mayam of* pure gold (1 *mayam* = 3,3 grams). The lowest amount of it is two *mayams* of pure gold. The amount of the dowry can exceed more than 8 *mayams*, when the *ijab qabul* (wedding contract) takes place, however only 8 *mayams* of the dowry amount are mentioned. The extra amount of the dowry is considered as the present of the groom to the bride.

[8]   *Perimpean* is the person who decorates with henna over the arms and hands of the bride. Normally, *perimpean* is the wife of the uncle's bride. In the tradition of Kluet, *perimpean* is called *puhun*, the daughter of whom is also mentioned as *perimpean*.

Chapter 8
Teachers' Perceptions of Islamic Religious Education in Arab High Schools in Israel

Najwan Saada
The Mofet Institute, Israel

ABSTRACT

In this multiple case study, the authors explore the purposes and significance of Islamic religious education as it is viewed and interpreted by Arab and Muslim teachers in Arab high schools in Israel. It interrogates how the Muslim teachers locate themselves and their pedagogy within a continuum of salafi (conservative) versus liberal conceptions of tarbiyya (the spiritual aspects of Islam) and ta`dib (the moral aspects of Islam) and why they do so. The results show that teachers support the salafi rather than the liberal conceptions of Islamic education. This means that they focus on the naql (the transmission of religious knowledge) rather than aql (rational thinking) in teaching the moral aspects of Islam. Also, teachers avoid the dealing with the intellectual diversity within Islam, the discussion of contemporary issues, and the tenets of other Abrahamic religions. They conclude that this may lead to religious illiteracy and argue that liberal Islamic education with critical and reflective reasoning is much appropriate for living in multicultural and multi-faith society.

INTRODUCTION

This study explores Muslim teachers' perceptions of Islamic education in Arab and secondary schools in Israel, of their own roles as Islamic educators, and of the aims of Islamic religious education in general. White (2009) emphasizes the need to do

DOI: 10.4018/978-1-5225-8528-2.ch008

more research in order to illuminate how teachers' religious identities impacts their views of schooling and their pedagogies. Another study has found that teachers' religious orientations influence their conceptions of citizenship education and their methods of teaching for democracy and national identity (author, 2013). In other words, teachers' religious orientations may influence their motivation to teach, their way of structuring their disciplines, their responsibilities towards their students, and their conceptualization of the purposes of education (White, 2010).

Very little is known about religious education in Arab schools in Israel. To date, most studies of Arab education have criticized civic and historical education from a critical multicultural perspective (Abu-Saad, 2006; Abu-Asba, 2001; Agbaria, 2010; Al-Haj, 1995; Makkawi, 2002; Pinson, 2007). Few studies have examined Islamic religious education in Arab schools (Agbaria, 2012; Mahajna & Kfir, 2013). According to Mahajna and Kfir (2013), religious education is a marginalized subject in the school's curriculum as students usually study one elective unit of Islamic studies (one hour per week starting from tenth until twelfth grade) compared to 3-5 units in other compulsory subjects. However, the situation has changed since 2014. In order to graduate, all Muslim students are now required to pass a matriculation (*Bagrut*) exam on Islamic religious education. For this purpose, a new textbook has been developed.

Agbaria (2012) finds that teaching Islam in Arab schools does not meet the needs of the Arab minority in Israel in terms of developing Muslim students' sense of collective community or their national (Palestinian) identity (Agbaria, 2012). This, Agbaria argues, serves the state's agenda in controlling and marginalizing Arab citizens through education for conformity, compliance, and discipline. Agbaria's work is important but limited to analyzing the official or explicit curriculum in Arab schools whereas the current study examines the taught or perceived curriculum (Goodlad, Klein, & Tye, 1979; Joseph, 2000). The taught curriculum, according to Joseph (2000) is "what individual teachers focus upon and choose to emphasize—often the choices represent teachers' knowledge, beliefs about how subjects should be taught, assumptions about students' needs, and interests in certain subjects" (p. 5). In addition, Agbaria's findings discuss the "what" of the curriculum and do not explore teachers' perceptions of how their practices serve their instructional goals. In other words, it does not focus on the role of teachers as possible social agents and intellectuals (Giroux, 1988) who may transform the curriculum based on their prior knowledge, their students' needs, and their personal ideologies. The current study aims to overcome the limitations of these studies by exploring the insider perspective on Islamic religious education as perceived and articulated by the teachers themselves. Before explaining the research procedures, we will explain in the next section the meanings of religious education from an Islamic perspective.

Conceptualizing Islamic Religious Education

According to Islamic theory of education, the purpose of education is to nurture the spiritual, intellectual, emotional, and physical faculties of the child (Attas, 1979). Also, the teachings of the Quran and the example of the Prophet Muhammad (his sayings and deeds) constitute the primary sources of education in Islam (Halstead, 1995). Thus, succeeding in this life and the hereafter requires following the Quran and the tradition of Prophet Muhammad (Cook & Malkāwī, 2010).

Scholars generally agree on three major purposes of Islamic education (Cook & Malkāwī, 2010; Halstead, 1995, 2004; Waghid & Smeyers, 2014; Waghid, 2011). These are *tarbiyya*, which means to grow and to rear the spiritual and ethical elements in students' lives in accordance with the commands of God; *ta`lim* which means to learn and receive knowledge transferred by teachers through instruction and teaching; and *ta`dib* which is the inculcating of good virtues and sound behaviors in Muslim students (Cook & Malkāwī, 2010).

Khan (1987) explains that *tarbiyya, ta`dib,* and *ta`lim* deal with the spiritual, moral, and intellectual components of Islamic education, respectively. The spiritual aspect of Islamic religious education aims to develop students' desires and capacities to seek wisdom and justice as they are clarified in the Quran (Halstead, 1995). It means worshiping God through obeying His instructions and doing good deeds. It encourages Muslims to make the connection between their lives on earth and eternal life after death.

Tarbiyya, for the purpose of this study, cares more about the *Ibadat* (God's worship) than *muamalat* (social obligations) (Zia, 2007). It is concerned with teaching Muslim students the tenets of their faith and the five pillars[1] of Islam. It challenges discourses and practices of materialism, consumerism, and rationalism in modern life (Hussain, 2004; Merry, 2006) by connecting Muslim believers to a transcendental power that provides answers to their existential questions and shows them the meaning of prayer, forgiveness, and salvation. *Tarbiyya* aims to help Muslims achieve inner peace by "developing and refining elements of love, kindness, compassion, and selflessness" (Cook & Malkāwī, 2010, p. xxviii). In addition, *tarbiyya* emphasizes the belief in and fear of one God (Allah) who is omnipotent, omniscient, and benevolent.

Ta`dib encourages Muslim students to be familiar with the moral teachings of Islam and its ethical code which relies on the Quran, the *ahadith* (prophetic traditions) and the *fiqh* (jurisprudence). Educating students to become good Muslims means to follow the divine law, the teachings of the prophet, and the contributions of authoritative Muslim scholars (*ulema*) (Zia, 2007). Students study within the *ta`dib* framework how to distinguish 'right' from 'wrong' behaviors and how to apply the recommended Islamic manners in everyday life. It is worth noting that Islam has

137

several moral teachings on topics such as marriage and divorce, sexual relationships, economics, and catering to the poor... Thus, *ta'dib* focuses on the *muamalat* or the Muslim duties towards fellow humans, society, and the environment (Niyozov & Memon, 2011). Also, it addresses the civic responsibilities of Muslims towards believers of other religions, non-believers, and members of different cultural, linguistic, socioeconomic, political and ethnic groups. Halstead (1995) explains that the divine law in Islam "integrates political, social, and economic life as well as individual life into a single religious worldview" (p.29).

Finally, *ta`lim* is related to the work of teachers and how they transmit Islamic religious content and theory of knowledge (Halstead, 1995) in their classrooms. In Islam, according to Halstead (1995), "the teachers were accountable to the community not only for transmitting knowledge and for developing their students' potential as rational beings, but also for initiating them into the moral, religious, and spiritual values which their community cherished" (p. 31). Although rote learning, memorization, and frontal teaching are very common in the Islamic world (Niyozov & Memon, 2011; Sahin, 2013), some philosophers of Islam, such as Ibn Khaldun, reject these methods of teaching and recommend nurturing skills of reasoning and critical thinking (Halstead, 1995).

Furthermore, over the last decade, there has been a growing critique of rigid and monolithic interpretations of Islamic ideals and a move towards adapting Islamic teachings to the values of modern and democratic life (Kunzman, 1998; Ramadan, 2004; Safi, 2003; author & Gross, 2017; Selcuk, 2012; Tan, 2011; Wilkinson, 2013; Waghid & Smeyers, 2014). Selcuk (2012), for instance, argues that "theology must be suitable to improve individual intellect and appropriate for the democratization process of society" (p. 224). She adds that the *sharia* must be understood from a historical perspective, thereby allowing Muslims to contextualize Islamic teachings based on their needs and the progress of their societies. In addition, Selcuk (2012) and Wilkinson (2013) question the blind imitation of previous Muslim scholars, the literal interpretation of the Quran, and the uncritical acceptance of the Islamic cultural heritage. By the same token, Waghid (2011), and Waghid and Smeyers (2014) recommend adapting the concepts of *tarbiyya, ta`dib,* and *ta`lim* to fit the demands of cosmopolitan and democratic citizenship, of living in modern and pluralistic societies, and of upholding the ideals of truth and justice. The following conceptual model (figure 1) summarizes the different positions on Islamic religious education mentioned above.

This conceptual model provides teachers and practitioners of education a framework to cultivate the spiritual, moral, and intellectual faculties of their students. In other words, teachers of Islamic education may provide their students with the learning experiences that highlight different levels of *tarbiyya, ta`dib,* and *ta`lim.*

Figure 1.

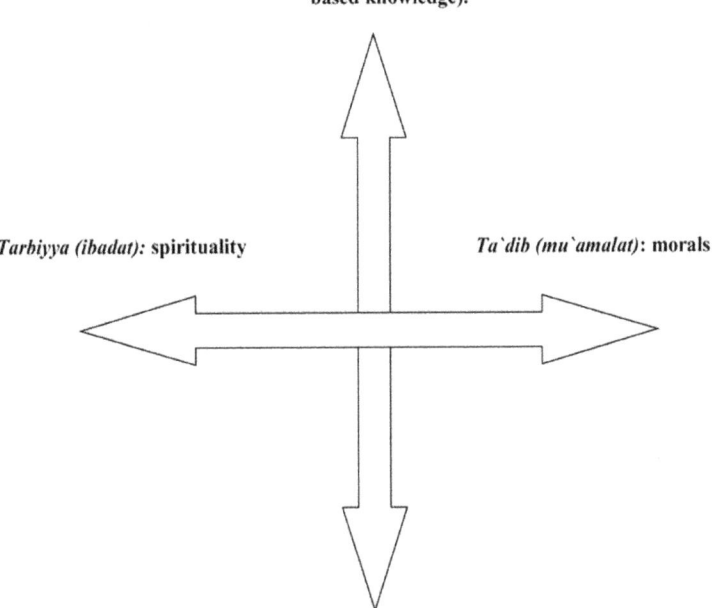

Critical *Ta'lim* (reflective, liberal, progressive, reformist, with an emphasis on *aql*—reason-based knowledge).

Tarbiyya (ibadat): spirituality

Ta`dib (mu`amalat): morals

Non-critical *Ta'lim* (conservative, fundamental, *salafi*, with an emphasis on *naql*—revelation-based knowledge).

Following the work of Waghid (2011), teachers could be divided into either critical or conservative groups based on whether they allow their students to 1) question religious ideas and concepts; 2) reconsider the contributions of religious authorities and scholars; 3) reflect upon their faith and develop their own religious identities; and 4) rethink the relationship between Islam, democracy, and modernity. Teachers who are more conservative represent the fundamental or the *salafi*[2] attitude in Islamic education. They prefer teaching the "what" and "how" of Islam (Waghid, 2011). By contrast, teachers who are more critical represent the progressive, liberal, and reformist outlook which engages students with the "why" of Islamic instructions.

Research Questions and Qualitative Method

The current study explores the Islamic religious education teachers' perceptions of the purposes and significance of Islamic religious education in their schools. It aims to answer the following questions:

- How do Islamic education teachers in Arab high schools in Israel perceive the purposes and significance of Islamic religious education?
- Where do Arab teachers locate themselves and their teaching within the spectrum of the salafi/liberal Islamic education?
- What are the knowledge, skills, and dispositions the teachers want to educate their students and why are these important?
- What do Arab teachers do in order to achieve their goals of Islamic religious education?

These questions are addressed in the study by means of a qualitative research design. Qualitative inquiry is the most appropriate method to use since these questions focus on the experiences, perspectives, and attitudes of the teachers and how they interpret their roles and their own perceptions of Islamic religious education. According to Guba and Lincoln (1982), the use of a qualitative paradigm assumes that participants' experiences cannot be fragmented into single variables as they are influenced by "multiple factors and conditions, all of which interact, with feedback and feedforward, to shape one another" (p. 242).

The specific approach to be used for this study is the multiple case method because "case studies strive to portray 'what it is like' to be in a particular situation, to catch the close up reality and thick description of participants' lived experiences of, thoughts about, and feelings for a situation" (Cohen, Manion, & Morrison, 2007, p. 254). Case studies draw upon in-depth exploration of the causes and motivations behind participants' beliefs and actions in their natural setting. Also, the case study methodology focuses on contemporary and real-life events, and answers questions of how and why the research participants think, interpret, or conceptualize the phenomenon under inquiry (Yin, 2009). The case study methodology focuses more on the explanatory power of doing the study than the predictive component. It helps us recognize "the complexity and embeddedness of social truths" (Cohen, Manion, & Morrison, 2007, p. 256) as well as the similarities and differences among the viewpoints held by the research participants. In explaining the logic of multiple case study research, Yin (2009) clarifies that:

Each individual case study consists of a "whole" study, in which convergent evidence is sought regarding the facts and conclusions for the case; each case's conclusions are then considered to be the information needing replication by other individual cases. Both the individual cases and the multiple-case results can and should be the focus of the summary report. (p. 56)

Each teacher selected in this study is considered one case to be analyzed as one unit. The multiple case method enables detailed description of the experiences and attitudes of informants in order to identify or discover important categories or patterns of meaning across their responses, their perceptions of Islamic religious education, and the knowledge, skills, and dispositions they wish to transfer to their students.

Research Setting and Participants

Arabs in Israel constitute a national, religious, and cultural minority (20.9% of the total population) which encompasses Muslims (81.3%), Christians (8.8%), and Druze (9.9%) (Rudnitzky, 2014). Arab citizens have their own schools and enjoy some level of cultural and religious autonomy (Abu- Asba, 2001; Maoz, 2007). Arab students learn in Arabic and their schools are run by Arab teachers and principals who are hired and supervised by the Israeli-Jewish Ministry of Education. However, Arab schools are not faith-based schools. They follow the core curriculum of the Ministry of Education, which guides the teaching of basic subjects such as math, language, and sciences as well as a religious education.

In this inquiry, five teachers are selected (3 males and 2 females) based on snowball sampling (Bryman, 2012) and literal replication (Yin, 2009, p. 54). The snowball sampling is "a sampling technique in which the researcher samples initially a small group of people relevant to the research questions, and these sampled participants propose other participants who have had the experience or characteristics relevant to the research" (Bryman, 2012, p. 424). Literal replication means that cases or units of analysis are chosen with the expectation that they share predictable and similar results (Yin, 2009). On this basis, we chose Arab teachers who teach Islamic religious education at the high school level and who agree to participate voluntarily in our study. For convenience considerations, we chose teachers who teach in eight different schools located at the center and north of Israel. The following table (figure 2) summarizes the background of the teachers selected. Pseudonyms are used for ethical considerations.

Data Collection and Analysis

Two in-depth interviews for 1.5 hours were conducted with each participant in his or her classroom at the end of the school day. These are semi-structured interviews with open-ended and follow up questions. The use of open-ended questions has the advantage of revealing "what is in the interviewees' mind as opposed to what the interviewer suspects is on the interviewees' mind" (Krueger & Casey, 2009, p. 57). The follow up questions are based on the dynamics of the interview, the participants' responses, and the guidelines of our inquiry. All the interviews will be recorded and transcribed later for further analysis. The interviews included questions such as:

Figure 2.

Name of teacher	Experience of teaching Islam	Grades	Sex	Education
T1	13 years	10-12	Male	Doctor in Islamic jurisprudence
T2	3	10-12	Female	B.A. in social sciences
T3	5	10-12	Female	B.A. in Islamic studies
T4	16	10-12	Male	M.A in Islamic studies
T5	10	10-12	Male	Doctor of Islamic

- What are the purposes of religious education in your opinion?
- What makes you believe what you believe about the goals of Islamic religious education?
- What is the knowledge you want your students to gain while studying in your classroom? Why?
- What are the skills you want your students to develop while studying in your classroom? Why?

- What are the dispositions/virtues you want your students to acquire while studying in your classroom?
- What are the difficulties that you face in achieving your goals of Islamic education?
- How do you appreciate the new curriculum of Islamic religious education? Does it meet your expectations? Why? Or why not?

Moreover, the materials used by informants in their classrooms were collected and analyzed, including handouts, assignment papers, exams, and the like. The analysis of these documents reveals how the teachers articulate or translate their religious and personal identities into a pedagogical framework. Drawing upon multiple sources of data achieves methodological triangulation, which reinforces the trustworthiness (Guba, 1981) of the findings. In other words, the convergence of data through using independent measures of the same phenomenon increases confidence in the "truth" of the research results. Respondents were also asked to give their validation (member check) of the accuracy and intentionality of the interview transcripts.

Data analysis followed the three stages of grounded theory research (Charmaz, 2006). The first step of analysis is based on an open and preliminary coding through which I read each interview transcript line by line in order to delineate units of general meaning in each interview. At the end of the open coding, the codes were reviewed to check for similarities and differences in order to figure out repeated patterns of meaning and categories. Categories "refer to such components as the conditions, causes, and consequences of a process—actions that let the researcher know if, when, how, and why, something happens" (Saldana, 2009, p. 159). In the second step, we did an axial analysis to build a logical chain of evidence, note causality, make inferences, and clarify the relationships between categories and subcategories. The purpose of the axial coding is to "strategically reassemble data that were split or fractured during the initial coding process (Saldana, 2009, p. 159). Here, the theoretical concepts described in the literature review, such as *tarbiyya* and *ta`dib,* were employed in order to describe the relationships among the categories in a theoretical and meaningful way. In the third step, we did a selective coding to clarify the key concepts and main themes of the study and subsume the main clusters of meaning into general and theoretical coherence. After writing the themes and their appropriate quotations, we compared/contrasted the results to the data once again in order to validate my analysis.

Findings

Interestingly, all teachers in this study report that they are satisfied with their jobs and with making Islamic religious education a compulsory subject in Arab schools.

They believe that this has increased the status of the religious education in the schools and in the eyes of their students. Teachers also report that they teach a total of three classes (distributed in the tenth and eleventh grades) and complain about the limited time and the extensive material that they have to cover for the matriculation exam. One teacher (T5) explains that students enjoy learning about Islam because they feel they do not know enough about their religion and because Islam is practical and relevant to everyday life. T4 expresses his concern that not passing the final exam of the obligatory Islamic education may do harm because students may think that Islam limits their success and their social mobility. As a result, he says, "I want them to think that they are rewarded not only by grades but also in the hereafter."

Teachers also agree that a teacher should function as a role model for his/her students and be knowledgeable about Islam so that he/she can answer the students' questions. In addition, our analysis reveals that most teachers apply non-liberal and non-critical Islamic religious education. The following themes depict the teachers' attitudes and patterns of thinking.

A'ql (rational thinking) vs. *Naql* (transmitted knowledge) in Islamic Character Education

In Islam, as mentioned in the conceptual model earlier, there is a debate over the place of *a'ql* (mind or reasoning) in understanding the *naql* (Islamic texts, transmitted exegesis, and materials from earlier commentators on how to understand the teachings of the Quran and the *Sunnah*[3]). The teachers in this study highlight the importance of *naql* in teaching the morals of Islam. Some of these morals can be considered universal while others are specific to the Islamic religion. Regardless of the type of moral, teachers insist on role modeling as a key feature in their pedagogy. For instance, one teacher (T3) states, "When I teach them that smoking cigarettes is *haram* (forbidden) in Islam, a student may ask, 'but how can you explain that another *sheikh* (religious scholar) is smoking?'." Therefore, teachers feel that they have to model what they are teaching in their own lives.

In addition, the majority of teachers frequently use examples from the life of Prophet Muhammad in order to show the mercy, kindness, and beauty of Islam. These examples are closely related to universal values, such as showing mercy, being tolerant, treating others the way one would like to be treated, and alleviating all kinds of human suffering. One teacher (T3) shares examples of how the Prophet treated his wives and his children in a merciful and respectful manner. She also highlights the values of honoring parents, upholding kinship and family ties, acting with integrity, showing kindness towards neighbors, and being gracious in every interaction with others.

The use of role-modeling in education for good virtues can be described as traditional character education, non-critical *ta`dib*, and conservative moralism (Gutmann, 1987) because it emphasizes the learning of socially-accepted values through direct instruction and the use of sanctions and awards. For example, the same teacher refers to God and other spiritual elements in order to inspire students to do good deeds and avoid bad ones. She explains, "If a person did a good deed, it will be written in his record by the angels, and if he did a bad deed, they (the angels) will be waiting for him to stop or regret before they write it down …even if you decide to steal something and you change your mind, you will be awarded for this." Another teacher (T5) requests that his students memorize some verses of the Quran and the *hadith* so that they remember and internalize good values, such as honesty and justice.

In another situation, three teachers (T3 and T1 and T4) draw a connection between personal piety and morality. One teacher asks, "Does it make sense for a person to make *wudu* (a type of ritual purification by washing parts of the body) to pray afterwards and continue doing bad stuff like *namima* (tattle) and *Istigabah* (gossip)"? T4 condemns teachers who teach Islam and do not apply its principles to their lives. For example, "How does it make sense that a teacher says that a female should wear the Islamic lawful dress while she does not do so herself"?

Yet, the transmission of "a bag of virtues" (Power, Higgins, & Kohlberg 1989) in character education is criticized for not developing the students' reflective capacities, their moral reasoning, and their political efficacy (Westheimer & Kahne, 2004). Lockwood (2001) argues, for example, that character education in schools should "address the reality of value controversy and not be limited by the view that value questions invariably have clear right answers… a view that is unrealistic, simplistic, and stifling of moral growth" (p. 60).

The use of *a`ql* (rational thinking) is more common in explaining some of the moral prohibitions than metaphysical issues in Islam. For instance, one teacher (T3) explains to her students that drinking alcohol is forbidden in Islam because it impairs one's judgment. Another teacher (T2) explains why eating pork is forbidden in Islam in this way: "Pork is full of germs and bacteria, so when you eat it, you cannot get rid of them…there are many studies confirming that … it is similar to eating a dead lamb which is forbidden for the same reason…God prevents us from eating what does harm to our bodies, health and souls." In another situation, a student posed a question about "why drugs are *haram* in Islam when this is not explicitly written in the Quran." The teacher (T3) explained, "That's true, but we have *qiyas*4 in the Islamic *fiqh* (Islamic jurisprudence), and since drugs affect people as much as alcohol, then it is forbidden by Muslim religion scholars." In a similar context, I asked a teacher (T2) about what happens if she does not have evidence to rely on from the Quran, the Sunnah or the *ijma* (a consensus of the Muslim scholars). The teacher answered, "Then we do not use the *qiyas*… I have to transfer evidence-based knowledge to my students… in fact, I have to follow the curriculum and what the curriculum says."

In explaining the prohibition of *zena* (sexual relationship before and outside of marriage), the teacher reasons, "But why do we have to give up the value of living in a stable family… where is the beauty of relatives and friends gathering on the day of marriage… unlike people in the West who celebrate Mother's Day and Woman's Day, we do appreciate the value of family." Another teacher (T5) warns students of the possible skin diseases transmitted as a result of intercourse with "people you do not know very well." He also cautions that smoking cigarettes, science confirms, may lead to a stroke, erectile dysfunction, and arteriosclerosis. The same teacher explains the dangers of watching porn as follows: "Watching porn causes a temporary pleasure, but doing so frequently leads to addiction…what is better to be addicted or to enjoy the real thing at the right time?"

When we ask the teachers if they bring different interpretations of the Quranic verses in the classroom, they have diverse opinions. For example, T3 says, "No… what I teach is what in the textbook, which is agreed by the majority of Muslims… there is no need to get into what the different *madahibs* (schools of thought within fiqh—Islamic jurisprudence) claim because it will confuse the students." Other teachers are willing to deal with disputed topics but only within the legitimate interpretations raised by authorized Muslim scholars (basically the four *madahibs*[5] in Islam). For instance, one teacher (T1) says, "I bring different interpretations of the Quran and sometimes different opinions on controversial *fiqh* matters, such as singing or listening to music, the wearing of *niqab* (the veiling of the face except the eyes), women's traveling without a *mahram* (an unmarriageable kin with whom marriage/sexual intercourse would be considered *haram* (illegal in Islam), drawing, and making of statues… but students are not qualified to disagree with the contribution of previous scholars." . The same teacher explains that reason should not be used to generate new metaphysical or Sharia judgments. To support this opinion, he states, "Ibn Taymiyyah (a theologian who died 1328 CE) says that the role of mind is to understand the scripture (the *naql*) and to transmit this understanding forward." Even when a teacher (T5) encourages rationalism in order to explain why listening to music is not *haram*, he does so in order to lead students to a pre-determined answer: "I tell my students that reciting the Quran properly requires knowing music notes… listening to music leads to human relaxation… and the Prophet himself did not prevent his wife Aisha from watching a musical performance." Another teacher (T4) says that thinking beyond the four *madahibs* in Islam or the *ijtihad* (contributions) of authorized Muslim scholars leads to conflict in the Muslim society.

T2 supports this way of thinking and prefers abiding by authorized religious scholars. She states, "I encourage my students not to accept all what they hear from *sheikhs* on the internet; they have to question these people and check if they are qualified to offer *fatwa* (an opinion on a legal matter given by a recognized authority), and they have to question their use of evidence from the legal sources of Islam." She adds that wearing gold and silk is forbidden for Muslim men. While this is in accordance with the Prophet Muhammad's teachings, yet, no additional argument or evidence is provided to explain why. Another teacher (T4) complains that "there are some students who access websites that do not recognize Allah or believe in Him, which makes my job harder in terms of transmitting the right information to these students".

We argue that this transmission and past-oriented interpretation of the Islam is incompatible with critical *ta`lim* (*tarbiyya* and *ta`dib*) or with living in the modern world. Unlike this perception of religious education, there are scholars who recommend encouraging students at the high school level to think critically about the reasonability of religious claims and to develop their own religious identities (Halstead, 2014; Thiessen, 2012). Halstead (2014) calls this "secondary values education," which means "teaching and learning to go beyond the present and particular values of the home and local community and beyond the acceptance of moral authority for its own sake" (p.77).

Education through critical *tarbiyya* and *ta`dib* becomes even more critical in light of the growing religious extremism in the Middle East and the rise of ISIS and other *jihadi* movements. One teacher (T3) reports, in support of this analysis, that she was shocked to know that a student supports ISIS:

Usually, I do not talk about ISIS because it has nothing to do with Islam, but one day I heard someone in the classroom speak in support of ISIS…I asked him why he thought so and he said because 'there is so much injustice in life'… what is painful, though, is that you do not know how many students believe in ISIS, you know, who knows what they hear and watch on YouTube or Facebook… since then, I have been talking about ISIS in my classrooms and I refute their arguments by showing the mercy of Islam, and how Prophet Muhammad treated prisoners of war and how he released them for teaching Muslims the skills of reading and writing.

This example illustrates the epistemological limitations of the *naql* (the uncritical transmission of religious knowledge) and its inadequacy in combating religious extremism.

The use of *a`ql* in explaining transcendental/spiritual issues is demonstrated by fewer teachers in this research. Mostly, the teachers use the intelligent design theory (Midgley, 2007) in order to prove the existence of God and His wisdom. This theory entails that "the living things in the world are so complex that they cannot have evolved by natural selection, so they must have had a designer" (p. 26). The designer is believed to be God. For instance, one teacher (T3) says, "In order to prove the existence of God, I never use a verse from the Quran at the beginning. I say look at the sky, who can hold it this way? Can you build a chair without legs? Look at the stars and how they are fixed in the sky day and night, look at your eyes and your body and see the coherence of your creation…think of the embryo in the belly of his mom and how it is protected by the uterine wall…imagine that there is more than one God, as Hindus believe, one for rain, one for marriage, one for love, and one for light… what's going to happen… a lot of problems and a chaos." Another teacher (T5) explains that *wudu* (the ritual of cleaning the body towards Muslim prayer) protects the body and keeps it healthy and claims that prayer itself releases the mind of bad electrical charges which prevents headaches. The same teacher explains that the purpose of wearing the *hijab* (the headscarf) and the *jilbab* (long and loose-fit coat or garment) is to protect women from sexual harassment. "Sexual harassment," he opines, "is not happening only in Muslim societies. It is happening in Christian and Jewish ones as well. In fact, all religions want to protect women against this violent behavior."

Nevertheless, the use of logical arguments in dealing with spiritual issues is not common. One teacher (T1) says, "Even if a student holds secular or atheist ideas, he would not share these with me… you know, because of the school's Islamic culture and community, but if he brings these issues up, I will have to engage so as not to impact other students… personally, I will never talk about these topics in my classroom." T2 shared another incident: "Students asked me if God has already determined before we were born who was going to be a Muslim and who was going to be an infidel, then why does He judge us now?" Her response is to remind students that people can still make up their minds and be responsible for their decisions. The same teacher adds that her students also ask, "Why would God punish the Jewish people for practicing a religion that does not follow the true Torah? There are nice Jews who help us… there are Jewish doctors who save our lives, so why would God punish them"? "If I see that the discussion is going so deep," she responds, "I say let us stop at this point since we do not have the right to debate or judge these matters"

T1's and T2's responses do not meet the demands of the critical *tarbiyya* because they silence students' epistemic curiosity regarding legitimate metaphysical and philosophical questions. One possible implication of this finding is the need for Islamic religion teachers who are qualified to deal with alternative ideologies of morality and spirituality in a confident and sophisticated manner. Thinking beyond the Islamic system of knowledge and dealing with alternative ways of knowing and being have the potential to improve students' cognitive, moral, and religious reasoning (Alexander, 2016b; Halstead, 2014, author, 2015; Tan, 2008, 2014). The following theme shows the limited and limiting understanding of diversity and multiculturalism in Islamic religious education.

Difference as *Fitnah* and the Missing Voice of Intellectual/Religious Pluralism

The missing point in teachers' responses is the civic purpose of religious education (Feinberg, 2006; author & Gross, 2017; Selcuk, 2012; Thiessen, 2012) and its possible contribution to living in a democratic and multicultural society. The teachers, for instance, do not see any need to learn about other sects or traditions in Islam or to learn about the worldviews of religious or non-religious people. One teacher (T1) mentions that he rejects the celebration of Christmas by Muslims and condemns this behavior in front of his students. Also, he does not believe in teaching about other religions because "in the past one scholar said neither a Muslim is going to become a Christian nor a Christian is going to become a Muslim… so why teach them about other religions… this is not necessary." In addition, the same teacher rejects the idea of inter-religious dialogue because he believes that there is a deep contradiction between religions at the creed level. The Quran says, he argues, "People of the Book! Come to a word common between us and you: That we shall serve none but Allah and shall associate none with Him in His Divinity and that some of us will not take others as lords other than Allah" (3:64).

Another teacher (T3) says that she teaches about other religions only in response to students' questions. She says, "Muslims are the only people who believe in Christianity and in Judaism whereas Jews believe in Moses and not in Jesus or Muhammad, and Christians believe in Moses and not in Prophet Muhammad… we believe in both… even the 'true' and old holy books of Christians and Jews maintain that Muhammad is the last prophet." She continues, "Even logically, it does not make sense to believe in Jesus as a god and as a son at the same time." She argues that the main purpose of the different religions is to refer to the oneness of God: "The Quran is the final holy book and it summarizes and expands the older holy books." T3 adds that she wants her students to be engaged in interfaith dialogue, but she wants them first to be able to talk about and defend their own religion.

This apologetic perception of Islam, we argue, may lead to religionism (Hull, 2000), which entails promoting a puritanical conception of one religion based on prejudice against other religions. Hull (2000, p. 76) explains, "The identity which is fostered by religionism depends upon rejection and exclusion. We are better than they. We are orthodox; they are infidel. We are believers; they are unbelievers. We are right; they are wrong. The other is identified as the pagan, the heathen, the alien, the stranger, the invader, the one who threatens us and our way of life." Another teacher (T2) teaches about other religions from an Islamic perspective: "We are (Muslims) obliged to protect our own religion… I tell my students that if you cannot convince believers of other religions that Islam is right, then you have to end the debate to avoid being swayed by their position."

Only one teacher (T5) in this study supports the teaching of other religions in Islamic education. He prefers to concentrate on the common elements between Islam, Christianity, and Judaism, arguing that they are similar in terms of the creed (coming from the same God) and different in their moral instructions (in order to meet the needs of people living in different time periods). He adds that all religions talk about marriage and divorce, prohibit drinking alcohol, and uphold values of tolerance, equality, integrity and justice. He points out, "They all come from the same origin and lead to the same end (salvation in the hereafter) ... why talk about the differences... the purpose is to reduce violence, to achieve mutual understanding, and to avoid destroying our society."

Not teaching about alternative conceptions of morality and/or spirituality in the multi-faith Israeli society may cause religious illiteracy, which may lead to hate crimes, antagonism, and violence (Moore, 2010). Furthermore, a quick look at ethno-religious conflicts in Muslim societies in the Middle East confirms this analysis. Critical scholars of religious education recommend developing students' intelligent consumption of religious knowledge or intelligent spirituality (Alexander, 2016b). This means the ability to think beyond the framework of a particular faith community and to challenge the clergy who may abuse their power or privilege in the name of Islam. Others discuss the significance of developing the students' informed empathy towards other religions and secular worldviews (Nord & Haynes, 1998; author & Gross, 2017). In addition, some scholars reject the indoctrinating nature of the exclusivist understanding of religion (author & Gross, 2017) because it does not meet the basic conditions of moral agency: "that people have the freedom to choose a life path [or an ethical vision] within reasonable limits, the intelligence to tell the difference between right and wrong according to such a path, and the capacity to err in the choices that they make according to the life they have chosen" (Alexander, 2016b, p. 14-15). Finally, they argue that not exposing the students to alternative communities of ethical practice threatens the liberal values of public education, including personal autonomy, equality of respect, and rationality (Feinberg, 2006; Halstead, 1996; Tan, 2008). Teachers may opt to avoid the problem of relativism, but they need to do so by examining the validity of the different religious arguments and letting their students decide for themselves.

Similarly, all teachers but one see no need to teach about the different intellectual traditions within Islam (Ala`wa, 2016) or to deal with contemporary events in Israel or the Islamic world. As one teacher claims, "There are many other important things to learn about Islam" and "who has time to deal with other traditions?" In addition, all teachers believe that teaching about other traditions may lead to confusion and conflict among students and ultimately to *fitnah* (a state of confusion, dissent, or chaos within the Muslim community) (Leaman & Ali, 2008, p. 39) in the Islamic community. One teacher (T4) argues, "I cannot provide an answer to controversial contemporary issues such as the war in Syria… or the divide in the Islamic movement regarding participation in the Israeli elections… this leads to *fitnah*… I avoid dialectical questions in my teaching because they may lead to a rift in the Muslim society…in order to prevent the *fitnah,* you do not talk about these issues." Later on, this teacher explained that he can teach what is known or agreed upon by the Muslim scholars who follow the Islamic methodology of religious reasoning (*ijtihad*) and that students may disagree within the limits of what is legitimately debated in Islam. Interestingly, the same teacher agrees with the contextualization of halal and *haram*[6] when it comes to new *fatwas* by scholars living in non-Islamic countries. This is because, he argues, not all Muslims live in societies where they can follow or apply the Islamic teachings of Sharia. He would also like the textbook to include the Islamic perspective on contemporary issues, such as car insurance, cloning, democracy and governance. He adds, "We should take the idea of democracy and analyze it, we should investigate whether Islamic governance includes elements of democracy under a different name…we should evaluate the idea of democracy according to the Islamic Sharia…and take what works for us and reject what does not."

Another teacher (T3) explains, "There are major differences between the Sunni[7] and the Shi`a creeds; they believe that God chose Ali to be the prophet and Gabriel (the angel) missed the point by choosing Prophet Muhammad… if we are so different about this basic thing, can you imagine the differences about other things… also they say bad things about the Prophet's wife Aisha, and his companions Umar and Uthman… If students learn about the Shi`a, they would hate them." The same teacher adds that she does not support the politicization of Islam because, "I believe in understanding Islam as it is revealed by God; it is a convenient and not a tough religion; the Islamic Sharia is comprehensible and Islam shouldn't be connected to a specific *sheikh*, stream or movement." Similarly, (T5) argues that he does not teach about different intellectual traditions in Islam unless he is asked by his students. He believes that students may accept the different interpretations of Islam as long as they meet the agreed instructions and principles of the Islamic Sharia.

Another teacher (T1) says, "I do not think that students at this age are able to learn about other Islamic traditions… If students ask about the Shi`a, I answer based on my own religious creed (Sunni)…I show the Sunni evidence that the Shi`a are wrong … I do not think schools should be a playground to combat the Shi`a, but if students ask, I tell them why Shi`as are wrong in their claims against Umar and Abu Baker (the Prophet Muhammad's companions) … I do not think Shi`as belong to Islam because they believe in a different religion." Another teacher (T4) contends that the current events in Syria and the killing of Sunni Muslims by the Shi`a have revealed their egoistic interests and their efforts to undermine Islam by re-establishing the pre-Islamic Persian nation. Another teacher (T2) says, "It is important to teach them the basic principles of Islam… they may learn and compare other streams of Islam in higher education… they have to have an absolute faith in the Sunni tradition and only afterwards they may learn about other schools of thought." By the same token, (T5) says that he avoids dealing with current and perhaps controversial issues, such as the outlawing of the northern faction of the Islamic Movement in Israel, because this may lead to distracting students from their goals. He adds, "I say you do not need to take a position on these matters because in either case you will have enemies."

Viewing difference as a deficit represents a reductionist, depoliticized, essentialised, and non-liberal conception of Islamic civilization, identity, and intellectual heritage. By so doing, we argue, students will miss the opportunity to exercise critical thinking about the validity and consistency of truth claims and to reflect upon their own beliefs and convictions. However, Tan (2008) and Halstead (2014) highlight the significance of allowing students to think critically from within their religious traditions. A critique from within occurs when students are exposed to the different interpretations of the religious text and its historical and contextual implications. This approach balances rootedness (respect for tradition) with openness in Islamic religious education (Tan 2008). When students are exposed to competing interpretations of Islamic teachings, they are, in fact, encouraged to exercise what Tan (2014) calls a "weak rationality." This means being engaged in critical reflection, filtering, evaluating, analyzing, appraising, and judging the claims of religion scholars and authorities and revising their own religiosity if necessary.

The idea of *fitnah* and the view of intellectual diversity as a threat to the Sunni tradition and the truth of Islam in Muslim-majority societies (Haddad, 1995) do not meet the demands of equality of respect, mutual understanding, and tolerance in deliberative democracy. The depoliticizing of Islam and the search for authentic identity reflect the Salafi ideology in Islam and this may silence alternative ways of knowing and of living according to Islam. In reality, Islam has been politicized, like many other religions (Moore, 2010). The rise of political Islam in Middle Eastern societies (Ayoob, 2008) as well as the active engagement of the Islamic movement in the local politics confirm this analysis.

Furthermore, dialogical dealing with controversy is one of the features of deliberative democracy and of the requirements of living in a multicultural and multi-faith society (Hess, 2009; Parker, 2003). Educationally, dealing with controversial issues in Islam through a critical pedagogy of *tarbiyya* and *ta`dib* will probably enhance students' critical self-reflection, their skills of perspective taking, and their tolerance towards different opinions. It will also enhance their cognitive reasoning, epistemic curiosity, problem solving capacities, collecting and evaluating data skills, and comparing/contrasting different attitudes (Avery, 2002; Avery & Simmons, 2013; Gutmann, 1987; Johnson & Johnson, 2009; Parker, 2003).

CONCLUSION

The findings of this study show the dominance of non-liberal and non-critical conceptions of Islamic education in Arab high schools in Israel. The first theme shows that teachers rely on traditional character education, which highlights obedience to Islamic law as a way for achieving the proper meaning of the good life. Teachers believe that there is a bag of virtues that should be transmitted to their students so that they become good believers and good people in their society. Even when the *a`ql* (rational thinking) is used, it aims to confirm the teachings of Islam. This kind of defensive rationality confirms the confessional nature of Islamic education. No other competing conceptions of morality are discussed and this, we believe, delimits the students' capacities of moral reasoning and the conduction of ethical dialogue with fellow (non-Muslim) citizens in the Israeli multicultural and multi-faith society.

The second theme shows that most teachers reject teaching about other religions or dealing with diversity within the Islamic intellectual heritage. This, as we have argued earlier, may lead to religionism and to religious illiteracy, which is a recipe for misunderstandings and possible tensions between Muslims and believers of other religions. When teachers try to deal with controversial issues or modern problems that Muslims face, they restrict themselves to the contribution of Muslim authorities. This makes us question the potential of Islamic education in developing the students' personal autonomy and their independent thinking. Education through deep immersion in the stories and practices of Islam might be appropriate for students at the elementary level where they acquire primary cultural and moral standards to establish their self-definition and build their basic autonomous being (Halstead, 2014). Alexander maintains that "the very idea of pursuing a moral life means appealing to standards by which to measure the worth of that life" (Alexander, 2000, p. 306). Yet, this religious initiation is inadequate at the high school level where students are expected to become intelligent consumers of their own religions; to develop as tolerant citizens of multiple conceptions of the good; and to exercise well-informed life choices and moral decisions.

One possible implication of these results is that more attention should be paid to preparing Islamic education teachers who are able to advocate for informed empathy towards believers of other religions, for thinking critically about religious authorities and interpretations, and for recognizing the existence of alternative and legitimate conceptions of the common good and the righteous life. Education through moral reasoning as well as reflective and dialogical thinking is crucial for living in a democratic and multi-faith society.

ACKNOWLEDGMENT

This research is sponsored and supported by the MOFET Institute as part of post-doctoral studies and it is supervised by Pr. Hanan Alexander- University of Haifa.

REFERENCES

Abu-Asba, K. (2001). Dilemmas in Arab education and in Arab schools in Israel. In Crossroads: Values and education in Israeli society (pp. 441-479). Jerusalem: The Israeli Ministry of Education. (in Hebrew)

Abu-Saad, I. (2006). Separate and unequal: The role of the state educational system in maintaining the subordination of Israel's Palestinian Arab citizens. *Social Identities, 10*(1), 101–127. doi:10.1080/1350463042000191010

Agbaria, A. (2010). Civic education for the Palestinians in Israel: Dilemmas and challenges. In H. A. Alexander, P. Halleli, & Y. Yonah (Eds.), *Citizenship, education, and social conflict: Israeli political education in global perspective* (pp. 217–237). Routledge.

Agbaria, A. K. (2012). Teaching Islam in Israel: On the absence of unifying goals and a collective community. In H. A. Alexander & A. K. Agbaria (Eds.), *Commitment, character, and citizenship: Religious education in liberal democracy* (pp. 181–198). New York: Routledge.

Al-Haj, M. (1995). *Education, Empowerment and Control: The Case of the Arabs in Israel*. Albany, NY: State University of New York.

Al-Jabri, M. (2009). *Democracy, human rights, and law in Islamic thought*. London: I. B. Tauris Publishers.

Al-Jabri, M. A. (1996). The religion, state, and the implementation of sharia. Markez Derasat Alwihda Alarabia. (in Arabic)

Al Zeera, Z. (2001). *Wholeness and holiness in education: An Islamic perspective*. Herndon: The International Institute of Islamic Thought.

Ala'wa, S. (2016). *The Islamic intellectual schools: From Khawarij to Muslim Brotherhood*. Beirut: Arab Network for Research and Publishing. (in Arabic)

Alexander, H. (2000). In search of a vision of the good: Values education and the postmodern condition. In R. Gardner. J. Cairns. & D. Lawton. (Eds.), Education for values (pp. 303-312). London: Kogan Page.

Alexander, H. (2009). Educating identity: Toward a pedagogy of difference. In S. Miedema (Ed.), *Religious Education as Encounter: A Tribute to John Hull* (pp. 45–52). Munster: Waxman.

Alexander, H. A. (2015). *Reimagining liberal education: Affiliation and inquiry in democratic schooling*. New York: Bloomsbury.

Alexander, H. A. (2016a). What is critical about critical pedagogy? Conflicting conceptions of criticism in the curriculum. *Educational Philosophy and Theory*. doi:10.1080/00131857.2016.1228519

Alexander, H. A. (2016b). What can go wrong in religious instruction? And what should go right? In B. Warnick (Ed.), *Philosophy: Education: Macmillan interdisciplinary Handbooks* (pp. 249–267). New York: Macmillan Reference.

Arthur, J., Gearon, L., & Sears, A. (2010). *Education, politics, and religion*. New York: Routledge. doi:10.4324/9780203846575

Ashraf, S. A. (1988). The conceptual framework of education: The Islamic perspective. *Muslim Education*, *5*(2), 8–18.

Attas, S. N. (1979). *Aims and objectives of Islamic education*. Jeddah: King Abd al Aziz University.

Avery, P. G. (2002). Political tolerance, democracy, and adolescents. In W. Parker (Ed.), *Education for democracy: Contexts, curricula, assessments* (pp. 113–130). Information Age Publishing.

Avery, P. G., Levy, S. A., & Simmons, A. M. (2013). Deliberating controversial public issues as part of civic education. *Social Studies*, *104*(3), 105–114. doi:10.1 080/00377996.2012.691571

Ayalon, H., & Yogev, A. (1996). The alternative worldview of state religious high schools in Israel. *Comparative Education Review*, *40*(1), 7–27. doi:10.1086/447353

Ayoob, M. (2008). *The many faces of political Islam: Religion and politics in the Muslim World*. Ann Arbor, MI: University of Michigan Press.

Barnes, P. (2001, October). (200). What is wrong with the phenomenological approach to religious education? *Religious Education (Chicago, Ill.)*, *96*(4), 445–461. doi:10.1080/0034408017753442366

Bryman, A. (2012). *Social research methods* (4th ed.). Oxford, UK: Oxford University Press.

Byrne, C. (2014). *Religion in secular education: What, in heaven's name, are we teaching our children?* Boston: Brill. doi:10.1163/9789004264342

Charmaz, K. (2006). *Constructing grounded theory: A practical guide through qualitative analysis*. London: Sage.

Cohen, L., Manion, L., & Morrison, K. (2007). *Research methods in Education*. New York: Routledge. doi:10.4324/9780203029053

Cook, B. J., & Malkāwī, F. H. (2010). *Classical foundations of Islamic educational thought: A compendium of parallel English-Arabic texts* (1st ed.). Brigham Young University Press.

Doumato, E., & Starrett, G. (2007). *Teaching Islam: Textbooks and religion in the Middle East*. Boulder, CO: Rienner.

Dwairy, M. (1997). *Personality culture and Arabic society: Psychological study*. New York: Haworth Press. (In Arabic)

Engebretson, K. (2006). Phenomenology and religious education theory. In M. de Souza (Ed.), *International handbook of the religious, moral and spiritual dimensions in education* (pp. 651–665). Dordrecht: Springer.

Erricker, C. (2010). *Religious education: A conceptual and interdisciplinary approach for secondary level*. London: Routledge.

Feinberg, W. (2006). *For goodness sake: Religious schools and education for democratic citizenry*. New York: Routledge.

Fisherman, S. (2011). Socialization agents influencing the religious identity of religious Israeli adolescents. *Religious Education (Chicago, Ill.)*, *106*(3), 272–298. doi:10.1080/00344087.2011.569653

Gearon, L. (2004). *Citizenship through secondary religious education*. New York: RoutledgeFalmer.

Giroux, H. (1988). *Teachers as intellectuals: Toward a critical pedagogy of learning*. Granby, MA: Bergin & Garvey.

Goodlad, J. I., Klein, M. F., & Tye, K. A. (1979). The domains of curriculum and their study. In *Curriculum Inquiry: The study of curriculum practice* (pp. 43–77). New York: McGraw Hill.

Gross, Z. (2003). State religious education in Israel: Between tradition and modernity. *Prospects*, *33*(2), 149–164. doi:10.1023/A:1023638728907

Gross, Z. (2010). Reflective teaching as a path to religious meaning-making and growth. *Religious Education (Chicago, Ill.)*, *105*(3), 265–282. doi:10.1080/00344081003772014

Guba, E., & Lincoln, Y. (1982). Epistemological and methodological bases of naturalistic inquiry. *Educational Communication and Technology*, *30*(4), 233–252.

Guba, E. G. (1981). Criteria for assessing the trustworthiness of naturalistic inquiries. *Educational Communication and Technology*, *29*(2), 75–91.

Gutmann, A. (1987). *Democratic education*. Princeton, NJ: Princeton University Press.

Habermas, J. (2006). Religion in the public sphere. *European Journal of Philosophy*, *14*(1), 1–25. doi:10.1111/j.1468-0378.2006.00241.x

Haddad, Y. Y. (1995). *Islamists and the challenge of pluralism*. Washington, DC: Center for Contemporary Arab Studies.

Halstead, M. (2014). Values and values education: Challenges for faith schools. In J. D. Chapman, S. McNamara, M. J. Reiss, & Y. Waghid (Eds.), *International handbook of learning, teaching and leading in faith-based schools* (pp. 65–83). Dordrecht: Springer Netherlands. doi:10.1007/978-94-017-8972-1_3

Halstead, M. J. (1995). Towards a unified view of Islamic education. *Islam & Christian-Muslim Relations*, *6*(1), 25–43. doi:10.1080/09596419508721040

Halstead, M. J. (1996). Liberal values and liberal education. In J. M. Halstead & M. J. Taylor (Eds.), *Values in education and education in values* (pp. 17–32). The Falmer Press.

Halstead, M. J. (2004). An Islamic concept of education. *Comparative Education*, *40*(4), 517–528. doi:10.1080/0305006042000284510

Hess, D. E. (2009). *Controversy in the classroom: The democratic power of discussion*. New York: Routledge.

Hull, J. M. (2000). The transmission of religious prejudice. *British Journal of Religious Education*, *14*(2), 69–72.

Hull, J. M. (2000). The transmission of religious prejudice. *British Journal of Religious Education*, *14*(2), 69–72.

Hull, J. M. (2003). The blessings of secularity: Religious education in England and Wales. *Journal of Religious Education*, *51*(3), 51–58.

Hussain, A. (2004). Islamic education: Why is there a need for it? *Journal of Beliefs & Values*, *25*(3), 317–323. doi:10.1080/1361767042000306130

Israeli Ministry of Education. (2014). *The modification of the curriculum of Islamic studies and culture to the policy of significant learning*. Hebrew.

Jackson, R. (1997). *Religious Education: An Interpretive Approach*. London: Hodder & Stoughton.

Jackson, R. (2004). *Rethinking religious education and plurality: Issues in diversity and pedagogy*. London: RoutledgeFalmer. doi:10.4324/9780203465165

Jackson, R. (2006). *Fifty key figures in Islam*. London: Routledge. doi:10.4324/9780203001387

Johnson, D. W., & Johnson, R. T. (2009). Energizing learning: The instructional power of conflict. *Educational Researcher*, *38*(1), 37–51. doi:10.3102/0013189X08330540

Joseph, P. B. (2000). Conceptualizing curriculum. In P. B. Joseph (Ed.), *Cultures of curriculum* (pp. 3–22). Mahwah, NJ: L. Erlbaum Associates.

Kamrava, M. (2009). Introduction: Reformist Islam in comparative perspective. In M. Kamrava (Ed.), *The new Voices of Islam: Reforming politics and modernity* (pp. 1–27). London: I.B. Tauris & Co. Ltd.

Kecia, A., & Leaman, O. (2008). *Islam: The key concepts*. New York: Routledge.

Khan, M. S. (1987). Humanism and Islamic education. *Muslim Education Quarterly*, *4*(3), 25–35.

Knowles, J. G. (1992). Models for understanding pre-service and beginning teachers' biographies: Illustrations from case studies. In I. Goodson (Ed.), *Studying teachers' lives* (pp. 99–152). New York: Teachers College Press. doi:10.4324/9780203415177_chapter_4

Krueger, R. A., & Casey, M. A. (2009). *Focus groups: A practical guide for applied research*. Los Angeles, CA: SAGE.

Kunzman, R. (2006). *Grappling with the good: Talking about religion and morality in public schools*. Albany, NY: State University of New York Press.

Kurzman, C. (1998). Liberal Islam and its Islamic context. In C. Kurzman (Ed.), *Liberal Islam: A source book* (pp. 3–26). New York: Oxford University Press.

Langeveld, M. (1983). Reflections on phenomenology and pedagogy. *Phenomenology + Pedagogy*, *1*(1), 5–7.

Leaman, O., & Ali, K. (2008). *Islam: The key concepts*. London: Routledge.

Lockwood, A. L. (2001). Blending civic decency and civic literacy. *The International Journal of Social Education, 16*(1), 55–61.

Mahajna, I., & Kfir, D. (2013). The status of Islamic religious studies in one academic college of Education and Israeli Arab schools today. [Arabic]. *Jamea'a, 17*(2), 97–124.

Makkawi, I. (2002). Role conflict and the dilemma of Palestinian teachers in Israel. *Comparative Education, 38*(1), 39–52. doi:10.1080/03050060120103847

Maoz, A. (2007). Religious education in Israel. *University of Detroit Mercy Law Review, 83*(5), 679–728.

McLaughlin, T. H. (1992). Citizenship, diversity, and education: A philosophical perspective. *Journal of Moral Education, 21*(3), 235–250. doi:10.1080/0305724920210307

Merry, M. (2006). Islamic philosophy of education and western Islamic schools: Points of tension. In F. Salili & R. Hoosain (Eds.), *Religion in multicultural education* (pp. 41–70). Greenwich, CT: IAP.

Merry, M. S. (2007). *Culture, identity, and Islamic schooling: A philosophical approach*. New York: Palgrave Macmillan. doi:10.1057/9780230109766

Midgley, M. (2007). Intelligent design theory and other ideological problems. *Journal of the Philosophy of Education Society of Great Britain, 15*, 1–48.

Moore, D. (2006a). Overcoming religious illiteracy: A cultural studies approach. *World History Connected, 4*(1). Retrieved from: http://worldhistoryconnected.press. illinois.edu/4.1/moore.html

Moore, D. (2010). *Guidelines for teaching about religion in K-12 public schools in the United States*. American Academy of Religion.

Moore, D. L. (2007). *Overcoming religious illiteracy: A cultural studies approach to the study of religion in secondary education*. New York: Palgrave Macmillan. doi:10.1057/9780230607002

Moore, J. R. (2006b). Teaching about Islam in secondary schools: Curricular and pedagogical considerations. *Equity & Excellence in Education, 39*(3), 279–286. doi:10.1080/10665680600788479

Nasr, S. (1989). *Knowledge and the sacred*. Albany, NY: State University of New York.

Niyozov, S., & Memon, N. (2011). Islamic education and Islamization: Evolution of themes, continuities and new directions. *Journal of Muslim Minority Affairs*, *31*(1), 5–30. doi:10.1080/13602004.2011.556886

Noddings, N. (1993). *Educating for intelligent belief or unbelief.* New York: Teachers College Press.

Nord, W. A. (1995). *Religion & American education: Rethinking a national dilemma.* Chapel Hill, NC: University of North Carolina Press.

Nord, W. A., & Haynes, C. C. (1998). *Taking religion seriously across the curriculum.* Nashville, TN: ASCD.

O'Grady, K. (2005). Professor Ninian Smart, phenomenology and religious education. *British Journal of Religious Education*, *27*(3), 227–237. doi:10.1080/01416200500141249

Parker, W. C. (2003). *Teaching democracy: Unity and diversity in public life.* New York: Teachers College Press.

Peleg, I., & Waxman, D. (2011). *Israeli's Palestinians: The conflict within.* New York: Cambridge University Press. doi:10.1017/CBO9780511852022

Pinson, H. (2007). Inclusive curriculum? Challenges to the role of citizenship education in a Jewish and democratic state. *Curriculum Inquiry*, *37*(4), 351–380. doi:10.1111/j.1467-873X.2007.00391.x

Power, F. C., Higgins, A., & Kohlberg, L. (1989). *Lawrence Kohlberg's approach to moral education.* New York: Columbia Press.

Ramadan, T. (2004). *Western Muslims and the future of Islam.* Oxford, UK: Oxford University Press.

Rosenblith, S. (2008). Beyond coexistence: Toward a more reflective religious pluralism. *Theory and Research in Education*, *6*(1), 107–121. doi:10.1177/1477878507086733

Rosenblith, S., & Priestmanm, S. (2004). Problematizing religious truth: Implications for public education. *Educational Theory*, *54*(4), 365–380. doi:10.1111/j.0013-2004.2004.00025.x

Rudnitzky, A. (2014). The Arab citizens of Israel at the start of the twenty-first century. Tel Aviv: The Institute for National Security Studies. (in Hebrew)

Sadaalah, S. (2004). Islamic orientations and education. In H. Daun & G. Walford (Eds.), *Educational strategies among Muslims in the context of globalization* (pp. 37–63). Boston: Brill.

Saeed, A. (2006). *Islamic thought: An introduction.* London: Routledge.

Safi, O. (2003). *Progressive Muslims on justice, gender, and pluralism.* Oxford, UK: Oneworld.

Sahin, A. (2013). *New Directions in Islamic education. Pedagogy and identity formation.* Kube Publishing Ltd.

Saldana, J. (2009). *The coding manual for qualitative researchers.* London: Sage.

Selcuk, M. (2012). The contribution of religious education to democratic culture. In H. A. Alexander & A. K. Agbaria (Eds.), *Commitment, character, and citizenship: Religious education in liberal democracy* (pp. 215–225). New York: Routledge.

Shamal, S. (2000). Cultural shift: The case of Jewish religious education in Israel. *British Journal of Sociology of Education, 21*(3), 401–417. doi:10.1080/713655352

Siegel, H. (1988). *Educating reason.* New York: Routledge.

Smart, N. (1987). *Religion in the western mind.* New York: Macmillan. doi:10.1007/978-1-349-08772-3

Sofian, K., Abu-Mokh, F. (2014). *The religious education book for the high school level: The first unit.* Haifa- Israel: Kul-Shee Library. (Arabic)

Stake, R. E. (1994). Case studies. In N. K. Denzin & Y. S. Lincoln (Eds.), *Handbook of qualitative research* (pp. 236–247). London: Sage.

Tan, C. (2008). *Teaching without indoctrination: Implications for values education.* Rotterdam: Sense Publishers.

Tan, C. (2011). *Islamic education and indoctrination: The case in Indonesia.* New York: Routledge.

Tan, C. (2014). Rationality and autonomy from the enlightenment and Islamic perspectives. *Journal of Beliefs and Values, 35*(3), 327-39.

Thiessen, E. J. (2012). Democratic schooling and the demands of religion. In H. A. Alexander & A. K. Agbaria (Eds.), *Commitment, character, and citizenship: Religious education in liberal democracy* (pp. 161–178). New York: Routledge.

Tibi, B. (2012). *Islamism and Islam.* New Haven, CT: Yale University Press.

Waghid, Y. (2011). *Conceptions of Islamic education: Pedagogical framings*. New York: Peter Lang.

Waghid, Y., & Smeyers, P. (2014). Re-envisioning the future: Democratic citizenship education and Islamic education. *Journal of Philosophy of Education, 48*(4), 539–558. doi:10.1111/1467-9752.12118

Westheimer, J., & Kahne, J. (2004). What kind of citizen? The politics of educating for democracy. *American Educational Research Journal, 41*(2), 237–269. doi:10.3102/00028312041002237

White, K. (2010). Asking sacred questions: Understanding religion's impact on teacher belief and action. *Religious Education (Chicago, Ill.), 37*(1), 40–59.

White, K. R. (2009). Connecting religion and teacher identity: The unexplored relationship between religion and teachers in public schools. *Teaching and Teacher Education, 25*(6), 857–866. doi:10.1016/j.tate.2009.01.004

Wilkinson, M. L. N. (2013). Introducing Islamic critical realism. *Journal of Critical Realism, 12*(4), 419–442. doi:10.1179/1476743013Z.00000000014

Wright, A. (2007). *Critical religious education, multiculturalism and the pursuit of truth*. Cardiff, UK: University of Wales Press.

Wright, R. (1996). Islam and liberal democracy: Two visions of reformation. *Journal of Democracy, 7*(2), 64–75. doi:10.1353/jod.1996.0037

Yin, R. K. (2009). *Case study research: Design and methods*. Thousand Oaks, CA: Sage Publications.

Zia, R. (2007). Transmission of values in Muslim countries: Religious education and moral development in school curricula. In A. Benavot, C. Braslavsky, & N. Truong (Eds.), *School knowledge in comparative and historical perspective* (pp. 119–134). Springer. doi:10.1007/978-1-4020-5736-6_8

ENDNOTES

[1] The performance of prayer five times a day, fasting in the month of *Ramadan*, giving alms to the poor (*zakat*), believing that there is one god (Allah) and that Prophet Muhammad his messenger, and performing the pilgrimage (*hajj*) to Makkah once in a lifetime (Waghid, 2011).

[2]   Salafism is the more conservative tradition of Islam. It supports literal and exclusivist interpretation of the Quran, the *hadith*, and Islamic law (Al-Jabri, 1996; Kecia & Leaman, 2008).

[3]   Sunnah means "normal practice, customary procedure or action, or norm sanctioned by tradition (Leaman & Ali, 2008, p. 135).

[4]   *Qiyas* is a fourth source for legal interpretation in Islam (after the Quran, the *hadith* and the *Ijma* (consensus of religion scholars). It means a personal opinion of a Muslim scholar—who knows and the Quran and *hadith* very well—it is "based upon making an analogy between a case in the Quran or Sunna and a newly arisen case" (Jackson, 2006, p. 43).

[5]   In Islam there are four major *madahibs* or schools of legal thinking. These are the Hanbali, Hanafi, Shafi'i, and Maliki jurists (Leaman and Ali, 2008)

[6]   The teacher here is referring to students who bring fatwas legitimizing the Reba (interest) in non-Muslim societies.

[7]   Somewhere between 80 and 90 percent of the world's Muslims identify as Sunni (Leaman and Ali, 2008).

Chapter 9
Islamic Education and Islamic Affinities in Precolonial West Africa

Ibrahima Diallo
University of South Australia, Australia

ABSTRACT

Evidence shows that in pre-colonial West Africa, Islamic education played a significant role following conversion of West Africans to Islam because of its impact on all spheres of life. With the establishment of theocratic states and communities, Islamic learning centers emerged to spread Islamic education and consolidate the Islamic way of life in West Africa. In this vast region where people of different ethnic, linguistic, and religious backgrounds lived and interacted for trade and commerce, Islamic education fostered Islamic affinities constructed on the universalism of Islam and Islamic injunction to form Muslim brotherhood and create the Ummah.

INTRODUCTION

Over the last four decades, research on Islam in pre-colonial West Africa has yielded ground-breaking findings. Now, there is robust evidence that demonstrates that pre-colonial West Africa was an important Islamic epicentre (Levtzion, 2000a; Levtzion, 2000b; Insoll, 1996; Trimingham, 1980). The existing body of academic and non-academic research shows that the establishment of Islamic theocracies and communities and world-class learning centres made pre-colonial West Africa attractive to Muslims from West Africa and beyond. With the spread of Islam, people of different ethnic, linguistic and cultural backgrounds lived and interacted for trade

DOI: 10.4018/978-1-5225-8528-2.ch009

and business as well as for Islamic education and religious pursuit in West Africa. The introduction of Islamic education in West Africa, on the one hand, and the subsequent development of *Ajami*, on the other hand, facilitated Islamic affinities among Muslims in the region. These Islamic affinities were mainly constructed on Islamic teachings such as the universalism of the Qur'anic message and the Qur'anic injunction to form brotherhood with Muslims and forge an Islamic *Ummah* or community of Muslims across the world. This article is about the ways in which Islamic education fostered Islamic affinities among African Muslims in precolonial West Africa. By Islamic affinity, I refer to the emotional, mystical, spiritual, and social relationship of affiliation, conviviality, and co-existence fostered by Islamic education for a shared membership to Islam. To address the ways in which Islamic education fostered Islamic affinities in pre-colonial Africa, the article is divided into four sections: In the first section, I provide the ethnic and linguistic context of West Africa in the precolonial situation. In the second section, I describe the place of Islam in the region. In the third, I analyse the ways in which Islamic education and, to certain extent, *Ajami* laid the foundations for Islamic affinities by providing the (basic) Islamic education that is essential for a person to identify and practice as a Muslim and to be able to forge affinities. In the fourth and last section, I discuss the ways in which Islamic education fostered Islamic affinities in West Africa.

The West African Context

Scholars of the history of Islam in Africa have often divided the continent into zones based on the ethno-cultural characteristics of the population, the geographic features of the region and the process of the penetration and spread of Islam in Africa. For example, in their studies of the history of Islam in Africa, Trimingham (1980) divided the continent into six zones while Insoll (1996) offered seven zones. For this article, I use West Africa to loosely refer to the current regional space that includes most country-members of the Economic Community of West Africa (ECOWAS)[1] (excluding Cabo Verde) and non-member countries such as Mauritania, Chad, and Cameroon. In the precolonial context, this vast region, with wide geographical contrasts and a heterogeneous landscape (forests, deserts, and savannahs), was divided into secular and theocratic states and communities (e.g.: kingdoms, empires, sultanates, and caliphates). Of these, the best known pre-colonial West African states were the Ghana Empire, the Mali Empire, the Songhay Empire, the Sokoto Caliphate, and the Kingdom of Dahomey. The arrival and the settlement of Arab and Berber traders and Islamic scholars in West Africa significantly contributed to the racial, cultural, linguistic and religious diversities of the region. As highlighted by Rebstock, it is indeed trade and religious motivations that brought Arabs and Berbers to the region:

[I]t was along the axes of this trade [oasis-horticulture, cattle and trade] that the first Muslim Arabs and proselytised Berbers advanced southward, setting up temporary trading-posts at the routes' intersections and bringing back with them as yet unheard reports of the 'land of the blacks' (bilād a-sūdān) (Rebstock, 2010, p. 145).

In other words, West Africa became an area of intense contact between people and communities of diverse backgrounds attracted mainly by trade and Islam. In addition to the African communities spread throughout West Africa (e.g.: the Mande, Dyala, Fula, Bambara, Hausa, and Mandinka, to name but a few) and the Arab and Berbers traders and proselytisers, there were also scholars from other parts of the world who were established in the various theocratic states and Islamic centres in West Africa. They engaged in Islamic scholarship and exchanges with the local Islamic scholars as well as with the Arab and Berber scholars established in West Africa. According to Bloom,

in the Western Bilad al-sudan, the arrival of large numbers of books and scholars can be dated from the period following the pilgrimage of the Malian ruler Mansa Musa (1312-37) to Mecca in 1324. While on pilgrimage, he is said to have met the Andalusian poet Abu Ishaq Ibrahim al-Sahili (d.1346), who accompanied him back to Mali (Bloom, 2008, p. 152).

In addition to the Andalusian poet brought to West Africa from Mecca to support Islamic scholarship in West Africa, Bloom mentioned another poet named al-Tuwayjin, the son of a businessman in Grenada, who also settled in Timbuktu (Bloom, 2008, p. 152).

There were important Islamic centres in West Africa, but Timbuktu was the best-known centre. It distinguished itself in the sixteenth century as the leading Islamic centre in West Africa and attracted students and scholars from all over the region; from the Saharan oases (from Walata to Awajila) and from North Africa (Hunwick, 1999), thus making Timbuktu one of the most multiethnic, multiracial and multilingual education centres in West Africa. According to Cleaveland,

the town of Timbuktu and Walata almost certainly began as small black settlements, Songhay or Sork in the case of Timbuktu, and Mande in the case of Walata. However, by the thirteenth or fourteenth century AD both towns were multiethnic, multiracial centres of commerce and Islamic scholarship (Cleaveland 2008, p. 79).

This shows that racial and ethnic diversities were a key feature of pre-colonial Islamic learning centres in West Africa. Cleaveland further argued that *one should resist the temptation to describe the scholarly institutions in Timbuktu and Walata as 'Black', as they clearly were multiethnic and multiracial, though they derived a substantial portion of their vitality from scholars of southern origin (Cleaveland 2008, p. 79).*

Linguistic diversity was also another important feature in pre-colonial West Africa. Cleaveland mentioned that Azay, a mixture of Mande and Berber, was an important language in Walata at the end of the sixteenth century, despite emigration from Timbuktu and the growing presence of Arabic speakers in the southern desert (Cleaveland 2008, p. 79).

As can be seen, Islam changed the outlook of West Africa. It brought together Muslims of different racial, cultural, and linguistic backgrounds from Africa and elsewhere in various sites, including the Islamic education centres and the theocratic states. In the next section, I describe Islam and its importance in pre-colonial Africa West Africa.

Islam in Pre-Colonial Africa

Archaeological evidence in Ethiopia and the Horn of Africa shows that the first contacts between Islam and the African continent can be traced back to the fourth or fifth century A.D. Insoll, 1996, p. 444. The Red Sea links between the Horn of African and the Arabian Peninsula served as the gateway through which Islam entered the African continent.

The early contacts were mainly facilitated by traders following pre-Islamic trade routes across the Red Sea. Around the seventh century Islam started to spread because of the intensification and diversification of trading activities in different parts of the African continent thanks to new trade routes (e.g.: the Trans Saharan route), trading posts and various settlements in the interior of the continent. Nevertheless,

first direct archaeological evidence we have for the presence of a Muslim community within the Horn of Africa is a group of over 200 Arabic funerary inscriptions on basalt, executed in the Kufic scripts (and later derivations), which date from A.D. 911 to AD 1539 (Insoll, 1996, p. 444).

In West Africa, intermittent contacts with Islam began from the late eighth century, but 'around the eleventh century [that] Islam ... started to take root in the sub-Saharan areas of the continent, West Africa and in East Africa' (Diagne, 2004, p. 375). Between the eleventh and fifteenth centuries, Islam in West Africa grew considerably grown, but was confined to coastal lines and river banks: for example, on the banks of Senegal and Niger rivers (Trimingham, 1980). With the combined work undertaken by several actors, including clerics, travellers, nomads, traders, pilgrims and settlers, on the one hand, and jihads and proselytising campaigns (Sanneh, 1976; Trimingham, 1980); on the other hand, the progression of Islam accelerated and reached almost all areas of West Africa. According to Trimingham, by the fifteenth century, Islam had reached almost all parts of North Africa, the coastlines of sub-Saharan Africa, various areas in modern Senegal, Mali, Nigeria, Niger, Chad and the Republic of Sudan. Islam spread further in West Africa, especially in Western Nigeria, Sierra Leone (30% Muslim) and Guinea (30% Muslim) (Trimingham, 1980, p. 37). By the end of the eighteenth century, "…Islam became a fully fledged African religion and the Qur'anic schools became wholly integrated with African social structures and adapted to their needs" (Hassane, 2008, p. 111).

Prior to the colonial conquest of West Africa, Islam was integrated in African societies and, as already highlighted, several well-established theocratic states were in place in various parts of West Africa. The most well-known pre-colonial Islamic states included the Futa Toro Empire (Senegal), the Macina and the Mali Empires (Mali), the Sokoto Caliphate and the Hausa Kingdoms (Nigeria), Kaneem-Bormu kingdom (spread across modern Chad, Cameroon, eastern Niger and northern Nigeria) and the Kingdom of Fuuta Jallon (Guinea). Following the establishment of these Islamic theocracies, religious devotion grew and Islamic education consolidated. It is safe to argue that in pre-colonial West Africa, Islam played an important part in the region because "…African Muslims reached their maximum density and Islam … made its deepest impact upon life" (Trimingham, 1980, p. 37). This section has discussed the spread and the place of Islam in pre-colonial West Africa. In the next I summarise the ways in which Islamic education and *Ajami* laid the foundations for Islamic affinities in West Africa.

The Foundations of Islamic Affinities

As mentioned before, the introduction and adoption of Islam in many parts of West Africa have had a deep impact on West African societies which included radical changes in the social structure, in everyday social interactions, in justice and law, in directions of trade, in types of education (religious or secular) and epistemologies (indigenous knowledge versus Islamic knowledge). In other words, Islam shaped the societies and became an integral part of the society and the way of life of many people in large parts of West Africa. As shown before, the Muslim population in the region was characterised by its ethnic, linguistic and cultural diversity. Islamic education laid the foundation for Islamic affinities in West Africa because to identify as a Muslim and engage with other Muslims one needs at least basic Islamic knowledge. Therefore, Islamic education, which developed as a corollary of Islam, provided the theological, linguistic and cultural knowledge needed to identify as a Muslim and to be able to forge Islamic affinities.

In West Africa, Islamic education that emerged to teach the Qur'an and the Arabic language and culture were conducted both in formal settings (such as madrasas, mosques, Islamic schools, etc.) and informal settings (such as the house of the marabou, under the shade of the village tree, temporary schools, the house of an individual volunteer, a benevolent, or a benefactor, etc.). Islamic education provided people with the Islamic knowledge and the skills they needed to live an Islamic way of life. It also provided opportunities to memorise the essential prayers, preparatory formulas, surah and verses needed to perform the compulsory daily prayers in Arabic[2]. For expert learners, Islamic education offered access to Islamic knowledge, through texts such as commentaries, poems, elegies and other religious works created by African as well as other Islamic scholars. A minority of learners continued their education to become expert users and could read and write fluent Arabic. Thanks to their advanced skills in Qur'anic literacy and Arabic, they were initiated into *tafsir* (Qur'anic interpretation), *fiqh* (Islamic law), *mantiq* (logic) and *bayan* (rhetoric) among other fields of advanced Islamic scholarship (Diallo, 2012). In short, Islamic education focused on teaching the (basic) literacy skills needed to read and use the Qur'an and live in accordance with Islamic codes and principles. With such skills and knowledge thanks to Islamic education, a person was able to identify as a Muslim and was able to forge Islamic affinities with African and non-African Muslims in West Africa.

As for *Ajami*, the writing of African languages using the Arabic alphabet, it developed in West Africa for secular functions relating mainly to private and mass communication. Introduced with Islam to teach the Qur'an, *Ajami* literacy developed from Islamic education. However, it significantly contributed to Islamic affinities in West Africa because with the *Ajami* that developed from Islamic education, a range of Islamic creative and literary texts in African languages flourished (e.g.: literary texts, memoirs, poems, songs, elegies, eulogies, etc.), thereby providing opportunities for Islamic affinities among West Africans by sharing the same linguistic and cultural repertoire.

In this section I have suggested that Islamic education was primarily delivered to provide Muslims with the literacy skills required to access (basic) Islamic knowledge to perform their daily religious rituals and gain Islamic knowledge. Fluency in Arabic was available only to advanced learners. As for *Ajami*, it developed for nonreligious purposes, but provided opportunity for creative religious texts in African languages to be shared by members of the same speech communities. The development of Islamic education to spread Islamic knowledge and skills, on the one hand, and the development of *Ajami*, as a language of creative Islamic texts in African languages, on the other hand, laid the foundations for the spread of Islamic knowledge and practices. These significantly contributed to fostering Islamic affinities in West Africa as they provided the knowledge and the skills needed to identity as a Muslim. In the next section, I discuss Islamic education and the ways in which it fostered Islamic affinities.

Islamic Affinities

To understand the extent to which Islamic education created Islamic affinities in pre-colonial West Africa, it is essential to understand the meaning of the word 'Islam' and the place the Qur'an occupies in the life of Muslims. The word Islam is derived from the Arabic root *s.l.m.*, which means *peace, security* and *surrender*. Translated into English, the word Islam has two distinct but complementary meanings. The first meaning is *salima* 'peace' and the second meaning is *aslama* 'to submit or to surrender'. Based on these two meanings, a Muslim can be defined as a peace-loving person "who surrenders to God's will, and the religion and society are based on this act of surrendering to God (or Allah)" (Akdere, Russ-Eft, & Eft, 2006). Islam is profoundly constructed on the Qur'an which was revealed to the Prophet Mohamad (Peace Be Upon Him; PBUH). In short, Islam primarily hinges on the Qur'an but also on the Prophetic traditions (*Sunnah* and *Hadith*[3]) and *Sharia* (divine Islamic law). Therefore, to be a Muslim is to adhere to Qur'anic teachings, the Prophetic traditions and Sharia. For example, for Muslims, there are five practices, the pillars of Islam, which are: the *Shahada* credo "there is no God but God and Muhamad is the Prophet of God", performing the five daily prayers (*Salat*), giving parts of one's wealth (2 to 10%) to the needy (*Zakat*), fasting during the month of Ramadan (S*aum*) and performing the pilgrimage (*Haj*) for those who can afford it.

In addition to these five pillars, Islam is grounded on key Qur'anic teaching principles. One is the *tawhidic* principle which is the doctrine of divine unity or the oneness of God. This principle hinges on the principle of *aqidah* which stipulates that Islamic teachings must remain unalterable and it emphasizes that faith remains always central and all-encompassing. In other words, the principle of *aqidah* "details what a Muslims should know, believe and inwardly understand about God and religion as prescribed by the Qur'an, and the Sunnah, the way of the Prophet Muhammad" (Annalakshmi & Abeer, 2011, p. 26). The other important Qur'anic principle is *tafakkur* which means using an Islamic perspective based on the revelation of the Qur'an and the teachings of the Hadiths as well as accepting every single Islamic truth. For example, rational knowledge (secular or not), and scientific reasoning are encouraged if they do not contradict Islamic teachings. Islamic principles are constructed on two other key Islamic principles, which are *al-haqiqa al-mutlaqa* and *Allahu a'lam*. The principle of *Al-haqiqa al-mutlaqa*, which means the 'absoluteness or the absolute truth', emphasizes the existence of one God only and one absolute ultimate truth. As for the principle of *Allahu a'lam,* which means 'only God knows', it intersects with the principles discussed before. In other words, absolute knowledge is not attainable by a simple human being; it is the privilege of God alone to know the ultimate truth. For these reasons, the Qur'an is the cornerstone of the Islamic way of life as highlighted by Haleem "the Qur'an is the supreme authority in Islam. It is the fundamental and paramount source of the creed, rituals, ethics, and laws of the Islamic religion" (Haleem, 2005). In summary, to be a Muslim involves preforming the five Islamic pillars of Islam and adhering to the Qur'anic teachings and principles contained in the Qur'an.

In pre-colonial West Africa, following conversion to Islam and the creation of theocratic states, Islam became an integral part of the daily life of Muslims. One of the best-known examples that highlights the religious devotion in West African was the Fuuta Jallon (Guinea), which was referred to as the 'diffusion centre for Islam in the region' (Trimingham, 1980, p. 70). According to Barry (1976)

... as pious Muslims, the almamis [Islamic clerics and/or political leaders], the princes or kings of the Fuuta Djallon, adhered strictly to the Qur'anic laws... from dawn to dusk, at prayer times, the Fuuta Djallon, from the deep valleys to the highlands, was only one supplication to Allah [God], the Unique, one only tribute to the Prophet] (Barry, 2005, p. 7. My translation.).

Given the important place of Islamic education, adherence to Islamic teachings facilitated Islamic affinities, especially in pre-colonial West Africa where Islam was the major regional banner to bring together people of different linguistic, social, and cultural backgrounds who interacted for trade and scholarship. In the next section, I will focus on the Islamic teachings that have fostered religious affinities in pre-colonial Africa, mainly the universalism of the Qur'anic message and the Qur'anic teachings to form brotherhood with Muslims and to establish the (Islamic) *ummah* with Muslims across the world. To illustrate the Islamic affinities references will be drawn primarily from the Qur'an teachings spread through Islamic education but reinforced by Hadiths and the Prophet's [PBUH] last sermon.

Universalism of Islam

The first tenet of Islamic education that fostered Islamic affinities in West Africa is the universalism found in the Qur'anic message. Islamic education taught that the Qur'an, in its very first surah, teaches all Muslims to adhere to one God who is the Lord of all, including mankind or the universe: "All the praises and thanks be to Allah, Lord of the '*Âlamîn*" (Qur'an 1:2). Islamic education taught that the Qur'an adds that God has sent the Prophet Mohamad (PBUH), his messenger, to all mankind in this following verse: "and We have not sent you (O Muhammad, PBUH) except as a giver of glad tidings and a warner to all mankind, but most of men know not." (Qur'an 34:28). In other words, God, the Lord of *Âlamîn,* has sent the Prophet to deliver His message to the whole world, i.e. the whole of mankind. These two verses on the Oneness of God and the universal nature of the Qur'anic message played a significant role in fostering Islamic affinities in West Africa. It calls for the belief in one God for all mankind. The statement of One Lord for all is stressed by the Qur'anic verse 49:13 which highlights the common origin of all mankind. The message of the Oneness of God, the universality of Qur'anic message, and the common origin of mankind resonate with the message of humanity of the Qur'an. The universality of Qur'anic message occupies an important place in the Islamic education "In fact, the Qur'an addresses human beings as *"Ya aiyuhal Nas"* (O Humankind) directly 306 times and indirectly more than two thousand times in its over 6,000 verses. In contrast the Qur'an specifically addresses Muslim men and women (*Ya aiyuhal Muslimun/Muslimat/Muslimatun/e*tc) by name only 49 times" (Abdullah, 2015). The Qur'an clearly expressed the Islamic perspective on diversity under one God among Muslims:

O mankind! We created you from a single (pair) of a male and a female, and made you into nations and tribes, that ye may know each other (not that ye may despise (each other). […]. (Qur'an 49:13)

Thus, any Muslim person would feel a bond of humanity with any other person, and even moreso with another Muslim, regardless of social position, ethnicity, nationality or language.

This Islamic education teaching of the Qur'anic message on the Oneness of God the Father of all was reiterated by the Prophet's (PBUH) final sermon, known as *Khutbatul Wada*, delivered at Mount Arafat on 6 March 632. The Prophet called upon Muslims saying: "people, your Lord is One, and your father is one: all of you are from Adam, and Adam was from the ground".

Islamic education teaches the Muslims to believe in one God who is the God of all and all mankind; or "*Âlamîn*". Islamic education also teaches that all human beings have a common origin and God is also the Creator of the diversity in the world. In other words, Islamic education calls for the belief of a universal God whose message is universal because it is destined to all; regardless of ethnicity or nationality.

Muslim Brotherhood

The Islamic affinities based on Qur'anic universality are reinforced by other Islamic teachings, namely the Islamic teaching on brotherhood among Muslims. From the

Islamic education perspective, all Muslims are brothers because Islam teaches that "the believers are but a single brotherhood…" (Qur'an 49:10). In addition to emphasising that all Muslims are part of a single family, Islamic education also reinforces Muslim brotherhood by encouraging forgiveness, compassion, reconciliation and peaceful relations among Muslims: "the believers are but brothers, so make reconciliation between your brothers and fear Allah that you may receive mercy." (Qur'an 49:10). The centrality of brotherhood in Islam is reiterated in Islamic education teaching as one *Hadith* reported by Ibn Malik says that "none of you has faith until he loves for his brother what he loves for himself" (Ṣaḥīḥ al-Bukhārī 13). Thus, from the Islamic education perspective, brotherhood is equated with Islamic faith. This encouragement and strengthening of brotherhood is also supported by another *Hadith* which recommends to Muslims:

Do not hate each other, do not envy each other, do not turn away from each other, but rather be servants of Allah as brothers. It is not lawful for a Muslim to boycott his brother for more than three days. (Ṣaḥīḥ Muslim 2559)

As can be seen, Islamic education teaches Muslims to be brothers. Also important is that Islamic education teaches brotherhood as an important part of being a Muslim and therefore as an important act of faith. For example, it is not 'lawful' for a Muslim to boycott another Muslim brother for more than three days. Islamic education teaches that this Islamic view is also confirmed in the Prophet's (PBUH) final sermon. He stated that "learn that every Muslim is a brother to every Muslim and that the Muslims constitute one brotherhood". Islamic education teaches that the Prophet added in the final sermon that

All mankind is from Adam and Eve, an Arab has no superiority over a non-Arab nor a non-Arab has any superiority over an Arab; also a White has no superiority over Black nor does a Black have any superiority over White except by piety and good action.

As discussed before, Islamic education also teachers that Allah is the Creator of all, including all mankind, and it also teaches that all mankind has a common origin. Therefore, all human beings are brothers regardless of their differences. Not only does Islamic education teach brotherhood and equality among people, but it also describes brotherhood as an important part of the Islamic faith.

Islamic Ummah

The third teaching of Islamic education that fostered Islamic affinity in West Africa is the teaching to creating the (Islamic) *Ummah*. In addition to recommending brotherhood among and between Muslims, Islamic education fostered Islamic affinities by encouraging Muslims to be part of an *Ummah*. This term generally is used to refer to an Islamic community that gathers Muslims across the world under one God. Despite a multiplicity in the interpretation of *Ummah*, Hassan found that it was used as "a framework for maintaining religious unity and accommodating the cultural diversities of the believers. This generated a strong sense of unity, which permeated the Muslim world and was instrumental in submerging, or overriding, the significant ethnic and cultural differences on the level of the ideal" (Hassan, 2006, p. 312). In West Africa, the concept of *Ummah* constituted an important tool for Islamic affinities among Muslims of different geographic locations, ethnicity, and linguistic backgrounds.

In this section I have shown not only that Islam has impacted on Muslim societies in West Africa, but also that following conversion to Islam, Islamic education influenced and shaped the life of the Muslims and became an important tool for Islamic affinities because Islamic education emphasised the universality of the Qur'anic message (destined to all mankind), taught Muslim brotherhood regardless of ethnic and linguistic backgrounds and recommended building an Islamic *ummah* to transcend geographic, racial and linguistic barriers. These teachings have influenced and shaped Islamic affinities in West Africa, namely among and between West African Muslims who live in a region marked by ethnic, cultural, linguistic and religious cleavages. The Islamic affinities fostered by the universalism of the Qur'anic message and its injunction to form brotherhood and forge an *ummah* were further strengthened and expanded by the Islamic education conducted by the various Sufi orders or brotherhoods who established Islamic education centres and schools in West Africa. The best-known in West Africa is the Tijaniyya order which significantly contributed to expanding and consolidating Islamic education in the region.

CONCLUSION

In this chapter, I have shown that in pre-colonial West Africa, when Islam was gradually introduced by Muslim traders and proselytisers and accepted in many parts of this region, Islamic education had a deep impact on the life of people and their societies. To live in accordance with Islamic teachings, Muslim theocracies and communities were established and Islamic education was started to spread the Qur'anic message. As a result, the Islamic way of life permeated all spheres of life of West African Muslims through the people's adherence to the Islamic teachings. However, as highlighted in a region marked by cleavages on linguistic, cultural, ethnic and religious lines, Islamic teachings became one of the most powerful messages for Islamic affinities among African Muslims of different backgrounds in pre-colonial West Africa. The Islamic affinities were fostered by Islamic education that focused on Qur'anic teachings and the Prophetic traditions (*Sunnah* and *Hadith*) reinforced by the Prophets' message in His last sermon at Mount Arafat. The strengthening of Islamic affinities in West Africa was facilitated by the establishment of Islamic education centres in West Africa (e.g. Timbuktu and Jenne) to spread the Qur'anic message and Arabic studies in its curriculum. In this chapter, I have shown that these Islamic affinities were constructed on such influential Islamic teachings as the universalism of the Qur'anic message, the injunction to form brotherhood with other Muslims, and the recommendation to forge the (Islamic) *ummah*. However, the Islamic teachings that served as vehicle for Islamic affinities in the West Africa, as in many parts of the world, were misappropriated to highlight differences and rivalries which led to jihads on doctrinal lines (orthodox vs unorthodox practices of Islam) and religious lines (against polytheists) in West Africa.

REFERENCES

Abdullah, A. (2015). *Qur'an's Message for Humanity*. Retrieved from http://www.islamicity.org/6509/Qur'ans-message-for-humanity/

Akdere, M., Russ-Eft, D., & Eft, N. (2006). The Islamic worldview of Adult learning in the workplace: Surrendering to God. *Advances in Developing Human Resources*, 8(3), 355–363. doi:10.1177/1523422306288428

Annalakshmi, N., & Abeer, M. (2011). Islamic worldview, religious personality and resilience among Muslim adolescent students in India. *Europe's Journal of Psychology*, 7(4), 716–738. doi:10.5964/ejop.v7i4.161

Barry, I. (2005). Fouta-Jalon: Nineteenth century. In K. Shillington (Ed.), *Encyclopaedia of African history* (pp. 538–539). New York: Fitzoroy Dearborn.

Bloom, J. M. (2008). Paper in Sudanic Africa. In S. Jeppie & S. B. Diagne (Eds.), *The meanings of Timbuktu* (pp. 77–92). Cape Town: HSRC Press.

Cleaveland, T. (2008). Timbuktu and Walata: lineages and higher education. In S. Jeppie & S. B. Diagne (Eds.), *The meanings of Timbuktu* (pp. 45–58). Cape Town: HSRC.

Diagne, S. (2004). Islam in Africa: Examining the Notion of an African Identity within the Islamic World. In K. Wiredu (Ed.), *A Companion to African Philosophy* (pp. 374–383). Oxford, UK: Blackwell Publishing.

Diallo, I. (2012). Qur'anic and Ajami literacies in pre-colonial West Africa. *Current Issues in Language Planning*, *13*(2), 91–104. doi:10.1080/14664208.2012.687498

Haleem, A. (2005). *The Qur'an*. Oxford, UK: Oxford University Press.

Hassan, R. (2006). Globalisation's challenge to the Islamic Ummah. *Asian Journal of Social Science*, *34*(2), 311–323. doi:10.1163/156853106777371184

Hassane, M. (2008). Ajami in Africa: The use of Arabic script in the transcription of African Languages. In S. Jeppie & S. B. Diagne (Eds.), (pp. 109–122). Cape Town: HSRC.

Hunwick, J. (1999). *Timbuktu and the Songhay Empire: Al-Sa'di's Tarikh al-Sudan down to 1613 and other Contemporary Documents*. Leiden: Brill.

Insoll, T. (1996). The archaeology of Islam in Sub-Saharan Africa: A review. *Journal of World Prehistory*, *10*(1), 439–504. doi:10.1007/BF02221202

Levtzion, N. (2000a). Islam in the Bilad al-Sudan to 1800. In N. Levtzion & P. Randall (Eds.), *History of Islam in Africa* (pp. 63–92). Ohio University Press.

Levtzion, N. (2000b). Patterns of Islamization and Varieties of Religious Experience among Muslims of Africa. In N. Levtzion & P. Randall (Eds.), (pp. 1–14). Ohio University Press.

Rebstock, U. (2010). West Africa and its early empires. In M. Fierro (Ed.), *The New Cambridge History of Islam* (pp. 144–158). Cambridge, UK: Cambridge University Press. doi:10.1017/CHOL9780521839570.007

Sanneh, L. (1976). The origins of clericalism in West African Islam. *Journal of African History*, *17*(1), 49–72. doi:10.1017/S0021853700014766

Trimingham, J. S. (1980). *The Influence of Islam upon Africa*. London: Longman.

ENDNOTES

[1]   The country members of ECOWAS are Benin, Burkina Faso, Cabo Verde, Ghana, Guinea, Guinea Bissau, Liberia, Mali, Niger, Nigeria, Senegal, Sierra Leone and Togo.

2   For example, for each daily prayer, it is crucial to know the pre-prayer (purification) and post-prayer formulas (dua rituals) as well as the prayer formulas themselves (which requires at the least the recitation (and understanding) of particular Qur'anic verses or surahs).

3   Sunnah and Hadith are the second most important sources of Islamic authority for Muslims. They both refer to actions and sayings of the Prophet Mohamad who lived and acted in accordance with God's teachings and, therefore, He represents the perfect model for all Muslims.

Chapter 10
English and Arabic Language Learning Environments:
Islamic Universities Undergraduates' Experiences

Noraisikin Sabani
https://orcid.org/0000-0003-1095-3094
Curtin University – Malaysia, Malaysia & Universiti Brunei Darussalam, Brunei

Anita Jimmie
Curtin University – Malaysia, Malaysia

Hanin Naziha Hasnor
Curtin University – Malaysia, Malaysia

ABSTRACT

The learning environment is defined as "external stimulants" that is exposed or reinforced in learners as a means to challenge their learning experiences. These reinforcements may include physical settings, teaching and learning endeavours, and even cultural and social determiners. This empirical study focuses on the perceived experiences that undergraduates from Brunei, Malaysia, and Indonesia experienced in their Arabic and English language learning environments. This qualitative study employed in-depth interviews with 60 informants that were selected through criterion sampling, snowballing technique. The analysis utilised template analysis. Emerging themes were compared and contrasted, to find similarities and differences. This chapter does not aim to seek the superiority of one learning environment over another but to appreciate the diversity and concord of these institutions. The findings illustrated overlapping, differentiated themes, which included the abovementioned.

DOI: 10.4018/978-1-5225-8528-2.ch010

INTRODUCTION

Bakhshialiabad, Bakshi, and Hassanshahi (2015) provide a comprehensive definition of the learning environment, which encompasses elements such as physical location and facilities, learning situation, and the ethos in which learning takes place for a learner. The overall educational setting, which also includes teaching approach, the way teachers interact with learners, and even the way the school is run or governed constitutes learning environment which can be enriching or detrimental to learner learning. Over the past two decades, researches done on learning environments has revealed that positive learning environments are significantly associated with positive outcomes. This, in turn, has created significant interest in understanding what motivates learners to learn and to engage in the learning process so educators can provide better learning experiences for them which will lead to successful learning outcomes.

Research on the learning environment and its consequent impact on learner learning has been primarily studied from a quantitative point of view (Roth, Tobin, & Zimmermann, 2002). These focus on studies that include the impact of technology on learners' learning environment (e.g. Huang, Chen, & Chou, 2016; Huda, Haron, Ripin, Hehsan, & Yaacob, 2017; Manca & Ranieri, 2016; Tang & Chaw, 2016). Recent studies, however, have seen the value of integrating a qualitative approach to investigating learner's perceptions on the learning environment and how they elements such as the classroom, learning resources and teaching approaches lead to better educational attainment. The relationship in which these elements occur helps to facilitate learning as it is imperative that learners' are deeply involved in learning (Hanrahan, 1998). Incorporating a qualitative view of understanding learners' perception and subsequently, their behaviour allows for more nuanced data to emerge and provides a "voice" for learners to share valuable insights with researchers. Thus this study takes a qualitative approach to understand how learning environments across three countries differ, and how learners perceive their learning environment and respond to it. This understanding coincides with social constructionism that believes that one's world or point of view is a mass of life puzzles that they have collected throughout their lifetime, which may rebuild, reconstruct or add on to their past experiences (Andrews, 2012; Boghossian, 2001; Cunliffe, 2008). It is a myriad of interactive events, which becomes a lifelong process, shaping one's way of thinking, their behaviour and outlook towards life. The study also seeks to identify the similarities or differences of Islamic Pedagogy in language teaching across the institutions in three countries. As highlighted by Seyyed Hossein Nasr, there is an appreciation of universal Islamic Pedagogy characteristics, and still, an even more acknowledgement in its diversity, in accordance to the social-cultural context of the learners' settings (Nasr, 2016).

BACKGROUND

Learning Environment: Multitude Influencing Factors

Personal and Situational Determiners in Learning Environment

In a study by Biggs (1989, cited in Lizzio, Wilson, & Simons, 2002), he argued that learners' perceptions are influenced by three dominant factors: the learning environment, learners' characteristics and approach to learning and also learning outcomes. He posited that both personal and situational factors shape a learner's approach to learning which then influences the kinds of outcomes that he or she achieves. Personal factors include elements such as experience, prior knowledge and learner competence whereas situational factors cover areas such as teaching approaches and strategies, course structure and workload (Aimes & Archer, 1988; Lizzio et al., 2002). Based on a study by Saljo (1979, cited in Richardson, 2005), he discovered that there exist five different conceptions of learning; one where learning is done for the increase of knowledge, learning by memorizing, learning to acquire facts and processes, learning as a process to understand realities and learning to interpret abstract knowledge. These types of learning fall into the deep versus surface approaches to learning (Entwistle, 1991). Entwisle (1991) also believed that learners' perceptions of the learning environment have positive correlations with how a learner approaches learning. This perception, in turn, moderates their experiences, as shown in this study on how receptive they are towards the learning as a whole.

More recent literature focuses on how personal learning environments, better known as PLE, is slowly evolving for learners. Learning now has become more demanding- learners are becoming more technologically inclined and dependent, whether they are seeking information for course content, doing research or even to gain knowledge. Learners are becoming adept at looking for information through various online sources including through SNS and other digital platforms (Dabbagh & Kitsantas, 2012). In this modern age, learners are no longer passive recipients of knowledge but also act as "active co-producers of content" (Dabbagh & Kitsantas, 2012, p.3). There is much focus on using learning management systems, and more recently, the use of different social media tools as learning platforms, which is seen to be of value due to its self-regulatory features. A learner's ability to control and personalise their learning is one of the most beneficial factors that motivate and encourage learning (Chiu & Gwo, 2016; Delen, Liew, & Willson, 2014).

Islam as Social and Cultural Determiners in Learning Environment

Knowledge-seeking, in Islam, is considered to be incumbent for every Muslim as they are placed in the world with duty as a vicegerent (Gunther, 2006; Halstead, 2007). The nobility of learned men are acknowledged, and that God consciousness can only be developed through knowledge (Al-Ghazali, 1898; Darussalam, 2004). Nonetheless, in Islam, the value of knowledge field differs, between religious or sacred knowledge, epitome through the study of the Quran and Hadith (prophetic traditions) as compared to other areas of expertise, including medicine, arithmetic and literature (Al-Ghazali, 1898; Seyyed Hossein Nasr, 1992, 2012).

Prophet Muhammad (Peace be upon Him) even encouraged his companions to learn other languages to ease communication between different races (Abu-Ghuddah, 2013). As Prophet Muhammad (Peace be upon Him) was known as the best teacher for humanity, studies have been made on his teaching and learning approaches and his sensitivity towards the learning environment, including the age and the needs of the person or group of people he was teaching (Abu-Ghuddah, 2013). Within the concept of Islamic Pedagogy, much focus is put on the heartfelt relationship between teacher and learners, orality and didactic approach as part of teaching and learning processes, the importance of *adab* or Islamic manners and the prominence of knowledge embodiment as moral compass (Al-Azem, 2016; Boyle, 2002; Sabani, Hardaker, Sabki, & Salleh, 2016).

In turn, the Islamic Pedagogy concept aims to focus on building a spiritually holistic person, with servitude towards God as one of its fundamental aims, and such understanding should transcend in all areas of life, including within their formal and non-formal learning processes.

Language Learning Environment

Teaching approaches, materials, reward system, the relationship between learners, teacher-learner relationship, classroom setting, and homework, are considered as components within a learning environment that affects the way learners learn a language (Kaylani, 1996, as cited in Kameli, Mostapha, & Baki, 2012). A study by Nakamura (2000) revealed that when learning the target language, learners are mostly affected by the EFL or ESL learning environment. As language is sociological and practical in nature, it can best be learnt in an ideal context characterised by a conducive, learner-centred and productive environment (Hannafin, Land, & Oliver, 1999). In another study, Sağlam and Salı (2013), defined foreign language learning environment as a multi-faceted setting containing the elements of physical, socio-psychological, pedagogical and linguistic. Emphasis is given to language teaching materials, instructional methods and techniques, linguistic elements of the foreign language environment (such as the use of the medium of instruction in the class, communication within the classroom and the exposure to the target language) and parental support.

Another term that is closely related to language learning environment would be Personal Learning Environment (PLE), which is an environment that is controlled by the learner to learn a language (Reinders, 2014). Furthermore, in PLE the teachers' roles become more of that of a facilitator, such as checking learner's online portfolios, replying the learners' posts, and providing feedback on out of the class language practice. In addition, Masaazi (2015), who coined the term Friendly and Productive Language Learning Environment (FPLE), suggested four dimensions of an effective and productive enriched learning environment as a focus on meaningful learning. Secondly, to align each person with their talents as a support for each learner. Thirdly, to create a clear structure for each person and lastly, to foster effective collaborations that add value to the language learners. When learning a language, FPLE has many educational, psychological and sociological advantages to both the learners and teachers. Most importantly, a conducive learning environment will help the learner to achieve maximum outputs and help improve learners' levels of attainment and performance in languages.

Setting the Context

The Malay Archipelago and Islam as Part of Geographical, Social and Religious Setups

The Malay Archipelago was a term, first coined by Alfred Russell Wallace (1863, 1869), referring to a set of a large group of islands, that shares similar geographical association and racial composition. The traits of living were also considered similar, focusing on its varieties of vegetations and wildlife. It was also noted that for many of these countries, the local languages were categorised as a variety from the Austronesian language family (Encyclopædia-Britannica, 2015).

There were multiple theories behind the conversion to Islam by many locals in the Malay Archipelago region, but it was predominantly associated with the traders from Arab (Hamid, 1965). Many of these traders spread Islam through intermarriage with the locals, and their willingness to not neglect the local cultures breed acceptance among the locals. Additionally, during the colonialism periods by both Portuguese and British, Islam becomes a uniting factor within the local Malay community and the foreign Muslims who married the locals (Alatas, 1985).

English and Arabic Language Learning as Part of the Educational Curriculum Setup

It is undeniable how powerful the English language has become in the 21st century. The global status of English as the language of communication, the language of science and technology and the language of commerce and trade has elevated the status of English as one of the most widely used languages in the world. However, this was not always the case, as acceptance towards the language as a medium for communication or indeed, a medium for instruction was frowned upon post-colonial occupation. One characteristic that these three countries have in common, from a cultural perspective is the fact that all three nations have Islam as its national religion or, in the case of Indonesia, having the majority of its people as Muslims, despite its stand as a secular country (Huda & Sabani, 2018). Thus, the practice of Islamic education and the role the Arabic language plays in aspects such as culture, identity and language education are somewhat similar, particularly in Islamic educational institutions.

There is a huge emphasis being placed on learning the Arabic language, and in essence, the importance of learning the Arabic language is vital as this language is associated to the Quran as the sacred text for the Muslims (Boutieri, 2013; Robinson, 1993). It is expected that at least for fundamental worship prayers, the Arabic language is used. On the other hand, the introduction of English as a tool for instruction initially created a tension, or a cultural conflict amongst the learners as English was perceived to be a tool of imperialism, and also a representation of Western values and ideologies (Mohd-Asraf, 2005; Umam, 2014) which goes sharply against the strong Islamic values instilled in the learners' lives. Also, at that time, as English is often seen as the 'language of Christianity' most parents were reluctant to allow their children to learn the language in schools (Ozog, 2005 cited in Mohd-Asraf, 2005).

In Malaysia for example, researchers such as Mohd Asraf (2005), Nair et al. (2012) and Yunus, Mohamad, and Waelateh (2016) have documented university learners' lack of receptiveness towards learning English, but recent literature has suggested that these views have changed in recent times (Che-Musa, Yew, & Azman, 2012; Thang, 2004; Thang, Ting, & Mohd Jaafar, 2011; Zubairi & Sarudin, 2009). The changes are partly due to the Malaysian Government's emphasis on improving English language proficiency in schools and universities within the nation (Mohd-Asraf, 2005).

In contrast, according to Lauder (2008), in 1950, the then Indonesian Government decided to make English the first foreign language in the country due to two reasons; its international status, and also because Dutch was a reminder of the colonialization in Indonesia. It is worth noting that Indonesia has given the English language the status Foreign Language, unlike Malaysia and Brunei which have awarded English the status of Second Language because this country was the only country in the Malay Archipelago that was colonialized by the Dutch instead of the British forces.

The Sultanate of Brunei however, has a very balanced approach to the teaching of English as the government decided to implement a bilingual education system in which Malay Language and English would be awarded equal importance in Brunei's secondary schools (Barry, 2011). Interestingly, since this strategy was implemented in 1985, there is little documentation of the cultural aspects and also learner experience with the teaching of English in a predominantly Muslim country. Similar findings may be observed for the neighbouring countries of Malaysia and Indonesia. Thus this study seeks to provide a snapshot of the undergraduates' experiences of learning English and Arabic language learning in Islamic Educational Institutions in each country.

METHODOLOGY AND DATA ANALYSIS

The data extracted for this book chapter is an extension of a research project, which substantially focuses on Islamic Pedagogy for Personalised Learning. It is an entirely qualitative study from a social constructionism epistemology viewpoint, which highlights the appreciation of one's lived experiences and its surrounding (Andrews, 2012). Through this viewpoint, the researchers consider the contextual references that are embedded within the informants' learning environment. Additionally, it aims to be receptive of similarities and differences within the three countries' sites, appreciating its diversity and uniformity. As such, it is not the aim of the paper to compare between sites due to their effectiveness, as the authors recognise and acknowledge their distinctive features and contributing factors. The research adopted a multisite, compacted fieldwork case studies approach (Creswell, 1998; Walker, 2010), involving three Islamic Higher Education Institutions in Brunei, Malaysia and Indonesia as part of the Malay Archipelago. The data collection was through in-depth interviews with 60 undergraduates in total. Template analysis was employed to seek main themes across all sites, with a focus on differentiated themes as well (King, 2004).

FINDINGS AND DISCUSSIONS

During the data analysis stage, which included interpreting and segregating data into themes, it was apparent that the themes were overlapping in one another, just as it illustrates the complexities of real lives. As such, considerations were made in deciding and selecting specific excerpts to represent the themes given. This consideration, does not, nonetheless, denote the exclusivity to a single theme for a particular reference.

While there are specific findings that point towards direct comparisons between English and Arabic language classrooms, some findings were exclusive to one of these subjects, based on informants' descriptions. Additionally, despite the overlapping central themes identified across all sites, there were also some distinctive features, which may be shared between two countries, or unique to a particular country. This section aims to focus on most prominent similarities, or outstanding distinctions, which were categorised into three main sections.

Situational and Personal Determiners in Learning Environment

Situational Determiners

The first common theme that relates to situational determiners in learning both Arabic and English language is its relation to the requirement of the university. For many of the informants across the three institutions, they described studying both Arabic and English language courses was as part of the University's requirement before graduation. IU1 indicated:

Yes, [the requirement is] for graduation. We have to sit for TOEFL for English language and IQLA for the Arabic language.

For many, this has become one of the most dominant external stimuli to perform well in these classes. This data is substantiated by ideas from Entwistle (1991) who differentiates one's conceptions of learning in gearing in their efforts in their studies. This data mirrors Suryasa, Prayoga, and Werdistira (2017), Rehman, Bilal, Sheikh, Bibi, and Nawaz (2014) and Mahadi and Jafari (2012) as instrumental motivation where learners learn a language for often pragmatic purposes, which in this case relates to future occupation and career preparedness. Gardner and Lambert (2012, cited in Rehman et al., 2014) posit that learners invest in learning a language for social and economic rewards, which may explain why learners are motivated to learn an additional language or perform well in language classes. According to Ahmed (2015), the learner's communicative needs and their perception towards learning are two essential determiners in language learning. If the learners are required to speak a language within different social settings, or even to achieve personal career plans, their perception towards the importance of language will shift, thus motivating them to learn the language better. This finding is mirrored in his study where learners demonstrate higher levels of motivation in acquiring the language and they work hard in language classes because they see the importance of language proficiency in future career plans.

The second point relates to the availability of these course offerings to undergraduates. Brunei's informants were the only group that indicated that their language-medium stream would determine which generic language course they will be undertaking. In other word, undergraduates who are from the English stream will only undertake Arabic language generic course and vice versa. To illustrate, BU6 indicated:

No, we don't have to take English classes, because we are already English medium, even Finance [course learners] are not taking it. But if [the learners are] from Arabic medium, [they have to take] ICT and English.

As for Indonesia and Malaysia, these generic language courses are compulsory to all, except for those who applied for credit transfer and was approved. There were also informants who mentioned the need to undertake a placement test before enrolling in these language classes, as a mean to evaluate their proficiency. MU2 and IU19, as an example, shared that for the classes, they will be placed in accordance with their level of proficiency. While the offer of credit transfer and generic language course may seem to be a matter of respective university's requirement, placement testing is seen as a mean to aid learners to learn effectively. If they are placed at the right level, which, may not only be limited to the language proficiency per se but inclusive of the learners' social background and pragmatic use of the target language as well (Thompson, 2015).

Additionally, many of the informants highlighted the overall differences in teaching strategies and approaches. For all of the Arabic language classes, most informants described it to have elements of the didactic and oral approach, where the lecturers taught in a didactic approach by teaching orally, while the learners listen and repeat, both in oral and written form. Additionally, many of the learners from these three cases indicated that the notes or work done by the learners are mostly handwritten. Finally, many of the classes required the learners to memorise as one of their learning efforts. These activities are conventional classical methods in Islamic pedagogy (Boyle, 2006; Hardaker & Sabki, 2015; Lukens-Bull, 2001; Sabani et al., 2016). In comparison, for some learners, especially in Brunei, there was also an indication of more technological inclusion in English classes, including the use of PowerPoint and emailing their work to their lecturers.

In the first semester, usually, our lecturer would teach the Arabic language like children. So the lecturer would read out, and we follow, and then we repeat, and we learn the meaning of the words, and sometimes he/she would ask the learner to read out one by one, and sometimes with notes and dialogue, like in the drama, like for children [lessons]... for assignments, if Arabic [classes], it's all handwritten, traditional way. No softcopy. It English, we have to use softcopy and email to the lecturer (BU5).

These findings allude to practices that suggest the presence of learning technology in aiding learners to improve their language learning through the use of many learning and teaching techniques, suited to their level of proficiency, current need as well as their social and cultural background (Ishihara & Cohen, 2010).

Meanwhile, English classes were often perceived to be communicative, which is commonly advocated for English classrooms (Azman, 2016). However, a few Indonesian and Malaysian informants mentioned that both Arabic and English language classes were conducted in a similarly communicative manner. Savignon (1991) contends there is a need for language classes to be more communicative and interactive as there is a need for learners to be more engaged in the learning process. Learners often have to participate in the "expression, interpretation and negotiation" (p. 4) of the language and its meaning in order for language learning to be effective and successful. Larsari (2011) argues that language functions not just as a communication tool but also a representation of one's social and cultural background, and immersion in the target language allows learners to use the language successfully if they can understand how languages are used contextually. These findings are supported in this study where English and Arabic classes are conducted in engaging, meaningful and interactive tasks that promotes learning, beyond the traditional drill and practice teaching approach to language learning.

MU4, when comparing between Arabic and English classes, mentioned:

During Arabic classes, the lecturer will teach us as usual. Do exercises, have a presentation, test... if English classes, it's also similar. We learn vocabulary and all, study literature, assignment, presentation and all. For the Arabic language, I memorise and understand how to use the word.

Md. Yasim et al. (2016) contend that vocabulary acquisition is a vital component in foreign language learning. The failure to master a language lies in having an adequate vocabulary for effective communication. In their study, they note that using various teaching aids such as electronic and non- electronic aids (i.e. textbooks and dictionaries) aids in teaching vocabulary for the Arabic language successfully. In a study by Che Haron (2014), she reported that implementing a communication approach to teaching Arabic in her classroom enhances learning because it encourages learners to get immersed in the language and practice in the meaningful use of the language. This, in turn, promotes a change in the perception of the use of a language which in turn facilitates language learning because learners are more comfortable and willing to learn. In a separate study, Mohd Hamidin (2015), reported that weak teaching approaches to the Arabic language are the main reasons why the teaching of this language is failing. She suggested that the use of ICT and Arabic based resources in the form of games, songs cartoons, Arabic comedy and social media can facilitate language learning. These form of communicative approaches to learning are both enjoyable and engaging, which is an essential aspect of encouraging learners to learn the language. These studies signal to similar teaching approaches to teaching where the emphasis is on learners' engagement and participation in learning language through the use of immersion and through the creation of meaning for successful language learning to happen (Che-Haron, Sheikh-Ahmad, Mamat, & Ahmed-Mohamed, 2010).

Perceived notions about whether the lecturers were native or non-native speakers to the target languages, as well as whether they are locals seem to affect the informants as well. For the data from Brunei, some of the informants mentioned that the availability of local lecturers to teach this targeted language is of an advantage, which may be due to the lecturers' familiarity to the nations' educational and social environments. This means some learners perceived strain when they are being taught the Arabic language by foreign lecturers (native speakers) as compared to the locals. Nonetheless, some informants preferred lecturers who do not use another language to support their language learning, as they find out that they can be more proficient because they are exposed to the targeted language more intensively. This finding may demonstrate two points, which is the locality of the lecturers, and the interference of another language to teach the target language. It has been noted that when language may be taught in a way that it considers the local context, it may improve learners' language proficiency (McKay, 2002).

For English, we can understand it more clearly. And we don't have a problem to understand, but for Arabic, we have difficulty to understand it, so how would we be able to respond if we don't understand? So what we do now is we will have a lecture in the Arabic language, and later it is explained in Malay (mother tongue). So, while it seems awkward, but the learners can understand better and perform better, rather than having the entire class in the Arabic language. So like, learners can get A+ when they are explained in Malay, while only get C, at its best if the classes are conducted thoroughly in Arabic language (MU3).

For Arabic, we have been taught by Ustaz...for Arabic class, we don't understand Arabic right, but Ustaz would speak only Arabic, even though we don't know Arabic 100% but most of the time we speak English so he will answer in Arabic, depends [on] our understanding (BU13).

Personal Determiners

In Arabic language classes, there were further distinctive features as compared to English language classes. An important thing to note is that for many of these learners, there was an inclination of favouring or understanding of one target language over another, based on their educational background. MU13's outlook demonstrated this point well:

The similarity is we are studying two diff language, which is quite interesting but the specific differences as well, the way of teaching. Well, I 'd say the Arabic class is complicated. To me, to me. Well, they say in Arabic, but sometimes I don't understand, but they keep saying in Arabic. So that's why I'm confused. But in English, I know English. So if they say something I don't know, I can just Google. So that's the diff between the difficulty of Arabic and English.

For learners who were from Islamic schools, for example, they may be more receptive towards the Arabic language, as they are more used to it and vice versa. IU11, as a sample, mentioned that such reception depends on the learners' previous background. In the case of him coming from an Islamic boarding school, the Arabic language was more natural for him, and for those who were studying in the national schools, they would be more proficient in English. Many informants in the three sites have indicated such implications. This point relates to one aspect of personalisation in Arabic language classrooms. In Indonesia, it was noted that some of the lecturers would often ask learners questions, to check their understanding of the lesson. For learners who were identified to be less proficient in the language course, much attention is given to them and are given more chance to communicate with the lecturers.

Throughout the sixty interviews, there were some occurrences that the learners indicated their preference in their approach to personalising their learning. One of them, an informant from Brunei reported his insistence to use the Arabic language in his informal sphere of education, including his interactions with the lecturers. Despite adverse responses by some of his peers, he still believed that this is the best way for him to improve his Arabic language proficiency.

I try I make an initiative for myself to learn Arabic as much as possible, so I would like to practice it, so its different from my friend because one time, I try to speak Arabic with my friend, just to learn more but they refuse to interact with me, give me feedback, so they replied in English language, ... my teachers, most of them can speak Arabic, I try to speak in Arabic even though my Arabic is not fluent enough, so I try to learn as much as possible (BU7).

Additionally, for learners in Indonesia, there were points about the use of community-based personal learning, through English language community, to study the target language informally. For example, IU6 utilised Facebook page to contact English native speakers and communicate with them.

The aspects relating to their personal determiners with their language learning may be related to their identity, as when a person is acquiring a new language, they often adopt "identity markers" of the new cultural groups (Ahmed, 2015). Lee (2011) also noted in his research on the three influencing factors in the way learners view language learning are the cultural, societal and educational aspects. While the focus group were Japanese, similar findings may be implied to Malaysia and Indonesia as part of South East Asian Countries.

Islam as Social and Cultural Determiners in Learning Environment

Regarding subject content, within the three research sites, the learners described their English classes as Business or Communication English classes. For many other learners, they also reported that their lessons' subject content also portrayed Islamic traits. These content may include Islamic history or specific subject content, for example, IU8 that indicated the content even included multiple aspects of the Middle East country, as the source of the Arabic language, while BU16 mentioned that even English classes have Islamic content. The Islamic materials selected may be in line with the concept of Islamic pedagogy itself, that is considered to be distinctive due to its religious influences in its teaching and learning processes and point of view (Zaman & Memon, 2016).

There were informants, across all institutions, that highlighted a certain level of differentiation, whereby English subject is often linked to Western countries contexts, as compared to Arabic with Middle Eastern countries. It was also mentioned that the lecturers' educational background might have also impacted this effect.

IU16 shared

Between these two classes, so happen for the Arabic class, the lecturer is from Mecca, while my English lecturer is from Indonesia, so, definitely, the way they teach and convey the lesson is totally different.

These points link to previous researches on the outlook and influence of the teachers towards their learners in their language learning approaches (Thang, Nambiar, Wong, Mohd Jaafar, & Amir, 2015). In the case of one Malaysian informant, she highlighted that she perceived the English language to the language of the world, while the Arabic language is related to the language of paradise.

In comparison, I feel like English is the language of the World. A language to communicate with everyone abroad. That is why it is known as the language of the World. But the Arabic language, it is the language of Paradise. A language that we Muslims must learn because, in Paradise, that is the language we will use, the language of Paradise.

Such perception may have been brought by one's association of the Arabic language to Islam's Sacred text (Boutieri, 2013; Robinson, 1993).

Furthermore, in all three case sites, the informants indicated that in Arabic classes, the informants were required to observe *ikhtilat* or segregation between two genders. Specifically, some of the informants mentioned that the male undergraduates were obliged to sit on one side, while the females were to sit on another side of the classroom.

In Arabic classes, even if [there are] males and females in a class, the males would sit in front, on the left side, while the females would sit slightly behind on the right side (BU14).

These learners also had separate group work according to their gender. Additionally, they were expected to observe the Islamic dress code, for example, as stated by IU14. It was highlighted by some that these practices are part of learning adab or Islamic manners that were taught by Prophet Muhammad (Peace be upon him) (Abu-Ghuddah, 2013). These kinds of expectations are standard for institutions that practice Islamic point of view as their spiritual compass (Boyle, 2000; Sabki & Hardaker, 2013). Nonetheless, mix responses were gathered from the undergraduates when asked about English classes regarding segregation, whereby they were allowed to mingle, but with specific boundaries, and one informant reported that their English lecturer did not pose such requirements. The informant later commented that it is possible that such scenarios may be likely because the lecturer was a part-timer.

Moreover, specific to Malaysian informants, one of the necessary activities that the undergraduates have to undertake is the turn-taking of giving tazkirah or Islamic reminders at the beginning of every class, for the first five minutes MU7 mentioned that, in English classes, the presentation of *tazkirah* is in English. This activity was seen not only as a way to practice their target language through impromptu or short speeches but in-line with Islamic based education that focuses on building on a spiritual dimension of the learners with the inculcation of Islamic content in many aspects of their learning experiences. Boyle (2000; 2006) indicated that learners' spirituality might be developed by instilling Islamic values in the learning environment. Additionally, it stated an understanding that the learning of nonreligious subjects for good, may reinforce a positive relationship between religious and rational subjects (Qureshi, 2016).

Teacher-learner relationships were one of the characteristics set within the priori in the data collection stage. Concerning the research paper scope, differentiated findings were reported by the informants. In Brunei, not many informants highlight on the teacher-learner relationships, formally and informally. Meanwhile, in Malaysia and Indonesia, there seems to be an indication of similar patterns in their experiences with their respective English and Arabic language lecturers. For English classes, these classes were often deemed as more engaging, and some undergraduates felt that they were closer to their lecturers, for example, as highlighted by MU2.

Additionally, the learners indicated that the activities in the English classes were more interesting as compared to Arabic language classes. This point may be to the communicative approach concept that is focused on English language classes. Findings indicated that communicative approaches in language learning allow learners to understand and utilise target language effectively for a specific purpose or context (Larsari, 2011; Savignon, 1991).

Meanwhile, while mentioned being of a more 'elderly' age group, or in some cases, came from the Middle East, there were also suggests that regarding approach, Arabic language lecturers are seen to be more passionate and patient in teaching. One informant said that the Arabic language lecturer was more heartfelt in their approach.

Between these two language classes, … I met a lecturer from Mecca, directly from Mecca, while my English lecturer is from Indonesia. At times, I found my general lecturer to be teaching like, "this is my job, this is my task", and at times, the emotion is not controllable, … to compare the Arabic language lecturer seems to be very patient, and it can be seen that the lecturer is genuinely passionate about teaching, so he/she really tries to make the learners understand. So you can really see how patient and honourable [the person is].

Such findings are aligned with many pieces of research relating to Islamic Pedagogy that highlights an intuitive and heartfelt connection between the teacher and the learner (Al-Azem, 2016; Boyle, 2000; Lukens-Bull, 2001; Sabki & Hardaker, 2013). As Imam Al-Ghazali (1898) noted in the *adab* or manner of teaching, it is expected that the teacher approaches their learners as if their own children.

As for the data from Indonesia and Malaysia, some informants from both countries highlighted on the use of 'old Arabic texts' as a reference, which was known as Kitab Arab Gundul and Kitab Arab in Malaysia.

We have Kitab Arab [arabic classical text]. The ustaz or ustazah (religious teachers) would translate [to Malaysian/English language] and give a speech [on the content] (MU7).

One aspect that was mentioned was, in the case of Indonesian undergraduates, some programs anticipate that by the time these learners graduate, they will be able to read these books without hesitation and it can be a source of reference to them. This relates heavily to the Islamic Pedagogy concept that highlight upon the need for the learners to align the fundamentals of the learners to Islamic knowledge (Al-Azem, 2016; Boyle, 2000; Sabani et al., 2016) and in this case, learning the Arabic language may be seen as one of the means of achieving this objective (Zaman & Memon, 2016).

Language Learning Environment

There were numerous accounts of the use of English or local language to support Arabic language learning. It was mentioned that this had eased the language learning process, as the undergraduates were able to grasp the subject content better. On the other hand, some lecturers did not utilise the support of any other language to teach Arabic, and the informants indicated mixed results. As for English language classes, many of the informants highlighted that due to earlier exposure to this language, many of them were able to cope with the subject content without the need of support from their local languages.

MU5 indicated

If English classes, it's the best and made me interested in English because the lecturer is very strict. Charismatic and have class. The way she teaches, she only speaks in English, and did not use the Malay language.... we have to present in front of everyone in English, and she encourages us to speak confidently, even if it's in broken English. She never tells us, "your grammar is incorrect" because she wants us to be confident (line 44).

The allowance to practice English language fully, even without proper grammar was also reported assisted in boosting the learners' confidence in speaking in English. These variable experiences may be linked to researches that relate to the involvement of the mother tongue or other languages, and their impact on targeted language learning (Snorradóttir, 2014).

Secondly, in relation to specific teaching techniques, informants provided differences between English and Arabic language classrooms. For the English language, many informants from Brunei and Indonesia indicated that they find the English lessons to be more interactive as compared to the Arabic language. It is described as the Arabic language to be more didactic, while the English language seems to be more communicative in their approaches. According to MU 10, he mentioned that the Arabic class tends to be classical and if English, it focusses on presentation and is more modern in its approaches, which focus on practising oral and written form. Ali, Daud, Juhary, and Raihanah (2018) claims that in the past, rote learning which stresses on the memorisation of information was widely used by teachers. The traditional didactic transmission teaching method for the Arab language was a popular method of instruction in Islamic pedagogy (Hardaker & Sabki, 2015). However, the recent curriculum has shifted to approaches emphasising meaningful learning through active, constructive and long-lasting learning experiences (DeWaelsche, 2015).

Meanwhile, in Malaysia, it was indicated that both language lessons were considered to be similarly interactive, as they have their language week, where undergraduates were provided with an opportunity to showcase their work at the university level. This included activities such as debate, games and choral speaking. One particular informant mentioned that the showcase for the Arabic language was more advanced than English. Meanwhile, some Indonesian undergraduates which highlighted the use variance in teaching techniques, ranging from songs, drama and role-play for English classes. In Malaysia, among the tasks given to English language learners is the task of preparing a video clip, that allowed the undergraduates to dramatise using the target language.

Regarding activities and the use of media in English classes, only Brunei informants indicated the use of digital technology to complete or send their work. It is also due to this, in Indonesia and Malaysia, the Arabic classes focus more on survival or basic conversational Arabic, which do not require an emphasis on immaculate grammar proficiency. In comparison, the informants in Brunei indicated that much attention is given to Arabic language grammar, that they have specific classes to teach *nahwu* or Arabic grammar. It can be related that the different degree of language learning objective and approaches may be associated with the social and cultural context of the language learners' setting, and the pragmatic solution to meet the needs of these learners (Ishihara & Cohen, 2010).

If Arabic classes, for example, the usual activity will be getting used to the grammar, and then the pronunciation is the most important, if we pronounce wrongly, the meaning will change. If English, mostly presentation, group work, communicate. Just for us to get used to talking in English (BU11).

On the other hand, the personalisation in the Malaysian Arabic language classrooms indicated that, as many of the learners have lower proficiency as compared to the English language, many of the lecturers teaching Arabic language took the initiative to be close to the learners and would provide extra classes to accommodate to the learners' needs. This shows that the main approach to improving learner curricular commitment and academic achievement is by personalising learning. This method's long-term aim is to improve learners' independence in learning and the shared responsibility between teachers and learners (Prain et al., 2013). Additionally, teachers, as subject expert signify the need for providing appropriate guidance to the learners as well.

Similarly, while both universities in Indonesia and Malaysia offered the respective English and Arabic language courses as generic, the intensity of the learning differs according to the proficiency of the learners. Learners with lower proficiency were offered a higher number of class-contact per week, as mentioned by IU10, for example. As for learner autonomy, the higher the level of competence, the more autonomy is given to me. This can be seen from the approaches that differ, in accordance to which degree they are placed. The findings echo the concept of learner autonomy in language learning that indicated that learners of lower proficiency is required to be guided, and given activities that will build upon their metacognitive skills, which in turn, will make the learners more autonomous. With more autonomy, the learners are given more flexibility whereby the learners can direct their learning and develop learner independence (Najeeb, 2013). While the University in Brunei may provide a similar outlook, none of the informants relates to this point during their interviews.

Finally, in language classrooms, regardless if is it Arabic or English language, there are multiple factors to be considered and many aspects of the learning environment that affects it. An extract from MU3 may encapsulate the whole idea of the overall perspective on teaching and learning process

Ok, the similarities, in the class, like if concerning comprehension, they both focus on comprehension and theory. But regarding understanding, that depends on the learners themselves. For the English language, it may seem more natural, because the language is universal. However, not all learners will be able to cope well with the Arabic language. For the English language, most of us learn it since young, but for the Arabic language, it is more and more complicated as it gets more advanced. And it can be confusing, as different lecturers seem to be teaching differently, by their level of mastery. But they will try to help clarify and so on. So, the difference probably will be learners' understanding, regarding materials, it's the same because both have its syllabus and the workload is quite similar.

CONCLUSION

Several conclusions may be resolved based on the discussions and findings elaborated. Firstly, learners' perception of the communicative goals influences how motivated they are in learning the language. If a learner can identify personal incentives and rewards in using the target language, this acts as a catalyst for acquisition in language learning. Educators need to raise awareness that language learning is both empowering and beneficial for learners beyond what they learn in the classroom.

Additionally, it has been noted that the language learning environment requires an interplay between the course design and organisation, relationships between learners and staffs, and learners' values. It can influence the way learners learn the language and the way the teachers teach the language. Therefore, emphasis should be given to the quality of the language learning environment that is supportive and can maximise learners' learning and achievement.

In general, it has also been noted that language classes are often interactive with a focus on communicative competence. It is crucial for learners to understand how languages work in context and within the communicative setting so they can acquire languages more effectively. For teachers this means using different teaching strategies that are interactive and engaging, using real-life situations and utilising resources used in the target language to improve proficiency.

Finally, for these Islamic higher educational institutions, it is noted that elements of Islamic Pedagogy are still evident. While it may variate from one language modules to another, and between institutions, such markings are of significance. There are elements, including heartfelt relationships between teachers and learners as well as the inculcation of Islamic content and traits, which may aid these learners to appreciate the applicability and embodiment of Islamic teachings, becoming their moral compass that transcends all spheres of life.

ACKNOWLEDGMENT

This research work is an extension of a PhD research project of Noraisikin Sabani, under the supervision of Professor Glenn Hardaker and Dr Sallimah Salleh, Universiti Brunei Darussalam.

REFERENCES

Abu-Ghuddah, A. A.-F. (2013). *Muhammad the Perfect Teacher: An Insight into His Teaching Methods*. Muslims at Work.

Ahmed, S. (2015). Attitudes towards English Language Learning among EFL Learners at UMSKAL. *Journal of Education and Practice*, *6*(18), 6–16.

Aimes, C., & Archer, J. (1988). Achievement Goals in the Classroom: Students' Learning Strategies and Motivation Processes. *Journal of Educational Psychology*, *80*(3), 260–267. doi:10.1037/0022-0663.80.3.260

Al-Azem, T. (2016). *The Transmission of Adab: Educational Ideals and their Institutional Manifestations. In Philosophies of Islamic Education* (pp. 124–138). Routledge.

Al-Ghazali, A. H. (1898). *Ihya' Ulum-Id-Din: Revival of Religious Learnings (Fazl-Ul-Karim, Trans.)*. Karachi: Darul Ishaat.

Alatas, S. F. (1985). Notes on various theories regarding the Islamization of the Malay Archipelago. *The Muslim World, 75*(3-4), 162–175. doi:10.1111/j.1478-1913.1985.tb02761.x

Ali, A. M., Daud, N. S. M., Juhary, J., & Raihanah, M. M. (2018). A MOOC for Literature Integrated Language Classroom: Pedagogical Suggestions for the Development of Higher Order Thinking Skills (HOTS). *Arab World English Journal., 4.* doi:10.24093/awej/call4.2

Andrews, T. (2012). What is social constructionism? *The Grounded Theory Review, 11*(1), 39–46.

Azman, H. (2016). Implementation and Challenges of English Language Education Reform in Malaysian Primary Schools. *3L: The Southeast Asian Journal of English Language Studies, 22*(3).

Bakhshialiabad, H., Bakshi, M., & Hassanshahi, G. (2015). Students' perceptions of the academic learning environment in seven medical sciences courses based on DREEM. *Advances in Medical Education and Practice, 6,* 195–203. doi:10.2147/AMEP.S60570 PMID:25848331

Barry, C. (2011). English Language Teaching in Brunei. *RELC Journal, 42*(3), 203–220. doi:10.1177/0033688211401255

Boghossian, P. (2001). What is social construction? Times Literary Supplement, February 23, 6-8. Boutieri, C. (2013). Inheritance, Heritage, and the Disinherited: Ambiguities of Religious Pedagogy in the Moroccan Public School. *Anthropology & Education Quarterly, 44*(4), 363–380. doi:10.1111/aeq.12037

Boyle, H. (2000). *Quranic Schools in Morocco: Agents of Preservation and Change (Doctorate in Philosophy in Education)*. Bell and Howell Information and Learning Company.

Boyle, H. (2006). Memorisation and Learning in Islamic Schools. *Comparative Education Review, 50*(3), 478–495. doi:10.1086/504819

Boyle, H. (2002). *The Growth of Qur'anic Schooling and the Marginalization of Islamic Pedagogy: The Case of Morocco.* Paper presented at the Annual Meeting of the Comparative and International Education Society, Orlando, FL.

Che-Haron, S. (2014). Using communicative approach in Arabic language classroom to develop Arabic speaking ability. *Journal of Education and Practice, 5*(39), 29–34.

Che-Haron, S., Sheikh-Ahmad, I., Mamat, A., & Ahmed-Mohamed, I. H. (2010). Understanding Arabic-speaking learning strategies among selected Malay learners: A case study at the International Islamic University Malaysia (IIUM). *Contemporary Issues in Education Research, 3*(8), 9–19. doi:10.19030/cier.v3i8.222

Che-Musa, N., Yew, L. K., & Azman, H. (2012). Exploring English Language Learning and Teaching in Malaysia. *GEMA Online Journal of Language Studies., 12*(1).

Chiu, L. L., & Gwo, J. H. (2016). A self-regulated flipped classroom approach to improving student's learning performance in a mathematics course. *Computers & Education*, 126–140.

Creswell, J. W. (1998). Qualitative inquiry and research design: Choosing among five approaches. *Sage (Atlanta, Ga.).*

Cunliffe, A. L. (2008). Orientations to social constructionism: Relationally responsive social constructionism and its implications for knowledge and learning. *Management Learning, 39*(2), 123–139. doi:10.1177/1350507607087578

Dabbagh, N., & Kitsantas, A. (2012). Personal Learning Environments, social media, and self-regulated learning: A natural formula for connecting formal and informal learning. *The Internet and Higher Education, 15*(1), 3–8. doi:10.1016/j.iheduc.2011.06.002

Darussalam, G. (2004). *Pedagogi Pendidikan Islam.* Kuala Lumpur: Utusan Publications and Distributions.

Delen, E., Liew, J., & Willson, V. (2014). Effects of interactivity and instructional scaffolding on learning: Self-regulation in online video-based environments. *Computers & Education, 78*, 312–320. doi:10.1016/j.compedu.2014.06.018

DeWaelsche, S. A. (2015). Critical thinking, questioning and student engagement in Korean university English courses. *Linguistics and Education, 32*, 131–147. doi:10.1016/j.linged.2015.10.003

Encyclopædia-Britannica. (2015). *Malay Archipelago.* Retrieved from http://www.britannica.com/place/Malay-Archipelago

Entwistle, N. J. (1991). Approaches to learning and perceptions of the learning environment. *Higher Education, 22*(3), 201–204. doi:10.1007/BF00132287

Gunther, S. (2006). Be Masters in That You Teach and Continue to Learn: Medieval Muslim Thinkers on Educational Theory. *Comparative Education Review, 50*(3), 367–388. doi:10.1086/503881

Halstead, J. M. (2007). Islamic values: A distinctive framework for moral education? *Journal of Moral Education, 36*(3), 283–296. doi:10.1080/03057240701643056

Hamid, I. (1965). *The Malay Islamic Hikayat*. Selangor: Universiti Kebangsaan Malaysia.

Hannafin, M., Land, S., & Oliver, K. (1999). Open learning environments: Foundations, methods, and models. *Instructional-design theories and models: A new paradigm of instructional theory, 2*, 115-140.

Hanrahan, M. (1998). The effect of learning environment factors on students' motivation and learning. *International Journal of Science Education, 20*(6), 737–753. doi:10.1080/0950069980200609

Hardaker, G., & Sabki, A. A. (2015). Islamic pedagogy and embodiment: An anthropological study of a British Madrasah. *International Journal of Qualitative Studies in Education: QSE, 28*(8), 873–886. doi:10.1080/09518398.2014.917738

Huang, T.-C., Chen, C.-C., & Chou, Y.-W. (2016). Animating eco-education: To see, feel, and discover in an augmented reality-based experiential learning environment. *Computers & Education, 96*, 72–82. doi:10.1016/j.compedu.2016.02.008

Huda, M., Haron, Z., Ripin, M. N., Hehsan, A., & Yaacob, A. B. C. (2017). Exploring innovative learning environment (ILE): Big data era. *International Journal of Applied Engineering Research, 12*(17), 6678–6685.

Huda, M., & Sabani, N. (2018). Empowering Muslim children's spirituality in Malay Archipelago: Integration between National Philosophical Foundations and Tawakkul (trust in God). *International Journal of Children's Spirituality, 23*(1), 81–94. doi: 10.1080/1364436X.2018.1431613

Ishihara, N., & Cohen, A. (2010). *Teaching and Learning Pragmatics: Where Langauge and Culture Meet*. Pearson Education Limited.

Kameli, S., Mostapha, G. B., & Baki, R. B. (2012). The Influence of Formal Language Learning Environment on Vocabulary Learning Strategies. *Journal of Language Teaching & Research, 3*(1). doi:10.4304/jltr.3.1.23-29

King, N. (2004). Using templates in the thematic analysis of texts. In C. Cassel & G. Symon (Eds.), *Essential guide to qualitative methods in organisational research* (pp. 256–270). London: Sage Publications. doi:10.4135/9781446280119.n21

Larsari, V. N. (2011). Learner's communicative competence in English as a Foreign Language. *Journal of English and Literature.*, *2*(7), 161–165.

Lauder, A. (2008). The Status and Function of English in Indonesia: A Review of the Key Factors. *Makara. Sosial Humanoira.*, *12*(1), 9–20.

Lee, P. (2011). Overview of Background Factors Which May Influence Japanese Learner Behaviour in the Communicative English Classroom. *Keiwa College Journal,* (20), 1-13.

Lizzio, A., Wilson, K., & Simons, R. (2002). University Students' Perceptions of the Learning Environment and Academic Outcomes: Implications for Theory and Practice. *Studies in Higher Education*, *27*(1), 27–52. doi:10.1080/03075070120099359

Lukens-Bull, R. A. (2001). Two Sides of the Same Coin: Modernity and Tradition in Islamic Education in Indonesia. *Anthropology & Education Quarterly*, *32*(3), 350–372. doi:10.1525/aeq.2001.32.3.350

Mahadi, T. S., & Jafari, S. M. (2012). Motivation, its types and its impacts in Language Learning. *International Journal of Business and Social Science*, *3*(24), 230–235.

Manca, S., & Ranieri, M. (2016). Facebook and the others. Potentials and obstacles of social media for teaching in higher education. *Computers & Education*, *95*, 216–230. doi:10.1016/j.compedu.2016.01.012

Masaazi, F. M. (2015). Developing a Friendly and Productive Language Learning Environment (FPLE) Using the Learner as a Resource. *Journal of Education and Training Studies*, *3*(5), 144–145. doi:10.11114/jets.v3i5.967

McKay, S. L. (2002). *Teaching English as an International Language: Rethinking Goals and Perspectives*. New York: OUP.

Mohd-Asraf, R. (2005). English and Islam: A Clash of Civilizations? *Journal of Language, Identity, and Education*, *4*(2), 103–118. doi:10.120715327701jlie0402_3

Mohd-Hamidin, N. (2015). *The teaching and learning strategies used in classroom: a case study in national religious secondary schools (SMKA) in Selangor*. The Teaching and Learning Strategies Used in Classroom.

Mohd-Yasim, I. M., Lubis, M. A., Mohd Noor, Z. A., & Kamaruddin, M. Y. (2016). The use of teaching aids in the teaching and learning of Arabic language vocabulary. *Creative Education, 7*, 443-448.

Nair, G., Rahim, R., Setia, R., Husin, N., Sabapathy, E., Jalil, N., ... Mohamed, N. (2012). Malaysian Graduates English Adequacy in the Job Sector. *Asian Social Science, 8*(4).

Najeeb, S. S. (2013). Learner autonomy in language learning. *Procedia: Social and Behavioral Sciences, 70*(70), 1238–1242. doi:10.1016/j.sbspro.2013.01.183

Nakamura, T. (2000). *The Use of Vocabulary Learning Strategies: the Case of Japanese EFL Learners in Two Different Learning Environments*. University of Essex.

Nasr, S. H. (1992). Oral transmission and the book in Islamic education: The spoken and the written word. *Journal of Islamic Studies, 3*(1), 1–14. doi:10.1093/jis/3.1.1

Nasr, S. H. (2012). Islamic Pedagogy: An Interview. *Islam & Science, 10*(1), 7–24.

Nasr, S. H. (2016). Philosophical Considerations of Islamic Education-Past and Future: Interview with Professor Seyyed Hossein Nasr. In M. Zaman & N. A. Memon (Eds.), *Philosophies of Islamic Education* (pp. 29–37). New York: Routledge.

Prain, V., Cox, P., Deed, C., Dorman, J., Edwards, D., Farrelly, C., ... Yagera, Z. (2013). Personalised learning: Lessons to be learnt. *British Educational Research Journal, 39*(4), 654–676.

Qureshi, O. A. (2016). Disciplinary and Islamic Education. In N. A. Memon & M. Zaman (Eds.), *Philosophies of Islamic Education: Historical Perspectives and Emerging Discourses*. New York: Routledge.

Rehman, A., Bilal, H. A., Sheikh, A., Bibi, N., & Nawaz, A. (2014). The role of motivation in learning English language for Pakistani learners. *International Journal of Humanities and Social Science, 4*(1), 254–258.

Reinders, H. (2014). Personal Learning Environments for Supporting Out-of-Class Language Learning. *English Teaching Forum, 52*(4), 14.

Richardson, J. T. E. (2005). Students' Approaches to Learning and Teacher's Approach to Teaching in Higher Education. *Educational Psychology, 25*(6), 673–680. doi:10.1080/01443410500344720

Robinson, F. (1993). Technology and religious change: Islam and the impact of print. *Modern Asian Studies, 27*(01), 229–251. doi:10.1017/S0026749X00016127

Roth, W. M., Tobin, K., & Zimmermann, A. (2002). Co-teaching/cogenerative dialoguing: Learning environments research as classroom praxis. *Learning Environments Research, 5*(1), 1–28. doi:10.1023/A:1015662623784

Sabani, N., Hardaker, G., Sabki, A., & Salleh, S. (2016). Understandings of Islamic pedagogy for personalised learning. *The International Journal of Information and Learning Technology, 33*(2), 78–90. doi:10.1108/IJILT-01-2016-0003

Sabki, A. i., & Hardaker, G. (2013). The madrasah concept of Islamic pedagogy. *Educational Review, 65*(3), 342–356. doi:10.1080/00131911.2012.668873

Sabki, A. A., & Hardaker, G. (2013). The madrasah concept of Islamic pedagogy. *Educational Review, 65*(3), 342–356. doi:10.1080/00131911.2012.668873

Sağlam, G., & Salı, P. (2013). The essentials of the foreign language learning environment: Through the eyes of the pre-service EFL teachers. *Procedia: Social and Behavioral Sciences, 93*, 1121–1125. doi:10.1016/j.sbspro.2013.09.342

Savignon, S. J. (1991). Communicative language teaching; state of the art. *TESOL Quarterly, 25*(2), 261–277. doi:10.2307/3587463

Snorradóttir, A. B. (2014). *Language use in the English classroom: the role of students' first language in grades 9 and 10 in English classrooms in Iceland.* University of Iceland.

Suryasa, W., Prayoga, G. P. A., & Werdistira, W. A. (2017). An analysis of students' motivation towards English learning as a second language among students in Pritchard English Academy. *International Journal of Social Science and Humanity*, (1): 2.

Tang, C. M., & Chaw, L. Y. (2016). Digital Literacy: A Prerequisite for Effective Learning in a Blended Learning Environment? *Electronic Journal of E-learning, 14*(1), 54–65.

Thang, S., Nambiar, R. K., Wong, F., Mohd Jaafar, N., & Amir, Z. (2015). A Clamour for More Technology in Universities: What Does an Investigation into the ICT Use and Learning Styles of Malaysian 'Digital Natives' Tell Us? *The Asia-Pacific Education Researcher, 24*(2), 353–361. doi:10.100740299-014-0185-2

Thang, S. M. (2004). Learning English in multicultural Malaysia: Are learners motivated? *Journal of Language and Learning, 2*(2).

Thang, S. M., Ting, S. L., & Mohd Jaafar, N. (2011). Attitudes and Motivation of Malaysian Secondary Students towards learning English as a Second Language. *3L: The Southeast Asian Journal of English Language Studies, 17*(1).

Thompson, G. L. (2015). Understanding the heritage language student: Proficiency and placement. *Journal of Hispanic Higher Education, 14*(1), 82–96. doi:10.1177/1538192714551277

Umam, C. (2014). Maintaining Islamic Values in English Language Teaching in Indonesian Pesantrens. *Didaktika Religia, 2*(1), 227–242.

Walker, R. (2010). The Conduct of Educational Case Study: Ethics, Theory and Procedures. In H. Torrance (Ed.), *Qualitative Research Methods in Education* (Vol. I, pp. 253–286). London: Sage Publications Ltd.

Wallace, A. R. (1863). On the physical geography of the Malay Archipelago. *Journal of the Royal Geographical Society of London, 33*, 217–234. doi:10.2307/1798448

Wallace, A. R. (1869). *The Malay Archipelago: the land of the orang-utan and the bird of paradise; a narrative of travel, with studies of man and nature.* London: Macmillan and Co.

Yunus, K., Mohamad, M., & Waelateh, B. (2016). The Breadth of Receptive Vocabulary Knowledge among English Major University Students. *Journal of Nusantara Studies, 1*(1), 7–17. doi:10.24200/jonus.vol1iss1pp7-17

Zaman, M., & Memon, N. A. (2016). *Philosophies of Islamic education: Historical perspectives and emerging discourses.* Routledge. doi:10.4324/9781315765501

Zubairi, A. M., & Sarudin, I. (2009). Motivation to learn a foreign language in Malaysia. *GEMA Online Journal of Language Studies, 9*(2), 73-87.

KEY TERMS AND DEFINITIONS

Adab: Refers to the Islamic moral or ethics formation, that complies with the will of God, partially through the utilisation of a Sacred Law that binds human to God and the rest of humanity.

Communicative Competence: Is outlined as the learner's proficiency and adeptness at conveying and sharing meaningful exchanges successfully in the target language within a given context.

Instrumental Motivation: Refers to the drive that learners possess to succeed in acquiring a language for utilitarian purposes.

Islamic Pedagogy: Is defined as an idea or concept that not only limits one to learn about the Islamic religion but with it as well, that should be encapsulated as an embodied learning dedicated to God.

Knowledge Embodiment: Relates to the concept that insinuates an understanding that when knowledge permeates within a person, it transcends in the interrelation of one's cognitive context and bodily expressions within a specific context.

Language Learning Environment: Is described as the materials, teaching approaches, the relationship between learners, learner-teacher interaction, reward system, teaching and learning setting, and assessment.

Learner Autonomy: Is defined as learner's capabilities to self-regulate their learning, which, among others, including deciding on the learning goals, learning contents and development of progress.

Personal Learning Environments (PLE): Is a new term typically used in e-learning systems where educators and learners collaborate with other users of PLE based applications to facilitate learning.

Personalized Learning: Is a concept that acknowledges learners' differences and individual inclination, and allowing them to pace their learning process individually, with the multiple support from their learning environment.

Chapter 11

Understanding Nasheed for Learning Strategy in Islamic Education

Muhammad Talhah Ajmain
Universiti Teknologi Malaysia, Malaysia

Jimaain Safar
Universiti Teknologi Malaysia, Malaysia

Ahmad Kilani Mohamed
Universiti Teknologi Malaysia, Malaysia

Miftachul Huda
ⓘD https://orcid.org/0000-0001-6712-0056
Universiti Pendidikan Sultan Idris, Malaysia

ABSTRACT

Nashid is one of various teaching methods and facilitator (PdPc). Teenagers nowadays are full of interest in entertainment in the form of songs and singing, and a good alternative is to bring them to God. Thus, this paper will be debating nashid as medium of education and missionary, nashid as a method of teaching and facilitating, the effectiveness of the method, and its implementation in teaching and learning. Aspects of creativeness in education are required in the 21st century. Nashid method is able to help students memorize facts and important things, strengthen memory, create high interest, build excitement, improve motivation and concentration, and enhance the confidence level among students. It will bring about a holistic student. However, the selection of the appropriate nashid must be considered to make sure the teaching objectives are achieved. Thus, teachers in Islamic teaching must look at this method as one of the important methods and apply it in their teaching and facilitating process.

DOI: 10.4018/978-1-5225-8528-2.ch011

INTRODUCTION

Nashid is one of the way of teaching and facilitation in learning process. Through this method, teacher could do teaching and facilitation (PdPc) that serves the purpose of enhancing the participation and interest of students. It is one of learning process in the form of entertainment that coherent with students' youth and lifestyle. Terms used for Islamic education in the lyrics could possibly engaged with the students through singing or nashid orally or with the assistance of audio equipment (Muhammad Said, 1998). Teacher will convey the information to the students with this simple and interesting method.

Nashid is one of the way to train the students to apply what did they learn in the form of song. This method will reduce the incidence of students being bored, increase the interactions among students and thus the teacher could identify strength and capabilities of their students. Students will have an affective learning when they learn about topics parallel to their interest, purpose and benefit that they will have. The teachers will be trained with variety of methods in teaching and learning but some of them are not using creativity in their teaching method. According to a research by Hairun Najuwah and Siti Nurhajariah (2014) shows that educators rarely use games and activities such as singing during teaching process. Deakin Handbook (2014) stated that students will develop skills and responds with art and singing activities. On top of that, singing will shape students' discipline, interactive and social skills (VCAA, 2015).

Thus, this paper will illustrates the importance of nashid especially for teenagers nowadays and how nashid method in Islamic education will act as an affective teaching and learning process.

Nashid As An Education Medium

Students among teenagers are prone to nashid or singing that is pleased to be heard with a good voice. According to Muhammad Kamil and Muhammed (2008), music art have an encouraging response from public especially teenagers. Through singing, they will feel contented and ease their mind (Suhana Udin, 2012). This is supported by Zainuddin et al. (2014) that stated as it is the nature of human to have an interest in music. In addition, teenagers are a group of people that is developing and searching for their own identity and love to explore new things.

Muslims are not separated from the art of sound through listening. Al Qaradhawi (1996) said that daily activities of muslims are related to the art of listening and feelings. For an instance, the sound wave in the Islamic art is through recitation of Al Quran and adzan (calling for prayers for muslims) that is a spiritual routine since the prophethood time. Furthermore, there are prayers and dzikir (routine oral habit in the remembrance of Allah) that will shake the heart and soul of the listeners.

We could not deny that teenagers nowadays love entertainment. Entertainment is not wrong as long as it does not cross the rules of religion. Ahmad Sharifuddin and Mohd Zain (2006) illustrates that the nature of human loves music. Entertainment is needed for each one of us as needed for our soul. Islam is not hindering muslims to adapt something from the west or the east, as long as it is parallel to the criteria and suits with cultural tradition that is not cross the limit of the religion (Mohammad Kamil and Muhammed, 2008).

Entertainment that is liked by teenagers are music and singing. Despite of that, teenagers need guidance so that the entertainment will not give a negative effect to them. This is because entertainment that is not being controlled will lead to negative impacts such as Ismaniza (2011) stated that Abd Ghafar Don (1997) shows that excessive entertainment will have a negative effects on the shape of teenagers' identity and mind especially adolescent and teenagers.

Nashid will also acts as da'wa. Ahmad Sharifuddin and Mohd Zain (2006) stated that a popular medium that fits the needs of da'wa is through music and singing. Nashid is the only one of Islamic music (Mohammad Kamil and Muhammed, 2008). When teenagers nowadays want to involve in public, they have an alternative in choosing nashid that is suitable for them. Thus, nashid is encouraged to be trained to teenagers so that they could be a daie even in their work setting in future ahead.

Nashid is among a music that can control listeners to get back to God. As stated by Mohamad Kamil and Muhammed (2008), if we take a look in the music industry currently, a part of muslims in Malaysia especially regard nashid as the only one Islamic music art and apart from nashid it is considered as non islamic. Nashid could be an alternative to muslims that love entertainment especially among teenagers. According to experts in islam that encourage music with certain condition, muslims have a massive input on how to make use of the benefit through music. This includes benefit of make a closer relationship with our creator, convey human rights messages, advices, identity, god, civilization, patriotism, nasionalisme, family, current issues and so on.

Among the advantages of nashid is that it will give calmness and relaxation in oneself. Calmness and relaxation is necessary to obtain comfort in spiritual need to Allah. According to Md Hashim, Md Afandi and Tuan Anuar (1999), art could bring happiness and entertainment to mankind and entertainment could serve the purpose of spiritual routine and needs as long as it will follow the rules of Islam. Among the entertainment that could entertain the soul and calm the heart with pleasant to the ear is singing (Nurul Huda, 2004). The exhausted soul will affect the quality of spiritual routine. The intelligence of Wali Songo in the use of benefit of entertainment for da'wa could be an example (Ahmad Sharifuddin and Mohd Zain, 2006).

Most entertainment at the moment could lead teenagers to negative impacts. If we could analyse music art, we could see a room for an improvement. For this purpose, we must not create or evolve a new music art. But we could focus mainly on make the music art Islamic that previously said as not parallel to religious need (Mohamad Kamil and Muhammed, 2008).

To make this as reality to fix the music art in islamic way, author could see that not only music art that need to be Islamic but it could be used for different purpose like education. But music art should serve parallel to subjects for example singing a song for non Islamic education and nashid for Islamic subjects.

Nashid As A Way Of Learning And Teaching

Learning method in 21st century not only focus on teaching skills but also need the creative skills from teachers in teaching session and facilitation (PdDc) to occur. According to Mohd Ali Muda (1994), paradigm shift in education system demand educators to make a change in which the essential element in this change is creativity. An excellent educator is not measured by skills of teaching only but also the creativity that we need in (PdPc) delivered (Siti Salwa and Muhammad Zahiri, 2014; Siti Salwa and Azlina, 2014).

The variety method in teaching and creative teacher could make the class alive with fun learning and motivates the students to follow the teaching process. Education currently focuses on learning environment that is interesting and effective that require the teacher to be a creative and innovative individual (Yong and Biramiah, 1996). Nor Farhanah (2011) stated that a creative teacher that acts as a motivator in learning for students.

Normally, information that could bring out the emotion and fun learning will easily make the students focus compare to boring information delivered (Abdul Fatah, 1990; Othman and Ali, 2012). Singing or nashid is seen as agent to enhance the emotion and increase the participation of an individual. This opinion is parallel with Savin (2001) and Rahman and Rahman (2013) that stated that the usage of familiar song in classroom that would give a great learning experience.

This is because singing as a usual routine in everyone no matter during happiness or sadness that could be implement in classroom. Mok Soon Sang and Lee Shok Mee (1989) stated that singing as an activity that happens in real life. This activity could be done in the classroom as an amusing oral activity and could act as the best medium in boost memory of students. Same as Noraini (2003), Nur Farhanah (2011), Rosli and Omar (2013) stated that the usage of rhythm and rhyme in teaching could strength the memory as well as reducing boredom, it can enhance interest and encourage convergence to learning.

Nashid method is suitable for use in Islamic education because nashid is more Islamic than singing. The thought has been mixed among Muslims in Malaysia as stated by Mohamad Kamil and Muhammed (2008), in view of today's music art scenario, some Muslims in Malaysia in particular have assumed that nashid is the only Islamic music art, while others are not Islamic. However, songs can also be used if they are in tune with situations such as unapproachable songs and keep the boundaries outlined by Islam in entertainment.

Usually students will have difficulty memorizing facts, or remember reading such as prayer recitation and prayer reading, things that involve the pillar or conditions and so on. This is because music is important in education because of its contribution to cognitive enabling a student to express his feelings (Eisner, 2003). Hermann, (1991) explains, the integration of music with other subjects will complement the development of the left and right brain.

If a student integrates both the functions of the brain in a harmonious way, learning will be fun, the power of concentration will increase, the memory will grow stronger, the imagination will improve for the problem, and the thinking will become more effective (Abdul Fatah, 1990) . The song itself requires a clear and correct sounding, according to the rhythm and delivered according to the pressure, intonation and specific tone. Teachers can provide song lyrics by selected content and materials (Suhana, 2012). From the intellectual aspect, students should remember the song lyrics and then understand the lyrics (Hisyamuddin, and Amir Hamzah, 2012).

In addition, using the nashid method in Islamic education also strengthens students' skills and builds the personality of the students. Mohd Soffwan (1998) states that in the context of strengthening the students' skills, singing is an activity that can help teachers achieve their goals. Likewise, the character of the students, through music and dance, can also help in developing their social skills (Hisyamuddin & Amir Hamzah, 2012). This will enable the teaching of Islamic education to achieve the desired goal and thus enable the students to have high moral character in their social skills. One of the eight major concepts in fast learning is fun learning using color-oriented activities, nashids, language games (Hairun Najuwah & Siti Nurhajariah, 2014). Based on the study, students are more likely to memorize reading when playing nashid accompanied by music and melody (Muhamad Zahiri, Noraini & Safira, 2016). However, it is a challenge for teachers to look for ideas in building new lyrics and songs because they will take time and need teachers' confidence, while building a new thing takes a long time (Baldwin & Beauchamp, 2014).

In conclusion, a challenging world now needs diversity to attract students to learning. The learning fun by using nashid method besides being able to attract students to learning, it also helps students to memorize the facts in learning easily and effectively. The effect of effective learning will help students develop their identity to develop their social skills and potentials.

The Effectiveness of Nashid Methods

In Islamic Education topics, there are important facts and contents that require the students' memorization. One of the most effective ways to remember the important facts and contents is through the nashid method. These important facts and contents are placed in the lyrics of the nashid lyrics that are song by certain melodies. This is in line with the views of Mok Soon Sang and Lee Shok Mee (1989) which state that singing is one of the best mediums in reinforcing student memories. The use of the song as a method to convey facts is an effective approach (Hisyamuddin Abdul & Amir Hamzah, 2012). According to Noraini (2003), the accompaniment of the rhythm of a song with certain rhythms reinforces the memory of a student. According to Nur Farhanah (2011), the use of the singing methods has helped students remember the 'Water Cycle' process. This is further supported by Muhamad Zahiri et al. (2016) stating that the accompaniment of nashid song rhythms can strengthen memory, as well as launch student readings.

The nashid method can help students memorizing skills. The wave of nashid melodies make it easier for students in memorizing process. In Goh's study (2011) it is proven that the method of singing is effective in memorizing song lyrics smoothly and helping Year Three students to master in tables multiplication from 6 to 8. According to Suhana Udin (2012) study shows the effectiveness of the combination of cartoon illustration method, movement and song used in helping and improving teaching practice remembering skills. The song is one of the facilitators in memorizing a suitable topic (Hisyamuddin Abdul & Amir Hamzah, 2012). This is supported by the study of Muhamad Zahiri et al. (2016) which shows that the nashid method can help students to read and memorize the reading of "tahiyyat" in prayers well and smoothly.

The nashid method also helps students' reading skills. Students are easy to say a word when it is waved in melodic nashid lyrics. Mohamad Lutfi's study (2011) states that the effectiveness of using the song method in learning improves word reading skills. The findings of the study by Suaini and Mohamed (2012) show that singing techniques can help teachers, especially special education teachers to enhance the smooth reading of two syllables for Slow Learner students. The results of Umi Kalsum and Mohamed (2012) study show that Music Chair Game Therapy can help students to recognizing and saying the syllables. The findings of Md. Nasir and Ain Hazwani (2014) show that the learning method while playing through singing activities are able to improve the oral reading skills of learning problem-students. This is in line with the study of Jamaiyah & Ramlah (2014) which shows the use of computers and songs can enhance the reading skills among students.

Apart from that, this method can cultivate interest, enjoyment and concentration of the students in the teaching and learning process making them eager to learn (D. Governor et al, 2012; Dawn Josep, 2015; Nihada & Alisa, 2016). This will lead to proficiency of the topic of learning. According to Noraini (2003), music background can boost up attentiveness, lessen boredom and promotes concentration of the students. This is aligned with a research conducted by Mohamad Lutfi (2011) who shows that students are interested and focus towards the singing method used in the learning and teaching process performed in classroom. Singing gives motivation and excitement to the students (Suhana Udin, 2012; D. Governor et al, 2012; Dawn Josep, 2015). Meanwhile, a research conducted by Md. Nasir & Ain Hazwani (2014) shows that students express engrossment and positive reaction towards the method of playing through singing activity implemented by the teacher. Nashid method not only help students to memorize and recall fluently, but also effective to attract student's attention (Muhamad Zahiri et al., 2016). Furthermore, it will be more exciting for the student to remember because they sing the nashid together.

Nashid method also can increase confidence level of the students and overcome their misunderstanding. They will be more convinced to give their answers for the problems related to the learning topic (Dawn Joseph, 2015). This is coincided with Mok Sang Sang (2010) who state that music is theraphy. It can overcome the problem of less convinced with the knowledge acquired. Students can answer with more assertiveness in shorter length of time after going through the singing method in the teaching and learning process (Tan Jun Ming & Chin Chee Keong, 2012). Research by Hisyamuddin Abdul dan Amir Hamzah (2012) proves that misconception or misunderstanding can be prevented by using singing method. When the students sing the nashid, they can build self-confidence through the emotion expression via the lyrics. (Jensen, 2008). This will then overcome their misunderstanding towards the content of the lesson.

Holistic student can be produced through nashid method. Students will follow the steps that will lead to the progression of intellect, spiritual, emotion, physical and social (Hisyamuddin Abdul & Amir Hamzah, 2012). From the intellect aspect, students are trained to remember and consequently understand the lyric of the nashid. As for the spiritual aspect, students will gain benefit from the divine lyrics. As for the emotion aspect, students are exposed to the value of the lyric. While for the physical aspect, students sing the nashid while doing style and movement based on the lyric of the nashid. Last but not least, for the social aspect,students can attain it by singing the song hormonally together.

Effectiveness of nashid method in teaching and learning provide the opportunity for teachers to choose this method in their learning session. This method is choosen because it benefits in the aspect of strengthening of memory and excitement in student's learning method that offers the individual holistic criteria fits the demand aligned with the National Education Philosophy. Therefore, to make learning process more efficient, teachers need to be exposed with the execution of this method so that PdPc process runs smoothly.

Implementation of Nashid Method

Method of nashid can be implement with various way in the Islamic education PdPc especially for students who are interested in music. The acceptance of the students toward music would be requirement to ensure that the song like nashid is effective (Hisyamuddin Abdul & Amir Hamzah, 2012). Nonetheless, students who are lack of interest towards music need to involve in the conducted activities in order to develop interest (Dawn Joseph, 2015). Method of nashid can be made as induction set, activities in the teaching, closing of the teaching and styling activities. Planning on setting nashid in particular aspect based on teaching objectives and suitability of the teaching topics. Purpose of the implementation is to assist students in relating new informations with old informations and integrated the informations in their mind by nashid activities applications (Gosling, 2006; Hairun Najuwah & Siti Nurhajariah, 2014).

Nashid can be set of induction (Norhaslina et al., 2014) by begin the teaching with selected nashid based on topics that will be teach. Teacher can used teaching aids such as laptop and speaker for playing the music without lyrics. Furthermore, teacher also can used computer and LCD to project lyrics of the nashid. Then, teacher can ask the student to sing along while appreciating the lyrics. According to Hisyamuddin Abdul and Amir Hamzah (2012), nashid activities can be done together with their friends to boost the student's spirit.

Beside, nashid can be set as activities in lesson step. Among the activities that can be done is by asking students to study and analyse the lyrics of nashid that have been given and relate the lyrics with the learning content which consist of topic, subtopics and important content. The results of this analysis will increase the appreciation of the students when sing the nashid. Another activities that can be done is by asking the student to invent their own lyrics based on important content regarding learning topic. This will be align with the Hisyamuddin Abdul & Amir Hamzah (2012) view which think that creating song's lyrics based on student's creativity is a transformation in method of learning and teaching.

Nashid can be closing for the lesson in order to strengthen students' understanding regarding the topics that have been learned. This method also will booster memory of the students towards topics if nashid's lyrics have connection with content of the lesson. It will make students to have motivation to revise content of the lesson. Hence, by putting nashid at the end of the lesson will give impact to student attitudes towards subjects after lesson session.

Nashid also can be set as styling activities by asking the students to search nashid which reated to the topic. Then, teacher will ask students to bring nashid's lyrics that relate to the next subject. The use of melody which is common to the students will make it easier for them to memorize the song (Muhamad Zahiri et al., 2016) then it will help to memorize content of the lesson. Nashid's lyrics will be share with others friends. In addition, modification of the method can be done by using simple music tools and easy to use (Hisyamuddin Abdul & Amir Hamzah, 2012). Thus, students will have opportunity given by the teacher to bring along nashid tools to expand their psychomotor. Hallam, et al (2009) said that "We need to empower the teacher for them to believe with successful and effective of the song in the lesson and accept new ideas for developing their students".

Method of Nashid in Islamic Education Topic

Application method of nashid in islamic education lesson is the teacher will play the nashid song trough audio tool or asking the students to create their own song. Teacher need to select any topics which are suitable for the activities. Certain topics are appropriate to conduct in nashid because it will make the lesson more interesting plus will enhance students' ability to memorise because it will make it easier if the activities is done in nashid.

In topic of verses understanding, student need to understand and memorise facts which is like verses interpretation such as speciality of the Quran, the nature and duties of the angel, characteristic of the people who are patient, the importance of prayer and some other topics. Thus, method of nashid which have interesting melody will assist student to memorise facts.

Moreover in aqidah part, students need to expose to facts that consist of the attributes of Allah, commandment of faith, knowing God, the nature of the angels, the death, the punishment of hell and the beauty of heaven and some other topics. Facts in the context include the purpose of language and terms, numbers, pronouncements and so on. In ibadah part, there are terms that need to be memorise by the student. For instances, ablutions, prayer, jumaah prayer, fasting, zakat fitrah, and many more. Prayers includes jumaah prayers, eidul fitri, eidul adha and tahajjud. All of the facts students need to memorise and remember important terms. If the terms and facts is memorise by using song and melody which are nice to hear, it will make the process to memorisation if more fun and easy.

Furthermore, in sirah there are so many facts need to be remember such as full name of the figure, date of birth, date of date of the figure, place of birth, date of war, the numbers of troops, name of sahabah who involve in the war, date of agreement, contribution of the figure and many more. There are several nashid song which are related to sirah topic in Islamic education which are suitable used as an example of a lesson to assist students in memorization. For instance topic regarding Rasulullah, students can used nashid song such as Rasulullah by Hijjaz as guidance. Besides, in adab part there are many fact that need to be master by the student which is quite simple compared to other topics. It is easier to be memorized and remembered by the students. However, the process of memorizing this part of adab will be easier if it is sing by using nashid method.

CONCLUSION

Facing the 21st century civilization era, teenage soul that prone to music and songs cannot be denied. Therefore, nashid is the form of song that can be the best alternative in occupying the emptiness of the teenager' soul. This need to be done to prevent them from choosing the form of music that can give negative impact towards their minds and behavior. Hence, teachers especially those who teach Islamic studies need to play their role in executing this responsibility.

Nashid not only can help student to excel in academic, it also can lighten their soul with the actual muslim living way. It can lead human's soul closer to its Creator. With lighted soul filled with eeman, these students can become preachers in the future. They can act as Islamic agents in various fields of career that they will go through. This desire cannot be achieved without early effort from early teenage stage.

In educating students through nashid, students need to be exposed with various types of nashid. This will help them to make the best choice in different situations. Teachers implement this by preparing various types of nashid from tremendous nashid groups in the learning and teaching process (PdPc). It also will be the foundation for the students to extend their creativity in the future within Islamic law. However, as an educator, teachers are responsible to ensure the aim of Islamic education remains, the method of using nashid cannot appear more prominent or important than the actual Islamic education and aligned with the cultivation of a student that is holistic as a muslim.

REFERENCES

Abdul Fatah Hassan. (1990). *Penggunaan Minda yang Optimum dalam Pembelajaran*. Skudai: Universiti Teknologi Malaysia.

Ahmad, N. (2003). *Menguatkan ingatan*. Retrieved from http://books.google.com.my

Ahmad Sharifuddin Mustapha & Mohd Zain Mubarak. (2006). *Dakwah melalui muzik dan nyanyian: satu perbincangan. Kertas kerja Seminar Serantau Dakwah dan Kesenian. Anjuran Jabatan Pengajian dakwah dan Kepimpinan.* Fakulti Pengajian Islam, Universiti Kebangsaan Malaysia.

Al-Qaradhawi, Y. (1996). *Al-Islam wa al-Fann.* Al-Qaherah: Matbaah al-Madani.

Baldwin, L., & Beauchamp, G. (2014). A study of teacher confidence in teaching music within the context of the introduction of the Foundation Phase (3–7 years) statutory Education Programme in Wales. *British Journal of Music Education, 31*(2), 195–208. doi:10.1017/S0265051714000060

(2008). Brain-based learning. InJensen, E. (Ed.), *The new paradigm of teaching* (2nd ed.). Thousand Oaks, CA: Corwin Press.

Deakin University. (2014). *ECA409-Primary Arts Education.* Retrieved from http://www.deakin.edu.au/current-students/courses/unitsearch.php?entunit=eca409&ent keyword=&year=2014

Džanić, N. D., & Pejić, A. (2016, October). The Effect of Using Songs On Young Learners and Their Motivation for Learning English. *An Interdisciplinary Journal, 1*(2), 40–54.

EisnerE. (2003). *The Function of Music In Education.* Retrieved from http://www.isme.org/article/view/89/1/26

Goh, M. L. (2011). Penggunaan Kaedah Nyanyian Dalam Penguasaan Sifir Darab 6 hingga 8 Pelajar Tahun Tiga. *Jurnal Penyelidikan Tindakan IPG KBL, 5,* 24–35.

Gosling, D. (2006). The value of pedagogic inquiry for improving teaching. *New Directions for Teaching and Learning, 107*(1), 99–108. doi:10.1038/bdj.2008.192

Governor, Hall, & Jackson. (2012). Teaching and Learning Science Through Song: Exploring the experiences of students and teachers. *International Journal of Science Education,* 1–24. doi:10.1080/09500693.2012.690542

Hallam, S., Burnard, P., Robertson, A., Saleh, C., Davies, V., Rogers, L., & Kokatsaki, D. (2009). Trainee primary-school teachers' perceptions of their effectiveness in teaching music. *Music Education Research, 11*(2), 221–240. doi:10.1080/14613800902924508

Hannan, A. (2007). *Interviews in Education Research.* Retrieved from http://www.edu.plymouth.ac.uk/resined/interviews/inthome.htm

Herman, N. (1991). The Creative Brain. *The Journal of Creative Behavior*, 25(4), 275–295. doi:10.1002/j.2162-6057.1991.tb01140.x

Hisyamuddin Abdul Razab & Amir Hamzah Sharaai. (2012). *Kaedah nyanyian dalam mengatasi masalah miskonsepsi dalam kalangan pelajar tahun tiga dalam topik magnet.* Persidangan Kebangsaan Pembangunan dan Pendidikan Lestari 2012. Institut Pendidikan Guru Kampus Tuanku Bainun, Bukit Mertajam, Pulau Pinang.

Ismaniza binti Ismail. (2011). *Peranan nashid sebagai medium dakwah.* Kertas Projek, Fakulti Pendidikan Universiti Teknologi Malaysia.

Jamali, H. N., & Isa, N. M. (2014). Aplikasi teknik pembelajaran pantas dalam pengajaran dan pembelajaran Bahasa Arab. *GSE E-Journal of Education*, 2(2), 1–11.

Josep, D. (2015). We did the how to teach it': Music teaching and learning in Higher Education in Australia. *Australian Journal of Teacher Education.*, 40(7), 1.

Mohamad, A. H., Baharudin, H., Jusoh, F., & Muda, Z. (2017). Pengajaran Dan Pembelajaran Pendidikan Islam Melalui Kaedah Nashid. *The International Seminar On Islamic Jurisprudence In Contemporary Society (Islac 2017).*

Mohamad Kamil Hj Ab Majid & Muhammed Yusof. (2008). Ke arah memperkasakan Islamisasi seni muzik sebagai satu alternatif: satu pengamatan awal. *Jurnal Hadhari Edisi Khas*, 105121.

Mohamad Lutfi Mat Saad. (2011). *Penggunaan kaedah nyanyian dapat menarik minat dan meningkatkan kemahiran membaca perkataan (vkv, kvkv, vkvk, kvkvk) pelajar prasekolah.* Seminar Penyelidikan Tindakan IPG Kampus Sultan Abdul Halim 2011.

Mok Soon Sang. (2010). *Bimbingan dan Kaunseling Kanak-Kanak.* Selangor: Penerbitan Multimedia Sdn. Bhd.

Mok Soon Sang & Lee Shok Mee. (1989). *Latihan Mengajar Untuk Maktab Perguruan.* Kuala Lumpur: Kumpulan Budiman Sdn Bhd.

Muda, M. A. (1994). Isu Kreativiti dan tuntutan Perubahan Dalam Pendidikan. Warta Pendeta. *Jurnal Pendidikan Terengganu*, 1(1), 53–60.

Muhamad, Z. A. M., Rahman, N. A., & Awang, S. (2016). Kajian tindakan kaedah nashid dalam membaiki bacaan tahiyyat dalam kalangan pelajar-pelajar sekolah rendah. *Journal of Islamic Studies in Indonesia and Southeast Asia*, 1(1), 29–36.

Muhid, S. J. N. A., & Jantan, R. (2014). Pengajaran membaca Bahasa Melayu berbantukan komputer dan nyanyian dalam kalangan pelajar-pelajar orang asli. *Asian Education Action Research Journal, 3*, 26–41.

Md. Nasir Masran & Ain Hazwani Abu Kasim. (2014). Keberkesanan kaedah belajar sambil main dalam meningkat kemahiran membaca lisan dalam kalangan pelajar-pelajar bermasalah pembelajaran. *Asian Education Action Research Journal*, (3), 79-95.

Norhaslina Kamarulzaman, Nazean Jomhari, & Mohd Yakub @ Zulkifli Mohd Yusoff. (2014). Membaca dan mempelajari al-Quran dengan teknik al-Jabari untuk pelajar dengan sindrom down. *The Fourth Annual International Quranic Conference 2014*. Retrieved from http://repository.um.edu.my/41337/1/Membaca%20dan%20 Mempelajari%20AlQuran%20dengan%20Teknik%20AlJabari%20untuk%20 Pelajar%20dengan%20Sindrom%20Down.pdf

Nur Farhanah Amin. (2011). *Keberkesanan Kaedah Nyanyian Dalam Meningkatkan Ingatan Pelajar Tahun 5 Bagi Tajuk 'Kitaran Air'. Tesis Ijazah Sarjana Muda Perguruan (dengan Kepujian)*. Institut Pendidikan Guru Dato' Razali Ismail.

Nurul Huda Adzis. (2004). *Nashid sebagai Hiburan alternatif dan peranannya dalam pembentukan peribadi remaja: kajian terhadap pelajar SPI, UTM*. Kertas Projek, Fakulti pendidikan Universiti Teknologi Malaysia.

Othman, N. S., & Ali, M. F. (2012). *Meningkatkan kemahiran mengingat nama-nama benua di dunia dan kedudukan Malaysia di peta dunia melalui kaedah nyanyian. Prosiding Seminar Penyelidikan Pendidikan IPG*. Kuala Lumpur: Institut Pendidikan Guru Malaysia.

Rahman, A. A. & Rahman, M. A. (2013). Keberkesanan kaedah nyanyian dalam meningkatkan daya ingatan pelajar tahun empat bagi topik jenis-jenis rumah tradisional di Malaysia. *Penyelidikan Tindakan PISMP 2013, 2*(4).

Rosli, M. F., & Omar, B. (2013). Penggunaan teknik nyanyian dan Mnemonik (Ndm) dalam meningkatkan penguasaan kata sendi nama dari pelajar tahun tiga. *Kajian Tindakan PISMP 2013, 2*(7).

Savin, C. F. (2001). *Tune-in to Biology: Music in the Science Classroom*. Retrieved from http://www.science.subaru.com/teaching_ideas/carolsavin

Seman, Z. C., Abdul, A. A. K., & Zaidul, A. S. A. (2014). *Nyanyian dan muzik mengikut pandangan hukum oleh Tuan Guru Hj. Abdul Rahman Pondok Sungai Durian Kuala Krai Kelantan*. International Research Management and Innovation Conference 2014 (IRMIC2014), Kuala Lumpur, Malaysia.

Siti, S. M. S., & Muhamad, Z. A. M. (2014). Harmonizing al-Qabisy's view and practice of J-Qaf programme in malaysian primary school. *Asian Journal of Management Sciences & Education*, *3*(1), 153–162.

Siti, S. M. S., & Mustaffa, A. (2014). Guru bersahsiah mulia menurut pandangan Ibn Sahnun: Analisa buku Adab Mu'allimin. *The Online Journal of Islamic Education*, *2*(2), 1–10.

Siti Suaini Yusoff & Mohamed Sulaiman@Wahid. (2012). Penggunaan teknik nyanyian untuk meningkatkan kelancaran membaca perkataan dua suku kata bagi pelajar 'Slow Learner'. *Prosiding Seminar Penyelidikan Tindakan PISMP, 3*(6).

Tan & Chin. (2012). Penggunaan Kaedah Nyanyian Untuk Meningkatkan Pengetahuan Tentang Cara Pengurusan Bahan Kitar Semula. *Persidangan Kebangsaan Pembangunan dan Pendidikan Lestari 2012*. Institut Pendidikan Guru Kampus Tuanku Bainun.

Suhana Udin. (2012). Meningkatkan kemahiran mengingat huruf Idgham Maal Ghunnah menggunakan gabungan kaedah ilustrasi kartun, pergerakan dan nyanyian. Koleksi artikel penyelidikan tindakan PISMP pendidikan Islam. *Seminar Penyelidikan Tindakan IPG KBL Tahun 2012*, 230-242.

Umi Kalsum Zakaria & Mohamed Sulaiman@Wahid. (2012). Aplikasi terapi permainan kerusi muzik dalam membantu pengecaman dan penyebutan suku kata KVKV. *Prosiding Seminar Penyelidikan Tindakan PISMP, 3*(6).

Victorian Curriculum and Assessment Authority (VCAA). (2015). *The Arts*. Retrieved from http://ausvels.vcaa.vic.edu.au/Overview/Strands-Domains-and-Dimensions

Yong, L. M. S., & Biramiah, K. (1996). *Dalam Guru Yang Kreatif: Isu-Isu Teoritikal dan Aplikasi Praktikal*. Kuala Lumpur: Arenabuku Sdn. Bhd.

Chapter 12
Strengthening Moral Responsibility for Learning Quality in Islamic Education

Miftachul Huda

iD https://orcid.org/0000-0001-6712-0056

Universiti Pendidikan Sultan Idris, Malaysia

Widhiya Ninsiana

State Institute for Islamic Studies (IAIN) Metro Lampung, Indonesia

Ulfatmi Ulfatmi

Universitas Islam Negeri Imam Bonjol Padang, Indonesia

Maragustam Siregar

Universitas Islam Negeri Sunan Kalijaga Yogyakarta, Indonesia

Febriyanto Febriyanto

Universitas Muhammadiyah Metro Lampung, Indonesia

Azmil Hashim

Universiti Pendidikan Sultan Idris, Malaysia

Afandi Salleh

Universiti Sultan Zainal Abidin Trengganu, Malaysia

Mohd Hilmi Rozali

Universiti Teknologi Malaysia, Malaysia

Ahmad Kilani Mohamed

Universiti Teknologi Malaysia, Malaysia

Mahyuddin Hassan

Universiti Teknologi Malaysia, Malaysia

Andino Maseleno

Universiti Tenaga Nasional, Malaysia

Nasrul Hisyam Nor Muhamad

Universiti Teknologi Malaysia, Malaysia

Kamarul Azmi Jasmi

Universiti Teknologi Malaysia, Malaysia

DOI: 10.4018/978-1-5225-8528-2.ch012

ABSTRACT

This chapter examines the distinctive point of view about moral responsibility as the main principle in maximizing the learning quality in the perspective of Islamic education. Moreover, the extensive details could be also discussed referring to the strategic comprehensive point of view to contribute into the modern age. Literature review has been adopted to critically examine the detailed overview of learning quality with a comprehensive enhancement in wide range of requirements to achieve quality learning referred to the Islamic education. The findings reveal that through addressing the contextual broad-basis in the learning process to follow up the strategic principles in the requirements combined into the modern age environment, the learning quality could be achieved through committing with the strategic comprehensive principles of moral responsibility. Those are moral responsibility as fundamental purpose of learning process, moral responsibility as strategic principles for learning quality, and moral responsibility as competence skills for learning quality. Thus, this chapter is expected to contribute into the outstanding point of view to enlarge the learning quality procedure in the context of Islamic education contribution into the modern age of education system.

INTRODUCTION

In the last decade, the potential value of Islamic education with the traditional heritage has been widely elucidated into the number of existing research as a response to maintain its distinctive trends and styles amidst the global challenges in the education system (Asadullah, 2016; Sabani et al., 2016). The dynamic system in Islamic education would particularly have a key driving space to incorporate the unique points to deal with the various issues and challenges to solve referring to both trends and traditions (Halstead, 2019). Such enhancements should be carried out in an appropriate manner standard in the basis of the aim of Islamic education. In particular, the predominant deal in the basis of solving the number of challenges within the education system needs to refer to the philosophical overview with a conceptual framework of Islamic education concern in ensuring the wise approach to apply for the fundamental principles guided to fit into the existing education system. Towards such various challenges faced amidst the education system, todays' situation of global education circumstance is potentially essential to give such impact of the number of concern like lack of moral engagement (Huda et al., 2016a), digital device addiction (Shen & Su, 2019), and less responsibility in any role in the learning process (Forbes & Baker, 2017).

Due to giving such cause of concern, the entire effort to respond the global education in the present situations has been reviewed to indicate in giving insights into the possibly appropriate point of view on the decision making to lead to the policy procedure standard to implement in the current education system. In the Islamic overview, the conditions to enlarge such influential concern in giving the core point into alternative decision of educational institutions could be viewed to the Islamic concept of education with providing a whole transmission from the planning to the implementation basis like (Halstead, 2004). Moreover, sustaining moral enhancement in teaching and learning basis assigned into traditional wisdom for sustainable learning in the Islamic point of view (Huda et al., 2017a) refers to the moral teaching in the record of world history. All these indicate the attempts to transmit the possible way to contribute into supplying an alternative point into the current education system. Through addressing the number of interrelated issues, such effort plays a key role in contributing the supplemental overview in advocating the strategic orientation of Islamic way of understanding as the main priority to gain the success in this life and hereafter amongst the Muslim society.

With achieving such alignment, the fundamental overview in the way to provide the strategic principles through addressing the outstanding guidelines of the personal and social concern with moral manner should be determined as an attempt to promote the individual performance as the first step to lead to create the societal condition. As a result, the attempts in guiding the human behaviour in assisting the intellectual, physical, and also moral enhancement in the context of teaching and learning (T&L) are potentially in line with conceiving the entire process of shaping and transforming the education quality itself (Fauzi et al., 2019; Othman et al., 2016). In particular, the fixed combination between the experiential basis and behavioural substance could play a supremacy point of view in determining the individual driving as a pivotal factor to contribute into the quality of education consequently through underlining the conditions towards the external educational environment.

In line with the attempts to determine the point of individual performance through conditioning to control the state of the educational environment, the pivotal role in this scheme would be enhanced in disseminating the information and knowledge transfer together with making influential towards the individual's moral manner. Moreover, the moral substance to outline the human condition whether they are in personal and social condition should bring along with strategic understanding towards Islamic values to enlarge the significant role in assisting to shape the surroundings with a systematic distribution about the environmental concern in the educational setting (Aminin et al., 2018; Forbes & Baker, 2017). In order to sustain such impact in attaining the fundamental aims as the pivotal dimension in the education setting, the augmented process could allow the teaching process in adopting the moral values appropriately referring to the situation and condition. In this view, attempts to impart the knowledge and moral manner in the Islamic point of view should start from aligning the strategic principles of comprehensive requirements for learning process in order to achieve the learning quality attribution into the education system (Huda et al., 2016b). Due to the main obligation of knowledge inquiry in the context of Islamic overview, such certain requirements have to do with determining the achievement extent to proceed 'what to do in fulfilling prior to the progress achieve in the certain stage'. In considering such attainment within the procedural context, both progressive level and number of requirements to explicate in the knowledge acquisition process needs to incorporate the design of main principles together with effective ways to carry out among the students and teachers in order to achieve the better result in their process.

In referring to the number of existing work on the way to enhance the strategic learning enhancement (Maseleno et al., 2019; Moksin et al., 2018; Naufal et al., 2017), there has been lack of concern about how Islamic education contribution to the modern age-education system, particularly in the context fulfilling the number of moral responsibility as the strategic principle disseminated into the comprehensive requirements for learning quality. In reviewing this, providing the crucial elements to monitor in the entire process of T&L is potentially a useful point in determining the valuable insights for human behaviour shaping mainly in supplying their balance between intellectual and moral dimension. Thus, this chapter attempts to examine the fundamental notion of principle about comprehensive requirement in the learning process with a strategic point to maximise the learning quality in the perspective of Islamic education. In this chapter, the presentation will be provided in referring expanding moral responsibility as a fundamental goal in the learning process. Moreover, the capability to enhance entirely serious consciousness for learning inquiry is potentially expanded with maintaining continuous commitment of controlling the emotional stability in learning. In particular, the learning enhancement with sustaining financial supplement could bring along with strengthening T&L engagement with strategic partnership through the planning strategy for learning management system (LMS). As a result, this chapter is expected to contribute into the outstanding point of view to enlarge the learning quality procedure in the context of Islamic education contribution into the modern age of education system. It is surely the learning quality should do with the commitment of taking a serious concern of moral responsibility awareness, brought to the contextual broad-basis combined into the modern age environment.

Aims of Learning Commitment in Islam

The learning commitment in Islamic point of view could be escaped from the extensive comprehension about the purpose of learning itself. In Islam, the essential basis to have the first understanding about the clear purpose in education itself has tree core points in the way to transmit the knowledge inquiry, knowledge transfer and also knowledge execution (Huda et al., 2016c). In other words, the entire attempts to understand the educational setting process should do with bringing along with the inextricable link between educating, coaching, and implementing in the sense that is tied into *ta'līm*, meaning of schooling, teaching or instruction), *tarbiyyah*, meaning of breeding, upbringing or nurturing, and *ta'dīb* meaning of knowledge or knowhow about something, learning, awareness about a piece of information (Halstead, 2004). In the point of referring to the apparent basis of aspects and dimensions of educational setting concept, the balanced combination between the human intellectuality and morality could facilitate the expansion of education quality in the sense that is endured with the knowledge and the good manners development (Huda et al., 2019). It is apparently that the aspects of human awareness in the distribution process of educating through the learning quality could give a feedback in facilitating the enlargement of the significant principles in producing the individual with moral, intellectual and spiritual balance.

In the overview of Islamic concept in transmitting the learning commitment to drive in the right path within bridging the spiritual and mental substance, the outstanding code of conducting the learning process should bring along with mutual understanding to enlarge the main priority of behaving the *Tawhid* (trust in God) orientation as the first goal (Choudhury, 2018; Huda and Sabani, 2018). Through a fixed combination of the purposeful orientation, the committed awareness in assisting the process of T&L could be organised into the tenets of religious sphere in upholding the belief to God. In supplying the orientation to have the balanced personality, both morality and intellectuality should be started with fitting the goal setting referring to the core foundation of all the process in absorbing the knowledge understanding appropriately (Huda & Kartanegara, 2015a; Rosli et al., 2018). Since the moral substance itself as in Islamic perspective contains the religious principles to adhere, it has a core point in serving as upholding the fundamental elements of nurturing the human behaviour with moral, spiritual and intellectual dimension to ensure their understanding stage of what is good, appropriate and wise act amidst their daily life circumstance. The sphere of behaving the obvious balance between religious understanding principle and moral manners way could ensure the potential pathway in nurturing the human personality substance fitted in the Islamic education aims. As a result, transmitting moral and intellectual dimension in the T&L process needs to expand the substantive value of making the goal decision more appropriately in the context of contemporary education system (Huda et al., 2018a). Attempts to have the mutual process combined between producing and sustaining the personal quality within Islamic education should bring along with promoting the morality with religiosity as a valuable insight into shaping the human character behaviour.

As such, the clear overview towards behaving the ultimate goal as a fundamental element to start with what is morally good refers to the way of comprehending the morality to link into the religious values. The valuable insights of ethical behaviour as indicated in the religious principles should do with determining the moral knowledge and moral understanding (Yusob et al., 2017). At this point of view, the religious personality will have a mutual link into the ethical engagement determined to consider in particular representing the essential basis of moral obligation in contributing into the society's development. The oriented necessity to enlarge the valuable determination of moral manner assigned with religious principles would lead to have a significant attribution of gaining the personal quality within Islamic point of view (Mohd Yusob et al., 2015). As a result, the essential presence of morality as indicated in the Islamic education refers to sustain the nurturance of morally religious sphere transmitted into preparing the learning process in achieving the obviously detailed goal as a fundamental element in continuing the further deal with the strategic process in the knowledge transfer and inquiry.

In the attempts to attain such level, the purpose in learning should be oriented to promote the wellbeing of individual quality and social responsibility awareness (Huda et al., 2018b). In this view, the strategic principle to bridge in transmitting the particular goal is designed into performing the central aspects, namely providing the beneficial value of societal concern and together with ensuring the quality of T&L assigned into the contemporary instruction trends, like digitalization, online based tool (Aminudin et al., 2018a; Aminudin et al., 2018b; Aminudin et al., 2018c; Anshari et al., 2017). In terms of the curriculum design of Islamic education aligned into the purpose as a fundamental element, the learning process should bring along with providing the students a wide range of competence and technics towards knowing the knowledge transfer while supplying their continuity sustenance of religious spirituality. In particular, the sustainability in managing the students' awareness to commit with the moral obligation referring to the Islamic principles should be considered in particular into the major concern in transforming the individual quality (Huda et al., 2018b). Moreover, the aspect of committed awareness in increasing the spiritual and physical aspects plays a key role in transmitting the generous continuity in expanding the baser-self in ensuring their personal quality and social concern in a balanced point of view. In the way to enhance in extent of educating and coaching in the learning process, there are a number of points to enlarge the purpose to deal with determining the mutual aspects of performing the generic strategy to commit into the continuity basis in the school basis. Those are

1. Seek for the knowledge of divine existence together with the concerns of the wide range of creation i.e. humankind;
2. Commit with pursuing the pleasing to Allah

3. Assist the success on this life and hereafter life
4. Make a clearance of ignorance towards oneself
5. Maintain the religious life circumstance to achieve peace life
6. Enhance the cognitive extent (*'aql*) to improve the better quality in the society (al-Zarnūjī, 2008).

The further exposure about the purpose shown above could be determined into three core parts, namely the purpose of gaining *'ibadah*, relation to God; obtaining *mu'amalah*, relation to the societal humankind; and the next purpose related to individual quality enhancement (Huda & Kartanegara, 2015). In particular, the wide range of purpose in learning process should do with combining individual, social and religious development in the sense that is transmit into T&L process, committed into the moral manner within the education system. As such, the motivation to sustain the purpose in determining the successful attainment refers to the entire ethical aspects.

Moral Responsibility as Fundamental Purpose of Learning Process

As indicated in the purposeful orientation in the learning process, both moral engagement and professional cognition should be balanced in the sense that enhances the responsible awareness among the learners in the context of school context. The particular essence of behaving moral manners to deal with the social community should be widely transmitted into incorporating the individual quality assurance. Emphasising the Islamic point of view in the moral ethics should do with enhancing their responsibility extent mainly in the context of teacher-students relationship in the learning process, such as in the certain study course (Huda et al., 2017b; Sabani et al., 2016). The ethical foundation should be emphasised in general discourse with maximising the responsible awareness for the self-orientation and social engagement process. In particular, attempts to determine the moral engagement should bring along with searching for the knowledge appropriately linked into the moral manner to implement in the real society at large.

In addition, the moral obligation to involve in the learning and teaching process has to start with addressing the continued engagement between them in obtaining the knowledge in line with enhancing the respectful awareness (Huda & Teh, 2018). The moral manners have the inextricable link towards the subject matters or whatever students learn. As a result for curriculum design, the first attention to apply for that case is on determining the goal orientation as an earlier point of forwarding the moral aspects, including the religious belief orientation. Through careful consideration of making sure towards achieving the particular purpose with maintaining the main principles of Islamic point of view, knowledge understanding should be balanced into the moral implication in facing the latest condition within the certain circumstance, such as making harmony in multiracial society (Wani, Abdullah & Chang, 2015), ethical commitment in the multi-background relationship (Tamam & Krauss, 2017), and also teaching and learning-based moral engagement (Huda et al., 2017c). Moreover, moral orientation as the main goal in underlying the process entirely within the wide range of subject courses is widely a key factor to enhance the continuity of program to benefit all the society at large, since in Islamic perspective all knowledge has the ethical point to determine in transmitting the value of information which will give an insightful point into the school platform.

In line with achieving the main principle of Islamic education orientation, attempts to determine the knowledge transfer into the benefitting value into the society have been widely transformed into the curriculum design assigned by the stakeholder in order to provide the useful platform to use amidst the T&L based instruction. In this view, the strategic determination in providing the quality of education refers to the way to manage the actual circumstance in the school environment by highlighting the main point of moral obligation to adhere as a result of the field based implementation from the conceptual framework designed by the stakeholder (Wulandari et al., 2018). As a point of ensuring the balance between morality and professionality to be transmitted in the T&L orientation, giving the key illustration of what subject matter will be delivered among the students is also a key point in enabling their learning orientation within the moral obligation. As a result, the usability of knowledge inquiry together with experience supplement in this essence should bring along with an important prerequisite of moral responsibility incorporated into the learning purpose orientation (Huda et al., 2018c). The committed awareness of careful engagement in considering the moral obligation amidst the learning courses has an absolute consequence to give the insightful value into the outcome-based learning quality (Maseleno et al., 2017; Susilowati et al., 2018a; Susilowati et al., 2018b; Susilowati et al., 2018c). Attempts to search for the personal and social quality standard in engaging the life circumstance whether they are in the school or in the societal concern are in line with the way they search for knowledge to understand the flow of condition and solution appropriately within the Islamic point of view.

In the effort to setting the moral responsibility together with learning purpose, the mutual involvement of supplying such enhancement of knowledge on what to do appropriately and wisely should be considered in particular in finding out the careful solution of problems taken into facing in the community at large, or even in the primary house case for instance. In this view, the mutual link between the life purposes for what they learn has the consequence to enlarge commitment of personal quality of human being and also their engaged empathy for instance refers to the entirely oriented education procedure in following the main foundation as the philosophical framework designed by the stakeholder (Fahriana & Huda, 2019). This particular attainment should do with giving the inextricable implication towards the determination of career to enhance their life in the economic growth in the society at large (Maseleno et al., 2019b; Sahlan, Abu-Hussin & Hehsan, 2018). In this view, any knowledge to search for in the learning process such as astronomy is potentially to have a beneficial value to give assistance of determining the position of *Qiblah*, the direction for Muslim prayer for worship. This is committed to that the most eligible to recommend among the knowledge fields is on the one with elevating the spiritual growth (Zarnūjī, 2008).

In terms of enhancing the learning quality with their strategic orientation as the dynamics to feature the mutual assistance of determining the appropriate fields of obtaining the learning goal, the synchronisation of that goal should be attempted with featuring the Islamic values in helping which fields still relevant to achieve the learning purpose. For instance, when the learner is committed to become an Engineer, then s/he should bring along with ethically engaged compatibility towards whether it is still reliable into the Islamic values in particular. As a result, the point of applying for the components of both mathematics sciences together with science become a prominent element to support the learning basic to engineering, with compounding the essential value of the Islamic values (Bakar, 2015; Othman et al., 2016). The entire process of engagement to commit with the mutual achievement of learning goal and program instruction is potentially an earlier part of nurturing the knowledge understanding of certain subject matters with tying the Islamic values essentials (Paramboor & Ibrahim, 2014; Huda & Kartanegara, 2015b). The continued inclination in sharing and receiving the knowledge from others would give the multiple time of comprehension stage than the one with keeping own wisdom based island in a convenient condition. Since the goal orientation in T&L process with imparting the knowledge understanding, such condition would assist in improving the personal quality of wisdom and also awareness. As such, this attainment has the mutual link that the most valuable person with the best virtuous is the one with continuing for learning and teaching to others.

Moral Responsibility as Strategic Personal Abilities for Learning Quality

These two oriented standard quality would have a subsequent point in determining the main principles of Islamic education T&L basis. The objective point of behaving the purpose as a basic orientation of applying for the indicators transmitted into the individual quality. Since learning quality has an optional discourse in determining the entire process of T&L instruction, the mutual benefit to achieve fitted into the philosophical goal has to do with brining the commitment of moral obligation as the mutual responsibility (Kirat, 2015). The specific objection refers to the way of looking at the certain issues together with finding the solution appropriately within the Islamic principles, *hikmah*, wisdom-oriented basic system (Hussien, Hashim & Mokhtar, 2017). This system will allow the appropriately useful ways to give the possible solution to respond the challenging issues, such as conflict. As a prominent component, this attainment of *hikmah* could be designed into the principle wisely within the stage of education together with the commitment of purpose determination in the T&L procedural context. The balanced orientation of giving the usefulness could start with expanding the specific purpose whether they are individual, social and religious concern. This should be widely addressed through the following accessibility on the assessment of beneficial components into the society and also measurement of teaching quality process. It is certain that attempts to prepare such quality standard to meet the challenges like moral decadences, irresponsibility involvement, and even ethical challenges could be transmitted into serving as the basic requirement to achieve the orientation of societal goal. Through educating and mentoring the quality basis setting on managing the dynamic systems in T&L, determining the individual development oriented purpose should bring along with the way of graduates to go through the steps provided in the curriculum design (Huda & Kartanegara, 2015c). In particular, the strategic encouragement has to follow the goal commitment set into the condition where the process should deal with a dynamic extent in enabling the wide range of material moment in facilitating the situation into a good typical circumstance to transform the human being to sustain their knowledge understanding in underlying their life.

In line with transmitting the performance quality for T&L, it is certain that the strategy with behaving a number of capabilities to give insights into assisting the achievement towards the goal orientation in its process could be accommodated through the entire putting into practice about the basic principles in the educational setting. Moreover, an attempt to formulate the strategic concern in T&L is necessarily supposed to contribute into the outcome basis where knowledge cognition and moral responsibility would be the main priority as the achievement basis (Maseleno et al., 2017; Sugiyarti et al., 2018). Led by setting the learning quality, moral commitment in underlying the entire process from designing the purpose to the outcome prospect should be considered in particular point of how the process go through the steps wisely within the Islamic values basis. All the efforts should focus on committing with the purpose-oriented design of instruction in the way which transforms the core aims to keep in mind as a particular consequence. It is the main point of targeting the human concern in the society in enabling the accessibility of the certain project in the social needs orientation together with preparing the growth possibility towards the demands in the society. In this view, the moral consideration as a prominent supplement in underlying such efforts is widely essential to sustain the Islamic values to give insights into the worldview framework which can give to transmit amidst the society at large. Bringing the committed ways of Islamic values could enhance the quality set through the purpose based instruction and the result expert basis (Bensaid et al., 2014; Huda et al., 2019). As such, Islamic point of view in providing the framework guidelines should be taken into consideration in managing its purposeful objectives for the social humanity benefit in the sense that is commanded in the responsible requirements. The above in transmitting the quality procedure context is required to bring along with Islamic worldview in ensuring the clear setting and implementation stage in an appropriate manner within the guided principles.

With providing the clear balance between learning quality and moral obligation, the committed awareness in enabling T&L to go through the appropriate manners is potentially convinced in the attempts to know what is right and responsibility in the context of educator and learner (Jonassen & Grabowski, 2012). This is to ensure that continuity process will run into an appropriate procedure in order to emphasise the strategic cooperation process in enabling the individual performances in T&L context to achieve the basic aims together with providing them the solving-based strategy by utilising their knowledge understanding and practical enhancement procedure. As such, the basic systems in educating the problem-based instruction for T&L should be transmitted into following the stage of educational aim as an objective point of view in assisting the development for the individual quality, which is a main concern to lead into the moral responsibility (Robinson & Smith, 2012). This attainment could potentially enhance the extent of transforming the quality of rational thinking in underlying their minds in facing the problems emerged in the life circumstance wisely and appropriately based on the Islamic point of view. By focusing on the character building to underlie the attitude basis, the spirituality substance might become a prominent element in creating the ideal basis of worthwhile objectives which refers to lead to the vision for the T&L instruction basis. In this view, the initiative of curriculum design in enabling the practical stage through a sufficient knowledge understanding with gaining information on providing the life guidance of what to do and how to do wisely and appropriately within Islamic point of view. In particular, the balance achievement through integrating the religious knowledge and sciences foundation could reflect the essential element of accelerating the wide range of components including spirituality, morality and ability to transmit into the performance quality for the individual basis and social concern. In conjunction with the moral responsibility and learning quality, there are three categories of individual performance in trying to understand in T&L context.

1. The first point refers to the personal quality with a virtuous extent (al-Zarnūjī, 2008). This type is usually oriented to have a sufficient good opinion, while tries to interact actively with consulting into the others with more experience and intelligence. This category of person with a knowledgeable potential would

give a sufficient contribution in offering the good guidance by providing the counselling basis into others (Huda & Kartanegara, 2015e). Moreover, the potentials to uphold in transforming the followers into the individual quality with morality, professionality and wisdom would lead to the tolerance. In this view, a sufficient knowledge on gaining good direction could be engaged in guiding to better interact into the peers within the instruction procedure.

2. The second type points out the lower stage than earlier one in the sense that the personal attribute in this category has nothing to direct the correct view and attitude (al-Zarnūjī, 2008). However, this person tried to perform an effort through consultation towards the one with knowing something about the certain update of subject matters. Through such indicators, this person has nothing to properly opine his own view in the way which expands his opinions to lead to the understanding stage of the certain issues. In this view, this category would always try to raise learning with being more analytic in looking at the certain issues. In other words, the wide capacity of critical thinking skills would enable him to carefully recognise the issues to find out the problem solving appropriately within their knowledge understanding scale (Paramboor & Ibrahim, 2014). In the attempts to have a look into the issues within a creative way, the opposite point of this category with possessing a weak analytical thinking towards somethings would potentially lead to achieve the close-minded basis since the learning process might only be sourced through listening from others which has no knowledge about certain subject at all. As such, this category of personal attribute would have a significance of turning-out for the conservative point of view together with uncreative scale in enabling their way to comprehend a whole towards the certain issues. By emphasising the necessary points of performing the procedural context of obtaining the ideas from the extent of knowledge understanding, the sufficient recognizance with a reasoning capacity might enhance the way of critical look into the object.

3. In further, the last type underlined the one with no correct ideas about something and also no effort to try consulting in seeking the information from others with more experience and knowledgeable basis (al-Zarnūjī, 2008). As such, this category of person might look into the arrogance with feeling better than others in the way to find out the solution appropriately and wisely. In the context of T&L procedure, the individual ability is supposed to look for the knowledge understanding from others with any background as long as their capacity to give the information is sufficiently supported by their experience level. Moreover, this personal attribute has usually nothing or perhaps lack of knowledge towards the certain object. In this view, through boosting the commitment to seek further about the knowledge, the potentials to bring along with possessing the sufficient information could be started with keeping trying the certain act in

a wisely procedural stage. As indicated in the following Arabic proverb, *man qāla lā adrī wa huwa yata'allam afḍalu miman yadrī wa huwa yata'ẓẓam*, it has the meaning that "He who states 'I have no idea' and learns is better than him who knows but puffs himself up"). As a result, the further consequence points out that it is necessary to have a scale of conscious effort together with continued learning from others, even if already known of certain object. In this view, the necessary point in searching for the knowledge sufficiently with information related would give the raise of worldview in looking at a whole context of certain issues (Huda et al., 2017d). As the particular attribution of gaining the better result in finding the one with more experience of the certain subject, this category would enable him to enhance their capacity through getting much more inquiry with listening. Since this attainment could be performed through within or outside the environment of formal instruction in the sense which upholds the update from others to elevate his or her own ideas, experience and expertise (Kartanegara & Huda, 2016). In particular, such potentials here refer to maintain the sustenance of open-mindedness in order to have a wide willingness to share with others from more experience. It is necessary to point out expanding the virtuous basis with intelligence in creating such individual quality.

In further, the implication to have the environmental basis could be performed through the systematic design of curriculum instruction involved into the virtuous open mindedness. Moreover, the point of particular basis on T&L instruction should be transmitted by continuing the extent of consistency on the specific goal transformed with the ethical engagement. Both moral responsibility and religious principle set into designing the better goal are in line with staying consistent towards focusing on giving the insightful value for the technical guideline in facilitating the wide achievement in responding the challenges within appropriate and wise approach (Huda et al., 2019; Huda et al., 2018a; Huda et al., 2018b; Weinberger et al., 2018). With enhancing the critical discourse in T&L instruction in leading to the learning quality, attempts to shape the individual quality to achieve the successful attainment should do with enabling the learning potentials through the wide range of mechanical process transformed in creating the strategic principles as the wide application to deal with the challenges for both todays' time and future unpredictable circumstance. In this view, both ethical and rational basis in the attempts to carry out the guidelines principle for the necessary acts need to perform the designed purpose in enabling the learning quality basis to maximise the expertise and experiences in enhancing the wide contribution for the beneficial value in the societal circumstance. As such, the extent of experience and expertise which the individual quality can perform refers to the point of ultimate goal on the way to manage wisely of the certain programs designed in the education system built-in to the fundamental strategic principles of Islamic values. Moreover, the comprehensive attainment of behaving the proper way in assisting to maintain the society might have a continued discipline engaged into the learning process context.

Moral Responsibility as Competence Skills for Learning Quality

As the prominent element in the learning process, the strategic principle in underlying the knowledge inquiry could be transmitted into the particular point involving the critical way of thinking together with solving skills for problematic discourse. The main feature here refers to make a beneficial value through giving the reminder to accelerate the active point to have a critical look towards the potential issues in the life circumstance such as moral decadence, distrust oriented attitude in T&L process, ethical challenges in digital tool use. In this view, the need to have a critical discourse in looking at a whole towards such phenomena potentially occurred should be taken into consideration in addressing the way of understanding clearly with capability and experience sufficiently. Looking at the contextual point of view in the way to manage well about the life circumstance would enable the individual quality's direct settings in ensuring the capacity of thinking skills (Huda & Teh, 2018). In particular, attempts to increase the period of learning process in the school context should determine the particular concern of dynamic environment together in elevating the experiential expert with rational skills behaviour. In the effort to perform the wide range of strategic principles assigned into the comprehensive requirement in the learning process, it is necessary to make a balanced combination between the scale of cognition and psychomotor basis in ensuring the knowledge understanding and professional ability in solving the emerging problem whether they are in the school or in the society context. As such, possessing a well-designed curriculum, in this context, should bring along with moral obligation in enabling the individual quality to have a sufficient knowledge understanding, so that such valuable insights on knowing what to do and how to do wisely could be achieved in a particular condition, like in emergency cases on careless issues or less empathy in the society (Lauermann, 2014; Levy, 2014). At this point of view, the wide ability to have an entirely critical look towards the certain issues is required to begin with learning by doing from others' more experience and expert in the related field. This is to ensure the potential value could be gained appropriately by considering the moral responsibility. Consequently, the teaching quality basis has to be generated into the current trends of digitalization such as social media or smartphone as the instruction medium (Anshari et al., 2017). Moreover, the comprehensive combination between mind and practice mapping could be determined in the T&L process entirely with providing the ability skills to solve the issues. Since the extent of individual quality is shaped by the environment basis condition, it is necessary to plan the basic value in managing the wide practice to ensure the potentials of behaviour in order to assist the sustenance of moral substance in line with Islamic values.

In line with granting the learning quality, the necessary point to transmit the wide opportunity of accessing the problem solving skills which the learners can adopt should bring along with the systematic principles in assisting the capable potentials. As such, the effort to apply for the additional programs planned in the curricula activities is potentially needed to get the assessment in underlying their implementation strategy by utilising the technological device in the basis of digital tool (Huda, 2019). Through extensive observation assigned into the curricular activities, the strategic principles should take a wide collaboration with expanding the networking alliance on T&L technology in ensuring the quality performance under the controlled management. Incorporating the teaching performance in enabling the moral enhancement transmitted into the well-being, both inside and outside circumstance could create the situation where they can support each other in elevating the entire process of knowledge transfer within the right path of strategic comprehensive learning (Huda et al., 2016). In the context of Islamic point of view, such comprehensive requirements may have an essential rule in enabling T&L under the required transmission incorporated into the distinctive feature of guidelines, so that the entire process could go through the curriculum design within the planning and management. In the basis of T&L, al-Zarnūjī (2008) suggests that there are wide range of distinctive approaches in enabling such process in the knowledge transfer collaborated into the subject matters, including lecture program, talk show or even public lecture, where the contextual approach may also be expanded referring to the contemporary situation. Attempts to achieve the main goal of T&L should do with preserving such comprehensive principles particularly through making a diary list apart from listening. Moreover, such core features derive from the way to observe carefully about the phenomenon wisely in the basis of behaving calmly within possessing trust in God (*tawakkul*), where such components could give an insightful value to manifest the moral values in underlying the interaction among them appropriately and properly (Huda et al., 2019). In the wide range of skills performance to enhance the learning oriented enhancement, the combination between wise-based problem solving and behavioural capability should be incorporated in transforming in planning and management.

In terms of incorporating the aims on developing the personal and social ability skills, making the condition where T&L can have a fundamental sphere in enabling the entire process to run appropriately and wisely, the wide ability in the stages of conditioning both inside and outside basis designed into the classroom with a holistic procedure should bring along with enhancing the learners' continuing personal-awareness. Moreover, an obligation to go through the entire processes of T&L in supporting the life circumstance outside the classroom basis could expand the point of view in transmitting the comprehensive requirements to underlie the learning process (Huda et al., 2016b). As an attempt to elucidate the potential value of fulfilling the requirements in expanding the strategic principles with a comprehensive scale, the learning comprehension could be largely transformed into the technological skills in the basis of appropriate and proper way. Expanding the comprehensive learning requirements refers to enhance the strategic basis on elucidating the wide range of potentials with a valuable point of view in enabling the learners to have fulfilment on such fundamental notion as the basic element of T&L process (Slade & Prinsloo, 2013). In this view, getting improved with such attempt through strengthening the initial expertise on problem-solving skills is required to behave in fulfilling the principles as a guideline for T&L in incorporating the number of skills capabilities. At this point of view, the abilities to have a good preparation to solve the complex issues possibly emerged along with the number of global trends as the challenges are in line with underlining the potential major of basic components adopted in the curriculum activities. As such, the customised skills on learning itself need to empower the training program in elevating the development procedure stages to make the substantive target towards the scale of mind and spirituality combination to enlarge the personal behaviour in underlying the social orientation activities. This would lead to all learners to have an enough planning to meet the emerging challenges in the sense that can be transformed into soul and physical orientation (al-Zarnūjī, 2008). In the attempts to design such training programs to develop the goal as a vision to achieve, bridging the connection of building the soul basis should bring along with expanding the spiritual path to support the discipline sustenance in underlying the social orientation. As a central element in enabling to work hard in both school basis and social context, managing the substance of discipline in continuing self-control may imply with carrying out responsibilities to enlarge the T&L process. In this view, having such components including careful arrangement together with reflection to apply for the assessment programs would lead to commit with achieving the skilful creativity assigned into discipline.

In further, the committed awareness of making careful arrangements to have a point of skilful abilities plays a key role in guiding the entire process of learning referring to the experiential basis of teaching performance. As such, showing the creative components in underlying the thinking skills and practical stage is widely necessary to commit with both ethical and technical features in ensuring all sides to move hand-in-hand basis orientation. In this view, the teaching performance could be a comprehensive role in educating, coaching, and transferring the knowledge with such information related to the learners' need (Huda et al., 2017e; Maseleno et al., 2017). While expounding the above corporations in leading ultimately into the all-inclusive programs, promoting the personal-based critical thinking skills to have a substantive motivation is undoubtedly the first stage of gaining the introspection committed to the willingness in enhancing the responsibility capacity. In the attempts to encourage the capacity of self-confidence, gaining the mutual commitment should bring along with quality performance of self-assurance assigned into compounding the valuable insights of self-determining thinking. In particular, the wide range of spiritual endurance in making the individual quality with the basis of *insān al-kāmil*, perfect element of spiritual and cognitive distinction (Ghorbani et al., 2016), refers to gather the extensive elaboration of experiential learning which the Muslim society can have access to deal with in the contemporary circumstance amidst the digital age (Huda et al., 2017f; Idris, 2017). Through incorporating beyond directing the mutual assistance of T&L basic performance, bringing together with managing the comprehensive instruction referring to the Islamic point of view is necessary to have sustenance of providing the mutual support to achieve outcome based instruction design fitting to the current demand within following the Islamic education goal (Halstead, 2004; Huda and Kartanegara, 2015). In terms of managing the development for the individual quality with nourishing the potential value of moral and spiritual behaviour attribution, the spirit of T&L should be taken into combining into the continued collective advance in the attempts to determine the education role through facilitating the all-inclusive wisdom. In particular, joining cooperation between stakeholders together with university partnership needs to release the responsibilities in ensuring the stages well performed in the controlled management. Moreover, possessing the committed initiative to achieve comprehensive learning principles should take the point of complete intelligence with learning competence. Moreover, this should be followed with having a wide learning inspiration embedded into the fortitude committed to the learning procedure orientation. In achieving the moral responsibility, fulfilling the economic sustenance has to be well prepared in providing the learning quality. Apart from this, gaining the teacher's motivation in determining the assurance should bring along with period organisation of the learning process with a crucial point of view in expanding the learning quality and moral responsibility in the educational setting platform.

CONCLUSION

This chapter examined the moral responsibility as a fundamental goal to achieve the learning quality. Through expounding the strategic principles to enhance the basis of the distinctive point of view about moral responsibility, the main principle in maximising the learning quality in the perspective of Islamic education could be transmitted into the T&L process followed with the extensive details of a comprehensive enhancement in wide range of requirements. Among such distinction, there are three core points of view as the main characteristics of the strategic principles for the requirements to achieve the learning quality committed into the comprehensive principles of moral responsibility. Those are moral responsibility as fundamental purpose of learning process, moral responsibility as strategic principles for learning quality, and moral responsibility as competence skills for learning quality. Thus, this chapter is expected to contribute into the outstanding point of view to enlarge the learning quality procedure in the context of Islamic education contribution into the modern age of education system. Moreover, the quality instruction could be achieved through fulfilling the extensive point of addressing a significant applied performance useful to improve in T&L process. Through presenting such implementation stage in the learning rules, bringing along with a knowledgeable nature to elevate the moral responsibility should be transformed into the societal concern by maintaining the moral values attribution. In particular, the mutual appreciation has to be properly provided referring to addressing the extent of T&L process. Through promoting the learning quality with addressing the principal requirements, the outcome based instruction could be determined in the mutual engagement for classroom basis and societal orientation as an attempt to achieve the moral responsibility.

REFERENCES

Abadi, S., Teh, K.S.M., Huda, M., Hehsan, A., Ripin, M.N., Haron, Z., ... Syarifudin, A. (2018b). Design of student score application for assessing the most outstanding student at vocational high school. *International Journal of Engineering and Technology*, *7*(2.27), 172-177.

Abadi, S., Teh, K.S.M., Nasir, B.M., Huda, M., Ivanova, N.L., Sari, T.I., ... Muslihudin, M. (2018a). Application model of k-means clustering: insights into promotion strategy of vocational high school. *International Journal of Engineering and Technology*, *7*(2.27), 182-187.

Abdullah, K., & Salleh, M. A. (2015). Conceptualizing Jihad Among Southeast Asia s Radical Salafi Movements. *Journal for the Study of Religions and Ideologies*, *14*(42), 121–146.

Abu-Hussin, M. F., Salleh, M. A., & Nasir, B. M. (2015). Beyond religious affinity: Malaysia's relations with countries in the Arab Gulf. *The Pacific Review*, *28*(4), 461–482. doi:10.1080/09512748.2015.1011213

Al-Zarnūjī, B. (Ed.). (2008). Ta'lim al Muta'allim (Pedoman belajar bagi penuntun ilmu secara Islami) [Islamic students' guide for learning]. Surabaya: Menara Suci.

Aminin, S., Huda, M., Ninsiana, W., & Dacholfany, M. I. (2018). Sustaining civic-based moral values: Insights from language learning and literature. *International Journal of Civil Engineering and Technology*, *9*(4), 157–174.

Aminudin, N., Fauzi, Huda, M., Hehsan, A., Ripin, M.N., Haron, Z., ... Fauzi, A.M. (2018c). Application program learning based on android for students experiences. *International Journal of Engineering and Technology*, *7*(2.27), 194-198.

Aminudin, N., Huda, M., Ihwani, S.S., Noor, S.S.M., Basiron, B., Jasmi, K.A., ... Rohmadi, D. (2018a). The family hope program using AHP method. *International Journal of Engineering and Technology, 7*(2.27), 188-193.

Aminudin, N., Huda, M., Mohamed, A.K., Embong, W.H.W., Mohamad, A.M., Basiron, B., ... Nungsiati. (2018b). Higher education selection using simple additive weighting. *International Journal of Engineering and Technology*, *7*(2.27), 211-217.

Anshari, M., Almunawar, M. N., Shahrill, M., Wicaksono, D. K., & Huda, M. (2017). Smartphones usage in the classrooms: Learning aid or interference? *Education and Information Technologies*, *22*(6), 3063–3079. doi:10.100710639-017-9572-7

Asadullah, M. N. (2016). Trust, trustworthiness, and traditional Islamic education. *Oxford Development Studies*, *44*(2), 152–166. doi:10.1080/13600818.2015.1104294

Bakar, O. (2015). *Islamic civilisation and the modern world: Thematic essays*. Bandar Seri Begawan, Brunei: UBD Press.

Bensaid, B., Machouche, S. B. T., & Grine, F. (2014). A Qur'anic framework for spiritual intelligence. *Religions*, *5*(1), 179–198. doi:10.3390/rel5010179

Choudhury, M. A. (2018). The ontological law of Tawhid contra 'Shari'ah-compliance' in Islamic portfolio finance. *International Journal of Law and Management*, *60*(2), 413–434. doi:10.1108/IJLMA-01-2017-0001

Fahriana, A. S., & Huda, M. (2019). Application of Analysis of Strengths, Weaknesses, Opportunities, and Threats in Islamic Education Institutions. *Istawa: Jurnal Pendidikan Islam*, *4*(1), 50–64. doi:10.24269/ijpi.v4i1.1670

Fauzi, I., Irviani, R., Muslihudin, M., Satria, F., Huda, M., Kamenez, N. V., & Maseleno, A. (2019). Revolutionizing Education through Artificial Intelligence: Fuzzy Multiple Attribute Decision Making Approach for Determining the Best Vocational High School. *Applied Mechanics and Materials*, *892*, 234–239. doi:10.4028/www.scientific.net/AMM.892.234

Forbes, M., & Baker, W. (2017). Moral Values and Market Attitudes. In Markets, Morals, and Religion (pp. 43-50). Routledge.

Ghorbani, N., Watson, P. J., Omidbeiki, M., & Chen, Z. J. (2016). Muslim attachments to God and the "perfect man"(Ensān-e Kāmel): Relationships with religious orientation and psychological adjustment in Iran. *Psychology of Religion and Spirituality*, *8*(4), 318–329. doi:10.1037/rel0000084

Halstead, M. (2004). An Islamic concept of education. *Comparative Education*, *40*(4), 517–529. doi:10.1080/0305006042000284510

Halstead, M. (2019). New Directions in Islamic Education: Pedagogy and Identity Formation By ABDULLAH SAHIN. *Journal of Islamic Studies*, *30*(2), 286–288. doi:10.1093/jis/etz006

Huda, M., Jasmi, K. A., Alas, Y., Qodriah, S. L., Dacholfany, M. I., & Jamsari, E. A. (2018c). Empowering civic responsibility: insights from service learning. *Engaged Scholarship and Civic Responsibility in Higher Education*, 144-165.

Huda, M., Jasmi, K. A., Basiran, B., Mustari, M. I. B., & Sabani, A. N. (2017a). Traditional Wisdom on Sustainable Learning: An Insightful View From Al-Zarnuji's Ta 'lim al-Muta 'allim. *SAGE Open*, *7*(1), 1–8. doi:10.1177/2158244017697160

Huda, M., Jasmi, K. A., Hehsan, A., Mustari, M. I., Shahrill, M., Basiron, B., & Gassama, S. K. (2017d). Empowering children with adaptive technology skills: Careful engagement in the digital information age. *International Electronic Journal of Elementary Education*, *9*(3), 693–708.

Huda, M., Jasmi, K. A., Mohamed, A. K., Wan Embong, W. H., & Safar, J. (2016a). Philosophical Investigation of Al-Zarnuji's Ta'lim al-Muta'allim: Strengthening Ethical Engagement into Teaching and Learning. *Social Science*, *11*(22), 5516–5551.

Huda, M., Jasmi, K. A., Mustari, M. I., Basiron, B., Mohamed, A. K., Embong, W., ... Safar, J. (2017). Innovative E-Therapy Service in Higher Education: Mobile Application Design. *International Journal of Interactive Mobile Technologies*, *11*(4), 83–94. doi:10.3991/ijim.v11i4.6734

Huda, M., Jasmi, K. A., Mustari, M. I. B., & Basiron, A. B. (2017c). Understanding of Wara' (Godliness) as a Feature of Character and Religious Education. *Social Sciences*, *12*(6), 1106–1111.

Huda, M., & Kartanegara, M. (2015a). Islamic Spiritual Character Values of al-Zarnūjī's Ta 'līm al-Muta 'allim. *Mediterranean Journal of Social Sciences, 6*(4S2), 229-235.

Huda, M., & Kartanegara, M. (2015b). Aim formulation of education: An analysis of the Book *Ta'lm al- Muta'allim*. *International Journal of Humanities and Social Science*, *5*(2), 143–149.

Huda, M., & Kartanegara, M. (2015c). Curriculum conception in the perspective of the book ta'lim al-muta'allim. *International Journal of Education and Research*, *3*(2), 221–232.

Huda, M., & Kartanegara, M. (2015d). Distinctive feature of Al-Zarnûjî's ideas: A philosophical inquiry into the book *Ta'lim al-Muta'allim*. *American International Journal of Contemporary Research*, *5*(2), 171–177.

Huda, M., & Kartanegara, M. (2015e). Ethical Foundation of Character Education in Indonesia: Reflections on Integration between Ahmad Dahlan and al-Zarnūjī. *International Conference of Malay Muslim Prominent Scholars. Selangor: Kolej Universiti Islam Antarbangsa (KUIS)*.

Huda, M., Maseleno, A., Jasmi, K. A., Mustari, I., & Basiron, B. (2017f). Strengthening Interaction from Direct to Virtual Basis: Insights from Ethical and Professional Empowerment. *International Journal of Applied Engineering Research*, *12*(17), 6901–6909.

Huda, M., Mulyadi, D., Hananto, A. L., Nor Muhamad, N. H., Mat Teh, K. S., & Don, A. G. (2018b). Empowering corporate social responsibility (CSR): Insights from service learning. *Social Responsibility Journal*, *14*(4), 875–894. doi:10.1108/SRJ-04-2017-0078

Huda, M., & Sabani, N. (2018). Empowering Muslim Children's Spirituality in Malay Archipelago: Integration between National Philosophical Foundations and Tawakkul (Trust in God). *International Journal of Children's Spirituality*, *23*(1), 81–94. doi:10.1080/1364436X.2018.1431613

Huda, M., Sabani, N., Shahrill, M., Jasmi, K. A., Basiron, B., & Mustari, M. I. (2017b). Empowering Learning Culture as Student Identity Construction in Higher Education. In A. Shahriar & G. Syed (Eds.), *Student Culture and Identity in Higher Education* (pp. 160–179). Hershey, PA: IGI Global. doi:10.4018/978-1-5225-2551-6.ch010

Huda, M., & Siregar, M., Rahman, S.K.A., Mat Teh, K.S., Said, H., Jamsari, E.A., … Ninsiana, W. (2017e). From Live Interaction to Virtual Interaction: An Exposure on the Moral Engagement in the Digital Era. *Journal of Theoretical and Applied Information Technology*, *95*(19), 4964–4972.

Huda, M., Sudrajat, S., Kawangit, R. M., Teh, K. S. M., & Jalal, B. (2019). Strengthening divine values for self-regulation in religiosity: Insights from *Tawakkul* (trust in God). *International Journal of Ethics and Systems*, IJOES-02-2018-0025. doi:10.1108/IJOES-02-2018-0025

Huda, M., & Teh, K. S. M. (2018). Empowering Professional and Ethical Competence on Reflective Teaching Practice in Digital Era. In K. Dikilitas, E. Mede, & D. Atay (Eds.), *Mentorship Strategies in Teacher Education* (pp. 136–152). Hershey, PA: IGI Global. doi:10.4018/978-1-5225-4050-2.ch007

Huda, M., Teh, K. S. M., Nor, N. H. M., & Nor, M. B. M. (2018a). Transmitting Leadership Based Civic Responsibility: Insights from Service Learning. *International Journal of Ethics and Systems*, *34*(1), 20–31. doi:10.1108/IJOES-05-2017-0079

Huda, M., Yusuf, J. B., Jasmi, K. A., & Nasir, G. A. (2016b). Understanding Comprehensive Learning Requirements in the Light of al-Zarnūjī's Ta'līm al-Muta'allim. *SAGE Open*, *6*(4), 1–14. doi:10.1177/2158244016670197

Huda, M., Yusuf, J. B., Jasmi, K. A., & Zakaria, G. N. (2016c). Al-Zarnūjī's Concept of Knowledge ('ilm). *SAGE Open*, *6*(3), 1–13. doi:10.1177/2158244016666885

Hussien, S., Hashim, R., & Mokhtar, N. A. M. (2017). Hikmah Pedagogy. In *Interfaith Education for All* (pp. 97–106). Rotterdam: SensePublishers. doi:10.1007/978-94-6351-170-4_8

Idris, S. (2017). Insan Kamil: Theological and Psychological Perspective. *Asian Journal of Social Science. Art and Humanities*, *5*(2), 9–28.

Jonassen, D. H., & Grabowski, B. L. (2012). *Handbook of individual differences, learning, and instruction*. London: Routledge.

Kartanegara, M., & Huda, M. (2016). Constructing civil society: an Islamic cultural perspective. *Mediterranean Journal of Social Sciences, 7*(1 S1), 126.

Kirat, M. (2015). The Islamic roots of modern public relations and corporate social responsibility. *International Journal of Islamic Marketing and Branding*, *1*(1), 97–112. doi:10.1504/IJIMB.2015.068144

Lauermann, F. (2014). Teacher responsibility from the teacher's perspective. *International Journal of Educational Research*, *65*, 75–89. doi:10.1016/j.ijer.2013.09.005

Levy, N. (2014). *Consciousness and moral responsibility*. Oxford University Press. doi:10.1093/acprof:oso/9780198704638.001.0001

Maseleno, A., Pardimin, Huda, M., Ramlan, Hehsan, A., Yusof, Y.M., ... Junaidi, J. (2018a). Mathematical Theory of Evidence to Subject Expertise Diagnostic. *ICIC Express Letters*, *12*(4), 369. doi:10.24507/icicel.12.04.369

Maseleno, A., Huda, M., Jasmi, K. A., Basiron, B., Mustari, I., Don, A. G., & Ahmad, R. (2019a). Hau-Kashyap approach for student's level of expertise. *Egyptian Informatics Journal*, *20*(1), 27–32. doi:10.1016/j.eij.2018.04.001

Maseleno, A., Huda, M., Siregar, M., Ahmad, R., Hehsan, A., Haron, Z., ... Jasmi, K. A. (2017). Combining the Previous Measure of Evidence to Educational Entrance Examination. *Journal of Artificial Intelligence*, *10*(3), 85–90. doi:10.3923/jai.2017.85.90

Maseleno, A., Sabani, N., Huda, M., Ahmad, R., Jasmi, K. A., & Basiron, B. (2018c). Demystifying Learning Analytics in Personalised Learning. *IACSIT International Journal of Engineering and Technology*, *7*(3), 1124–1129. doi:10.14419/ijet.v7i3.9789

Maseleno, A., Shankar, K., Huda, M., Othman, M., Khoir, P., & Muslihudin, M. (2019b). Citizen Economic Level (CELL) using SAW. *Expert Systems in Finance: Smart Financial Applications in Big Data Environments*, 97.

Mohd Yusob, M. L., Salleh, M. A., Haron, A. S., Makhtar, M., Asari, K. N., & Jamil, L. S. M. (2015). Maqasid al-Shariah as a Parameter for Islamic Countries in Screening International Treaties Before Ratification: An Analysis. *Pertanika Journal of Social Science & Humanities*, 23.

Moksin, A. I., Shahrill, M., Anshari, M., Huda, M., & Tengah, K. A. (2018). The Learning of Integration in Calculus Using the Autograph Technology. *Advanced Science Letters*, *24*(1), 550–552. doi:10.1166/asl.2018.12067

Naufal, M. A., Atan, N. A., Abdullah, A. H., & Abu, M. S. (2017). Problem Solving, Based On Metacognitive Learning Activities, To Improve Mathematical Reasoning Skills Of Students. *Man in India*, *97*(12), 213–220.

Osguthorpe, R. D. (2015). On the reasons we want teachers of good disposition and moral character. *Journal of Teacher Education*, *59*(4), 288–299. doi:10.1177/0022487108321377

Othman, R., Shahrill, M., Mundia, L., Tan, A., & Huda, M. (2016). Investigating the Relationship Between the Student's Ability and Learning Preferences: Evidence from Year 7 Mathematics Students. *The New Educational Review*, *44*(2), 125–138.

Paramboor, J., & Ibrahim, M. B. (2014). Educational leadership as a manifestation of 'Adab' in education: Conception of Zarnuji. *International Journal of Education and Research, 2*(3), 1–12.

Robinson, S. J., & Smith, J. (2012). Exploring responsibility. *Journal of Global Responsibility, 3*(1), 151–166.

Rosli, M. R. B., Salamon, H. B., & Huda, M. (2018). Distribution Management of Zakat Fund: Recommended Proposal for Asnaf Riqab in Malaysia. *International Journal of Civil Engineering and Technology, 9*(3), 56–64.

Runesson, U. (2015). Pedagogical and learning theories and the improvement and development of lesson and learning studies. *International Journal for Lesson and Learning Studies, 4*(3), 186–193. doi:10.1108/IJLLS-04-2015-0016

Sabani, N., Hardaker, G., Sabki, A., & Salleh, S. (2016). Understandings of Islamic pedagogy for personalised learning. *The International Journal of Information and Learning Technology, 33*(2), 78–90. doi:10.1108/IJILT-01-2016-0003

Sahlan, M. K., Abu-Hussin, M. F., & Hehsan, A. (2018). Market coopetition: Implications of religious identity in creating value added partnership within halal mart retailers. *Journal of Islamic Marketing.*

Shen, L., & Su, A. (2019). Intervention of Smartphone Addiction. In *Multifaceted Approach to Digital Addiction and Its Treatment* (pp. 207–228). IGI Global. doi:10.4018/978-1-5225-8449-0.ch010

Sugiyarti, E., Jasmi, K. A., Basiron, B., Huda, M., Shankar, K., & Maseleno, A. (2018). Decision support system of scholarship grantee selection using data mining. *International Journal of Pure and Applied Mathematics, 119*(15), 2239–2249.

Susilowati, T., Dacholfany, M.I., Aminin, S., Ikhwan, A., Nasir, B.M., Huda, M., … Wulandari. (2018b). Getting parents involved in child's school: using attendance application system based on SMS gateway. *International Journal of Engineering and Technology, 7*(2.27), 167-174.

Susilowati, T., Jasmi, K.A., Basiron, B., Huda, M., Shankar, K., Maseleno, A., & Julia, A. (2018a). Determination of Scholarship Recipients Using Simple Additive Weighting Method. *International Journal of Pure and Applied Mathematics, 119*(15), 2231–2238.

Susilowati, T., Teh, K.S.M., Nasir, B.M., Don, A.G., Huda, M., Hensafitri, T., … Irawan, D. (2018c). Learning application of Lampung language based on multimedia software. *International Journal of Engineering and Technology, 7*(2.27), 175-181.

Tamam, E., & Krauss, S. E. (2017). Ethnic-related diversity engagement differences in intercultural sensitivity among Malaysian undergraduate students. *International Journal of Adolescence and Youth*, 22(2), 137–150. doi:10.1080/02673843.2014.881295

Wani, H., Abdullah, R., & Chang, L. (2015). An Islamic perspective in managing religious diversity. *Religions*, 6(2), 642–656. doi:10.3390/rel6020642

Weinberger, A., Biedermann, H., Patry, J. L., & Weyringer, S. (Eds.). (2018). *Professionals' Ethos and Education for Responsibility*. BRILL.

Wulandari, Aminin, S., Dacholfany, M.I., Mujib, A., Huda, M., Nasir, B.M., … Masrur, M. (2018). Design of library application system. *International Journal of Engineering and Technology*, 7(2.27), 199-204.

Yusob, M. M., Salleh, M. A., Ariffin, M. R., & Mohamed, A. N. H. (2017). International Religious Freedom Act 1998 and the Issues of Religious Freedom in Muslim Countries. *Pertanika Journal of Social Science & Humanities*, 25, 231–239.

Chapter 13
Empowering Learning Ethics Culture in Islamic Education

Miftachul Huda
ⓘD https://orcid.org/0000-0001-6712-0056
Universiti Pendidikan Sultan Idris, Malaysia

Khoirurrijal Khoirurrijal
State Institute for Islamic Studies (IAIN) Metro Lampung, Indonesia

M. Ihsan Dacholfany
Universitas Muhammdiyah Metro Lampung, Indonesia

Susminingsih Susminingsih
State Institute of Islamic Studies (IAIN) Pekalongan, Indonesia

Azmil Hashim
Universiti Pendidikan Sultan Idris, Malaysia

Nurazmalail Marni
Universiti Teknologi Malaysia, Malaysia

Ahmad Kilani Mohamed
Universiti Teknologi Malaysia, Malaysia

Madheil Azaeim Ahmad Puad
Universiti Kebangsaan Malaysia, Malaysia

Mohd Hilmi Rozali
Universiti Teknologi Malaysia, Malaysia

Andino Maseleno
Universiti Tenaga Nasional Malaysia, Malaysia

Nasrul Hisyam Nor Muhamad
Universiti Teknologi Malaysia, Malaysia

Afiful Ikhwan
ⓘD https://orcid.org/0000-0002-6412-3830
Universitas Muhammadiyah Ponorogo, Indonesia

DOI: 10.4018/978-1-5225-8528-2.ch013

INTRODUCTION

In the educational field, the learning acquisition has an important role to play in enhancing the personal growth and social responsibility (Aminin et al., 2018; Huda et al., 2018a; Rosli et al., 2018). This can be seen from the curriculum design prepared for the learning process from a variety of sides, such as content of book, learning strategy appointment and also the spiritual processing which underlies the students' emotional and creative thinking (Furnham, Monsen & Ahmetoglu, 2009). The latter would become an important part to the inner state management. Among the school holders, they need to take care in performing the inner state among their students, since it can improve the individual inner to drive their deed between learning and other activities well in the way that can be balanced to the societal and individual concern (Wenger, 2010).

Moreover, it may become an outstanding concern which needs to pay attention on how to actually manage the goal itself to enable in getting well. Since every deed is inextricable link to the process to get possessing a goal, learning strategy activity is necessary to have a clear purpose to implement well in the way that can guide students in the school context (Huda & Kartanegara, 2015a; Slade & Prinsloo, 2013). Moreover, there has been scholarly attention to concern further on managing ethical and strategical consideration in the learning goal. To get the value to run the learning goal in the inner process among the students, the need to employ well on the learning acquisition in the perspective of Islamic classical heritage is significant to underlie the way on pursuing the foundational element to drive a goal in learning in the Islamic perspective. With this regard, this chapter will explore the ethics and strategy which can be implemented with considering attention to the learning goal among the students.

LITERATURE REVIEW

Significance of Learning Goal in Islam

As priming mechanism to design the learning purpose through its content, it can be prepared to achieve expectations for the learning outcome. Since learning purpose is the outcome which is supposed to enhance the standard of human quality in terms of cognitive, affective and psychomotor aspect, it can be employed from the curriculum design which underlies to drive the educational process with understanding the rules as in the guidelines (Elliott, 2015). In other words, it enables students to understand the content designed in the curriculum. In particular, the attempts to emphasise the knowledge inquiry and transfer in enabling to grow into achieving the maturity should bring along with developing the potentials for committing with the virtuous behaviours (Halstead, 2004). With this regard, the educational concern of the learning goal needs to always getting tied with a significant essence of the inner and outer management on the students learning. It is necessary to have a wide commitment with an attempt to create the good personality by which to address the stage of understanding the rules of Islamic behaviour together with committed awareness of sufficient knowledge and information shaped into the learning purpose (Huda & Kartanegara, 2015b). In particular, it has a meaning to do with morality to underlie an effort to create the good human personality. The personality resulted from the learning goal may enhance the expectations of students in providing the support to their performance between within and outside learning.

Since learning purpose in education should be prepared with an effort to attain the expectation, the implementation needs to be considered with forming the commitment oriented to the well-made plan (Mohd Yusob et al., 2015; Roorda et al., 2011). As a component of education to prepare early period of learning and teaching, the learning qualified with the effort to prepare in facing the challenges and prospects becomes a basic foundation to achieve the learning goal. It is important to consider that as the termination of all the activity, the learning goal has a characteristic on the dynamic nature to the development of human life (Salleh et al., 2015; Slade & Prinsloo, 2013). It refers to an essential dimension to achieve the successful attainment in the extent of learning process and teaching performance. In this view, getting improvement with the balance between technique and achievement target should bring along with designing the purpose oriented give an insightful value in guiding the process and action on the right way. In terms of the purpose with the role to control such implementation in teaching and learning process, focusing on the effort with the measurement and evaluation can be integrated to give the enlightenment to these endeavours in education (Anshari et al., 2017; Wenger, 2010). In particular, the well appropriate combination between goal orientation and implementation form should bring along with making positive feedback into the human potency, the needs for society, and the model point of Islamic life aspect (Huda and Sabani, 2018). To implement in nowadays education system through these four kinds, the learning goal could be attained to the focus lesson in demonstrating concepts balanced with skills.

With regard to educating students a clear purpose prepared to recognise the right and responsibility it is important to consider an effort to study in cooperation between both achieving the goal purpose and solving the problems (Jonassen & Grabowski, 2012). The quality to measure the success of education becomes significant to cultivate the person with knowledge and values oriented to the self-arrangement in facing the challenges (Brophy, 2013). In the Islamic point of view, the dimension of Islamic education is coverage into morality, spirituality and knowledge ability in the sense that can give valuable insights into the experiential paths of life guidance in order to achieve the successful attainment between life here and hereafter. Consequently, the extent of curriculum together with its practical implication needs to be performed appropriately to achieve the human personality incorporated into the dimensional part among spirituality, morality and cognitive ability.

Comprehensive Process Learning in Islamic Education

Learning could be conceived at a whole as an attempt to acquire knowledge to be critical thinking and also to pursue the skill which can be practised for doing something useful (Slade & Prinsloo, 2013). The ability to learn can happen continuously within the person's lifetime as the most outstanding characteristics for the human being (Huda et al, 2016a). It indicates that the entire attempts to have a mutual line of creating the personal quality needs to have a wide combination between experiential basis and knowledge understanding with an insightful value of the way on transforming the beginning until the result of such process. With this regard, the intellectual and spiritual aspect should be formed into pointing out the behavioural skills in building the extent of experiential paths, in the sense that can be improved to exercise judgement through such characteristics to solve problems (Fahriana & Huda, 2019). Enhancing the significant part of the certain principles to implement amidst the society orientation refers to adopt the potential skills, knowledge understanding, and behavioural attitudes in a particular point of view explored to get improve the entire process of learning.

In line with such process, the extent of learning process could be determined in developing the core stages towards what the teachers transfer through giving the lecture of certain subject, and also giving the students' commitment to conduct their certain assignment, where all such process should bring along with forming the committed awareness of divine involvement (*tawakkal*) (Al-Zarnūjī, 2008). These should become a core point of view in terms of such stages based on the way which should be considered in particular (Huda et al., 2019a). Since the learning process could adopt the number of activities from planning until implementation management, the wide combination between knowledge, behaviour and skills has to be incorporated in resulting the development stage in underlying the performance in the context of training and schooling (Jonassen & Grabowski, 2012). It can be seen that learning is actually a process through procedural stages (Brophy, 2013). Approached by several experiments, it is essential to point out that considering the guidelines rules to interact entirely with an environmental sphere, the classroom quality in the experience context is central to improve the extent of learning commitment in the holistic process in achieving the extent of committed awareness together with an in-depth understanding stage of certain phenomena, in the sense that can give insights into the social and individual balance.

In terms of enhancing the balance between social and individual side, the need to empower spiritual and mental ethics should be taken into consideration in attaining the particular efforts with the opportunities to take benefit of learning process. Attempts to shape the way of seeking knowledge by incorporating the appropriate approach refers to the particular initiative by which the goals will be associated with the method of learning (Mu'izzuddin, 2014; Paramboor & Ibrahim, 2014). The adoption of getting the recommendation towards the learning method needs to have the instructional basis with a practical stage commended into maximizing the time given to drive a right path of cognitive, spiritual and mental substance in the basis of outcome orientation to give insightful value of putting the moral message from what teachers have been conducting into practice (Grunebaum & Abel, 1947; Hafidzah, 2014; Huda & Kartanegara, 2015c). In this view, al-Zarnūjī proposed the conceptual framework as stated in his work that the learning benefit can be taken seriously in producing the intellectual circumstance committed into the strategic principles in enhancing the moral developments amongst the students.

In order to understand how the students should learn which can be caused by learning environment, it is necessary to further elucidate integrated principles as core guideline which addresses instructions through program and training which may be seriously concerned with how they learn. This can become an occasion to consider in particular solving through wise approach in the sense that an alternative tool through incorporating peers management may have chance to accelerate the extent of networking in giving the influential platform to have a significant point of view in supporting the learning instruction process (Atmotiyoso and Huda, 2018). Therefore, the optimization on both should be considered in a particular way as an attempt to assist in producing the environmental basis in enabling the students to maximise their potentials to have a sufficient experience of learning and also to have wide support from their peers as well. It is significant to take a point of view that the role of certain guideline is actually needed to keep on learning with conditioning moral purpose.

Learning Ethics With Personal Qualities as Learning Goal

About ethical consideration in the learning goal, choosing the portion of the study and the teachers is determined as students' responsibility. As al-Zarnūjī pointed out, having a wide commitment of gaining the purpose should be clearly arranged with designing the time management in dealing with the learning process. This indicates that attempts to consider in particular way towards the moral aspect needs to bring along with careful attention to determine the extent of knowledge benefit, together with teaching guidance and also their peer experience (Huda & Kartanegara, 2015d; Yahya, 2005). He draws a picture on the key point to how the student should manage his or her self-determination in choosing peers and teachers as indicated in the basis of needs and demands. As a result, the student should be wisely determined in particular in the sense that the person has to consider carefully thinking and rethinking through consultation.

In this regard, al-Zarnūjī points out that the particular initiative in searching for personal qualities with the balance of moral, spiritual and intellectual substance criteria could give a point of view in enabling the performance orientation to achieve the goal of learning itself. Those include the fully personal determination, partly determined personality and totally ignorant quality, where all these have been the one particular stage of personal orientation. These three main kinds of human being with regard to quality of learning dynamics refer to how some potencies and supervised vision could be united and developed within the instruction (Nor & Malim, 2014; Mansor et al., 2015; Paramboor & Ibrahim, 2014). In terms of the three kinds of human being, al-Zarnūjī (2008) addresses these as in the following. The first is perfect human who possesses a right opinion and often consults with the intelligent people. It means the good potency with good counselling will result the good personality with wise view and tolerance. Through considering a special attention to the good supervision and counselling, the students for example will feel engaged with the school's instruction and teacher's guidance (Roorda et al, 2011). The second one is half human referring to the one with a right opinion but no effort to consult with people. In particular, he is the one who consults with others, but no opinion for himself. When student has an opinion in line with good analysis, critical views and ability to recognise, answer and solve the problems and certain case, but it is not balance with open-minded where the personal quality should open to listen, see and consider receipt, then the new idea which may perhaps be not recognised to further identify from others would not ever come to his or her part of knowledge (Salleh et al., 2015; Salleh, 2013a). The third one is the one with neither else of knowledge information involving a right opinion nor consultation and seeking information with others.

As a result, there should be any effort to search for the knowledge information by retrieving the one with experience in any subject. The main effort of this person lies on referring to whomever with expertise and experience to always open minded combined with controlling careful view (Mohd Yusob et al., 2015; Mansor et al., 2015; Rissanen, 2012; Salleh, 2013a). Moreover, the blessings will come to the study model with this manner, where there would be much knowledge to come up with thinking and feeling. The point of view is that the education, learning and teaching should be considered to refer such effort through goal setting and prayer setting as a significant role for being a wise person with ethical consideration in the learning process. Al-Zarnūjī believes that the moral purpose underlying learning process should make much more on the core point of general view where the student must have some aspiration and goal to reach all the perseverance and repetitive study (Huda et al, 2016a). From this perspective, recognizing learning as a mechanical aid and rule through such core elements such as guidelines, programs and instruction terms is particularly a part of pursuing the learning achievements (Othman et al., 2016). In this regard, learning achievement comes from learning feeling with such purposes well prepared. In terms of cognitive, affective and psychomotor aspect, the gap area still needs to further develop how the way used to increase learning achievement through instruction becomes a point of view to make students get engaged with core element in learning where both considering intention and paying special attention to the perseverance is a key point of successful instruction.

Since ethical consideration has a significant role to play a wide scale in spurring the student learning instruction, the moral purpose underlying learning process should make much more on well preparing general nature for future life with such challenges (Al-Zarnūjī, 2008). Similarly to contemporary's perspective, when the student is supposed to have some aspiration and goal, an effort from the perseverance and repetitive study is taken to account together with his or her will (Elliott, 2015; Huda et al., 2016b). For example, incorporating a high aspiration leading to assiduity, interest and exertion, the students will acquire the goal as arranged with prayer setting through divine involvement. It means that making an effort with considering and comprehending the sphere and condition should be engaged together with undertaking and approaching a task of learning process. Al-Zarnūjī points out that frequently the need to tackle learning process to encourage students' interest and motivation in learning should be taken account with action wholeheartedly by a combination undertaking his or her learning with underlying ethical consideration such as discipline, spirit value and respect. Thus, these key points of knowledge are taken as ethical and strategical consideration of personal qualities with sufficient incentive for intelligence in learning goal by endeavouring perseverance and removing the ignorance from him and the society.

METHODOLOGY

This chapter attempts to examine learning ethics commitment for learning achievement in Islamic education. Through elucidating the wide initiative of enhancing the strategic principles for learning quality referring to the contribution from Islamic education tradition, such extensive sustainability could be arranged into the learning quality through empowering the comprehensive principles to deal with. Through the strategic effort to promote ethical and strategical commitment with enhancing the learning quality to enhance among the students, the distinction of strategic principles are in line with the attempts to have a wide transmission committed to follow the foundational conception to support the entire process of learning quality. As the point of incorporating the learning quality enhancement rooted into the way to perform the strategic principles to deal with, attempts to demonstrate the wide range of such initiatives has to go through looking critically at the patterns and trends existed around the academia. The literature review from referred journals was conducted using keywords on examine learning commitment and learning achievement in the Islamic education. Getting such literature, an analysis was conducted by organizing substantive keywords. Then, extracting data with deep literature analysis was also employed to interpret the findings. In further, the key elements were analysed with synthesizing into new interpretations, conceptualizations, and modelling of outstanding value of strategic principles for learning quality in the basis of learning ethics commitment for learning achievement in Islamic education point of view.

ANALYSIS AND DISCUSSION

Learning Ethics Culture for Learning Achievement in Islamic Education

The learning purpose has an outstanding value to direct the outcome in in enhancing the value through the students' learning orientation. This kind of direction can be seen through the content balanced to the standard of competence which has been designed in the curriculum. In this view, al-Zarnūjī believed that the substantive message of the subject material has to be taught in a particular way in enabling the balance to commit with the moral integrity as indicated in the behaviour together with the intellectual capacity development process (Huda et al., 2016c). Moreover, the intellectual ability with problem reasoning skills has to be involved with addressing the dynamics of learning instruction to enhance the balance in monitoring process and ethical wisdom to underlie the interactional basis in the society at large. Moreover, the need to determine the contextual approach together with committed awareness of purpose orientation, knowledge understanding stage, and implementation guidelines. As such, this initiative should bring together with the entire commitment into the ethical standards in determining personal ability of recognising the problem root, for instance, so that the problem solution could be taken in the basis of needs with a wise approach (Mohamed, 2014). With this regard, cognitive ability in adopting the ability to get the clear reason may give a chance to collaborate into conceptualising the learning purpose as the main commitment to underlie in achieving the balance in all the learning process dynamics in the sense that can be maintained with producing the personal quality of wisdom and intellectual capability.

In terms of the mutual integrity between stakeholder and actor involvement in enabling the commitment to have the sufficient stage of understanding to respond the society problems, it is necessary to incorporate the Islamic education in the basis of society needs in providing the problem solving identification referring to the extent of knowledge understanding and experiential concern. In achieving the stage of clear understanding towards the real community for instance, the need to have a mutual commitment in collaborating with other partnerships has to prioritise in ensuring the wise based practice referring to the curriculum instruction together with practical stage. In this view, educating and coaching would give a chance in transmitting the value of educational purpose related to the Islamic education vision (Huda and Kartanegara, 2015d; Nuryatno, 2011). Moreover, the basis of theoretical framework which Islamic education offers is especially referring to the morality and spirituality substance in the sense that guides into the personal quality with a divine direction in underlying the life (Huda and Sabani, 2018; Jamaluddin, 2013). Among moral attitude and spiritual belief, these two particular points of view could be determined concisely to give a worthwhile consideration to expect in gaining the clear understanding towards the vision and curriculum instruction in leading to take implication into the practice. In the attempts to observe the personal quality with spiritual and intellectual balance, the integration between religious sciences and conventional knowledge in underlying the Muslim educators to make their own commitment in transferring their capacity should be taken into consideration in achieving the main goal in the teaching and learning process.

In addition, obtaining the personality development in the context of integrating both spiritual awareness and knowledge ability in achieving the human excellence need to take an essence of building the spiritual, moral and intellectual capacity (Al Hamdani, 2016; Huda et al., 2019). In the attempts to deliver the information related to develop the human capacity of such balance, designing the curriculum construction has to be fitted to the goal and vision as planned in the stakeholder's decision making within the advice under the educational council referring to the Islamic education guidelines (Al-Sharaf, 2013; Aşlamacı & Kaymakcan, 2017). Planning management referring to the goal orientation should be well prepared in fitting to condition of teaching and learning performance together with professional skills and knowledge ability as indicated in the context of competent and technical point of view. In achieving the attempts to maximise their performance, sustaining spiritual skills and religious understanding could be transmitted as the driving path of typical path in the teaching and learning purpose as indicated in the Islamic education (Izfanna & Hisyam, 2012; Tan & Ibrahim, 2017). In particular, the theoretical level needs to consider in particular in shaping the model standard of human quality with having moral and spiritual abilities. Through sustaining the goal determined in the curriculum design, the importance in building the elements of individual and social capacity balance incorporated to grow the intellectual performance in underlying the practical stage in the social interaction.

In addition, al-Zarnūjī (2008) believes that a learner who has the endeavour to learning must have the true intention as in the following:

1. To achieve the God's pleasure;
2. To attain the life success in the hereafter;
3. To remove unawareness from himself and others;
4. To recover the religious substances;
5. To sustain the Islamic faith;
6. To nurture the cognitive ability;
7. To rise the appreciation of the physical abilities.

With this regard, such intentions can be classified into three main concerns. The first is achieving divine engagement with spiritual control on every deed; the second is assisting personal development to assure the capability growth in the skill performance; applying knowledge in contributing to get involved among the society. Both social and individual development can be determined to have a significant role to the education now days. As a result, the learning purpose has extrinsically the meaning that the main point of such process of education setting should bring along with forming the clear understanding towards what to do in the context of spiritual and intellectual balance to achieve holistically.

Achieving Divine Engagement-Based Spiritual Commitment

In the attempts to achieve the learning performance together with the competent skills, the components of spiritual control in underlying the learning outcome should be determined in creating the balance extent in supporting the productive essence. Through inextricable basis on achieving this initiative, teaching and learning should start with working into building the virtuous relation in the context of attempting to consider in managing individual and social concern as the main ability to perform in both inside and outside of learning process (Abu-Hussin et al., 2015; Al Hamdani, 2016; Aşlamacı & Kaymakcan, 2017; Halstead, 2007). In the context of Islamic education perspective, both teaching and learning context should be comprehended as an attempt to gain the pleasure of worship to God, in the sense that can be attained through continued practice together with committed awareness of active participation in spiritual and social conduct (Choudhury, 2016a; Huda et al., 2019a). It is pivotal for them as a spiritual control in the learning process to enable them in paying serious attention to the immoral behaviour. This initiative has to begin with determining the early point of entire process about teaching and learning process to be reflected to have a wide component of worship path into God (Choudhury, 2016b). Inspired by the emotional state to have the reflection into worship to God, the key point of practical stage in underlying such process of teaching and learning process refers to the extent of worshipping God as indicated to be the main point of the obligation amidst the Muslim society. This refers to the Qur'an verse (al-Dzariyat: 56) that and I (God) do not create human being and genie, except for worshipping to me (God). In this view, attempts to achieve the divine engagement in the basis of spiritual commitment could be embedded as the adaptive submission to go further in the divine involvement, where the potential value to deal with such acts needs to begin with sustaining the intention as the first step on conducting the worship.

In addition, the first is the main act of worship like praying, fasting, paying zakat and performing hajj (pilgrimage). All these refer to the basic requirements as the individual capacity. Moreover, the next point here refers to the practical stage of commending to worship, one of which example could be seen such as additional prayers and fasting, making a gift to others and also performing additional task strongly recommended. In particular, the social context as valued into the worship in the context of Islamic economic growth, political decision with a wise approach of Islamic point of view, social involvement with integrity nurturance and also the social development context of comprehensive appointment in producing the spiritual growth and knowledge understanding towards the social community development (Halstead, 2007; Huda et al., 2017b; Izfanna & Hisyam, 2012). The learning process employed in sincerity to seek for the God's pleasure as the divine involvement is basically an observance (Huda et al, 2019). Moreover, the committed awareness to value the practical stage in enabling all these concise enhancements of education to run well appropriately in line with divine engagement needs to point out bringing along with the *tawakkul* as the trust in God together with the *tawhid* as the belief in God, in underlying all the activities including learning and teaching process within the balance amongst the spiritual and intellectual to lead to the moral development stage (Choudhury, 2016c; Jamaluddin, 2013). This process should be determined to underlie the development stage in transferring the knowledge understanding together with the commitment to potentially get involved in the social community as an attempt to contribute as the responsible awareness.

In order to possess the commitment of having the mutual trust and understanding in the context of social interaction, for instance, the potential capacity to enhance the personal quality to commit with the responsibility and morality has to be oriented to deal optimally with a sufficient knowledge understanding and practical continuity. At this point of view, attempts to perform in providing the inner substance of spiritual and moral spirit should be made in a particular way integrated into sustaining the responsibility engaged in expanding the society at large as the main contribution of worship in the social context (Choudhury, 2016d; Huda and Kartanegara, 2015f). In short, the significant essence of learning purpose is to give the facility to have a wide connection in worshipping to God together with performing righteousness, benevolence and exquisite goal where this may also be implementation of Divine attribute (Choudhury, 2018). It is important to take a particular point of view that the basic element as the purpose in the learning process is to seek the continued blessing and pleasure of Divine involvement as the Islamic education stressed in the main goal. This reminds us that concerning the Divine involvement as the basic element to gain the central elements to deploy in the worldly matters context. All these effort could be explored in further to have a mutual line in underlying the necessary to inculcate among the students in the educational institution today. In particular, the main emphasis as Al-Zarnūjī concerned is delivered to give the direction with both spiritual and moral obligation in nurturing the committed awareness in the learning process with such purpose (Huda et al., 2017a). As the central orientation considered in particular in both social and individual capacity development, the ultimate point in determining the educational setting is entirely on the attempts to realise the complete decision to have the continued submission to God. It is worthwhile to consider in particular getting benefit in such a way to give insights into the individual and social responsibility in the educational setting as an attempt to underlie the skill performance.

Assisting Skill Performance for Personal Capability Development

The next main point of educational goal refers to assist the personal development as one of the main goals determined in the learning process. This attempt should be inculcated into the individual capacity in the context of social community at large. The core element to be assigned with integrating both knowledge and values would assist the individual capacity to enhance the personal and social quality with a sufficient understanding towards what to do appropriately and wisely in line with committing to conduct the goodness between individual and social context. Moreover, the wide experiential capacity through learning initiative together with teaching competence should bring along with attaining the committed awareness of responsibility and duty (Huda et al., 2017b; Jamaluddin, 2013). Such quality indicator refers to the virtues of human beings who can accept the obligation and duty as the individual and social level. Amongst the key indicators to achieve the personal quality in the context of Islamic education, the needs to have the mutual acceptance between divine stewardship obligation and the real attempts through worship in both God and society transmitted with *hikmah* (wise basis). In particular, the balance between wise approach and appropriate priority could give the particular way in enhancing the competent skills together with integrity scale amongst personal commitment, spiritual spirit, intellectual ability, social feeling and heart essence to lead to reach the level of *insan kamil* (complete personal capacity), in the sense that is oriented to uphold the contextual basis in Islamic education approach (Halstead, 2019). In this view, developing the individual capacity in the context of social concern refers to the mutual line of giving the way to live within adhering the Islamic guidelines, where all such these would become a key point of worship.

In line with obliging the basic orientation to assist the individual quality, attempts to cultivate the direction path to enable the person to become good personality refers to the orientation of learning process in the view in enhancing the individual development capacity. It is pivotal to note it as a consequence to address the individual development for intellectual and physical endowment. As a result, the students should have the orientation that the learning process where both students and teachers have a relationship can be employed through comprehending and mastering the knowledge. At the same, this process can be also engaged to eliminate the scale of ignorance from the individual basis. In particular, the scale of lack of intelligence amongst the persons refers to the capacity on accessing the information available mainly in the text book in particular. This is to ensure the accuracy of information from the early part, assessed through knowledge from within and outside learning process (Huda et al, 2016b). With regard to the health body, it can give a feedback to the process among the personal level to support the learning process, so that everybody can contribute to their circumstance with knowledge. In this view, influencing the learning process of the person can be employed when the condition of both mind and body is well stabilised, since the good mind quality is situated in the good body condition. As such, empowering the mindfulness would lead to the learners to concentrate to accept knowledge which can make them gain cognitive development with intellectual ability. As a result, making concentration in accepting the knowledge is really dependent on how to manage the spirit and cognitive essence where this can be enhanced to achieve the intellectuality of individual development.

With regard to the potential essence which can be carried out through making habituation and giving example in any educational institution such as *Madrasa* (Islamic boarding) and the school, the strategic existence of the natural tendency to optimise the individual development is potentially determined to play a key role in giving the mandate to sustain the human quality. In particular, attempts to take a beneficial value through utilising the effectiveness in giving the service indicate the two main parts. One is about the task to lead in managing the world, and another one is on the real servant of God (Huda et al., 2019a). As such, it is necessary to elucidate the capacity scale of responsible awareness on achieving the experience emphasised through potentials from God to the human society at large.

By accommodating the clear understanding in enabling to continue the learning orientation through emphasising to the learners in the educational process, the commitment of eliminating the ignorance from individuality has to be continually incorporated from the inner state of enabling the learners to work their assignment appropriately. In expanding the continued basis of taking consideration towards what to do and how to achieve as the responsibility, the lifelong learning could be indicated through building the timeless and anywhere basis freely with the teaching guidance as stated in the Islamic education rules (Halstead, 2019; Mu'izzuddin, 2014). Consequently, the need to continuously learn anytime and anywhere basis has to be reflected to apply for in the wide range of conditions, since the human is nothing when born in this world. It is argued that learning can influence to the conditional shape because nobody born in this world brings knowledge. In this view, the distinctive significance of personal quality with knowledge is that such deal is opposite from the ignorant one in the sense which enable to have access the wide understanding about the phenomena. In terms of fulfilling the educational process in enabling the individual quality to access the knowledge understanding to elevate their capability, the two possible platforms, both formal and informal scheme could give the reflection in exploring the potencies and the result achievement.

Applying Knowledge for Active Involvement in the Society

As the attempts to elaborate the learning ethics commitment to achieve the learning process, the responsible awareness to look at the society needs could be determined in valuing the knowledge understanding on what to do and how to do wisely in the context of social community. Since the educational orientation can actually be directed through the curriculum design, the possible instrument to apply for refers to the particular approach contributed in preserving the society values in enabling the practical stage more concisely and clearly viewed. The effort to transmit the social community engagement through reflecting the cultural legacy together with traditional principles could play a significant role in giving the direction path to continuously innovate following the global context and contemporary needs (Huda et al., 2017c; Mansor et al., 2015; Mohd Yusob et al., 2015). As such, the appropriate tool for social community development should be directed to the worldwide context of local stage through maximising the innovation capacity. In particular, the mutual concern about living together in the local level context and also with the family membership should be committed to ensure the learning process to cover the worldwide community needs. The mutual concern of contributing into the active involvement in the society context could be incorporated into the service learning to elevate the capacity of social responsibility within the corporate management basis (Huda et al., 2018; Mu'izzuddin, 2014). In terms of enhancing the capacity scale of having the commitment on learning process, attempts to sustain the religious understanding through *Tawakkul* and *Tawhid* integration could play a key to drive the direction the concern about reviving the matters of religious point of view together with maintaining the experiential learning basis in looking at the whole context. Moreover, the notion of Islamic education to apply for the active involvement in the society at large could be given a chance to rebuild the individual quality in the social orientation in enabling the quality assurance. In this view, the level to get involved into the social community at large where the three functions above is matched points out the clear description to transmit the piety with the skilful ability in providing the experiential stage in underlying the social interaction.

In the attempts to concisely build the learning process in conducive basis, the learning style with such distinct characteristic should be appropriately prepared in giving chance amongst the students to maximise their readiness to sustain their talents of intellectual and spiritual elements (Nuryatno, 2011; Rissanen, 2012; Tan & Ibrahim, 2017). As such, the continued application refers to provide guidelines in elevating the personal and social aspect in underlying their necessary task in the context of learning, community and also the nation building. In particular, it is necessary to nurture the individual development in the attempts to optimise their ability to accept information to result in their knowledge capacity. Through facilitating the learners with managing the information received to be analysed, the sufficient experience is also needed especially when giving the chance to learn to get involved in the social community (Huda et al., 2018; Wenger, 2010). With this regard, enhancing the capacity of individual development to underlie the social community engagement should bring along with transmitting the experiential paths to enlarge the knowledge understanding on what to do and how to do wisely in the context of social community at large. Moreover, the orientation of self-management in underlying the social interaction refers to have a wide commitment to build the knowledge to fulfil based on the needs to spread along with the societal condition (Anshari et al., 2017; Huda et al., 2016d; Slade & Prinsloo, 2013). It means that this transmission of knowledge which can belong to the surrounding people has a concern to assure that they can accept the rules in keeping away from chasms out of ignorance. It is pivotal to possess the intention that the scale of knowledge understanding about self-condition refers to arrange the commitment to concisely communicate, interact and socialise with others wisely in line with maintaining the divine engagement. This is to ensure the transmission process of personal development in Islamic education would have a tremendous contribution into the societal context.

In addition, the scale of social orientation as the outcome which can be supposed to consider in further in the reality needs to maintain the professional based social orientation where this point of view can make a benefit for the person with qualification in contributing the social community (Huda et al., 2019b). It is aimed at getting the perfection involved to achieve the knowledge in gaining the position in an institution where this professionalism has a significant role to drive the attainment of that position. At this point of view, to get a position in a place can be achieved through the knowledge, since the learning achievement is prioritised for the hereafter life, in the sense that can be determined to give insights into supporting an important bridge in facilitating the religious supplement to underlie the social interaction context (Huda et al., 2017d; Mohd Yusob et al., 2015). Through dealing with the worldly life, it is worthwhile to consider in particular having an access of Islamic way as the main commitment in Islamic education through attaining '*amr ma'rūf nahī munkar*', which has the meaning that the commitment of applying for the righteousness together with revitalizing the religious act and also avoiding the denial act potency. Moreover, the arrangement of such commitment refers to play a key role in transmitting the attainment in looking at the problem to give the solution appropriately in line with the condition. In the attempts to enable the experiential learning basis, possessing the mature essence among the learners needs to go beyond the passion on surrounding condition. It can strengthen the personal ability to contemplate the beneficial values which could be achieved as a necessity for the social engagement.

CONCLUSION AND RECOMMENDATION

This chapter has dealt with the elucidation of learning ethics commitment in sustaining the learning achievement, as al-Zarnūjī (2008) points out through six core learning commitment stages as discussed early. It is worthwhile to take note in a particular way that the wider context of recognising the clear indication of certain learning commitment has to be embedded in the process of teaching and learning process. In this view, the key point valued into fulfilling the main subject to give insights in strengthening the knowledge understanding stage refers to the essential inclusion in transmitting the educational value. It is important to keep in mind that such attempts to convince such principles in the learning process need to form the intellectual capacity to elevate the thinking skills. This should be also at the same time prepared with constructing the moral responsibility to measure in the process of teaching and learning. The specific contribution of outlining the extent of professional and moral obligation refers to expand to take benefit about the entre process of educational pedagogue. This initiative would give a chance to transmit the basic element of soul and mind, in the sense that can be achieved to contribute into the individual development and social community. At this point of view, the need to apply for an appropriate way should be determined in referring to the society needs. The moral educator in distributing the knowledge amongst the students should do with expanding the intellectual capability assigned with the spiritual development in underlying the enlightening treatment to provide the appropriate guideline based on the Islamic education point of view. Since every deed is an inextricable link to the process which is well prepared with a goal, possessing the initiative of implementing the learning needs to have a good strategy committed into the clear determination in enabling the stakeholder to deal with in the school context.

Through critical exploration about the learning ethics commitment for learning achievement, paying serious attention on balance between intellectual, moral, and spiritual skills should be determined as the main point of the learning goal. Attempts to expand the learning ethics commitment for learning achievement in Islamic education could be indicated into three core paths: achieving divine engagement-based spiritual commitment, assisting skill performance for personal capability development, and applying knowledge for active involvement in the society. This chapter is expected to enrich the conceptual framework of learning acquisition with paying particular attention to strategical and ethical engagement. It indicates that the greater prominence of having the commitment on learning process in Islamic education refers to expand in a particular way in bridging the balance of moral and spiritual basis to underlie the social interaction within the environmental context. The main guideline principle is expected to give the contribution in providing the theoretical framework of procedural rules of self-arrangement on learning ethics commitment for learning achievement referring to Islamic education point of view. Both teaching competency strategy and learning enhancement should begin with building the inner state of recognising the whole context of certain phenomena. This is to ensure the accuracy of such information to be achieved in line with fundamental basis in Islamic education. As a result, addressing the wide range of principle guidelines would offer the category in expanding the rational thinking in the attempts to respond the emerging challenges to solve wisely together with enhancing the spiritual basis in underlying wisely the entire process of Islamic point of view across time and space. Through applying for the knowledge understanding of what to do and how to do wisely and appropriately, it is worthwhile to take a necessary point in transmitting the intellectual capacity, moral responsibility and spiritual belief in the sense which can give the direction to have the particular attention in working hard together with professionally ensuring to gain the beneficial value of knowledge achieved in the process.

Thus, the transmission of knowledge understanding and moral responsibility could develop the individual capacity and social community through addressing the worldly benefit together with hereafter life orientation. In this view, attempts to gain the passion of learning integrated into the rational thinking as the indicator of individual development capacity could give the facilitation of moral learning through construction the principle guideline. In the attempts to recognise the valuable insights of Islamic morality together with spiritual skills, the learning ethics commitment needs to pursuit the knowledge understanding of what to do and how to do wisely in relation between God and society at large. Consequently, the committed awareness of learning enhancement here should be determined in particular way on giving the point of encouraging the learners to have a look at the particular view about the social dimension. The educational setting in this context could begin with concerning the detailed point of view in expanding the balance amongst the intellectual, moral and spiritual elements in driving the paths of human direction, mainly in interacting with others and also in the teacher and students relationship. Both social and individual development should be balance in the context of strengthening the potential value to underlie the ability skills to concern the social community at large. Integrating the practical and theoretical path is supposedly strengthened in line with committing the individual and social development. Attempts to pay particular attention through curriculum design possibly applied for referring to divine engagement, individual development, and social responsibility would give an alternative solution to sustain the soul construction as the main point of directing the knowledge understanding.

ACKNOWLEDGMENT

This work is partly based on the research project entitled Kaedah pengajaran tafsir al-quran dan hubungannya dengan amalan penghayatan akhlak al-Quran [The teaching method for Quranic interpretation and its relation to the reflective practice of the Quran]. The author(s) would like to extend their gratitude to the Research Management and Innovation Centre (RMIC), Sultan Idris Education University, Perak, Malaysia for the University Research Grant (Code 2018-0241-107-01).

REFERENCES

Abdullah, K., & Salleh, M. A. (2015). Conceptualizing Jihad Among Southeast Asia s Radical Salafi Movements. *Journal for the Study of Religions and Ideologies*, *14*(42), 121–146.

Abu-Hussin, M. F., Salleh, M. A., & Nasir, B. M. (2015). Beyond religious affinity: Malaysia's relations with countries in the Arab Gulf. *The Pacific Review*, *28*(4), 461–482. doi:10.1080/09512748.2015.1011213

Al Attas, S. M. N. (1979). *Aims and Objectives of Islamic Education*. Jeddah: King Abdul Aziz University.

Al Hamdani, D. (2016). The character education in islamic education viewpoint. *Jurnal Pendidikan Islam UIN Sunan Gunung Djati*, *1*(1), 98–109. doi:10.15575/jpi.v1i1.614

Al Qur'an al Karim. (2005). *Madinah: King Fahd Complex for the Printing of the Holy Qur'an*. Author.

Al-Sharaf, A. (2013). Developing scientific thinking methods and applications in Islamic education. *Education*, *133*(3), 272–282.

Al-Zarnūjī, B. (2008). *Ta'lim al-Muta'allim: Tariq al-Ta'allum* [Learning instruction for students' learning]. Surabaya, Indonesia: Al Miftah.

Aminin, S., Huda, M., Ninsiana, W., & Dacholfany, M. I. (2018). Sustaining civic-based moral values: Insights from language learning and literature. *International Journal of Civil Engineering and Technology*, *9*(4), 157–174.

Anshari, M., Almunawar, M. N., Shahrill, M., Wicaksono, D. K., & Huda, M. (2017). Smartphones usage in the classrooms: Learning aid or interference? *Education and Information Technologies*, *22*(6), 3063–3079. doi:10.100710639-017-9572-7

Aşlamacı, İ., & Kaymakcan, R. (2017). A model for Islamic education from Turkey: The Imam-Hatip schools. *British Journal of Religious Education*, *39*(3), 279–292. doi:10.1080/01416200.2015.1128390

Atmotiyoso, P., & Huda, M. (2018). Investigating Factors Influencing Work Performance on Mathematics Teaching: A Case Study. *International Journal of Instruction*, *11*(3), 391–402. doi:10.12973/iji.2018.11327a

Brophy, J. E. (2013). *Motivating students to learn*. London: Routledge. doi:10.4324/9780203858318

Choudhury, M. A. (2016a). Technically integrating Al-Wasatiyyah and Maqasid As-Shari'ah with a Tawhidi methodological worldview. *Absolute Reality in the Qur'an*, 101-111.

Choudhury, M. A. (2016b). Introduction: Foundations of the Qur'anic Worldview. *Absolute Reality in the Qur'an*, 3-18.

Choudhury, M. A. (2016c). Analytical Precept of Absolute Reality in the Qur'an. *Absolute Reality in the Qur'an*, 19-37.

Choudhury, M. A. (2016d). *Absolute Reality in the Qur'an*. Academic Press.

Choudhury, M. A. (2018). The ontological law of Tawhid contra 'Shari'ah-compliance'in Islamic portfolio finance. *International Journal of Law and Management*, *60*(2), 413–434. doi:10.1108/IJLMA-01-2017-0001

Elliott, J. (2015). Towards a comprehensive pedagogical theory to inform lesson study: An editorial review. *International Journal for Lesson and Learning Studies*, *4*(4), 318–327. doi:10.1108/IJLLS-08-2015-0028

Fahriana, A. S., & Huda, M. (2019). Application of Analysis of Strengths, Weaknesses, Opportunities, and Threats in Islamic Education Institutions. *Istawa: Jurnal Pendidikan Islam*, *4*(1), 50–64. doi:10.24269/ijpi.v4i1.1670

Furnham, A., Monsen, J., & Ahmetoglu, G. (2009). Typical intellectual engagement, Big Five personality traits, approaches to learning and cognitive ability predictors of academic performance. *The British Journal of Educational Psychology*, *79*(4), 769–782. doi:10.1348/978185409X412147 PMID:19245744

Gilliot, C. (2012). *Education and learning in the early Islamic world*. London: Ashgate Variorum.

Grunebaum, G. E. V., & Abel, T. M. (1947). *Instruction of the student: The method of learning*. New York: King's Crown Press.

Hafidzah, L. (2014). Textbooks of Islamic Education in Indonesia's Traditional Pesantren: The Use of Al-Zarnūjī 's Ta'lim Al-Muta'allim Tariq At-Ta'alum and Hasyim Asy'ari's Adab Al-'Âlim Wa Al-Muta'alim. *Al-Albab Journal*, *3*(2), 199-212.

Halstead, J. M. (2007). Islamic values: A distinctive framework for moral education? *Journal of Moral Education*, *36*(3), 283–296. doi:10.1080/03057240701643056

Halstead, J. M. (2017). Islamic Education in England. Handbook of Islamic Education, 1-17.

Halstead, J. M. (2018). Islamic Education in the West and Its Challenges. Handbook of Contemporary Islam and Muslim Lives, 1-15.

Halstead, M. (2004). An Islamic concept of education. *Comparative Education*, *40*(4), 517–529. doi:10.1080/0305006042000284510

Halstead, M. (2019). *New Directions in Islamic Education: Pedagogy and Identity Formation By Abdullah Sahin*. Academic Press.

Huda, M. (2018). Empowering Application Strategy in the Technology Adoption: Insights from Professional and Ethical Engagement. *Journal of Science and Technology Policy Management*. . doi:10.1108/JSTPM-09-2017-0044

Huda, M., Anshari, M., Almunawar, M. N., Shahrill, M., Tan, A., Jaidin, J. H., ... Masri, M. (2016). Innovative Teaching in Higher Education: The Big Data Approach. *The Turkish Online Journal of Educational Technology, 15*(Special issue), 1210–1216.

Huda, M., Jasmi, K. A., Alas, Y., Qodriah, S. L., Dacholfany, M. I., & Jamsari, E. A. (2017d). Empowering Civic Responsibility: Insights From Service Learning. In S. Burton (Ed.), *Engaged Scholarship and Civic Responsibility in Higher Education* (pp. 144–165). Hershey, PA: IGI Global. doi:10.4018/978-1-5225-3649-9.ch007

Huda, M., Jasmi, K. A., Embong, W. H., Safar, J., Mohamad, A. M., Mohamed, A. K., ... Rahman, S. K. (2017c). Nurturing Compassion-Based Empathy: Innovative Approach in Higher Education. In M. Badea & M. Suditu (Eds.), *Violence Prevention and Safety Promotion in Higher Education Settings* (pp. 154–173). Hershey, PA: IGI Global. doi:10.4018/978-1-5225-2960-6.ch009

Huda, M., Jasmi, K. A., Mohamed, A. K., Wan Embong, W. H., & Safar, J. (2016c). (in press). Philosophical Investigation of al- Zarnūjī's Taʿlīm al-Mutaʿallim: Strengthening Ethical Engagement into Teaching and Learning. *Social Science*.

Huda, M., Jasmi, K. A., Mustari, I., Basiron, B., & Sabani, N. (2017a). Traditional wisdom on sustainable learning: An insightful view from Al-Zarnuji's Ta 'lim al-Muta 'allim. *SAGE Open, 7*(1), 2158244017697160. doi:10.1177/2158244017697160

Huda, M., & Kartanegara, M. (2015a). Aim formulation of education: An analysis of the book *Ta'lim al-Muta'allim. International Journal of Humanities and Social Science, 5*(2), 143–149.

Huda, M., & Kartanegara, M. (2015b). Curriculum Conception In The Perspective Of The Book Ta'lim Al-Muta'allim. *International Journal of Education and Research, 3*(2), 221–232.

Huda, M., & Kartanegara, M. (2015c). Distinctive feature of al-Zarnûjî's ideas: A philosopical inquiry into the book *Ta'lim al-Muta'allim. American International Journal of Contemporary Research, 5*(2), 171–177.

Huda, M., & Kartanegara, M. (2015d). Islamic spiritual character values of al-Zarnūjī's *Taʿlīm al-Mutaʿallim. Mediterranean Journal of Social Sciences, 6*(4), 229–235.

Huda, M., & Kartanegara, M. (2015e). Ethical foundation of character education in indonesia: reflections on integration between Ahmad Dahlan and Al-Zarnūjī. *Persidangan Antarabangsa Tokoh Ulama Melayu Nusantara (PanTUMN).* Doi:10.13140/RG.2.1.5082.1605

Huda, M., & Kartanegara, M. (2015f). The Significance of Educative Environment to the Character Development: A Study of al-Zarnūjī's Ta'līm al-Muta'allim. *International Journal of Innovation Education and Research*, *3*(3), 191–200.

Huda, M., Mulyadi, D., Hananto, A. L., Nor Muhamad, N. H., Mat Teh, K. S., & Don, A. G. (2018). Empowering corporate social responsibility (CSR): Insights from service learning. *Social Responsibility Journal*, *14*(4), 875–894. doi:10.1108/SRJ-04-2017-0078

Huda, M., Qodriah, S. L., Rismayadi, B., Hananto, A., Kardiyati, E. N., Ruskam, A., & Nasir, B. M. (2019). Towards Cooperative with Competitive Alliance: Insights into Performance Value in Social Entrepreneurship. In *Creating Business Value and Competitive Advantage with Social Entrepreneurship* (p. 294). Hershey, PA: IGI Global. doi:10.4018/978-1-5225-5687-9.ch014

Huda, M., & Sabani, N. (2018). Empowering Muslim Children's Spirituality in Malay Archipelago: Integration between National Philosophical Foundations and Tawakkul (Trust in God). *International Journal of Children's Spirituality*, *23*(1), 81–94. doi:10.1080/1364436X.2018.1431613

Huda, M., Sabani, N., Shahrill, M., Jasmi, K. A., Basiron, B., & Mustari, M. I. (2017b). Empowering learning culture as student identity construction in higher education. *Student Culture and Identity in Higher Education*, 160-179.

Huda, M., Sudrajat, S., Kawangit, R.M., Teh, K.S.M., & Jalal, B. (2019). Strengthening divine values for self-regulation in religiosity: insights from *Tawakkul* (trust in God). *International Journal of Ethics and Systems*. Doi:10.1108/IJOES-02-2018-0025

Huda, M., Yusuf, J. B., Jasmi, K. A., & Nasir, G. A. (2016a, October). Understanding comprehensive learning requirements in the light of al-Zarnūjī's Ta'līm al-Muta'allim. *SAGE Open*, 1–14.

Huda, M., Yusuf, J. B., Jasmi, K. A., & Zakaria, G. N. (2016b, July). Al-Zarnūjī's concept of knowledge ('ilm). *SAGE Open*, 1–13.

Izfanna, D., & Hisyam, N. A. (2012). A comprehensive approach in developing akhlaq: A case study on the implementation of character education at Pondok Pesantren Darunnajah. *Multicultural Education & Technology Journal*, *6*(2), 77–86. doi:10.1108/17504971211236254

Jamaluddin, D. (2013). Character Education in Islamic Perspective. *International Journal of Scientific & Technology Research, 2*(2), 187-189.

Jonassen, D. H., & Grabowski, B. L. (2012). *Handbook of individual differences, learning, and instruction.* London: Routledge.

Mansor, N., Ariffin, R., Nordin, R., & Salleh, M. A. (2015). Mosque Tourism Certification in Waqf Management: A Model by Ukhwah Samara. *Social Sciences and Humanities, 23,* 291–304.

Mohamed, N. (2014). Islamic education, eco-ethics and community. *Studies in Philosophy and Education, 33*(3), 315–328. doi:10.100711217-013-9387-y

Mohd Yusob, M. L., Salleh, M. A., Haron, A. S., Makhtar, M., Asari, K. N., & Jamil, L. S. M. (2015). Maqasid al-Shariah as a Parameter for Islamic Countries in Screening International Treaties Before Ratification: An Analysis. *Pertanika Journal of Social Science & Humanities, 23.*

Mu'izzuddin, M. (2014). Etika belajar dalam kitab ta'līm muta'allim [Learning ethics of Ta'līm al-Muta'allim]. *Jurnal Al-Ittijah, 4*(01), 1–18.

Nor, M. R. M., & Malim, M. (2014). Revisiting Islamic education: The case of Indonesia. *Journal for Multicultural Education, 8*(4), 261–276. doi:10.1108/JME-05-2014-0019

Nuryatno, M. A. (2011). Islamic Education in A Pluralistic Society. *Al-Jami'ah. Journal of Islamic Studies, 49*(2), 411–431.

Paramboor, J., & Ibrahim, M. B. (2014). Educational leadership as a manifestation of 'Adab' in education: Conception of Zarnuji. *International Journal of Education and Research, 2*(3), 1–12.

Rissanen, I. (2012). Teaching Islamic education in Finnish schools: A field of negotiations. *Teaching and Teacher Education, 28*(5), 740–749. doi:10.1016/j.tate.2012.02.001

Roorda, D. L., Koomen, H. M., Spilt, J. L., & Oort, F. J. (2011). The influence of affective teacher–student relationships on students' school engagement and achievement: A meta-analytic approach. *Review of Educational Research, 81*(4), 493–529. doi:10.3102/0034654311421793

Rosli, M. R. B., Salamon, H. B., & Huda, M. (2018). Distribution Management of Zakat Fund: Recommended Proposal for Asnaf Riqab in Malaysia. *International Journal of Civil Engineering and Technology, 9*(3), 56–64.

Salleh, M. A., Abu-Hussin, M. F., Azeez, Y. A., Adam, F., & Muhamad, N. H. N. (2015). The Emergence of Non-State Actors in Enhancing Malaysia's Relationship with the Gcc Countries. *Pertanika Journal of Social Science & Humanities*, *23*, 267–280.

Salleh, M. S. (2013a). Philosophical Foundations of Islamic Development : Khurshid Ahmad's Conception Revisited. *International Journal of Education and Research*, *1*(7), 1–16.

Salleh, M. S. (2013b). Strategizing Islamic Education. *International Journal of Education and Research*, *1*(6), 1–14.

Slade, S., & Prinsloo, P. (2013). Learning analytics, ethical issues, and dilemmas. *The American Behavioral Scientist*, *57*(10), 1510–1529. doi:10.1177/0002764213479366

Tan, C., & Ibrahim, A. (2017). Humanism, Islamic Education, and Confucian Education. *Religious Education (Chicago, Ill.)*, *112*(4), 394–406. doi:10.1080/00 344087.2016.1225247

Wenger, E. (2010). Communities of practice and social learning systems: the career of a concept. In *Social learning systems and communities of practice* (pp. 179–198). London: Springer. doi:10.1007/978-1-84996-133-2_11

Yahya, M. S. (2005). Atmosfir Akademis dan Nilai Estetik Kitab Ta'līm al-Muta'allim [Academic atmosphere and ethical values of Ta'līm al-Muta'allim]. *Journal Ibda*, *3*(2), 1–10.

Chapter 14
Understanding *Istifadah* (Utilizing Time and Chance) for Personality Development in Islamic Education

Miftachul Huda

https://orcid.org/0000-0001-6712-0056

Universiti Pendidikan Sultan Idris, Malaysia

M. Ikhsan Nawawi

Institute for Islamic Studies Agus Salim, Indonesia

Liberty Liberty

State Institute for Islamic Studies (IAIN) Metro Lampung, Indonesia

Jarkawi Jarkawi

https://orcid.org/0000-0002-7846-3983

Universitas Islam Kalimantan Muhammad Arsyad Al Banjari, Indonesia

Azmil Hashim

Universiti Pendidikan Sultan Idris, Malaysia

Muhamad Mustaqim Ahmad

Universiti Kebangsaan Malaysia, Malaysia

Mohd Hilmi Rozali

Universiti Teknologi Malaysia, Malaysia

Nurazmalail Marni

Universiti Teknologi Malaysia, Malaysia

Bushrah Basiron

Universiti Teknologi Malaysia, Malaysia

Ahmad Kilani Mohamed

Universiti Teknologi Malaysia, Malaysia

Andino Maseleno

Universiti Tenaga Nasional Malaysia, Malaysia

Noorhaswari Ismail

Universiti Teknologi Malaysia, Malaysia

DOI: 10.4018/978-1-5225-8528-2.ch014

INTRODUCTION

During the last decade, the number of behaviour challenges could be viewed into the certain phenomena of student involvement in the criminal task as reported by the local authority (Afriyanti and Siti, 2015; Arifin, 2015; Khalisotussurur and Ramidi, 2015). Moreover, it is reported that there is such crisis in character with a rampant occurrence of phenomena. Such indicators include violence, vandalism and adolescent mischief, dishonesty, disrespect and cruelty to peers. These incidents point out a worrying condition with declining of characters of students. The decline of the students' morality encourages the researchers to examine the problem through the perspective of character education.

With respect to the problems of character values facing the community in general, and among the students in particular, it is necessary to make a 'foundational concept' as an effort to perform character education. On this regard, both general and character education are necessary as the ultimate component in the effort to instil noble characters and values (Attaran, 2015; Halstead, 2014; Tan, Naidu & Jamil, 2018). This acts as a significant attempt to equip students not only with the qualities of knowledge in the sense of cognitive aspects, but also to reflecting how mental and spiritual aspects become a basic element to develop them in order to be generations with noble character. Through implementing character education, some ways, one of which is how students should do, in terms of managing time and maximizing time for virtues inquiry, become a significant effort to instil ethical foundations for the students.

However, it is unfortunate, not many studies have been taken to particular address the point of how the students should do in the 'specifically shared ways' in the context of utilizing time and chance, known as concept of *istifādah* as a part of ethical foundation for the students. This chapter attempts to examine *istifādah* as moral education through taking the first stage in satisfying this gap through critical exploration. Moreover, the essentials of moral education referring to the *istifādah* context with a comprehensive approach is potentially explored in utilizing time and chance to enhance the quality for students interaction. The integrative morality to be implemented in the educational process refers to most encourage transforming individual qualities with spiritual and intellectual skills. The main discussion of this chapter refers to the theoretical conception of al-Zarnūjī's *Ta'līm al-Muta'allim,* which has the wider influential basis with its crucial guidelines in giving insights into teaching and learning practice in the context of Islamic education (Hafidzah, 2014; Huda and Kartanegara, 2015a; Mansor et al., 2015). Moreover, the distinctive point of this conceptual framework is indicated into the following. Those are the alternative practice amongst the teaching of morality amidst the *pesantren* (Islamic boarding), its unique model of teaching and learning appropriately advanced as the basic foundation of how to do in respect to the learning and teaching process

Conceptualising *Istifādah* (Utilizing Time and Chance)

Prior to further discussion about the concept of *istifādah*, as al-Zarnuji proposed, it is worthwhile to comprehend its definition first. It comes from Arabic word, which actually means 'taking benefit' or advantages (Yunus, 1990). It means that there can be carried out some principles to be employed through utilising some priorities given, such as time, chance and virtues. On this view, this can be understood that in the order for character education, the students should be with 'favourable feels' in accordance with managing daily list of school, for example, and make discipline for every certain activity, learning schedule outside from school, by always providing some schools' tools and equipment.

In regard to what is meant about *istifādah*, according to al-Zarnuji's *Ta'līm al-Muta'allim*, there are two main aspects, at which all these are particularly concerned to prioritising both two fundamental points, 'time' and 'chance' (p.114-115). On this point of view, there has been clearly outlined in the Qur'an, (al-'Aṣr, v.1-3), 'For the sake of time, behold, the man is really in loss: except those who believe in and do righteous deeds (*amal sālih*) and counsel's advice (*naṣihat*) to obey the truth (*haq*) and to comply with patience and constancy (*ṣabr*)'. From this verse, there contain two main virtues as the ultimate point of stressing on utilising such potentials being a sequence of the process of *istifādah*, at which each has the sustainability, namely time management with discipline and also wisdom through virtues inquiry from experienced personality. As outlined in the verse, the virtues should come from the individual managing well balancing between righteous deeds (*'amal sālih*) and counsel's advice in order to achieve the truth (*tawā ṣawb al-haq*).

In line with understanding the basis of *istifādah*, the attempts to utilise time and chance refer to enhance the moral quality as the responsible awareness in action management, where the planning should be incorporated in gaining the wisdom-based experiential virtues. With this regard, the basis of understanding behavioural manners in leading to the goodness from the personal and social context should begin with flourishing the accountability standard to put into the universal level in enabling the accessibility to achieve the main point. The balance between productivity achievement and entire process in guiding the advanced principles to the people manners refers to apply for the theoretical and practical capability within identifying what to do appropriately and wisely into the particular condition (Brownlee et al., 2016; Tan & Ibrahim, 2017). In this perspective, it is sure to make understanding about the moral virtues supplement to give the positive feedback in assisting the life, for example, as the praise of such individual development. Other chance to be utilised is about 'the time for praying at night' in the order for making it as 'soul-reflective thinking' (Al-Zarnuji, 2008). With this regard, there are many opportunities actually being able to utilize for the students or adolescents, as the effort to conduct whatever should come in the attempts to achieve the moral quality virtues. This ensures to yield the main concern which will later become the soul conduction to the heart. In the real discourse, the point could be viewed in particular including the process of learning to fit into the contemporary needs which the student could have chance in understanding the certain subject.

Through moral quality development with a significant attribution to underlie the discipline among the persons, it is worthwhile to take note in a particular way that the scale of understanding to do further towards the behavioural attitude refers to transform the beneficial value which can uphold the personality trait in responding the certain situations wisely within maintaining the human character behaviour (Lubis, 2015; Rahim, 2013; Robinson, 2015). It is true that the essential element of moral behaviour together with applying the extent of knowledge in assessing the appropriate act will consequently lead to the practical habituation which is fundamental to give a feedback with a significant consequence to the personal qualities. In the effort to asses the suitability of acting and realising with the certain practice to become the particular habituation of moral quality development, the manners management in the way to drive the path of direction should bring along with understanding to look at the certain phenomena to provide the solution basis wisely referring to the Islamic way of life in particular (Choudhury, 2016a; Watt, 2017). With this regard, the mutual involvement of action management through planning to give the sustenance committed into the discipline of manners in underlying the human behaviour.

Integrating *Hikmah* (Wisdom) on Moral Quality for Personal Development in Islamic Education

As the wise approach in underlying professional practice with moral responsibility, *hikmah* (wisdom) has the link to expand the capacity of personal quality including knowledge understanding together with certain technique in dealing with the emerging challenges (Önal, 2010; Proctor, 2013). The key point of gaining the information related in supporting the active involvement in the society at large should bring along with spiritual and moral substance. The point of this attainment refers to underlie the personal quality transmitted into upholding the complex condition in the wide range of many levels to solve the problem wisely within the Islamic principles (Fahriana & Huda, 2019; Huda and Sabani, 2018; Lovat, 2016; Suharto, 2018). In the attempts to determine the wise basis to elevate the experience and knowledge understanding, it is necessary to build the quality assurance of the ability to determine whether it is correct and false or right and wrong. In particular, the action plan management needs to monitor from the entire process with the sufficient knowledge capacity in underlying the responsible commitment towards what to do and how to achieve appropriately (Ferrari et al, 2011). Conceptualised as the extensive knowledge in looking at the whole context of certain phenomena, attempts to recognise the root of problems with sufficient information refer to determine the accuracy of how such solution could be effective within the action plan management (Demirel Ucan & Wright, 2019). Subsequently, the extent of knowledge skills and understanding stage plays a key role in transmitting the decision point of interacting, socialising and acting wisely in the social community at large. Thus, wisdom as a virtue which has the potential qualities in determining which appropriate manners should be performed well.

In terms of learning field, the ethical foundation of socialising the interaction together with its characteristics should build the attempts emphasise the core elements in underlying the social interaction across human relationship. Those are the knowledge understanding about the way to achieve the learning process, the way to do wisely within the Islamic education principle guidelines, the way to become a pious quality of personal and social orientation, and also the way to live peacefully with getting involved into others concisely. As such, the awareness capacity to enlarge the mutual trust in the human relationship refers to point out supporting to conduct the certain task in school context, environmental concern and also nation building (Balakrishnan, 2017; Kartanegara, & Huda, 2016; Mohd Khambali@ Hambali et al., 2017; Tan et al., 2018). As a result, wisdom should be comprehended well in order to being performed in such a way and manner for life. Much whatever should be employed means that the chance given to increase such virtues in search for *hikmah* (wisdom) is required from the 'person with experiences' (al-Zarnuji, 2008, p.117). It means that the extents of potentials which the person has have the coherence extent to give the influential basis through worldview. Moreover, *hikmah* should be maintained to embed in a particular way in underlying the personal quality in managing their time wisely based on the need. The combination amongst the expert knowledge refers to enhance the reflecting practice in terms of teaching and learning process, working experience and also the vacation program at the certain place. With this regard, the extent of wise way to view the reality is the potential effect to how a person should react wisely with in any condition. It means that a person with the wise view should reach one of such characteristics, including an extensive factual and theoretical knowledge, being successful at living well and knowing how to live.

In line with the measurement, operation and definition of *hikmah*, the wide range of elements including integration point of intellectual capacity, reflective practice, and also affective personality characteristics refers to the foundational substance that virtues as emphasised at which its sources derive from the nature are concerned to the acquisition of *hikmah*. Consequently, achieving this *hikmah*, which is a central notion for noble values, should be oriented through virtues inquiry (Choudhury, 2016a). The wisdom-based moral virtues could be identified into measuring the manner assigned with the awareness extent to link the relationships between personal and social quality skills in giving the insights into promising the peaceful orientation integrated amidst community. In particular, attempts to offer the principle guidelines through the initiative of pathway of instructional process in achieving harmony and integrity in the balance between personal and social orientation behaviour substance (Huda et al., 2017a; Maseleno et al., 2018). With deploying the wisdom-based manner as the way to deal with the certain challenges in the social interaction for instance, it is necessary to point out giving the function as the particular chance to ensure in overcoming the integrated perspectives of the behavioural paths together with critical thinking skills. As a result, the sufficient supplement to give the feedback in giving the direction to go forward could be determined to enhance the experiential basis in the life circumstance in achieving the happiness. Moreover, the broader context of assessing the realities in perceiving the principle of direction towards what to do and how to do wisely with committed awareness of having look at the whole into the certain issue refers to play a key role in ensuring the way to achieve the happiness (Bergsma and Ardelt, 2012; Huda et al., 2017b). In particular, the wise basis here could be taken to give a point of contributing the direction as a pathway to transmit the mutual feeling, concern and also understanding in the sense that can be concentrating a vision to be aware of issues around the social life amidst the community at large.

In addition, the mutual line of moral quality principles refers to sustaining the essential value of distinctive form of Islamic point of view in stressing the discourse of developing the personality traits with having the maturity-based experiential scale together with knowledge understanding. This is important to take note that the basic elements of moral quality with pointing out the virtue ethics refer to the main principles which direct persons to give on directing the pathway the addressing the human consciousness towards emerging global context. Emphasising the virtue ethics refers to take a beneficial value of moral responsibility committed to flourish the dimension of human behaviour together with skilful ability to lead to the manner management (Intezari, 2016; Huda et al., 2017c). In particular, it is necessary to enlarge the way of ethical discourse in underlying both person and community at large to be aware of recognition of the relationship between personal and social level to represent the behavioural substance oriented to the interaction. With this regard, the ethics to supplement as the dimension of human manner incorporated into the essential principles of Islamic education could be emphasised in transmitting the valuable insights of stressing both human harmony and multiplicity.

Moreover, the critical discourse could be comprehended with the essential point of assessing the moral behaviour to represent the orientation of building the balance between personal development and social responsibility in the context of recognising what is appropriately good to conduct in further. This is to ensure that the availability of experiential scale together from the integration between moral obligation and intellectual discourse could be enhanced to drive a pathway to determine wisely in line with embodying the rationality, spirituality and also cognitive ability in underlying the interaction basis. The circumstance of personal quality gathered from experiential level and also the knowledge understanding of religion and sciences may have a portion to give insights into directing the wise technique on the way to have a look at what is true and wrong in a whole context (Huda et al., 2017d; Tan et al., 2018). In the attempts to enable the process of interacting, socialising and acting with others appropriately within Islamic principles, it is worthwhile to consider in particular that the arrangement to show the integrity commitment into moral, spiritual and intellectual skills has to be determined to provide a clear picture of having a sense in looking at the issues in a broader context, so that the way to give solution could appropriately be prepared in fitting to the condition. As a result, the determination process should bring along with an appropriate technique combined into the wise approach to which extent of the knowledge expert person has would result in the typical way to see the choices.

Sustaining Continuous Discipline

According to al-Zarnuji (2008), *istifādah* (taking benefits) for the students should be performed at any time to acquire 'virtues' (p.114). In terms of building the commitment to have the continuous discipline, the essential components of virtue ethics to underlie the value of responsibility engagement places a key role as the bases of wisdom. It indicates the consistent awareness of managing the personal quality through the knowledge understanding in underlying to give the direction path in what to do and how to do appropriately and wisely in line with expanding the capacity the human belongs (Huda & Teh, 2018). In consequence, this deliberation provides a broader significance of scriptures in religious consciousness. From this perspective, personality development qualities with a sufficient commitment to build the experiential basis should bring along with an entire approach to give insights into personal development in transmitting the social responsibility awareness (Rahim, 2013; Robinson, 2015). Moreover, the particular attention should be pointed out in determining the intellectual capacity together with spiritual ability as a basic assumption contributing to the educational field (Othman et al., 2016). In terms of learning, student has to prioritise the best commitment to employ utilising time management with 'discipline'. It is important to note that the discipline is not only to do whatever students are really concerned, but also to make the reflection for the soul refinement, namely by conceptualising such virtues to be manifested in learning, as an effort for inculcating noble character values, in particular.

In addition, transmitting the essence of discipline refers to the training of intellectual capacity together with accepting the principle rules towards the certain lesson that can be learnt from the life circumstances, such social interaction. Similarly, discipline as believed in an individual life is the main requirements of creating a condition where the person can learn to control one's feelings, emotions and behaviour (Intezari, 2016; Swartwood, 2013). As a result, it enables whoever can manage it well to think maturely about some phenomena, act maturely towards such problems and to take decisions responsibly with self-awareness through self-propelled, self-controlled and self-guiding persons (Proctor, 2013; Choudhury, 2016c). In other words, discipline, which can make us responsible and conscious, is one of the essential traits required for social life.

Consequently, discipline in a society becomes a particular decision which might determine whether spirit and the key-note of the worldly order are in accordance with a part of life style. In particular, discipline should be taught earlier as a virtue ethics necessary to be instilled within the children to be a personality habituated to do right path and to have a spirit way. Since being a part of virtues, discipline is the pre-requisite for growth and development for further process for one lesson which has to be in imbibed at a very young age (Foucault, 2018). It is necessary to point out the significance of committing with the discipline could give the point in enabling the learners to have access in continuing the tasks appropriately within the wise approach. In particular, it is the responsibility of the teachers to inculcate in them the value of discipline. Simply, discipline will be consequently taught through giving the commitment towards the certain appointment in the sense that could be given a chance into self-control management together with obtaining the obedience as the responsibility awareness (Michael, Storey & Thomas, 2008). From this perspective, it is clear that discipline is not only as a good virtue which adds colour and charm to the personality, but also as an essential quality of life required by every one of our society to make social, professional and family life.

In further, discipline, which is essential for life in terms of different forms in many different situations, refers to establish the extent of personal quality in enabling to learn in controlling one's feelings, emotions and behaviour (Evertson & Weinstein, 2013). The ability to manage self-controlled behaviour means that discipline is the condition of having all experienced personally and socially. In other words, discipline is also an ultimate component as the supreme importance of the heart and mind which enables to perform such activities in life (McCullough and Willoughby, 2009). As the professional standard for the key components to uphold the development of knowledge understanding and competence skills, it is the main character in the sense that without discipline there is nothing to be achieved in life with a variety of purposes. Simply, discipline is an ultimate factor which affects such spirit way for the human life in terms of work, study and other activities, and is an essential habit that everyone should possess as a civilized citizen.

In terms of the reason of discipline, there are many reasons for why it is necessary as a part of life conduct. The main reason is that with a discipline it is a particular way that we need to exercise discipline to be successful in life (Duckworth et al., 2011). As a result, discipline can mean various kinds of purposes to different people and students, for example. Thus, discipline is concerned to motivate the individual and make concentrate on learning to get best assignments in on time (Lu et al., 2016). It can, thus, be analysed that discipline has two main purposes, to give the nice situation for students and teachers in order to manage their needs and to create circumstance enabling to learn well. In other words, its significance has been vary in line with a variety of purposes, and also has the significant impact to academic success, or success in careers.

Nurturing Effective Time Management

Time management refers to concisely attempt the entire process of establishing the planning together with utilizing the appropriate way to employ the certain activities, by which to achieve the effectiveness, efficiency and productivity (Adair, 2009). In addition, time management needs to adopt the committed awareness of transforming the wide focus on what to do wisely. It means that the effectiveness in some time that a person has may seem more dependent on the particular manner to dedicate precious time to learning about time management. As for one of the potential components in managing time, a further investigation on how to utilise time with necessary and useful matter is an effective strategy to manage time appropriately in the balance of fulfilling the demands amidst the society needs. As such, it indicates to give the point of view in enhancing the necessary supplement to complete many other aspects of life, such as time for study, work, relax, etc. (Thomas et al., 2017). In particular, the necessary act in the useful matter here depends on the technique in organising the plan to spend on specific activities. Simply, it is usually a necessity in any project development designed with combination of processes, tools, techniques, and methods, as it determines the project completion time and scope.

In terms of learning, time management in specific strategies need to be considered in particular, since an appropriate conceptual framework may be used to conceive a fundamental understanding of managing time wisely. As a result, the manner for condensing and memorizing an important material becomes one particular necessity to self-evaluative standards for learning preparation accurately. In particular, al-Zarnuji (2008) points out whoever gets memorise at any time will surely get lost about his/ her memory, and thus through writing down he/she will get it forever, since the knowledge is information, skills and understanding obtained from such experiences as the theoretical or practical understanding of a subject. On this view, the knowledge is something which is obtained from scholars' understanding of any subject in the form of talk or discourse, since they memorised well on what they have ever heard, and showed to the best they memorised.

In addition, the reason why time management is importance is that the personal quality in managing the time consequently has the potency in making successful (Morden, 2017). There are many ways to do in terms of managing time wisely for learning. One manner is with making a note for recording such events involving experience, understanding to something new and even some unique and interesting phenomena. In addition, this can be implemented by providing 'stationery to record all new information' about the knowledge which the person had just heard in accordance with the scientific avail (al-Zarnuji, 2008). In particular, the students should be concisely aware to make up date something regarding their needs during the process of learning, even as being part of character education, by always alerting all regards related to the school needs, such as making diary notes in the order for being taken a reflective essence and also considered as potential enhancement. The particular skill involving the manner of managing the detailed goal refers to enhance the commitment in building the appropriate approach to submit the planning in line with concentrating on a crucial point of view in transmitting the progress of the goals (Chase et al., 2013). In terms of taking the priority in managing the active involvement into the social community as an attempt to take benefit of the time, making the action planning should be determined in enhancing the individual development and social responsibility development. Obtaining the important task in organising the careful engagement of performing what to do and how to do wisely refers to the mutual line with covering the action planning as indicated in the time management.

Empowering Strategic Effort With Experiential Foundations

Personal qualities involving knowledge, skills, and experience become factors that play a role in developing self-regulation. It means that such skill, knowledge and experience function as one of the most significant variables as an ability to monitor and control our own behaviour, emotions and thoughts in accordance with particular situation. As such, levels of skill and experience to ensure suitability with accumulated experience is influenced many factors, one of which is religious qualities which may serve as the most important factor (Foucault, 2018; Greene, 2018). In particular, McCullough and Willoughby (2009) determine the distinguished theoretical framework that the role of religious consciousness gave the influences on development of self-regulatory power, social behaviour and self-monitoring control.

Subsequently, from this perspective, few steps at the process to carry out are necessary, mainly in self-regulatory power to monitoring control. One of them is 'caring' with such experienced person (al-Zarnuji, 2008). This notion essentially has the consequence from understanding (*istifhām*), feeling (*ihsās*) and implementing (*'isti'māl*), at which caring is located between *istifhām* and *isti'māl*. In terms of 'caring', it can be with such analysis on how adolescents and students should have the feeling, being part of those with more experience, such as discussing or sharing about the constraints, which may usually be confronted from any way unknown. This is similar with a poetry 'how much I deeply regret and loss to get anything from a noble knowledgeable person, and what has passed not being able to return (Choudhury, 2016c). The other ways as the effort necessary to achieve such virtues in learning are to 'always memorise and reflect whatever about the virtues and knowledge' (al-Zarnuji, 2008, p.116). It means that moral quality that person do refer to actually endowment from God by means of human action, since the good process for gaining the virtue (…). Pertaining to the emphasis on virtues inquiry from experienced personality, it seems to have been a key point about the significance of anyone who has more learned, as al-Zarnuji (2008) points out that 'one learned with more experience will be more significantly difficult for the *shaytan* (devil) to encourage disturbing with such earnest than one thousand worshippers'. The further explanation of difficult for *shaytan* (devil) here is that a willingness to manage and control mentality from immoral or wicked behaviour, such as arrogance in terms of both inward and outward, since this is a very crucial thing which needs to be considered in particular (Huda and Kartanegara, 2015). It means that with remarkable elucidation, virtue ethics encourages people to develop their character to become the fundamental basis for the good life.

In terms of *mashaqqah*, it can actually be defined as 'an apprehensive sense for learning' (Yunus, 1990, p.201). In other words, there should be any effort to conduct during the process of education with the meaning that such effort can be outlined as the form of 'readiness to have the responsibility and duty' as the students who have consciousness and awareness in a whole. With this regard, it can be understood as readiness and consciousness in accepting the duty and responsibility for the students, in the order for completing such requirements. Al-Zarnuji (2008) believes that achieving the knowledge will be glorious if implemented with a contemptible essence assigned into the earnest effort, and thus could be attained through such struggle with various divergences of requirements. It means that during acquisition of knowledge, readiness to bear various kinds of tests to endure, essentially known as 'an earnest effort' should be performed well (Michael, Storey & Thomas, 2008). This should become an underlying component in taking into spirit manner as an attempt to make some desirable traits of character (Choudhury, 2016d). In particular, the commitment to sustain obligation through the wide range of the moral responsibility and professional practice will give the chance to resolve the challenges involving such ethical questions in terms of obligations and options to the spirit way in a practice in new community.

The original definition of *tamalluq*, according to al-Zarnuji's *Ta'līm al-Muta'allim*, is flirting (Yunus, 1990, p.428). In other words, it can be understood that there such a divergence of tasks and obstacles should be made as the challenges for the students in order to achieve the wisely mature thinking and caring. Al-Zarnuji believes that someone with continually determined attempt will have more chance to achieve the glory as he says 'I knew you are desired to be glory, but you will not achieve it until making yourself lowly'. It means that in terms of consequences during the process of education, some obstacles are necessarily required to resolve, and thus making a person with continuous effort until pursuing such knowledge and readiness for managing any risk. In other words, some obstacles during the educational process will become the main elements to make maturity in thinking. This is to construct the learners in the order for encourage on dynamic thinking how to resolve the problems.

Implication Into Islamic Education

Istifādah is a particular concept as the ethical foundation for character education, since it contains such psychological sections. The necessary point in the attempt of measuring the psychological components depends on a variety of approaches including the quality of belief qualities in Gods. In particular, the wider experience from gaining the spiritual quality would also have the consequence towards the extent of responsible awareness into the human life condition. In this view, the mutual involvement of personal and social qualities in the sense that can be deployed amidst the social community activities whether it is from traditional or modern motives should be incorporated into building the awareness together with strengthening the Islamic principles (Choudhury, 2016e; Huda et al., 2019a; Mohd Khambali@ Hambali et al., 2017). This is to ensure the extents of expanding the wide range of services provided into the social activities in running well appropriately under the prayer setting and management appointment. Moreover, the balance between personal development and social responsibility awareness should be taken into consideration in a particular way to enhance the commitment in contributing into the community service for instance (Tan et al., 2018). With this regard, the responsible capacity transmitted into the practical capability to deliver the information sufficiently has to be involved with building the moral obligation in underlying the way of persons in interacting, acting and socialising with their partnerships wisely within Islamic education principles (Arjmand, 2017; Fahriana, & Huda, 2019; Halstead, 2004; Halstead, 2007). As such, the spiritual capacity within Islamic principles to underlie the service in shaping the moral responsibility in terms of individual and social performance should bring along with strengthening the commitment in building a wise approach in facilitating the balance circumstance. Such variety of kinship through constituting the balance condition with such a convenient interaction in the personal and social level is necessary as an effort to construct the character building for the students.

In line with building the moral principles in Islamic education, character building refers to the strategic system of cultivating the moral values amongst the students. This process involves knowledge, consciousness or volition, and action to implement these values, both to Almighty God, ourselves, others, environment. In particular, this attempth can make human perfect man who has the wise view. Attempts to cultivate the moral quality with the good orientation refer to the universal value in enabling the global context to have a look at the whole context (Alavi, 2008; Ali, 2011; Choudhury, 2016e; Kumar & Che Rose, 2012). Moreover, it is worthwhile to take note that both parents and educators need to adopt the mutual relationship to provide the basis of having such understanding to the certain phenomena through reflecting all the life circumstance components (Proctor, 2013). As a result, ethics has become the upholding elements for enhancing a good character. It results a quality improvement, which aims at the realisation of generations with a vision, fixed into the social responsibility with giving the valuable insights into the nation building awareness. In order to achieve that process, it is necessary for character education implemented at school to cover all the components based on its curriculum, learning process and achievement, relation quality, subject matter, school management, activity and curricular, maintenance of facilities, payment and hard work from all educational environment.

Through implementing character education, some ways, one of which is quality of relationship among either school environment or family circumstance, become a significant effort to instil ethical foundations for the students. In terms of the significance of instilling characters and values, as underlined in al-Zarnuji's *Ta'līm al-Muta'allim*, the character is required with noble values cooperation between mental and physical aspect, as referred in his essentials of *niyyah* (motivation) in education. In other words, the role of considering *niyyah* being point of view for managing the soul and mind, has been a central element, prior to further direction for constructing educational process, particularly among the students (Halstead, 2014; Huda and Kartanegara, 2015a). Moreover, it is also seen as an attempt to pass on moral and religious values to the students. In this context, moral and religious principles should be determined to give an insightful value in the education system, since the criteria, as stated, have appropriately been designed to the citizenship, for example belief and devotion to God, responsibility, respect, competence and skills and possession of high moral quality (Mabud, 2018; Lubis, 2015; Parrott, 2017; Robinson, 2015). In particular, such values need to be embedded into the context of teaching and learning procedure through designing the curriculum with various activities as its components implemented in the school. Thus, the role of the institution where student and teacher interact with has a quite significant potency to help them virtuous, knowledgeable, balanced and harmonious development in their individuals.

CONCLUSION

This chapter did examine the essential value of *istifādah* for personality development through elucidating the thoughtful dialogues within the conceptual level in enabling the transmission into the practical desires with its specifications. Based on the significant effort to practise for the students, being such tasks of character education, through utilisation or taking benefit (*istifādah*), to instil such noble character values, there are three fundamental basis emphasised in the process for education. In terms of the powerful construction of al-Zarnuji's concept of *istifādah*, understanding, feeling and implementing such proposed conceptual frameworks are necessary as the effort to attain the moral values, *hikmah*, through virtues inquiry. The findings reveal that there four core stages to examine istifādah for personal development in Islamic education context. Those are sustaining continuous discipline, nurturing effective time management, integrating *Hikmah* (wisdom) based moral quality for personal development, and empowering strategic effort with experiential foundations. Moreover, this study is supposed to give the contribution mainly in supplementing the theoretical basis on personality development in Islamic education context. For conceptual recommendation of education, it is hoped to contribute particularly in constructing the personal development.

REFERENCES

Abdullah, K., & Salleh, M. A. (2015). Conceptualizing Jihad Among Southeast Asia s Radical Salafi Movements. *Journal for the Study of Religions and Ideologies*, *14*(42), 121–146.

Abu-Hussin, M. F., Salleh, M. A., & Nasir, B. M. (2015). Beyond religious affinity: Malaysia's relations with countries in the Arab Gulf. *The Pacific Review*, *28*(4), 461–482. doi:10.1080/09512748.2015.1011213

Adair, J. (2009). *Effective time management: How to save time and spend it wisely*. Pan Macmillan.

Afriyanti, D., & Ruqoyah, S. (2015). *Berbagai jenis kejahatan seperti pencurian, tawuran, dan pelecehan seks dilakukan siswa* [A variety of violence such as brawl, theft and sexual harassment involving some students]. Retrieved from http://metro. news.viva.co.id/news/read/312779-2-008-kasus-kriminal-dilakukan-anak-anak

Al-Qur'an al-Karim. (2005). *Madinah: King Fahd Complex for the Printing of the Holy Qur'an.* Author.

Al-Zarnūjī, B. (2008). Pedoman Belajar Bagi Penuntun Ilmu Secara Islami [Students' Islamic Guide for Learning] (M. Thaifuri, Trans.). In Ta'lim al Muta'allim. Surabaya: Menara Suci.

Alavi, H. R. (2008). Nearness to God: A perspective on Islamic education. *Religious Education (Chicago, Ill.)*, *103*(1), 5–21. doi:10.1080/00344080701807361

Ali, M. M. (2011). *The religion of Islam.* Ahmadiyya Anjuman Ishaat Islam Lahore USA.

Anshari, M., Almunawar, M. N., Shahrill, M., Wicaksono, D. K., & Huda, M. (2017). Smartphones usage in the classrooms: Learning aid or interference? *Education and Information Technologies*, *22*(6), 3063–3079. doi:10.100710639-017-9572-7

Arifin, N. (2015). *Video Kekerasan Pelajar di Jawa Timur Beredar* [videos of violence involving students scattered in East Java]. Retrieved from http://daerah.sindonews. com/read/934611/23/video-kekerasan-pelajar-di-jawa-timur-beredar-1418038066

Arjmand, R. (2017). Islam and Education in the Modern Era: Social, Cultural, Political Changes and Responses from Islamic Education. Handbook of Islamic Education, 1-17.

Attaran, M. (2015). Moral education, habituation, and divine assistance in view of Ghazali. *Journal of Research on Christian Education*, *24*(1), 43–51. doi:10.1080/ 10656219.2015.1008083

Balakrishnan, V. (2017). Making moral education work in a multicultural society with Islamic hegemony. *Journal of Moral Education*, *46*(1), 79–87. doi:10.1080/0 3057240.2016.1268111

Bergsma, A., & Ardelt, M. (2012). Self-reported wisdom and happiness: An empirical investigation. *Journal of Happiness Studies*, *13*(3), 481–499. doi:10.100710902- 011-9275-5

Brownlee, J. L., Scholes, L., Walker, S., & Johansson, E. (2016). Critical values education in the early years: Alignment of teachers' personal epistemologies and practices for active citizenship. *Teaching and Teacher Education*, *59*, 261–273. doi:10.1016/j.tate.2016.06.009

Chase, J. A. D., Topp, R., Smith, C. E., Cohen, M. Z., Fahrenwald, N., Zerwic, J. J., ... Conn, V. S. (2013). Time management strategies for research productivity. *Western Journal of Nursing Research*, *35*(2), 155–176. doi:10.1177/0193945912451163 PMID:22868990

Choudhury, M. A. (2016a). An ethical worldview of Moral-Social reconstruction. *Absolute Reality in the Qur'an*, 149-180.

Choudhury, M. A. (2016b). *Absolute Reality in the Qur'an*. Basingstoke, UK: Palgrave Macmillan. doi:10.1057/978-1-137-58947-7

Choudhury, M. A. (2016c). Technically integrating Al-Wasatiyyah and Maqasid As-Shari'ah with a Tawhidi methodological worldview. *Absolute Reality in the Qur'an*, 101-111.

Choudhury, M. A. (2016d). Introduction: foundations of the qur'anic worldview. *Absolute Reality in the Qur'an*, 3-18.

Choudhury, M. A. (2016e). Analytical precept of absolute reality in the qur'an. *Absolute Reality in the Qur'an*, 19-37.

Choudhury, M. A. (2018). Endogenous Ethics in Evolutionary Learning Model Contra Utilitarianism: Endogenous Ethics. *Ethics and Decision-Making for Sustainable Business Practices*, 55-72.

Demirel Ucan, A., & Wright, A. (2019). Improving the pedagogy of Islamic religious education through an application of critical religious education, variation theory and the learning study model. *British Journal of Religious Education*, *41*(2), 202–217. doi:10.1080/01416200.2018.1484695

Duckworth, A. L., Grant, H., Loew, B., Oettingen, G., & Gollwitzer, P. M. (2011). Self-regulation strategies improve self-discipline in adolescents: Benefits of mental contrasting and implementation intentions. *Educational Psychology*, *31*(1), 17–26. doi:10.1080/01443410.2010.506003

Evertson, C. M., & Weinstein, C. S. (Eds.). (2013). *Handbook of classroom management: Research, practice, and contemporary issues*. Routledge. doi:10.4324/9780203874783

Fahriana, A. S., & Huda, M. (2019). Application of Analysis of Strengths, Weaknesses, Opportunities, and Threats in Islamic Education Institutions. *Istawa: Jurnal Pendidikan Islam*, *4*(1), 50–64. doi:10.24269/ijpi.v4i1.1670

Ferrari, M., Kahn, A., Benayon, M., & Nero, J. (2011). Phronesis, sophia, and hochma: Developing wisdom in Islam and Judaism. *Research in Human Development*, *8*(2), 128–148. doi:10.1080/15427609.2011.568869

Foucault, M. (2018). Discipline. In *Rethinking The Subject* (pp. 60–69). Routledge. doi:10.4324/9780429497643-4

Greene, R. J. (2018). *Rewarding performance: Guiding principles; custom strategies*. Routledge. doi:10.4324/9780429429019

Hafidzah, L. (2014). Textbooks of Islamic Education in Indonesia's Traditional Pesantren: The Use of al-Zarnuji's Ta'lim al-Muta'allim Tariq at-Ta'alum and Hasyim Asy'ari's Adab al-'Alim Wa al-Muta'alim. *AL ALBAB*, *3*(2).

Halstead, J. M. (2007). Islamic values: A distinctive framework for moral education? *Journal of Moral Education*, *36*(3), 283–296. doi:10.1080/03057240701643056

Halstead, J. M. (2014). Values and Values Education: Challenges for Faith Schools. In International Handbook of Learning, Teaching and Leading in Faith-Based Schools (pp. 65-81). Springer Netherlands.

Halstead, M. (2004). An Islamic concept of education. *Comparative Education*, *40*(4), 517–529. doi:10.1080/0305006042000284510

Hambali, K., Sintang, S., Awang, A., Mat Karim, K. N., Abdul Rahman, N. F., Wan Ramli, W. A., ... Md. Noor, R. (2017). al-Wasatiyyah in the practice of religious tolerance among the families of new Muslims in sustaining a well-being society. *Humanomics, 33*(2), 211-220.

Huda, M., Anshari, M., Almunawar, M. N., Shahrill, M., Tan, A., Jaidin, J. H., ... Masri, M. (2016a). Innovative Teaching in Higher Education: The Big Data Approach. *The Turkish Online Journal of Educational Technology*, *15*(Special issue), 1210–1216.

Huda, M., Jasmi, K. A., Alas, Y., Qodriah, S. L., Dacholfany, M. I., & Jamsari, E. A. (2017d). Empowering Civic Responsibility: Insights From Service Learning. In S. Burton (Ed.), *Engaged Scholarship and Civic Responsibility in Higher Education* (pp. 144–165). Hershey, PA: IGI Global. doi:10.4018/978-1-5225-3649-9.ch007

Huda, M., Jasmi, K. A., Basiran, B., Mustari, M. I. B., & Sabani, A. N. (2017b). Traditional Wisdom on Sustainable Learning: An Insightful View From Al-Zarnuji's Ta 'lim al-Muta 'allim. *SAGE Open*, *7*(1), 1–8. doi:10.1177/2158244017697160

Huda, M., Jasmi, K. A., Embong, W. H., Safar, J., Mohamad, A. M., Mohamed, A. K., ... Rahman, S. K. (2017c). Nurturing Compassion-Based Empathy: Innovative Approach in Higher Education. In M. Badea & M. Suditu (Eds.), *Violence Prevention and Safety Promotion in Higher Education Settings* (pp. 154–173). Hershey, PA: IGI Global. doi:10.4018/978-1-5225-2960-6.ch009

Huda, M., Jasmi, K. A., Mohamed, A. K., Wan Embong, W. H., & Safar, J. (2016d). Philosophical Investigation of Al-Zarnuji's Ta'lim al-Muta'allim: Strengthening Ethical Engagement into Teaching and Learning. *Social Science, 11*(22), 5516–5551.

Huda, M., & Kartanegara, M. (2015a). Islamic Spiritual Character Values of al-Zarnūjī's Ta 'līm al-Muta 'allim. *Mediterranean Journal of Social Sciences, 6*(4S2), 229-235.

Huda, M., & Kartanegara, M. (2015b). Ethical Foundation of Character Education in Indonesia: Reflections on Integration between Ahmad Dahlan and al-Zarnuji. In Persidangan Antarabangsa Tokoh Ulama Melayu Nusantara (PanTUMN) (pp. 404–420). Selangor: Kolej Universiti Islam Antarabangsa Selangor (KUIS) Malaysia.

Huda, M., Kartanegara, M., & Zakaria, G. A. N. (2015c). The effect of learning strategy of reading aloud on students' achievement in the subject of Islamic studies at secondary school in Semarang. *International Journal of Education and Research, 3*(2), 577–588.

Huda, M., Mulyadi, D., Hananto, A. L., Nor Muhamad, N. H., Mat Teh, K. S., & Don, A. G. (2018). Empowering corporate social responsibility (CSR): Insights from service learning. *Social Responsibility Journal, 14*(4), 875–894. doi:10.1108/SRJ-04-2017-0078

Huda, M., & Sabani, N. (2018). Empowering Muslim Children's Spirituality in Malay Archipelago: Integration between National Philosophical Foundations and Tawakkul (Trust in God). *International Journal of Children's Spirituality, 23*(1), 81–94. doi:10.1080/1364436X.2018.1431613

Huda, M., Sabani, N., Shahrill, M., Jasmi, K. A., Basiron, B., & Mustari, M. I. (2017a). Empowering Learning Culture as Student Identity Construction in Higher Education. In A. Shahriar & G. Syed (Eds.), *Student Culture and Identity in Higher Education* (pp. 160–179). Hershey, PA: IGI Global. doi:10.4018/978-1-5225-2551-6.ch010

Huda, M., Sudrajat, S., Kawangit, R.M., Teh, K.S.M., & Jalal, B. (2019). Strengthening divine values for self-regulation in religiosity: insights from *Tawakkul* (trust in God). *International Journal of Ethics and Systems*. Doi:10.1108/IJOES-02-2018-0025

Huda, M., & Teh, K. S. M. (2018). Empowering professional and ethical competence on reflective teaching practice in digital era. *Mentorship Strategies in Teacher Education*, 136-152.

Huda, M., Yusuf, J. B., Jasmi, K. A., & Nasir, G. A. (2016b). Understanding Comprehensive Learning Requirements in the Light of al-Zarnūjī's Ta'līm al-Muta'allim. *SAGE Open*, *6*(4), 1–14. doi:10.1177/2158244016670197

Huda, M., Yusuf, J. B., Jasmi, K. A., & Zakaria, G. N. (2016c). Al-Zarnūjī's Concept of Knowledge ('ilm). *SAGE Open*, *6*(3), 1–13. doi:10.1177/2158244016666885

Intezari, A. (2016). Conceptualizing wisdom: theoretical perspectives. *Practical Wisdom in the Age of Technology*, 23-37.

Kartanegara, M., & Huda, M. (2016). Constructing Civil Society: An Islamic Cultural Perspective. *Mediterranean Journal of Social Sciences*, *7*(1), 126–135.

Khalisotussurur, L., & Ramidi. (2015, March 10). *Kasus Kriminalitas Anak Meningkat pada tahun 2014* [Criminal cases involving children and adolescents increased]. Retrieved from http://www.gresnews.com/berita/sosial/21041-kasus-kriminalitas-anak-meningkat-pada-2014/

Kumar, N., & Che Rose, R. (2012). The impact of knowledge sharing and Islamic work ethic on innovation capability. *Cross Cultural Management*, *19*(2), 142–165. doi:10.1108/13527601211219847

Lovat, T. (2016). Islamic morality: Teaching to balance the record. *Journal of Moral Education*, *45*(1), 1–15. doi:10.1080/03057240.2015.1136601

Lu, Y. Y., Wu, H. Y., Chen, H. C., Lin, H. L., & Chang, Y. L. (2016). The analysis of situational positive discipline strategies by positive discipline awarded teachers. *Bulletin of Educational Psychology*, *48*(2), 159–184.

Lubis, M. A. (2015). Effective implementation of the integrated Islamic education. *Global Journal Al-Thaqafah*, *5*(1), 59–68. doi:10.7187/GJAT792015.05.01

Mabud, S. A. (2018). The Emergence of Islamic Schools: A Contextual Background. In *Islamic Schooling in the West* (pp. 11–33). Cham: Palgrave Macmillan.

Mansor, N., Ariffin, R., Nordin, R., & Salleh, M. A. (2015). Mosque Tourism Certification in Waqf Management: A Model by Ukhwah Samara. *Social Sciences and Humanities*, *23*, 291–304.

Maseleno, A., Sabani, N., Huda, M., Ahmad, R., Jasmi, K. A., & Basiron, B. (2018). Demystifying learning analytics in personalised learning. *IACSIT International Journal of Engineering and Technology*, *7*(3), 1124–1129. doi:10.14419/ijet.v7i3.9789

McCullough, M. E., & Willoughby, B. L. (2009). Religion, self-regulation, and self-control: Associations, explanations, and implications. *Psychological Bulletin*, *135*(1), 69–93. doi:10.1037/a0014213 PMID:19210054

Michael, S. C., Storey, D., & Thomas, H. (2008). Discovery and Coordination in Strategic Management and Entrepreneurship. In *Strategic Entrepreneurship: Creating a New Mindset* (pp. 45–65). Wiley.

Mohd Yusob, M. L., Salleh, M. A., Haron, A. S., Makhtar, M., Asari, K. N., & Jamil, L. S. M. (2015). Maqasid al-Shariah as a Parameter for Islamic Countries in Screening International Treaties Before Ratification: An Analysis. *Pertanika Journal of Social Science & Humanities*, 23.

Morden, T. (2017). *Principles of management*. Routledge.

Önal, M. (2010). Wisdom (Hikmah) as a Holistic Basis for Inter-religious Education. In International Handbook of Inter-religious Education (pp. 221-234). Springer Netherlands.

Othman, R., Shahrill, M., Mundia, L., Tan, A., & Huda, M. (2016). Investigating the Relationship Between the Student's Ability and Learning Preferences: Evidence from Year 7 Mathematics Students. *The New Educational Review*, *44*(2), 125–138.

Parrott, J. (2017). Al-Ghazali and the golden rule: Ethics of reciprocity in the works of a Muslim sage. *Journal of Religious & Theological Information*, *16*(2), 68–78. doi:10.1080/10477845.2017.1281067

Proctor, C. (2013). The Importance of Good Character. In Research, Applications, and Interventions for Children and Adolescents: A Positive Psychology Perspective (pp. 13–21). Academic Press. doi:10.1007/978-94-007-6398-2_2

Rahim, A. A. (2013). Understanding Islamic Ethics and Its Significance on the Character Building. *International Journal of Social Science and Humanity*, *3*(6), 508–513.

Robinson, S. (2015). Islam, responsibility and business in the thought of Fethullah Gülen. *Journal of Business Ethics*, *128*(2), 369–381.

Salleh, M. A., Abu-Hussin, M. F., Azeez, Y. A., Adam, F., & Muhamad, N. H. N. (2015). The Emergence of Non-State Actors in Enhancing Malaysia's Relationship with the Gcc Countries. *Pertanika Journal of Social Science & Humanities, 23,* 267–280.

Suharto, T. (2018). Transnational Islamic education in Indonesia: An ideological perspective. *Contemporary Islam, 12*(2), 101–122. doi:10.100711562-017-0409-3

Swartwood, J. D. (2013). Wisdom as an Expert Skill. *Ethical Theory and Moral Practice, 16*(3), 511–528. doi:10.100710677-012-9367-2

Tan, B. P., Naidu, N. B. M., & Jamil, Z. (2018). Moral values and good citizens in a multi-ethnic society: A content analysis of moral education textbooks in Malaysia. *Journal of Social Studies Research, 42*(2), 119–134. doi:10.1016/j.jssr.2017.05.004

Tan, C., & Ibrahim, A. (2017). Humanism, Islamic Education, and Confucian Education. *Religious Education (Chicago, Ill.), 112*(4), 394–406. doi:10.1080/00 344087.2016.1225247

Thomas, T., Wallace, J., Allen, P., Clark, J., Jones, A., Lawrence, J., ... Sheridan Burns, L. (2017). Strategies for leading academics to rethink humanities and social sciences curricula in the context of discipline standards. *The International Journal for Academic Development, 22*(2), 120–133. doi:10.1080/1360144X.2017.1285239

Watt, W. M. (2017). *Islamic philosophy and theology.* Routledge.

Yunus, M. (1990). *Kamus bahasa Arab- Indonesia* [A Dictionary of Arab to Indonesia]. Jakarta: Bulan Bintang.

Compilation of References

(2008). Brain-based learning. InJensen, E. (Ed.), *The new paradigm of teaching* (2nd ed.). Thousand Oaks, CA: Corwin Press.

Aan Komariah dan Cepi Triatna. (2008). Visionary Leadership: Menuju Sekolah Efektif terj. Ahmad Ali Riadi & Fahrurozi. Jakarta: Bumi Aksara.

Abadi, S., Teh, K.S.M., Huda, M., Hehsan, A., Ripin, M.N., Haron, Z., … Syarifudin, A. (2018b). Design of student score application for assessing the most outstanding student at vocational high school. *International Journal of Engineering and Technology*, *7*(2.27), 172-177.

Abadi, S., Teh, K.S.M., Nasir, B.M., Huda, M., Ivanova, N.L., Sari, T.I., … Muslihudin, M. (2018a). Application model of k-means clustering: insights into promotion strategy of vocational high school. *International Journal of Engineering and Technology*, *7*(2.27), 182-187.

Abdul Fatah Hassan. (1990). *Penggunaan Minda yang Optimum dalam Pembelajaran*. Skudai: Universiti Teknologi Malaysia.

Abdullah, A. (2015). *Qur'an's Message for Humanity*. Retrieved from http://www.islamicity.org/6509/Qur'ans-message-for-humanity/

Abdullah, O. (2007). *The role of madrasah education in Singapore: A study on the philosophy and practice of madrasah education in a secular state and plural society* (Unpublished masters dissertation). International Institute of Islamic Thought and Civilization (ISTAC), Kuala Lumpur.

Abdullah, K., & Salleh, M. A. (2015). Conceptualizing Jihad Among Southeast Asia s Radical Salafi Movements. *Journal for the Study of Religions and Ideologies*, *14*(42), 121–146.

Abu Ghuddah, A. (2003). *Prophet Muhammad–the teacher and his teaching methodologies*. Karachi: Zam Zam Publishers.

Abu Guddah, A. (1996). *Al-Rasūl al-Mu'allim wa asālibuhu fi al-t'alīm* [Prophet Muḥammad the Teacher]. Halab: Maktabah al-matbuāt al-Islamiyyah.

Abu Hamid, A.-G. (2005). *Ihya' ulum al-din: The Book of the purification of the self*. Beirut, Lebanon: Dar Ibn Hazm.

Abu-Asba, K. (2001). Dilemmas in Arab education and in Arab schools in Israel. In Crossroads: Values and education in Israeli society (pp. 441-479). Jerusalem: The Israeli Ministry of Education. (in Hebrew)

Abu-Ghuddah, A. A.-F. (2013). *Muhammad the Perfect Teacher: An Insight into His Teaching Methods*. Muslims at Work.

Abu-Hussin, M. F., Salleh, M. A., & Nasir, B. M. (2015). Beyond religious affinity: Malaysia's relations with countries in the Arab Gulf. *The Pacific Review*, *28*(4), 461–482. doi:10.1080/09 512748.2015.1011213

Abu-Saad, I. (2006). Separate and unequal: The role of the state educational system in maintaining the subordination of Israel's Palestinian Arab citizens. *Social Identities*, *10*(1), 101–127. doi:10.1080/1350463042000191010

Adair, J. (2009). *Effective time management: How to save time and spend it wisely*. Pan Macmillan.

Adnan, A. (2006). *A study of Islamic leadership theory and practice in K-12 Islamic schools in Michigan* (Unpublished doctoral dissertation). Brigham Young University.

Afriyanti, D., & Ruqoyah, S. (2015). *Berbagai jenis kejahatan seperti pencurian, tawuran, dan pelecehan seks dilakukan siswa* [A variety of violence such as brawl, theft and sexual harassment involving some students]. Retrieved from http://metro.news.viva.co.id/news/read/312779-2-008-kasus-kriminal-dilakukan-anak-anak

Agbaria, A. (2010). Civic education for the Palestinians in Israel: Dilemmas and challenges. In H. A. Alexander, P. Halleli, & Y. Yonah (Eds.), *Citizenship, education, and social conflict: Israeli political education in global perspective* (pp. 217–237). Routledge.

Agbaria, A. K. (2012). Teaching Islam in Israel: On the absence of unifying goals and a collective community. In H. A. Alexander & A. K. Agbaria (Eds.), *Commitment, character, and citizenship: Religious education in liberal democracy* (pp. 181–198). New York: Routledge.

Ahmad Sharifuddin Mustapha & Mohd Zain Mubarak. (2006). *Dakwah melalui muzik dan nyanyian: satu perbincangan. Kertas kerja Seminar Serantau Dakwah dan Kesenian. Anjuran Jabatan Pengajian dakwah dan Kepimpinan*. Fakulti Pengajian Islam, Universiti Kebangsaan Malaysia.

Ahmad, N. (2003). *Menguatkan ingatan*. Retrieved from http://books.google.com.my

Ahmad, I. (2001). Teaching Islamic Studies in the Non-Arab World: With or Without Arabic? *Journal of Muslim Minority Affairs*, *21*(2), 273–285. doi:10.1080/1360200120092851

Ahmed, S. (2015). Attitudes towards English Language Learning among EFL Learners at UMSKAL. *Journal of Education and Practice*, *6*(18), 6–16.

Aimes, C., & Archer, J. (1988). Achievement Goals in the Classroom: Students' Learning Strategies and Motivation Processes. *Journal of Educational Psychology*, *80*(3), 260–267. doi:10.1037/0022-0663.80.3.260

Ajem, R., & Memon, N. A. (2011). *Principles of Islamic Pedagogy, a Teacher's Manual. Islamic Teacher Education Program.* Toronto: Canada Razi Group.

Akdere, M., Russ-Eft, D., & Eft, N. (2006). The Islamic worldview of Adult learning in the workplace: Surrendering to God. *Advances in Developing Human Resources, 8*(3), 355–363. doi:10.1177/1523422306288428

Al Attas, S. M. N. (1979). *Aims and Objectives of Islamic Education.* Jeddah: King Abdul Aziz University.

Al Hamdani, D. (2016). The character education in islamic education viewpoint. *Jurnal Pendidikan Islam UIN Sunan Gunung Djati, 1*(1), 98–109. doi:10.15575/jpi.v1i1.614

Al Qur'an al Karim. (2005). *Madinah: King Fahd Complex for the Printing of the Holy Qur'an.* Author.

Ala'wa, S. (2016). *The Islamic intellectual schools: From Khawarij to Muslim Brotherhood.* Beirut: Arab Network for Research and Publishing. (in Arabic)

Alatas, S. F. (1985). Notes on various theories regarding the Islamization of the Malay Archipelago. *The Muslim World, 75*(3-4), 162–175. doi:10.1111/j.1478-1913.1985.tb02761.x

Al-Attas, S. M. N. (1979). Aims and objectives of Islamic education. Hodder and Stoughton.

Al-Attas, S. (1979). *Aims and objectives of Islamic education.* Jeddah: Hodder & Stoughton.

Alavi, H. R. (2008). Nearness to God: A perspective on Islamic education. *Religious Education (Chicago, Ill.), 103*(1), 5–21. doi:10.1080/00344080701807361

Al-Azem, T. (2016). *The Transmission of Adab: Educational Ideals and their Institutional Manifestations. In Philosophies of Islamic Education* (pp. 124–138). Routledge.

Al-Bani, M. N. (2008). *Ringkasan Shahih Muslim, terj., Elly Lathifah.* Jakarta: Gema Insani.

Al-Bukhārī, M. I. (1986). *The Translation of the meaning of Sahīh Al-Bukhārī* (6th ed.). (M. M. Khan, Trans.). Lahore: Kāzi Publications.

Alexander, H. (2000). In search of a vision of the good: Values education and the postmodern condition. In R. Gardner. J. Cairns. & D. Lawton. (Eds.), Education for values (pp. 303-312). London: Kogan Page.

Alexander, H. (2009). Educating identity: Toward a pedagogy of difference. In S. Miedema (Ed.), *Religious Education as Encounter: A Tribute to John Hull* (pp. 45–52). Munster: Waxman.

Alexander, H. A. (2015). *Reimagining liberal education: Affiliation and inquiry in democratic schooling.* New York: Bloomsbury.

Alexander, H. A. (2016a). What is critical about critical pedagogy? Conflicting conceptions of criticism in the curriculum. *Educational Philosophy and Theory.* doi:10.1080/00131857.2016 .1228519

Alexander, H. A. (2016b). What can go wrong in religious instruction? And what should go right? In B. Warnick (Ed.), *Philosophy: Education: Macmillan interdisciplinary Handbooks* (pp. 249–267). New York: Macmillan Reference.

Alexander, R. J. (2017). *Towards Dialogic Teaching: rethinking classroom talk* (5th ed.). Dialogos.

Al-Ghazali, A. H. (1898). *Ihya' Ulum-Id-Din: Revival of Religious Learnings (Fazl-Ul-Karim, Trans.)*. Karachi: Darul Ishaat.

Al-Ghazālī, A. H. (1993). *'Ihyā 'Ulūm-ud-Dīn* [The Revival of Religious Sciences] (F. Karim, Trans.). Karachi: Dārul Ishaat.

Al-Haj, M. (1995). *Education, Empowerment and Control: The Case of the Arabs in Israel*. Albany, NY: State University of New York.

Al-Ḥākim, M. A. (1990). Mustadrak Al-Ḥākim. Beirut: Dar al-Kutub al-'Ilmiyyah.

Al-Hilaalee, S. (1999). *The Manners of the Scholar & Student of Knowledge*. Birmingham, UK: Salafi Publications.

Ali, A. (2003). *Kamus Inggris-Indonesia-Arab*. Yogyakarta: Mukti Karya Grafika.

Ali, A. M., Daud, N. S. M., Juhary, J., & Raihanah, M. M. (2018). A MOOC for Literature Integrated Language Classroom: Pedagogical Suggestions for the Development of Higher Order Thinking Skills (HOTS). *Arab World English Journal.*, *4*. doi:10.24093/awej/call4.2

Ali, M. M. (2011). *The religion of Islam*. Ahmadiyya Anjuman Ishaat Islam Lahore USA.

Al-Jabri, M. A. (1996). The religion, state, and the implementation of sharia. Markez Derasat Alwihda Alarabia. (in Arabic)

Al-Jabri, M. (2009). *Democracy, human rights, and law in Islamic thought*. London: I. B. Tauris Publishers.

Aljunied, S. M. K., & Dayang, I. H. (2005). Estranged from the ideal past: Historical evolution of madrassahs in Singapore. *Journal of Muslim Minority Affairs*, *25*(2), 249–260. doi:10.1080/13602000500350694

Al-Qabisi, A. H . (1986). *Al-Risalah al-Mufassalah li-Ahwal al-Muta'alimin wa- Ahkam al-Mu'allimmin wa al-Muta'allimin*. Tunis: al-Sharikah al-Tunisiyyah li-Tawzi'.

Al-Qaradhawi, Y. (1996). *Al-Islam wa al-Fann*. Al-Qaherah: Matbaah al-Madani.

Al-Qazwinī, M. Y. (1996). *Sunan Ibn-i-Majah* (M. T. Ansari, Trans.). Lahore: Kazi Publications.

Al-Qur'an al-Karim. (2005). *Madinah: King Fahd Complex for the Printing of the Holy Qur'an*. Author.

Al-Qushayrī, M. H. (1971). *Ŝahih Muslim* (A. H. Siddiqī, Trans.). Dār al Manār.

Al-Sharaf, A. (2013). Developing scientific thinking methods and applications in Islamic education. *Education, 133*(3), 272–282.

Alshareef, M. (2007). *Humanity's Teacher: 21 Teaching Techniques of the Prophet.* Retrieved August 31, 2017, from http://www.khutbah.com/en/ed_know/humanity_teacher.php

Al-Sijistānī, S. A. (1984). *Sunan Abū Dāwūd* (A. Hasan, Trans.). Lahore: Sh. Muḥammad Ashraf.

Al-Tabarī, M. J. (1990). *The Commentary on the Qur'ān.* Oxford, UK: Oxford University Press.

Al-tafakkur fi khalq Allah (Ed.). (1995). *Maher al-Munjid.* Beirut: Dar al-Fikr al-Mu'asir.

Al-Talbi, A. (1993). Al-Farabi (259-339 AH/872-950 AD). *Prospects: The Quarterly Review of Comparative Education, 23*(1/2), 353–372.

Al-Yaḥṣubī, `I. M. (1991). *Muhammad the Messenger Ash-Shifa of Qadi `Iyad* (A.A. Bewley, Trans.). Granada: Madinah Press.

Al-Zarnūjī, B. (2008). Pedoman Belajar Bagi Penuntun Ilmu Secara Islami [Students' Islamic Guide for Learning] (M. Thaifuri, Trans.). In Ta'lim al Muta'allim. Surabaya: Menara Suci.

Al-Zarnūjī, B. (Ed.). (2008). Ta'lim al Muta'allim (Pedoman belajar bagi penuntun ilmu secara Islami) [Islamic students' guide for learning]. Surabaya: Menara Suci.

Al-Zarnūjī, B. (2008). *Ta'lim al-Muta'allim: Tariq al-Ta'allum* [Learning instruction for students' learning]. Surabaya, Indonesia: Al Miftah.

Al-Zeera, Z. (2001). *Wholeness and holiness in education: An Islamic perspective.* Herndon, VA: The International Institute of Islamic Thought.

Aminin, S., Huda, M., Ninsiana, W., & Dacholfany, M. I. (2018). Sustaining civic-based moral values: Insights from language learning and literature. *International Journal of Civil Engineering and Technology, 9*(4), 157–174.

Aminudin, N., Fauzi, Huda, M., Hehsan, A., Ripin, M.N., Haron, Z., … Fauzi, A.M. (2018c). Application program learning based on android for students experiences. *International Journal of Engineering and Technology, 7*(2.27), 194-198.

Aminudin, N., Huda, M., Ihwani, S.S., Noor, S.S.M., Basiron, B., Jasmi, K.A., … Rohmadi, D. (2018a). The family hope program using AHP method. *International Journal of Engineering and Technology, 7*(2.27), 188-193.

Aminudin, N., Huda, M., Mohamed, A.K., Embong, W.H.W., Mohamad, A.M., Basiron, B., … Nungsiati. (2018b). Higher education selection using simple additive weighting. *International Journal of Engineering and Technology, 7*(2.27), 211-217.

Andrews, T. (2012). What is social constructionism? *The Grounded Theory Review, 11*(1), 39–46.

Andriani, R. (2015). Nilai-Nilai Pendidikan Budaya dan Karakter Bangsa. Retrieved from http://www.membumikanpendidikan.com/2015/03/nilai-nilai-pendidikan-budaya-dan.html

Annalakshmi, N., & Abeer, M. (2011). Islamic worldview, religious personality and resilience among Muslim adolescent students in India. *Europe's Journal of Psychology, 7*(4), 716–738. doi:10.5964/ejop.v7i4.161

Anshari, M., Almunawar, M. N., Shahrill, M., Wicaksono, D. K., & Huda, M. (2017). Smartphones usage in the classrooms: Learning aid or interference? *Education and Information Technologies, 22*(6), 3063–3079. doi:10.100710639-017-9572-7

Apriliawati, R. (2011). *Panduan Pintar Ibu Hamil. Cet. Ke-1*. Yogyakarta: Moncer Publisher.

Aqsha, M., Melor, M., Tajul, M., & Mohd, N. (2011). The Perception and Method in Teaching and Learning Islamic Education. *International Journal of Education and Information Technologies, 5*(1).

Arifin, N. (2015). *Video Kekerasan Pelajar di Jawa Timur Beredar* [videos of violence involving students scattered in East Java]. Retrieved from http://daerah.sindonews.com/read/934611/23/video-kekerasan-pelajar-di-jawa-timur-beredar-1418038066

Arifin, M., & Khambali, K. B. M. (2016). Islam dan akulturasi budaya lokal di Aceh (Studi terhadap ritual *rah ulei* di kuburan dalam masyarakat Pidie Aceh). *Jurnal Ilmiah Islam Futura, 15*(2), 251–284. doi:10.22373/jiif.v15i2.545

Arjmand, R. (2017). Islam and Education in the Modern Era: Social, Cultural, Political Changes and Responses from Islamic Education. Handbook of Islamic Education, 1-17.

Armstrong, K. (1993). *Muḥammad: A Western attempt to understand Islam*. London: Victor Gollancz Ltd.

Arthur, J. (2010). Of good character: Exploration of virtues and values in 3-25 year-olds. Exeter, UK: Imprint Academic.

Arthur, J., & Wilson, K. (2010). New research directions in character and values education in the UK. In T. Lovat, R. Toomey & N. Clement (Eds.), International research handbook on values education and student wellbeing (pp. 339-358). Dordrecht, The Netherlands: Springer. doi:10.1007/978-90-481-8675-4_21

Arthur, J. (2003). *Education with character: The moral economy of schooling*. London: Routledge. doi:10.4324/9780203220139

Arthur, J., Gearon, L., & Sears, A. (2010). *Education, politics, and religion*. New York: Routledge. doi:10.4324/9780203846575

Asadullah, M. N. (2016). Trust, trustworthiness, and traditional Islamic education. *Oxford Development Studies, 44*(2), 152–166. doi:10.1080/13600818.2015.1104294

Ashaari, M. F., Ismail, Z., Puteh, A., Samsudin, M. A., Ismail, M., Kawangit, R., ... Ramzi, M. I. (2012). An Assessment of Teaching and Learning Methodology in Islamic Studies. *Procedia: Social and Behavioral Sciences, 59*, 618–626. doi:10.1016/j.sbspro.2012.09.322

Ashraf, S. A. (1988). The conceptual framework of education: The Islamic perspective. *Muslim Education*, *5*(2), 8–18.

Aşlamacı, İ., & Kaymakcan, R. (2017). A model for Islamic education from Turkey: The Imam-Hatip schools. *British Journal of Religious Education*, *39*(3), 279–292. doi:10.1080/01416200.2015.1128390

Assegaf, A. R., Zakaria, A. R., & Sulaiman, A. M. (2012). *The Closer Bridge towards Islamic Studies in Higher Education in Malaysia and Indonesia*. Creative Education; doi:10.4236/ce.2012.326149

Asyafah, A. (2014). Research based instruction in the teaching of islamic education. *SpringerPlus*, *3*(1), 755. doi:10.1186/2193-1801-3-755 PMID:25674481

Asy-Syarbini, M. A. (1995). *Mughni Al Muhtaj Ila Ma'rifat Al Ma'ani Al Fadhul Minhaj, Juz V*. Baerut: Dar Al Kutub Al Ilmiyah.

Atmotiyoso, P., & Huda, M. (2018). Investigating Factors Influencing Work Performance on Mathematics Teaching: A Case Study. *International Journal of Instruction*, *11*(3), 391–402. doi:10.12973/iji.2018.11327a

Attaran, M. (1987). *Great Muslim mentors' views about the upbringing of children*. Tehran: Ministry of Education Press.

Attaran, M. (2015). Moral education, habituation, and divine assistance in view of Ghazali. *Journal of Research on Christian Education*, *24*(1), 43–51. doi:10.1080/10656219.2015.1008083

Avery, P. G. (2002). Political tolerance, democracy, and adolescents. In W. Parker (Ed.), *Education for democracy: Contexts, curricula, assessments* (pp. 113–130). Information Age Publishing.

Avery, P. G., Levy, S. A., & Simmons, A. M. (2013). Deliberating controversial public issues as part of civic education. *Social Studies*, *104*(3), 105–114. doi:10.1080/00377996.2012.691571

Ayalon, H., & Yogev, A. (1996). The alternative worldview of state religious high schools in Israel. *Comparative Education Review*, *40*(1), 7–27. doi:10.1086/447353

Ayoob, M. (2008). *The many faces of political Islam: Religion and politics in the Muslim World*. Ann Arbor, MI: University of Michigan Press.

Azami, M. M. (1992). *Studies in Hadith Methodology and Literature*. American Trust Publications.

Azman, H. (2016). Implementation and Challenges of English Language Education Reform in Malaysian Primary Schools. *3L: The Southeast Asian Journal of English Language Studies, 22*(3).

Bakar, O. (2015). *Islamic civilisation and the modern world: Thematic essays*. Bandar Seri Begawan, Brunei: UBD Press.

Bakhshialiabad, H., Bakshi, M., & Hassanshahi, G. (2015). Students' perceptions of the academic learning environment in seven medical sciences courses based on DREEM. *Advances in Medical Education and Practice*, *6*, 195–203. doi:10.2147/AMEP.S60570 PMID:25848331

Balakrishnan, V. (2017). Making moral education work in a multicultural society with Islamic hegemony. *Journal of Moral Education*, *46*(1), 79–87. doi:10.1080/03057240.2016.1268111

Baldwin, L., & Beauchamp, G. (2014). A study of teacher confidence in teaching music within the context of the introduction of the Foundation Phase (3–7 years) statutory Education Programme in Wales. *British Journal of Music Education*, *31*(2), 195–208. doi:10.1017/S0265051714000060

Barakāt Badr al-Dīn al-Ghazī, A. (2009). *Al-Dduru al-Nadid fi adab al-mufid wal- mustafid. Annotated by Abu Ya'qub Nash'at Kamal Al-Misri*. Al-Jizah, Egypt: Maktabat al-Taw'iyah al-Islamiyah.

Barnes, P. (2001, October). (200). What is wrong with the phenomenological approach to religious education? *Religious Education (Chicago, Ill.)*, *96*(4), 445–461. doi:10.1080/003440801753442366

Barry, C. (2011). English Language Teaching in Brunei. *RELC Journal*, *42*(3), 203–220. doi:10.1177/0033688211401255

Barry, I. (2005). Fouta-Jalon: Nineteenth century. In K. Shillington (Ed.), *Encyclopaedia of African history* (pp. 538–539). New York: Fitzoroy Dearborn.

Bass, B. M. (1998). *Transformational leadership: Industrial, military, and educational impact*. Mahwah, NJ: Erlbaum.

Bass, B. M., & Avolio, B. J. (Eds.). (1994). *Improving organisational effectiveness through transformational leadership*. Thousand Oaks, CA: Sage Publications.

Bauben, J. M. (1996). *Image of the Prophet Muḥammad in the West – A Study of Muir, Margoliouth and Watt*. Leicester, UK: The Islamic Foundation.

Beekun, R. I., & Badawi, J. (1999). *Leadership: An Islamic perspective*. Amana Publications.

Bennett, C. (1998). *In Search of Muḥammad*. London: Cassell.

Benninga, J., Berkowitz, M., Kuehn, P., & Smith, K. (2006). Character and academics: What good schools do. *Phi Delta Kappan*, *87*(6), 448–452. doi:10.1177/003172170608700610

Bensaid, B., & Machouche, S.T. (1406). *Memorizing the Words of God: Special Reference to 'Abdul Rahman Ibn Khaldun'*.

Bensaid, B., Machouche, S. B. T., & Grine, F. (2014). A Qur'anic framework for spiritual intelligence. *Religions*, *5*(1), 179–198. doi:10.3390/rel5010179

Bergsma, A., & Ardelt, M. (2012). Self-reported wisdom and happiness: An empirical investigation. *Journal of Happiness Studies*, *13*(3), 481–499. doi:10.100710902-011-9275-5

Bloom, J. M. (2008). Paper in Sudanic Africa. In S. Jeppie & S. B. Diagne (Eds.), *The meanings of Timbuktu* (pp. 77–92). Cape Town: HSRC Press.

Boghossian, P. (2001). What is social construction? Times Literary Supplement, February 23, 6-8. Boutieri, C. (2013). Inheritance, Heritage, and the Disinherited: Ambiguities of Religious Pedagogy in the Moroccan Public School. *Anthropology & Education Quarterly*, *44*(4), 363–380. doi:10.1111/aeq.12037

Boyle, H. (2002). *The Growth of Qur'anic Schooling and the Marginalization of Islamic Pedagogy: The Case of Morocco.* Paper presented at the Annual Meeting of the Comparative and International Education Society, Orlando, FL.

Boyle, H. (2000). *Quranic Schools in Morocco: Agents of Preservation and Change (Doctorate in Philosophy in Education).* Bell and Howell Information and Learning Company.

Boyle, H. (2006). Memorisation and Learning in Islamic Schools. *Comparative Education Review*, *50*(3), 478–495. doi:10.1086/504819

Brock, L. L., Nishida, T. K., Chiong, C., Grimm, K. J., & Rimm-Kaufman, S. E. (2008). Children's perceptions of the classroom environment and social and academic performance: A longitudinal analysis of the contribution of the Responsive Classroom approach. *Journal of School Psychology*, *46*(2), 129–149. doi:10.1016/j.jsp.2007.02.004 PMID:19083354

Brophy, J. E. (2013). *Motivating students to learn.* London: Routledge. doi:10.4324/9780203858318

Brownlee, J. L., Scholes, L., Walker, S., & Johansson, E. (2016). Critical values education in the early years: Alignment of teachers' personal epistemologies and practices for active citizenship. *Teaching and Teacher Education*, *59*, 261–273. doi:10.1016/j.tate.2016.06.009

Bruer, J. (1999). In search of . . . brain-based education. *Phi Delta Kappan*, *80*, 648–657.

Bryman, A. (2012). *Social research methods* (4th ed.). Oxford, UK: Oxford University Press.

Burke, C., & Grosvenor, I. (2003). *The School I'd like.* London: RoutledgeFalmer. doi:10.4324/9780203439074

Burns, J. M. (1978). *Leadership.* New York: Harper & Row.

Burton, J. (1994). *An Introduction to the Hadith.* Edinburgh, UK: Edinburgh University Press.

Byrne, C. (2014). *Religion in secular education: What, in heaven's name, are we teaching our children?* Boston: Brill. doi:10.1163/9789004264342

Campbell, R. J., Kyriakides, L., Muijs, R. D., & Robinson, W. (2004). Effective teaching and values: Some implications for research and teacher appraisal. *Oxford Review of Education*, *30*(4), 451–465. doi:10.1080/0305498042000303955

Carnegie Corporation. (1996). *Years of promise: A comprehensive learning strategy for America's children.* Executive summary. Available at: http://www.carnegie.org/sub/pubs/execsum.html

Carr, D. (2006). Professional and personal values and virtues in education and teaching. *Oxford Review of Education*, *32*(2), 171–183. doi:10.1080/03054980600645354

Carr, D. (2007). Character in teaching. *British Journal of Educational Studies, 55*(4), 369–389. doi:10.1111/j.1467-8527.2007.00386.x

Carr, D. (2010). Personal and professional values in teaching. In T. Lovat, R. Toomey, & N. Clement (Eds.), *International research handbook on values education and student wellbeing* (pp. 63–74). Dordrecht, The Netherlands: Springer. doi:10.1007/978-90-481-8675-4_4

Charmaz, K. (2006). *Constructing grounded theory: A practical guide through qualitative analysis.* London: Sage.

Chase, J. A. D., Topp, R., Smith, C. E., Cohen, M. Z., Fahrenwald, N., Zerwic, J. J., ... Conn, V. S. (2013). Time management strategies for research productivity. *Western Journal of Nursing Research, 35*(2), 155–176. doi:10.1177/0193945912451163 PMID:22868990

Cheddadi, A. (Ed.). (2005). Al-muqaddimah. Morocco: Dār al-Funūn wa-al-'Ulūm wal-Adab.

Che-Haron, S. (2014). Using communicative approach in Arabic language classroom to develop Arabic speaking ability. *Journal of Education and Practice, 5*(39), 29–34.

Che-Haron, S., Sheikh-Ahmad, I., Mamat, A., & Ahmed-Mohamed, I. H. (2010). Understanding Arabic-speaking learning strategies among selected Malay learners: A case study at the International Islamic University Malaysia (IIUM). *Contemporary Issues in Education Research, 3*(8), 9–19. doi:10.19030/cier.v3i8.222

Che-Musa, N., Yew, L. K., & Azman, H. (2012). Exploring English Language Learning and Teaching in Malaysia. *GEMA Online Journal of Language Studies., 12*(1).

Chiu, L. L., & Gwo, J. H. (2016). A self-regulated flipped classroom approach to improving student's learning performance in a mathematics course. *Computers & Education*, 126–140.

Choudhury, M. A. (2016a). An ethical worldview of Moral-Social reconstruction. *Absolute Reality in the Qur'an*, 149-180.

Choudhury, M. A. (2016a). Technically integrating Al-Wasatiyyah and Maqasid As-Shari'ah with a Tawhidi methodological worldview. *Absolute Reality in the Qur'an*, 101-111.

Choudhury, M. A. (2016b). Introduction: Foundations of the Qur'anic Worldview. *Absolute Reality in the Qur'an*, 3-18.

Choudhury, M. A. (2016c). Analytical Precept of Absolute Reality in the Qur'an. *Absolute Reality in the Qur'an*, 19-37.

Choudhury, M. A. (2016c). Technically integrating Al-Wasatiyyah and Maqasid As-Shari'ah with a Tawhidi methodological worldview. *Absolute Reality in the Qur'an*, 101-111.

Choudhury, M. A. (2016d). *Absolute Reality in the Qur'an*. Academic Press.

Choudhury, M. A. (2016d). Introduction: foundations of the qur'anic worldview. *Absolute Reality in the Qur'an*, 3-18.

Choudhury, M. A. (2016e). Analytical precept of absolute reality in the qur'an. *Absolute Reality in the Qur'an*, 19-37.

Choudhury, M. A. (2018). Endogenous Ethics in Evolutionary Learning Model Contra Utilitarianism: Endogenous Ethics. *Ethics and Decision-Making for Sustainable Business Practices*, 55-72.

Choudhury, M. A. (2016b). *Absolute Reality in the Qur'an*. Basingstoke, UK: Palgrave Macmillan. doi:10.1057/978-1-137-58947-7

Choudhury, M. A. (2018). The ontological law of Tawhid contra 'Shari'ah-compliance' in Islamic portfolio finance. *International Journal of Law and Management*, *60*(2), 413–434. doi:10.1108/IJLMA-01-2017-0001

Cleaveland, T. (2008). Timbuktu and Walata: lineages and higher education. In S. Jeppie & S. B. Diagne (Eds.), *The meanings of Timbuktu* (pp. 45–58). Cape Town: HSRC.

Cohen, L., Manion, L., & Morrison, K. (2007). *Research methods in Education*. New York: Routledge. doi:10.4324/9780203029053

Cook, J. (2010). Classical Foundations of Islamic Education. Brigham Young University Press.

Cook, B. J., & Malkāwī, F. H. (2010). *Classical foundations of Islamic educational thought: A compendium of parallel English-Arabic texts* (1st ed.). Brigham Young University Press.

Creswell, J. W. (1998). Qualitative inquiry and research design: Choosing among five approaches. *Sage (Atlanta, Ga.)*.

Crotty, R. (2010). Values education as an ethical dilemma about sociability. In T. Lovat, R. Toomey, & N. Clement (Eds.), International research handbook on values education and student wellbeing (pp. 631-644). Dordrecht, the Netherlands: Springer. doi:10.1007/978-90-481-8675-4_36

Cunliffe, A. L. (2008). Orientations to social constructionism: Relationally responsive social constructionism and its implications for knowledge and learning. *Management Learning*, *39*(2), 123–139. doi:10.1177/1350507607087578

Dabbagh, N., & Kitsantas, A. (2012). Personal Learning Environments, social media, and self-regulated learning: A natural formula for connecting formal and informal learning. *The Internet and Higher Education*, *15*(1), 3–8. doi:10.1016/j.iheduc.2011.06.002

Dalmeri. (2014). Pendidikan Untuk Pengembangan Karakter, Telaah terhadap Gagasan Thomas Lickona dalam Educating for Character. Jurnal Al-Ulum IAIN Sultan Amai Gorontalo, 14(14), 278.

Damasio, A. R. (2003). *Looking for Spinoza: Joy, sorrow, and the feeling brain*. New York: Harcourt.

Damasio, H., & Damasio, A. (2007). Social conduct, neurobiology, and education. In M. M. Suárez-Orozco (Ed.), *Learning in the global era: International perspectives on globalization and education* (pp. 104–117). Berkeley, CA: The University of California Press and the Ross Institute.

Darussalam, G. (2004). *Pedagogi Pendidikan Islam*. Kuala Lumpur: Utusan Publications and Distributions.

Darwis, R. (2015). Tradition of Hileyiya: The interaction between religion and traditions in Gorontalo in sociology of Islamic law perspective. *Analisa: Journal of Social Science and Religion*, *22*(1), 57–68.

Davidson, M., Khmelkov, V., & Lickona, T. (2010). The power of character: Needed for, and developed from, teaching and learning. In T. Lovat, R. Toomey & N. Clement (Eds.), International research handbook on values education and student wellbeing (pp. 427-454). Dordrecht, The Netherlands: Springer.

Deakin University. (2014). *ECA409-Primary Arts Education*. Retrieved from http://www.deakin. edu.au/current-students/courses/unitsearch.php?entunit=eca409&entkeyword=&year=2014

DEEWR. (2008). *At the heart of what we do: Values education at the centre of schooling*. Report of the Values Education Good Practice Schools Project – Stage 2. Melbourne: Curriculum Corporation. Available at: http://www.curriculum.edu.au/values/val_vegps2_final_report,26142.html

Delen, E., Liew, J., & Willson, V. (2014). Effects of interactivity and instructional scaffolding on learning: Self-regulation in online video-based environments. *Computers & Education*, *78*, 312–320. doi:10.1016/j.compedu.2014.06.018

Deliverance from Error. (1980). Boston: Twayne.

Demirel Ucan, A., & Wright, A. (2019). Improving the pedagogy of Islamic religious education through an application of critical religious education, variation theory and the learning study model. *British Journal of Religious Education*, *41*(2), 202–217. doi:10.1080/01416200.2018.1484695

Dermawan, Y. G. (2013). *Tabu dan Mitos Seputar Wanita Hamil Pada Etnik Jawa di Desa Bakaran Batu Kabupaten Deli Serdang* (Unpublished undergraduate thesis). UNIMED.

Desai, M. S., & Johnson, R. A. (2014). Integrated systems oriented student-centric learning environment: A framework for curriculum development. *Campus-Wide Information Systems*, *31*(1), 24–45. doi:10.1108/CWIS-01-2013-0002

DEST. (2003). *Values education study* (Executive summary final report). Melbourne: Curriculum Corporation. Available at: http://www.curriculum.edu.au/verve/_resources/VES_Final_Report14Nov.pdf

DEST. (2005). *National framework for values education in Australian schools*. Canberra: Australian Government Department of Education, Science and Training. Available at: http://www.curriculum.edu.au/verve/_resources/Framework_PDF_version_for_the_web.pdf

DEST. (2006). *Implementing the national framework for values education in Australian schools: Report of the Values Education Good Practice Schools Project – Stage 1*. Melbourne: Curriculum Corporation. Available at: http://www.curriculum.edu.au/verve/_resources/VEGPS1_FINAL_REPORT_081106.pdf

DeWaelsche, S. A. (2015). Critical thinking, questioning and student engagement in Korean university English courses. *Linguistics and Education*, *32*, 131–147. doi:10.1016/j.linged.2015.10.003

Dewan Redaksi Ensiklopedia Islam. (1997). Ensiklopedia Islam Cet. IV. Jakarta: PT. Ichtiar Baru Van Hoeve,.

Dewey, J. (1964). *John Dewey on education: Selected writings*. New York: Modern Library.

Diagne, S. (2004). Islam in Africa: Examining the Notion of an African Identity within the Islamic World. In K. Wiredu (Ed.), *A Companion to African Philosophy* (pp. 374–383). Oxford, UK: Blackwell Publishing.

Diallo, I. (2012). Qur'anic and Ajami literacies in pre-colonial West Africa. *Current Issues in Language Planning*, *13*(2), 91–104. doi:10.1080/14664208.2012.687498

Direktorat Pendidikan Tinggi Agama Islam (Ditpertais) STAIN Kudus. (2014). Kurikulum Berbasis Kompetensi. Retrieved from http://www.ditpertais.net/stainkudus/kdsprodi03.htm

Dodge, B. (1961). *Al-Azhar: A millennium of Muslim Learning*. Washington, DC: The Middle East Institute.

Doğan, R. (2002). The Usage of the metaphor in the Prophet Muḥammad's (pbuh) ḥadīths as an educational method. *Muslim Educational Quarterly*, *19*(3), 4–15.

Don, A. G., Muhamat Kawangit, R., Hamjah, S. H., Sham, M. F., Nasir, B., Asha'ari, M. F., & Abd Ghani, M. Z. (2012). Teaching Da'wah as Islamic studies (Teds) in higher learning institutions: Malaysian experience. *Advances in Natural and Applied Sciences, 6*. Retrieved from http://www.scopus.com/inward/record.url?eid=2-s2.0-84876710611&partnerID=40&md5=5505f41683251e6b765bec1531003443

Doumato, E., & Starrett, G. (2007). *Teaching Islam: Textbooks and religion in the Middle East*. Boulder, CO: Rienner.

Duckworth, A. L., Grant, H., Loew, B., Oettingen, G., & Gollwitzer, P. M. (2011). Self-regulation strategies improve self-discipline in adolescents: Benefits of mental contrasting and implementation intentions. *Educational Psychology*, *31*(1), 17–26. doi:10.1080/01443410.2010.506003

Dumont, H., Istance, D., & Benavides, F. (2014). The nature of learning: An OCED stocktake. In A. Pollard (Ed.), *Readings for reflective teaching in schools* (pp. 102–105). London: Bloomsbury.

Dwairy, M. (1997). *Personality culture and Arabic society: Psychological study*. New York: Haworth Press. (In Arabic)

Džanić, N. D., & Pejić, A. (2016, October). The Effect of Using Songs On Young Learners and Their Motivation for Learning English. *An Interdisciplinary Journal*, *1*(2), 40–54.

Eaude, T. (2011). *Thinking through pedagogy for Primary and Early Years*. Exeter, UK: Learning Matters.

Eaude, T. (2016). *New Perspective on Young Children's Moral Education: developing character through a virtue ethics approach*. London: Bloomsbury.

EisnerE. (2003). *The Function of Music In Education*. Retrieved from http://www.isme.org/article/view/89/1/26

Elkins, D. N., Hedstrom, J. L., Hughes, L. L., Leaf, J. A., & Saunders, C. (1988). Toward a Humanistic-Phenomenological Spirituality: Definition, Description and Measurement. *Journal of Humanistic Psychology*, *28*(4), 5–18. doi:10.1177/0022167888284002

Elliott, J. (2015). Towards a comprehensive pedagogical theory to inform lesson study: An editorial review. *International Journal for Lesson and Learning Studies*, *4*(4), 318–327. doi:10.1108/IJLLS-08-2015-0028

Enan, M. A. (1961). *Ibn Khaldun: His life and work*. Lahore, Pakistan: Ashraf Press.

Encyclopædia-Britannica. (2015). *Malay Archipelago*. Retrieved from http://www.britannica.com/place/Malay-Archipelago

Engebretson, K. (2006). Phenomenology and religious education theory. In M. de Souza (Ed.), *International handbook of the religious, moral and spiritual dimensions in education* (pp. 651–665). Dordrecht: Springer.

Entwistle, N. J. (1991). Approaches to learning and perceptions of the learning environment. *Higher Education*, *22*(3), 201–204. doi:10.1007/BF00132287

Erricker, C. (2010). *Religious education: A conceptual and interdisciplinary approach for secondary level*. London: Routledge.

Ervina, I. (2017). *Ritual Peutron Aneuk dan Dampaknya Terhadap Kehidupan Masyarakat di Gampong Tokoh Kecamatan Manggeng Kabupaten Aceh Barat Daya* (Unpublished Undergraduate Thesis). UIN Ar-Raniry.

Evertson, C. M., & Weinstein, C. S. (Eds.). (2013). *Handbook of classroom management: Research, practice, and contemporary issues*. Routledge. doi:10.4324/9780203874783

Ewens, T. (2014). *Reflective Primary Teaching*. Critical Publishing.

Fahriana, A. S., & Huda, M. (2019). Application of Analysis of Strengths, Weaknesses, Opportunities, and Threats in Islamic Education Institutions. *Istawa: Jurnal Pendidikan Islam*, *4*(1), 50–64. doi:10.24269/ijpi.v4i1.1670

Fakhry, M. (2001). *Averroes: His life and influence*. London: One World Publications.

Faryadi, Q. (2015). An Islamic perspective of teaching philosophy: A personal justification. *Journal of Research & Method in Education*, *5*(6), 49–60.

Fattah, N. (2001). *Landasan Manajemen Pendidikan*. Bandung: Remaja Rodaskarya.

Fauzi, I., Irviani, R., Muslihudin, M., Satria, F., Huda, M., Kamenez, N. V., & Maseleno, A. (2019). Revolutionizing Education through Artificial Intelligence: Fuzzy Multiple Attribute Decision Making Approach for Determining the Best Vocational High School. *Applied Mechanics and Materials*, *892*, 234–239. doi:10.4028/www.scientific.net/AMM.892.234

Fears of Radicalism Constrains Scholars. (2007, February 9). *Times Higher Education Supplement*.

Feinberg, W. (2006). *For goodness sake: Religious schools and education for democratic citizenry.* New York: Routledge.

Ferrari, M., Kahn, A., Benayon, M., & Nero, J. (2011). Phronesis, sophia, and hochma: Developing wisdom in Islam and Judaism. *Research in Human Development*, *8*(2), 128–148. doi:10.1080/15427609.2011.568869

Fisherman, S. (2011). Socialization agents influencing the religious identity of religious Israeli adolescents. *Religious Education (Chicago, Ill.)*, *106*(3), 272–298. doi:10.1080/00344087.2011.569653

Flay, B., & Aldred, C. (2010). The positive action program: Improving academics, behaviour, and character by teaching comprehensive skills for successful learning and living. In T. Lovat, R. Toomey, & N. Clement (Eds.), *International research handbook on values education and student wellbeing* (pp. 471–502). Dordrecht, The Netherlands: Springer. doi:10.1007/978-90-481-8675-4_28

Forbes, M., & Baker, W. (2017). Moral Values and Market Attitudes. In Markets, Morals, and Religion (pp. 43-50). Routledge.

Foucault, M. (2018). Discipline. In *Rethinking The Subject* (pp. 60–69). Routledge. doi:10.4324/9780429497643-4

Fromherz, A. J. (2010). *Ibn Khaldun: Life and time*. Edinburg University Press.

Fuadi, T. M. (2018). Mengkontruksi kearifan lokal dalam pengobatan tradisional reproduksi oleh dukun bayi di Aceh. *Prosiding Biotik*, *2*(1), 279–283.

Fullan, M. (2001). *Leading in a culture of change*. Jossey Bass.

Furnham, A., Monsen, J., & Ahmetoglu, G. (2009). Typical intellectual engagement, Big Five personality traits, approaches to learning and cognitive ability predictors of academic performance. *The British Journal of Educational Psychology*, *79*(4), 769–782. doi:10.1348/978185409X412147 PMID:19245744

Gardner, H. (1983). *Frames of mind: The theory of multiple intelligences*. New York: Basic Books.

Gearon, L. (2004). *Citizenship through secondary religious education*. New York: RoutledgeFalmer.

Ghorbani, N., Watson, P. J., Omidbeiki, M., & Chen, Z. J. (2016). Muslim attachments to God and the "perfect man"(Ensān-e Kāmel): Relationships with religious orientation and psychological adjustment in Iran. *Psychology of Religion and Spirituality*, *8*(4), 318–329. doi:10.1037/rel0000084

Ghuddah, A. (2010). *Prophet Muhammad, the teacher: And his teaching methodologies.* Dubai: Zam Zam Publishing.

Gil'adi, A. (2017). *Children of Islam.* Dordrecht, The Netherlands: Springer Nature.

Gilliot, C. (2012). *Education and learning in the early Islamic world.* London: Ashgate Variorum.

Giroux, H. (1988). *Teachers as intellectuals: Toward a critical pedagogy of learning.* Granby, MA: Bergin & Garvey.

Goh, M. L. (2011). Penggunaan Kaedah Nyanyian Dalam Penguasaan Sifir Darab 6 hingga 8 Pelajar Tahun Tiga. *Jurnal Penyelidikan Tindakan IPG KBL, 5,* 24–35.

Göl, A. (2011). Constructing Knowledge: An Effective Use of Educational Technology for Teaching Islamic Studies in the UK. *Education and Information Technologies, 17*(4), 399–416. doi:10.100710639-011-9165-9

Goleman, D. (1996). *Emotional intelligence: Why it can matter more than IQ.* New York: Bantam Books.

Goleman, D. (2001). *The emotionally intelligent workplace.* San Francisco: Jossey Bass.

Goleman, D. (2006). *Social intelligence: The new science of social relationships.* New York: Bantam Books.

Goodlad, J. I., Klein, M. F., & Tye, K. A. (1979). The domains of curriculum and their study. In *Curriculum Inquiry: The study of curriculum practice* (pp. 43–77). New York: McGraw Hill.

Gosling, D. (2006). The value of pedagogic inquiry for improving teaching. *New Directions for Teaching and Learning, 107*(1), 99–108. doi:10.1038/bdj.2008.192

Governor, Hall, & Jackson. (2012). Teaching and Learning Science Through Song: Exploring the experiences of students and teachers. *International Journal of Science Education,* 1–24. doi:10.1080/09500693.2012.690542

Greene, R. J. (2018). *Rewarding performance: Guiding principles; custom strategies.* Routledge. doi:10.4324/9780429429019

Gross, Z. (2003). State religious education in Israel: Between tradition and modernity. *Prospects, 33*(2), 149–164. doi:10.1023/A:1023638728907

Gross, Z. (2010). Reflective teaching as a path to religious meaning-making and growth. *Religious Education (Chicago, Ill.), 105*(3), 265–282. doi:10.1080/00344081003772014

Grunebaum, G. E. V., & Abel, T. M. (1947). *Instruction of the student: The method of learning.* New York: King's Crown Press.

Guba, E. G. (1981). Criteria for assessing the trustworthiness of naturalistic inquiries. *Educational Communication and Technology, 29*(2), 75–91.

Guba, E., & Lincoln, Y. (1982). Epistemological and methodological bases of naturalistic inquiry. *Educational Communication and Technology, 30*(4), 233–252.

Guillaume, A. (1955). *The Life of Muḥammad: A Translation of Ibn Isḥāq's Sīrat Rasūl Allāh.* Karachi: Oxford University Press.

Gülen, M. F. (2000). *Prophet Muḥammad: Aspects of his life.* The Fountain.

Gunther, S. (2006). Be Masters in That You Teach and Continue to Learn: Medieval Muslim Thinkers on Educational Theory. *Comparative Education Review, 50*(3), 367–388. doi:10.1086/503881

Gutmann, A. (1987). *Democratic education.* Princeton, NJ: Princeton University Press.

Habermas, J. (1974). *Theory and practice* (J. Viertal, Trans.). London: Heinmann.

Habermas, J. (1972). *Knowledge and human interests* (J. Shapiro, Trans.). London: Heinemann.

Habermas, J. (1990). *Moral consciousness and communicative action* (C. Lenhardt & S. W. Nicholsen, Trans.). Cambridge, MA: Massachusetts Institute of Technology Press.

Habermas, J. (2006). Religion in the public sphere. *European Journal of Philosophy, 14*(1), 1–25. doi:10.1111/j.1468-0378.2006.00241.x

Haddad, Y. Y. (1995). *Islamists and the challenge of pluralism.* Washington, DC: Center for Contemporary Arab Studies.

Hafidzah, L. (2014). Textbooks of Islamic Education in Indonesia's Traditional Pesantren: The Use of Al-Zarnūjī 's Ta'lim Al-Muta'allim Tariq At-Ta'alum and Hasyim Asy'ari's Adab Al-ʿĀlim Wa Al-Muta'alim. *Al- Albab Journal, 3*(2), 199-212.

Hafidzah, L. (2014). Textbooks of Islamic Education in Indonesia's Traditional Pesantren: The Use of al-Zarnuji's Ta'lim al-Muta'allim Tariq at-Ta'alum and Hasyim Asy'ari's Adab al-ʿAlim Wa al-Muta'alim. *AL ALBAB, 3*(2).

Haleem, A. (2005). *The Qur'an.* Oxford, UK: Oxford University Press.

Hallam, S., Burnard, P., Robertson, A., Saleh, C., Davies, V., Rogers, L., & Kokatsaki, D. (2009). Trainee primary-school teachers' perceptions of their effectiveness in teaching music. *Music Education Research, 11*(2), 221–240. doi:10.1080/14613800902924508

Hallinger, P. (2003). *Reshaping the landscape of school leadership development: A global perspective.* Portland, OR: Swets & Zeitlinger.

Halstead, J. M. (2014). Values and Values Education: Challenges for Faith Schools. In International Handbook of Learning, Teaching and Leading in Faith-Based Schools (pp. 65-81). Springer Netherlands.

Halstead, J. M. (2017). Islamic Education in England. Handbook of Islamic Education, 1-17.

Halstead, J. M. (2018). Islamic Education in the West and Its Challenges. Handbook of Contemporary Islam and Muslim Lives, 1-15.

Halstead, M. (2019). *New Directions in Islamic Education: Pedagogy and Identity Formation By Abdullah Sahin*. Academic Press.

Halstead, J. M. (2007). Islamic values: A distinctive framework for moral education? *Journal of Moral Education, 36*(3), 283–296. doi:10.1080/03057240701643056

Halstead, M. (2004). An Islamic concept of education. *Comparative Education, 40*(4), 517–529. doi:10.1080/0305006042000284510

Halstead, M. (2014). Values and values education: Challenges for faith schools. In J. D. Chapman, S. McNamara, M. J. Reiss, & Y. Waghid (Eds.), *International handbook of learning, teaching and leading in faith-based schools* (pp. 65–83). Dordrecht: Springer Netherlands. doi:10.1007/978-94-017-8972-1_3

Halstead, M. (2019). New Directions in Islamic Education: Pedagogy and Identity Formation By ABDULLAH SAHIN. *Journal of Islamic Studies, 30*(2), 286–288. doi:10.1093/jis/etz006

Halstead, M. J. (1995). Towards a unified view of Islamic education. *Islam & Christian-Muslim Relations, 6*(1), 25–43. doi:10.1080/09596419508721040

Halstead, M. J. (1996). Liberal values and liberal education. In J. M. Halstead & M. J. Taylor (Eds.), *Values in education and education in values* (pp. 17–32). The Falmer Press.

Hamalik, O. (2010). *Manajemen Pengembangan Kurikulum*. Bandung: Remaja Rodaskarya.

Hamarneh, S., Jochi, S., & Wuli, H. (2017). al-Tabari. In H. Selin (Ed.), Encyclopaedia of the history of science, technology, and medicine in non-Western cultures (pp. 930-931). Dordrecht, The Netherlands: Springer Nature. doi:10.1007/978-94-007-7747-7

Hambali, K., Sintang, S., Awang, A., Mat Karim, K. N., Abdul Rahman, N. F., Wan Ramli, W. A., ... Md. Noor, R. (2017). al-Wasatiyyah in the practice of religious tolerance among the families of new Muslims in sustaining a well-being society. *Humanomics, 33*(2), 211-220.

Hamid, I. (1965). *The Malay Islamic Hikayat*. Selangor: Universiti Kebangsaan Malaysia.

Hannafin, M., Land, S., & Oliver, K. (1999). Open learning environments: Foundations, methods, and models. *Instructional-design theories and models: A new paradigm of instructional theory, 2*, 115-140.

Hannan, A. (2007). *Interviews in Education Research*. Retrieved from http://www.edu.plymouth.ac.uk/resined/interviews/inthome.htm

Hanrahan, M. (1998). The effect of learning environment factors on students' motivation and learning. *International Journal of Science Education, 20*(6), 737–753. doi:10.1080/0950069980200609

Hardaker, G., & Sabki, A. A. (2015). Islamic pedagogy and embodiment: An anthropological study of a British Madrasah. *International Journal of Qualitative Studies in Education: QSE, 28*(8), 873–886. doi:10.1080/09518398.2014.917738

Hashim, R., & Hattori, M. (2015). The decline of intellectualism in higher Islamic traditional studies: Reforming the curriculum. In Critical Issues and reform in Muslim higher education. IIUM Press.

Hashim, R. (1997). The construction of an Islamic-based teacher education programme. *Muslim Education Quarterly, 14*(2), 57–68.

Hasibuan, M. (2008). *Manajemen Sumber Daya Manusia.* Jakarta: Bumi Aksara.

Hassane, M. (2008). Ajami in Africa: The use of Arabic script in the transcription of African Languages. In S. Jeppie & S. B. Diagne (Eds.), (pp. 109–122). Cape Town: HSRC.

Hassan, R. (2006). Globalisation's challenge to the Islamic Ummah. *Asian Journal of Social Science, 34*(2), 311–323. doi:10.1163/156853106777371184

Haykal, M. H. (1989). *The Life of Muḥammad* (I. R. Al-Faruqi, Trans.). Karachi: Dārul Ishaat.

Herman, N. (1991). The Creative Brain. *The Journal of Creative Behavior, 25*(4), 275–295. doi:10.1002/j.2162-6057.1991.tb01140.x

Hermansen, M. K. (1991). The State of the Art of Islamic Studies in the United States and Canada. *Islamic Culture, 65*(1).

Hess, D. E. (2009). *Controversy in the classroom: The democratic power of discussion.* New York: Routledge.

Hisyamuddin Abdul Razab & Amir Hamzah Sharaai. (2012). *Kaedah nyanyian dalam mengatasi masalah miskonsepsi dalam kalangan pelajar tahun tiga dalam topik magnet.* Persidangan Kebangsaan Pembangunan dan Pendidikan Lestari 2012. Institut Pendidikan Guru Kampus Tuanku Bainun, Bukit Mertajam, Pulau Pinang.

Huang, T.-C., Chen, C.-C., & Chou, Y.-W. (2016). Animating eco-education: To see, feel, and discover in an augmented reality-based experiential learning environment. *Computers & Education, 96,* 72–82. doi:10.1016/j.compedu.2016.02.008

Huda, M. (2018). Empowering Application Strategy in the Technology Adoption: Insights from Professional and Ethical Engagement. *Journal of Science and Technology Policy Management.* . doi:10.1108/JSTPM-09-2017-0044

Huda, M., & Kartanegara, M. (2015a). Islamic Spiritual Character Values of al-Zarnūjī's Ta 'līm al-Muta 'allim. *Mediterranean Journal of Social Sciences, 6*(4S2), 229-235.

Huda, M., & Kartanegara, M. (2015b). Ethical Foundation of Character Education in Indonesia: Reflections on Integration between Ahmad Dahlan and al-Zarnuji. In Persidangan Antarabangsa Tokoh Ulama Melayu Nusantara (PanTUMN) (pp. 404–420). Selangor: Kolej Universiti Islam Antarabangsa Selangor (KUIS) Malaysia.

Huda, M., & Kartanegara, M. (2015e). Ethical foundation of character education in indonesia: reflections on integration between Ahmad Dahlan and Al-Zarnūjī. *Persidangan Antarabangsa Tokoh Ulama Melayu Nusantara (PanTUMN).* Doi:10.13140/RG.2.1.5082.1605

Huda, M., & Teh, K. S. M. (2018). Empowering professional and ethical competence on reflective teaching practice in digital era. *Mentorship Strategies in Teacher Education*, 136-152.

Huda, M., Jasmi, K. A., Alas, Y., Qodriah, S. L., Dacholfany, M. I., & Jamsari, E. A. (2018c). Empowering civic responsibility: insights from service learning. *Engaged Scholarship and Civic Responsibility in Higher Education*, 144-165.

Huda, M., Sabani, N., Shahrill, M., Jasmi, K. A., Basiron, B., & Mustari, M. I. (2017b). Empowering learning culture as student identity construction in higher education. *Student Culture and Identity in Higher Education*, 160-179.

Huda, M., Anshari, M., Almunawar, M. N., Shahrill, M., Tan, A., Jaidin, J. H., ... Masri, M. (2016). Innovative Teaching in Higher Education: The Big Data Approach. *The Turkish Online Journal of Educational Technology*, *15*(Special issue), 1210–1216.

Huda, M., Haron, Z., Ripin, M. N., Hehsan, A., & Yaacob, A. B. C. (2017). Exploring innovative learning environment (ILE): Big data era. *International Journal of Applied Engineering Research*, *12*(17), 6678–6685.

Huda, M., Jasmi, K. A., Alas, Y., Qodriah, S. L., Dacholfany, M. I., & Jamsari, E. A. (2017d). Empowering Civic Responsibility: Insights From Service Learning. In S. Burton (Ed.), *Engaged Scholarship and Civic Responsibility in Higher Education* (pp. 144–165). Hershey, PA: IGI Global. doi:10.4018/978-1-5225-3649-9.ch007

Huda, M., Jasmi, K. A., Basiran, B., Mustari, M. I. B., & Sabani, A. N. (2017a). Traditional Wisdom on Sustainable Learning: An Insightful View From Al-Zarnuji's Ta 'lim al-Muta 'allim. *SAGE Open*, *7*(1), 1–8. doi:10.1177/2158244017697160

Huda, M., Jasmi, K. A., Embong, W. H., Safar, J., Mohamad, A. M., Mohamed, A. K., ... Rahman, S. K. (2017c). Nurturing Compassion-Based Empathy: Innovative Approach in Higher Education. In M. Badea & M. Suditu (Eds.), *Violence Prevention and Safety Promotion in Higher Education Settings* (pp. 154–173). Hershey, PA: IGI Global. doi:10.4018/978-1-5225-2960-6.ch009

Huda, M., Jasmi, K. A., Hehsan, A., Mustari, M. I., Shahrill, M., Basiron, B., & Gassama, S. K. (2017d). Empowering children with adaptive technology skills: Careful engagement in the digital information age. *International Electronic Journal of Elementary Education*, *9*(3), 693–708.

Huda, M., Jasmi, K. A., Mohamed, A. K., Wan Embong, W. H., & Safar, J. (2016a). Philosophical Investigation of Al-Zarnuji's Ta'lim al-Muta'allim: Strengthening Ethical Engagement into Teaching and Learning. *Social Science*, *11*(22), 5516–5551.

Huda, M., Jasmi, K. A., Mohamed, A. K., Wan Embong, W. H., & Safar, J. (2016c). (in press). Philosophical Investigation of al- Zarnūjī's Ta'līm al-Mutaʻallim: Strengthening Ethical Engagement into Teaching and Learning. *Social Science*.

Huda, M., Jasmi, K. A., Mustari, M. I. B., & Basiron, A. B. (2017c). Understanding of Wara' (Godliness) as a Feature of Character and Religious Education. *Social Sciences*, *12*(6), 1106–1111.

Huda, M., Jasmi, K. A., Mustari, M. I., Basiron, B., Mohamed, A. K., Embong, W., ... Safar, J. (2017). Innovative E-Therapy Service in Higher Education: Mobile Application Design. *International Journal of Interactive Mobile Technologies*, *11*(4), 83–94. doi:10.3991/ijim.v11i4.6734

Huda, M., & Kartanegara, M. (2015a). Aim formulation of education: An analysis of the book *Ta'lim al-Muta'allim*. *International Journal of Humanities and Social Science*, *5*(2), 143–149.

Huda, M., & Kartanegara, M. (2015b). Aim formulation of education: An analysis of the Book *Ta'lm al- Muta'allim*. *International Journal of Humanities and Social Science*, *5*(2), 143–149.

Huda, M., & Kartanegara, M. (2015b). Curriculum Conception In The Perspective Of The Book Ta'lim Al-Muta'allim. *International Journal of Education and Research*, *3*(2), 221–232.

Huda, M., & Kartanegara, M. (2015c). Curriculum conception in the perspective of the book ta'lim al-muta'allim. *International Journal of Education and Research*, *3*(2), 221–232.

Huda, M., & Kartanegara, M. (2015c). Distinctive feature of al-Zarnûjî's ideas: A philosopical inquiry into the book *Ta'lim al-Muta'allim*. *American International Journal of Contemporary Research*, *5*(2), 171–177.

Huda, M., & Kartanegara, M. (2015d). Distinctive feature of Al-Zarnûjî's ideas: A philosophical inquiry into the book *Ta'lim al-Muta'allim*. *American International Journal of Contemporary Research*, *5*(2), 171–177.

Huda, M., & Kartanegara, M. (2015d). Islamic spiritual character values of al-Zarnūjī's *Ta'līm al-Muta'allim*. *Mediterranean Journal of Social Sciences*, *6*(4), 229–235.

Huda, M., & Kartanegara, M. (2015e). Ethical Foundation of Character Education in Indonesia: Reflections on Integration between Ahmad Dahlan and al-Zarnūjī. *International Conference of Malay Muslim Prominent Scholars. Selangor: Kolej Universiti Islam Antarbangsa (KUIS)*.

Huda, M., & Kartanegara, M. (2015f). The Significance of Educative Environment to the Character Development: A Study of al-Zarnūjī's Ta'līm al-Muta'allim. *International Journal of Innovation Education and Research*, *3*(3), 191–200.

Huda, M., Kartanegara, M., & Zakaria, G. A. N. (2015c). The effect of learning strategy of reading aloud on students' achievement in the subject of Islamic studies at secondary school in Semarang. *International Journal of Education and Research*, *3*(2), 577–588.

Huda, M., Maseleno, A., Jasmi, K. A., Mustari, I., & Basiron, B. (2017f). Strengthening Interaction from Direct to Virtual Basis: Insights from Ethical and Professional Empowerment. *International Journal of Applied Engineering Research*, *12*(17), 6901–6909.

Huda, M., Mulyadi, D., Hananto, A. L., Nor Muhamad, N. H., Mat Teh, K. S., & Don, A. G. (2018b). Empowering corporate social responsibility (CSR): Insights from service learning. *Social Responsibility Journal*, *14*(4), 875–894. doi:10.1108/SRJ-04-2017-0078

Huda, M., Qodriah, S. L., Rismayadi, B., Hananto, A., Kardiyati, E. N., Ruskam, A., & Nasir, B. M. (2019). Towards Cooperative with Competitive Alliance: Insights into Performance Value in Social Entrepreneurship. In *Creating Business Value and Competitive Advantage with Social Entrepreneurship* (p. 294). Hershey, PA: IGI Global. doi:10.4018/978-1-5225-5687-9.ch014

Huda, M., & Sabani, N. (2018). Empowering Muslim children's spirituality in Malay Archipelago: Integration between National Philosophical Foundations and Tawakkul (trust in God). *International Journal of Children's Spirituality*, *23*(1), 81–94. doi:10.1080/1364436X.2018.1431613

Huda, M., Sabani, N., Shahrill, M., Jasmi, K. A., Basiron, B., & Mustari, M. I. (2017b). Empowering Learning Culture as Student Identity Construction in Higher Education. In A. Shahriar & G. Syed (Eds.), *Student Culture and Identity in Higher Education* (pp. 160–179). Hershey, PA: IGI Global. doi:10.4018/978-1-5225-2551-6.ch010

Huda, M., & Siregar, M., Rahman, S.K.A., Mat Teh, K.S., Said, H., Jamsari, E.A., ... Ninsiana, W. (2017e). From Live Interaction to Virtual Interaction: An Exposure on the Moral Engagement in the Digital Era. *Journal of Theoretical and Applied Information Technology*, *95*(19), 4964–4972.

Huda, M., Sudrajat, S., Kawangit, R. M., Teh, K. S. M., & Jalal, B. (2019). Strengthening divine values for self-regulation in religiosity: Insights from *Tawakkul* (trust in God). *International Journal of Ethics and Systems*, IJOES-02-2018-0025. doi:10.1108/IJOES-02-2018-0025

Huda, M., & Teh, K. S. M. (2018). Empowering Professional and Ethical Competence on Reflective Teaching Practice in Digital Era. In K. Dikilitas, E. Mede, & D. Atay (Eds.), *Mentorship Strategies in Teacher Education* (pp. 136–152). Hershey, PA: IGI Global. doi:10.4018/978-1-5225-4050-2.ch007

Huda, M., Teh, K. S. M., Nor, N. H. M., & Nor, M. B. M. (2018a). Transmitting Leadership Based Civic Responsibility: Insights from Service Learning. *International Journal of Ethics and Systems*, *34*(1), 20–31. doi:10.1108/IJOES-05-2017-0079

Huda, M., Yusuf, J. B., Jasmi, K. A., & Nasir, G. A. (2016a, October). Understanding comprehensive learning requirements in the light of al-Zarnūjī's Taʻlīm al-Mutaʻallim. *SAGE Open*, 1–14.

Huda, M., Yusuf, J. B., Jasmi, K. A., & Nasir, G. A. (2016b). Understanding Comprehensive Learning Requirements in the Light of al-Zarnūjī's Taʻlīm al-Mutaʻallim. *SAGE Open*, *6*(4), 1–14. doi:10.1177/2158244016670197

Huda, M., Yusuf, J. B., Jasmi, K. A., & Zakaria, G. N. (2016b, July). Al-Zarnūjī's concept of knowledge ('ilm). *SAGE Open*, 1–13.

Huda, M., Yusuf, J. B., Jasmi, K. A., & Zakaria, G. N. (2016c). Al-Zarnūjī's Concept of Knowledge ('ilm). *SAGE Open*, *6*(3), 1–13. doi:10.1177/2158244016666885

Hull, J. M. (2000). The transmission of religious prejudice. *British Journal of Religious Education*, *14*(2), 69–72.

Hull, J. M. (2003). The blessings of secularity: Religious education in England and Wales. *Journal of Religious Education*, *51*(3), 51–58.

Hunwick, J. (1999). *Timbuktu and the Songhay Empire: Al-Sa'di's Tarikh al-Sudan down to 1613 and other Contemporary Documents*. Leiden: Brill.

Husain, S. S., & Ashraf, S. A. (1979). Crisis in Muslim Education. King 'Abdulaziz University.

Hussain, A. (2004). Islamic education: Why is there a need for it? *Journal of Beliefs & Values*, *25*(3), 317–323. doi:10.1080/1361767042000306130

Hussien, S., Hashim, R., & Mokhtar, N. A. M. (2017). Hikmah Pedagogy. In *Interfaith Education for All* (pp. 97–106). Rotterdam: SensePublishers. doi:10.1007/978-94-6351-170-4_8

Ibn 'Abd Rabbih, A. (1983). *Al-'Iqd al-farid*. Beirut, Lebanon: Dar al Kutub al- 'Ilmiyah.

Idris, S. (2017). Insan Kamil: Theological and Psychological Perspective. *Asian Journal of Social Science. Art and Humanities*, *5*(2), 9–28.

Ikhwan, A. (2013). Pengembangan Kurikulum Pendidikan Agama Islam (PAI). Malang: Insan Cita Press dan STAIM Tulungagung. Retrieved from https://scholar.google.co.id/scholar?hl=id&as_sdt=0,5&cluster=10168247928958272298

Ikhwan, A. (2014). Integrasi Pendidikan Islami (Nilai-Nilai Islami dalam Pembelajaran). Ta'allum: Jurnal Pendidikan Islam, 2(2), 184. Retrieved from http://ejournal.iain-tulungagung.ac.id/index.php/taalum/article/view/574

Ikhwan, A. (2017). Development Of Quality Management Islamic Education In Islamic Boarding School (Case Study Madrasah Aliyah Ash Sholihin). Al-Hayat. *Journal of Islamic Education*, *1*(1), 117. Retrieved from http://alhayat.or.id/index.php/alhayat/article/view/7

Immordino-Yang, M. H., & Damasio, A. R. (2007). We feel, therefore we learn: The relevance of affect and social neuroscience to education. *Mind, Brain and Education: the Official Journal of the International Mind, Brain, and Education Society*, *1*(1), 3–10. doi:10.1111/j.1751-228X.2007.00004.x

Insoll, T. (1996). The archaeology of Islam in Sub-Saharan Africa: A review. *Journal of World Prehistory*, *10*(1), 439–504. doi:10.1007/BF02221202

Institute of African Studies. (n.d.). *Islamic Studies*. Retrieved February 20, 2016, from http://www.ias.uni-bayreuth.de/en/subject_groups/h_islamic_studies/

Intezari, A. (2016). Conceptualizing wisdom: theoretical perspectives. *Practical Wisdom in the Age of Technology*, 23-37.

Ishihara, N., & Cohen, A. (2010). *Teaching and Learning Pragmatics: Where Langauge and Culture Meet*. Pearson Education Limited.

Ismaniza binti Ismail. (2011). *Peranan nashid sebagai medium dakwah*. Kertas Projek, Fakulti Pendidikan Universiti Teknologi Malaysia.

Israeli Ministry of Education. (2014). *The modification of the curriculum of Islamic studies and culture to the policy of significant learning*. Hebrew.

Izfanna, D., & Hisyam, N. A. (2012). A comprehensive approach in developing akhlaq: A case study on the implementation of character education at Pondok Pesantren Darunnajah. *Multicultural Education & Technology Journal*, *6*(2), 77–86. doi:10.1108/17504971211236254

Jackson, R. (1997). *Religious Education: An Interpretive Approach*. London: Hodder & Stoughton.

Jackson, R. (2004). *Rethinking religious education and plurality: Issues in diversity and pedagogy*. London: RoutledgeFalmer. doi:10.4324/9780203465165

Jackson, R. (2006). *Fifty key figures in Islam*. London: Routledge. doi:10.4324/9780203001387

Jamali, H. N., & Isa, N. M. (2014). Aplikasi teknik pembelajaran pantas dalam pengajaran dan pembelajaran Bahasa Arab. *GSE E-Journal of Education*, *2*(2), 1–11.

Jamaluddin, D. (2013). Character Education in Islamic Perspective. *International Journal of Scientific & Technology Research*, *2*(2), 187-189.

Jawad, H. (1990). Muḥammad the Educator: An Authentic Approach. *The Islamic Quarterly*, *34*(2), 115–122.

Johnson, D. W., & Johnson, R. T. (2009). Energizing learning: The instructional power of conflict. *Educational Researcher*, *38*(1), 37–51. doi:10.3102/0013189X08330540

Jonassen, D. H., & Grabowski, B. L. (2012). *Handbook of individual differences, learning, and instruction*. London: Routledge.

Josep, D. (2015). We did the how to teach it': Music teaching and learning in Higher Education in Australia. *Australian Journal of Teacher Education.*, *40*(7), 1.

Joseph, P. B. (2000). Conceptualizing curriculum. In P. B. Joseph (Ed.), *Cultures of curriculum* (pp. 3–22). Mahwah, NJ: L. Erlbaum Associates.

Juhnke, G. A., Watts, R. E., Guerra, N. S., & Hsieh, P. (2009). Using Prayer as an Intervention with Clients who are Substance Abusing and Addicted who Self-Identify Personal Faith in God and Prayer as Recovery Resources. *Journal of Addictions & Offender Counseling*, *30*(1), 16–23. doi:10.1002/j.2161-1874.2009.tb00053.x

Juma'at, M. (1990). *Principal and teacher perceptions of the principal's instructional leadership role in primary schools* (Unpublished masters dissertation). National Institute of Education, Nanyang Technological University, Singapore.

Jusoh & Jusoff. (2009). Using Multimedia in Teaching Islamic Studies. *Journal Media and Communication Studies, 1*.

Jusoh, K. A. (2009). *Siri Kepimpinan: Evolusi Kepimpinan 1, Tinjauan Teori-Teori Terpilih* [Leadership Series: The evolution of leadership, a study on selected theories]. Kuala Lumpur: Kasturi Jingga Corporation Sdn Bhd, 75.

Kameli, S., Mostapha, G. B., & Baki, R. B. (2012). The Influence of Formal Language Learning Environment on Vocabulary Learning Strategies. *Journal of Language Teaching & Research*, *3*(1). doi:10.4304/jltr.3.1.23-29

Kamrava, M. (2009). Introduction: Reformist Islam in comparative perspective. In M. Kamrava (Ed.), *The new Voices of Islam: Reforming politics and modernity* (pp. 1–27). London: I.B. Tauris & Co. Ltd.

Kartanegara, M., & Huda, M. (2016). Constructing civil society: an Islamic cultural perspective. *Mediterranean Journal of Social Sciences, 7*(1 S1), 126.

Kartanegara, M., & Huda, M. (2016). Constructing Civil Society: An Islamic Cultural Perspective. *Mediterranean Journal of Social Sciences*, *7*(1), 126–135.

Kartikowati, S., & Hidir, A. (2015). Sistem kepercayaan di kalangan ibu hamil dalam masyarakat Melayu. *Jurnal Parallela*, *1*(2), 159–167.

Kazmi. (2006). Instructional Technology and Islamic Education: Intimation of Islamic Pedagogy. *Islamic Studies Journal*.

Kecia, A., & Leaman, O. (2008). *Islam: The key concepts*. New York: Routledge.

Khaldūn, I. A. (1967). The Muqaddimah (F. Rosenthal, Trans.; N. J. Dawood, Ed.). Princeton University Press.

Khaldun. (1979). *Al-Ta'rif bi Ibn Khaldun wa-rihlatuhu gharban wa-sharqan*. Dar al- Kitab al-Lubnani li Tiba'ah wa al-Nashr.

Khalisotussurur, L., & Ramidi. (2015, March 10). *Kasus Kriminalitas Anak Meningkat pada tahun 2014* [Criminal cases involving children and adolescents increased]. Retrieved from http://www.gresnews.com/berita/sosial/21041-kasus-kriminalitas-anak-meningkat-pada-2014/

Khan, M. S. (1987). Humanism and Islamic education. *Muslim Education Quarterly*, *4*(3), 25–35.

Khir, B. M. S. (2007). Islamic Studies within Islam: Definition Approaches and Challenges of Modernity. *Journal of Beliefs & Values*, *28*(3), 257–266. doi:10.1080/13617670701712430

King, N. (2004). Using templates in the thematic analysis of texts. In C. Cassel & G. Symon (Eds.), *Essential guide to qualitative methods in organisational research* (pp. 256–270). London: Sage Publications. doi:10.4135/9781446280119.n21

Kirat, M. (2015). The Islamic roots of modern public relations and corporate social responsibility. *International Journal of Islamic Marketing and Branding*, *1*(1), 97–112. doi:10.1504/IJIMB.2015.068144

Knowles, J. G. (1992). Models for understanding pre-service and beginning teachers' biographies: Illustrations from case studies. In I. Goodson (Ed.), *Studying teachers' lives* (pp. 99–152). New York: Teachers College Press. doi:10.4324/9780203415177_chapter_4

Krathwohl, D. (1993). *Methods of Educational and Social Science Research*. New York: Longman.

Krueger, R. A., & Casey, M. A. (2009). *Focus groups: A practical guide for applied research.* Los Angeles, CA: SAGE.

Kumar, N., & Che Rose, R. (2012). The impact of knowledge sharing and Islamic work ethic on innovation capability. *Cross Cultural Management, 19*(2), 142–165. doi:10.1108/13527601211219847

Kunzman, R. (2006). *Grappling with the good: Talking about religion and morality in public schools.* Albany, NY: State University of New York Press.

Kurnia, I. (2008). *Perkembangan Belajar Peserta Didik.* Jakarta: Direktorat Jenderal Pendidikan Tinggi Departemen Pendidikan Nasional.

Kurzman, C. (1998). Liberal Islam and its Islamic context. In C. Kurzman (Ed.), *Liberal Islam: A source book* (pp. 3–26). New York: Oxford University Press.

Kyriacou, C. (2018). *Essential Teaching Skills* (5th ed.). Oxford, UK: OUP.

Langeveld, M. (1983). Reflections on phenomenology and pedagogy. *Phenomenology + Pedagogy, 1*(1), 5–7.

Lansu, A., Boon, J., Sloep, P. B., & van Dam-Mieras, R. (2013). Changing professional demands in sustainable regional development: A curriculum design process to meet transboundary competence. *Journal of Cleaner Production, 49*, 123–133. doi:10.1016/j.jclepro.2012.10.019

Larsari, V. N. (2011). Learner's communicative competence in English as a Foreign Language. *Journal of English and Literature., 2*(7), 161–165.

Lauder, A. (2008). The Status and Function of English in Indonesia: A Review of the Key Factors. *Makara. Sosial Humanoira., 12*(1), 9–20.

Lauermann, F. (2014). Teacher responsibility from the teacher's perspective. *International Journal of Educational Research, 65*, 75–89. doi:10.1016/j.ijer.2013.09.005

Lee, P. (2011). Overview of Background Factors Which May Influence Japanese Learner Behaviour in the Communicative English Classroom. *Keiwa College Journal,* (20), 1-13.

Leithwood, K., & Jantzi, D. (2000). *Making schools smarter: A system for monitoring school and district progress.* Thousand Oaks, CA: Corwin Press.

Lembaga Ilmu Dakwah & Publikasi Sarana Keagamaan. (2011). Kitab Hadits 9 Imam. Jakarta Timur: Lidwa Pusaka i-Software.

Levtzion, N. (2000a). Islam in the Bilad al-Sudan to 1800. In N. Levtzion & P. Randall (Eds.), *History of Islam in Africa* (pp. 63–92). Ohio University Press.

Levtzion, N. (2000b). Patterns of Islamization and Varieties of Religious Experience among Muslims of Africa. In N. Levtzion & P. Randall (Eds.), (pp. 1–14). Ohio University Press.

Levy, N. (2014). *Consciousness and moral responsibility*. Oxford University Press. doi:10.1093/acprof:oso/9780198704638.001.0001

Lickona, T. (2010). 11 Principles of Character Education. Retrieved from http://www.character.org/uploads/PDFs/ElevenPrinciples_new2010.pdf

Lickona, T. (2013). *Educating for Character, Mendidik Untuk Membentuk Karakter, terjemahan Juma Abdu Wamaungo*. Jakarta: Bumi Aksara.

Lings, M. (1991). *Muḥammad His Life Based on Earliest Sources* (2nd ed.). The Islamic Texts Society.

Lizzio, A., Wilson, K., & Simons, R. (2002). University Students' Perceptions of the Learning Environment and Academic Outcomes: Implications for Theory and Practice. *Studies in Higher Education, 27*(1), 27–52. doi:10.1080/03075070120099359

Lockwood, A. L. (2001). Blending civic decency and civic literacy. *The International Journal of Social Education, 16*(1), 55–61.

Lovat, T. (2010). Synergies and balance between values education and quality teaching. *Educational Philosophy and Theory, 42*(4), 489–500. doi:10.1111/j.1469-5812.2008.00469.x

Lovat, T. (2016). Islamic morality: Teaching to balance the record. *Journal of Moral Education, 45*(1), 1–15. doi:10.1080/03057240.2015.1136601

Lovat, T. (2017). Values education as good practice pedagogy: Evidence from Australian empirical research. *Journal of Moral Education, 46*(1), 88–96. doi:10.1080/03057240.2016.1268110

Lovat, T. (2018). Spirituality in Australian education: A legacy of confusion, omission and obstruction. In M. de Souza & L. Halafoff (Eds.), *Re-enchanting education and spiritual wellbeing* (pp. 36–47). London: Routledge.

Lovat, T., & Clement, N. (2008a). The pedagogical imperative of values education. *Journal of Beliefs & Values, 29*(3), 273–285. doi:10.1080/13617670802465821

Lovat, T., & Clement, N. (2008b). Quality teaching and values education: Coalescing for effective learning. *Journal of Moral Education, 37*(1), 1–16. doi:10.1080/03057240701803643

Lovat, T., & Clement, N. (2008c). Values education: Bridging the religious and secular divide. *Journal of Religious Education, 56*, 40–49.

Lovat, T., Clement, N., Dally, K., & Toomey, R. (2010b). Values education as holistic development for all sectors: Researching for effective pedagogy. *Oxford Review of Education, 36*(6), 1–17. doi:10.1080/03054985.2010.501141

Lovat, T., Clement, N., Dally, K., & Toomey, R. (2010c). Addressing issues of religious difference through values education: An Islam instance. *Cambridge Journal of Education, 40*(3), 213–227. doi:10.1080/0305764X.2010.504599

Lovat, T., Dally, K., Clement, N., & Toomey, R. (2011). *Values pedagogy and student achievement: Contemporary research evidence*. Dordrecht, The Netherlands: Springer. doi:10.1007/978-94-007-1563-9

Lovat, T., & Toomey, R. (Eds.). (2009). *Values education and quality teaching: The double helix effect*. Dordrecht, Netherlands: Springer. doi:10.1007/978-1-4020-9962-5

Lovat, T., Toomey, R., & Clement, N. (Eds.). (2010a). *International research handbook on values education and student wellbeing*. Dordrecht, The Netherlands: Springer. doi:10.1007/978-90-481-8675-4

Lovat, T., Toomey, R., Dally, K., & Clement, N. (2009). *Project to test and measure the impact of values education on student effects and school ambience. Report for the Australian Government Department of Education, Employment and Workplace Relations by The University of Newcastle*. Canberra: DEEWR. Available at http://www.curriculum.edu.au/verve/_resources/Project_to_Test_and_Measure_the_Impact_of_Values_Education.pdf

Lubis, M. A. (2015). Effective implementation of the integrated Islamic education. *Global Journal Al-Thaqafah*, *5*(1), 59–68. doi:10.7187/GJAT792015.05.01

Lubis, M. A., Yunus, M. M., Lampoh, A. A., & Ishak, N. M. (2011). The Use of ICT in Teaching Islamic Subjects in Brunei Darussalam. *International Journal of Education and Information Technologies*, *1*(5).

Lukens-Bull, R. A. (2001). Two Sides of the Same Coin: Modernity and Tradition in Islamic Education in Indonesia. *Anthropology & Education Quarterly*, *32*(3), 350–372. doi:10.1525/aeq.2001.32.3.350

Lu, Y. Y., Wu, H. Y., Chen, H. C., Lin, H. L., & Chang, Y. L. (2016). The analysis of situational positive discipline strategies by positive discipline awarded teachers. *Bulletin of Educational Psychology*, *48*(2), 159–184.

Mabud, S. A. (2018). The Emergence of Islamic Schools: A Contextual Background. In *Islamic Schooling in the West* (pp. 11–33). Cham: Palgrave Macmillan.

Mahadi, T. S., & Jafari, S. M. (2012). Motivation, its types and its impacts in Language Learning. *International Journal of Business and Social Science*, *3*(24), 230–235.

Mahajna, I., & Kfir, D. (2013). The status of Islamic religious studies in one academic college of Education and Israeli Arab schools today. [Arabic]. *Jamea'a*, *17*(2), 97–124.

Mahmud, J. (2010). How the Messenger Taught his Students. Lahore: Al-Misbah.

Makkawi, I. (2002). Role conflict and the dilemma of Palestinian teachers in Israel. *Comparative Education*, *38*(1), 39–52. doi:10.1080/03050060120103847

Manan, A. (2015). *The ritual calendar of South Aceh, Indonesia*. Wissenschaftliche Schriften der WWU Münster, Reihe X, Band 22, MV-Verlag-Germany.

Manan, A. (2016). The ritual of death in Aceh: an ethnographic study in Blangporoh village, West Labuhan Haji, South Aceh, Indonesia. In Parts and Whole. Muenster: Lit Verlag.

Manan, A. (2014). The ritual of marriage (An ethnographic study in West Labuhan Haji, South Aceh). *Jurnal Ilmiah Peuradeun-International Multidiciplinary Journal*, 2(2), 17–44.

Manca, S., & Ranieri, M. (2016). Facebook and the others. Potentials and obstacles of social media for teaching in higher education. *Computers & Education*, 95, 216–230. doi:10.1016/j.compedu.2016.01.012

Mansoorpuri, M. S. (1988). *Mercy for the Worlds* (A. J. Siddiqui, Trans.). Karachi: Dārul Ishaat.

Mansor, N., Ariffin, R., Nordin, R., & Salleh, M. A. (2015). Mosque Tourism Certification in Waqf Management: A Model by Ukhwah Samara. *Social Sciences and Humanities*, 23, 291–304.

Manuty, M. N. (2011). Islamic Studies Programs in Malaysia's Higher Learning Institutions: Responses to Contemporary Challenges of Modernity, Globalization and Post 9/11. In K. Bustamam-Ahmad & P. Jory (Eds.), *Islamic Studies and Islamic Education in Contemporary Southeast Asia*. Kuala Lumpur: Yayasan Ilmuwan.

Maoz, A. (2007). Religious education in Israel. *University of Detroit Mercy Law Review*, 83(5), 679–728.

Martin, R. C., Empey, H. J., Arkoun, M., & Rippin, A. (2016). Islamic Studies. In *The Oxford Encyclopedia of the Islamic World. Oxford Islamic Studies Online*. Retrieved from http://www.oxfordislamicstudies.com/article/opr/t236/e0395

Masaazi, F. M. (2015). Developing a Friendly and Productive Language Learning Environment (FPLE) Using the Learner as a Resource. *Journal of Education and Training Studies*, 3(5), 144–145. doi:10.11114/jets.v3i5.967

Maseleno, A., Shankar, K., Huda, M., Othman, M., Khoir, P., & Muslihudin, M. (2019b). Citizen Economic Level (CELL) using SAW. *Expert Systems in Finance: Smart Financial Applications in Big Data Environments*, 97.

Maseleno, A., Pardimin, Huda, M., Ramlan, Hehsan, A., Yusof, Y.M., … Junaidi, J. (2018a). Mathematical Theory of Evidence to Subject Expertise Diagnostic. *ICIC Express Letters*, 12(4), 369. doi:10.24507/icicel.12.04.369

Maseleno, A., Huda, M., Jasmi, K. A., Basiron, B., Mustari, I., Don, A. G., & Ahmad, R. (2019a). Hau-Kashyap approach for student's level of expertise. *Egyptian Informatics Journal*, 20(1), 27–32. doi:10.1016/j.eij.2018.04.001

Maseleno, A., Huda, M., Siregar, M., Ahmad, R., Hehsan, A., Haron, Z., ... Jasmi, K. A. (2017). Combining the Previous Measure of Evidence to Educational Entrance Examination. *Journal of Artificial Intelligence*, 10(3), 85–90. doi:10.3923/jai.2017.85.90

Maseleno, A., Sabani, N., Huda, M., Ahmad, R., Jasmi, K. A., & Basiron, B. (2018c). Demystifying Learning Analytics in Personalised Learning. *IACSIT International Journal of Engineering and Technology, 7*(3), 1124–1129. doi:10.14419/ijet.v7i3.9789

Mattson, I. (2013). *The Story of the Qur'an: Its History and place in Muslim Life*. Oxford, UK: Wiley-Blackwell.

Maulana, M. M. (2013). Upacara daur hidup dalam pernikahan adat Sunda. *Refleksi, 13*(5), 623–640.

Mayer, E. (Ed.). (n.d.). Key competencies: Report of the committee to advise the Australian Education Council and Ministers of Vocational Education, Employment and Training on employment-related key competencies for post-compulsory education and training. Canberra: AEC & MOVEET. Available at: file:///C:/Users/Tjl607/Downloads/scpp-00129-nat-1992.pdf

McCullough, M. E., & Willoughby, B. L. (2009). Religion, self-regulation, and self-control: Associations, explanations, and implications. *Psychological Bulletin, 135*(1), 69–93. doi:10.1037/a0014213 PMID:19210054

MCEETYA. (1999). *Adelaide declaration on national goals for schooling in the twenty-first century*. Canberra: Ministerial Council on Education, Employment, Training and Youth Affairs. Available at: http://www.curriculum.edu.au/mceetya/nationalgoals/

MCEETYA. (2008). *Melbourne declaration on educational goals for young Australians*. Canberra: Ministerial Council on Education, Employment, Training and Youth Affairs. Available at: http://www.curriculum.edu.au/verve/_resources/National_Declaration_on_the_Educational_Goals_for_Young_Australians.pdf

McKay, S. L. (2002). *Teaching English as an International Language: Rethinking Goals and Perspectives*. New York: OUP.

McLaughlin, T. H. (1992). Citizenship, diversity, and education: A philosophical perspective. *Journal of Moral Education, 21*(3), 235–250. doi:10.1080/0305724920210307

Md. Nasir Masran & Ain Hazwani Abu Kasim. (2014). Keberkesanan kaedah belajar sambil main dalam meningkat kemahiran membaca lisan dalam kalangan pelajar-pelajar bermasalah pembelajaran. *Asian Education Action Research Journal*, (3), 79-95.

Memon, N. A. (2011). What Islamic school teachers want: Towards developing an Islamic teacher education programme. *British Journal of Religious Education, 33*(3), 285–298. doi:10.1080/01416200.2011.595912

Merry, M. (2006). Islamic philosophy of education and western Islamic schools: Points of tension. In F. Salili & R. Hoosain (Eds.), *Religion in multicultural education* (pp. 41–70). Greenwich, CT: IAP.

Merry, M. S. (2007). *Culture, identity, and Islamic schooling: A philosophical approach*. New York: Palgrave Macmillan. doi:10.1057/9780230109766

Michael, S. C., Storey, D., & Thomas, H. (2008). Discovery and Coordination in Strategic Management and Entrepreneurship. In *Strategic Entrepreneurship: Creating a New Mindset* (pp. 45–65). Wiley.

Midgley, M. (2007). Intelligent design theory and other ideological problems. *Journal of the Philosophy of Education Society of Great Britain, 15*, 1–48.

Mogra, I. (2010). Teachers and teaching: A contemporary Muslim understanding. *Religious Education (Chicago, Ill.), 105*(3), 317–329. doi:10.1080/00344081003772089

Mohamad Kamil Hj Ab Majid & Muhammed Yusof. (2008). Ke arah memperkasakan Islamisasi seni muzik sebagai satu alternatif: satu pengamatan awal. *Jurnal Hadhari Edisi Khas*, 105121.

Mohamad Lutfi Mat Saad. (2011). *Penggunaan kaedah nyanyian dapat menarik minat dan meningkatkan kemahiran membaca perkataan (vkv, kvkv, vkvk, kvkvk) pelajar prasekolah.* Seminar Penyelidikan Tindakan IPG Kampus Sultan Abdul Halim 2011.

Mohamad, A. H., Baharudin, H., Jusoh, F., & Muda, Z. (2017). Pengajaran Dan Pembelajaran Pendidikan Islam Melalui Kaedah Nashid. *The International Seminar On Islamic Jurisprudence In Contemporary Society (Islac 2017).*

Mohamed, N. (2014). Islamic education, eco-ethics and community. *Studies in Philosophy and Education, 33*(3), 315–328. doi:10.100711217-013-9387-y

Mohamed, Y. (2015). The Duties of the Teacher *Al-Iṣfahānī's* Dharī'a *as a Source of Inspiration for al-Ghazālī's* Mīzān al-'Amal. In G. Tamer (Ed.), *Islam and Rationality: The Impact of al-Ghazālī.* Leiden: Brill.

Mohd Yusob, M. L., Salleh, M. A., Haron, A. S., Makhtar, M., Asari, K. N., & Jamil, L. S. M. (2015). Maqasid al-Shariah as a Parameter for Islamic Countries in Screening International Treaties Before Ratification: An Analysis. *Pertanika Journal of Social Science & Humanities*, 23.

Mohd-Asraf, R. (2005). English and Islam: A Clash of Civilizations? *Journal of Language, Identity, and Education, 4*(2), 103–118. doi:10.120715327701jlie0402_3

Mohd-Hamidin, N. (2015). *The teaching and learning strategies used in classroom: a case study in national religious secondary schools (SMKA) in Selangor.* The Teaching and Learning Strategies Used in Classroom.

Mohd-Yasim, I. M., Lubis, M. A., Mohd Noor, Z. A., & Kamaruddin, M. Y. (2016). The use of teaching aids in the teaching and learning of Arabic language vocabulary. *Creative Education, 7*, 443-448.

Mok Soon Sang & Lee Shok Mee. (1989). *Latihan Mengajar Untuk Maktab Perguruan.* Kuala Lumpur: Kumpulan Budiman Sdn Bhd.

Mok Soon Sang. (2010). *Bimbingan dan Kaunseling Kanak-Kanak.* Selangor: Penerbitan Multimedia Sdn. Bhd.

Moksin, A. I., Shahrill, M., Anshari, M., Huda, M., & Tengah, K. A. (2018). The Learning of Integration in Calculus Using the Autograph Technology. *Advanced Science Letters*, *24*(1), 550–552. doi:10.1166/asl.2018.12067

Moleong, J. L. (2000). *Metode Penelitian Kualitatif.* Bandung: Remaja Rosdakarya.

Moore, D. (2006a). Overcoming religious illiteracy: A cultural studies approach. *World History Connected, 4*(1). Retrieved from: http://worldhistoryconnected.press.illinois.edu/4.1/moore.html

Moore, D. (2010). *Guidelines for teaching about religion in K-12 public schools in the United States.* American Academy of Religion.

Moore, D. L. (2007). *Overcoming religious illiteracy: A cultural studies approach to the study of religion in secondary education.* New York: Palgrave Macmillan. doi:10.1057/9780230607002

Moore, J. R. (2006b). Teaching about Islam in secondary schools: Curricular and pedagogical considerations. *Equity & Excellence in Education, 39*(3), 279–286. doi:10.1080/10665680600788479

Morden, T. (2017). *Principles of management.* Routledge.

Moulton, J. (2009). Madrasah education: Negotiating belief and value differences in Islamic schools around the world. *Beliefs and Values, 1*(1), 94–120. doi:10.1891/1942-0617.1.1.94

Mu'izzuddin, M. (2014). Etika belajar dalam kitab ta'lîm muta'allim [Learning ethics of Ta'lîm al-Muta'allim]. *Jurnal Al-Ittijah, 4*(01), 1–18.

Muda, M. A. (1994). Isu Kreativiti dan tuntutan Perubahan Dalam Pendidikan. Warta Pendeta. *Jurnal Pendidikan Terengganu, 1*(1), 53–60.

Muhamad, Z. A. M., Rahman, N. A., & Awang, S. (2016). Kajian tindakan kaedah nashid dalam membaiki bacaan tahiyyat dalam kalangan pelajar-pelajar sekolah rendah. *Journal of Islamic Studies in Indonesia and Southeast Asia, 1*(1), 29–36.

Muhammad Eliyasin & Nanik Nurhayati. (2012). *Manajemen Pendidikan Islam.* Yogyakarta: Aditya Media Publishing.

Muhammad, N. (2007). *Antropologi Agama.* Banda Aceh: Ar-Raniry Press.

Muhid, S. J. N. A., & Jantan, R. (2014). Pengajaran membaca Bahasa Melayu berbantukan komputer dan nyanyian dalam kalangan pelajar-pelajar orang asli. *Asian Education Action Research Journal, 3*, 26–41.

Mulyono. (2008). Manajemen Administrasi dan Organisasi Pendidikan. Yogyakarta: Ar-Ruzz Media.

Mustaffa. (1996). *Leadership dynamism: Instilling vision for the future century.* Kuala Lumpur: TerajuDinamikSdn.

Myint, S. K., & Salleh, I. M. (2009). *Transformative leadership and educational excellence.* Rotterdam: Sense Publishers.

Nair, G., Rahim, R., Setia, R., Husin, N., Sabapathy, E., Jalil, N., ... Mohamed, N. (2012). Malaysian Graduates English Adequacy in the Job Sector. *Asian Social Science*, 8(4).

Najeeb, S. S. (2013). Learner autonomy in language learning. *Procedia: Social and Behavioral Sciences*, 70(70), 1238–1242. doi:10.1016/j.sbspro.2013.01.183

Nakamura, T. (2000). *The Use of Vocabulary Learning Strategies: the Case of Japanese EFL Learners in Two Different Learning Environments*. University of Essex.

Nanji, A. (1997). Mapping Islamic studies: Genealogy. *Continuity and Change, 38*.

Nasr, S. (1989). *Knowledge and the sacred*. Albany, NY: State University of New York.

Nasr, S. (2010). *Islam in the modern world*. New York: Harper One.

Nasr, S. H. (1992). Oral transmission and the book in Islamic education: The spoken and the written word. *Journal of Islamic Studies*, 3(1), 1–14. doi:10.1093/jis/3.1.1

Nasr, S. H. (2012). Islamic Pedagogy: An Interview. *Islam & Science*, 10(1), 7–24.

Nasr, S. H. (2016). Philosophical Considerations of Islamic Education-Past and Future: Interview with Professor Seyyed Hossein Nasr. In M. Zaman & N. A. Memon (Eds.), *Philosophies of Islamic Education* (pp. 29–37). New York: Routledge.

Naufal, M. A., Atan, N. A., Abdullah, A. H., & Abu, M. S. (2017). Problem Solving, Based On Metacognitive Learning Activities, To Improve Mathematical Reasoning Skills Of Students. *Man in India*, 97(12), 213–220.

Nawawi, M. (1987). *Adab al-'alim wal muta'allim*. Tanta, Egypt: Maktabat al- Sahabah.

Newman, J. H. (1921). *Apologia pro vita sua*. London: Everyman.

Newman, J. H. (1927). *The idea of a university defined and illustrated*. Chicago, IL: Loyola University Press.

Newmann, F., & ... (1996). *Authentic achievement: Restructuring schools for intellectual quality*. San Francisco: Jossey Bass.

Niyozov, S., & Memon, N. (2011). Islamic education and Islamization: Evolution of themes, continuities and new directions. *Journal of Muslim Minority Affairs*, 31(1), 5–30. doi:10.1080 /13602004.2011.556886

Noddings, N. (1993). *Educating for intelligent belief or unbelief*. New York: Teachers College Press.

Noddings, N. (2002). *Educating moral people: A caring alternative to character education*. New York: Teachers College Press.

Nord, W. A. (1995). *Religion & American education: Rethinking a national dilemma*. Chapel Hill, NC: University of North Carolina Press.

Nord, W. A., & Haynes, C. C. (1998). *Taking religion seriously across the curriculum.* Nashville, TN: ASCD.

Norhaslina Kamarulzaman, Nazean Jomhari, & Mohd Yakub @ Zulkifli Mohd Yusoff. (2014). Membaca dan mempelajari al-Quran dengan teknik al-Jabari untuk pelajar dengan sindrom down. *The Fourth Annual International Quranic Conference 2014.* Retrieved from http://repository. um.edu.my/41337/1/Membaca%20dan%20Mempelajari%20AlQuran%20dengan%20Teknik%20 AlJabari%20untuk%20Pelajar%20dengan%20Sindrom%20Down.pdf

Nor, M. R. M., & Malim, M. (2014). Revisiting Islamic education: The case of Indonesia. *Journal for Multicultural Education, 8*(4), 261–276. doi:10.1108/JME-05-2014-0019

Nowrozi, R., Nasrabadi, H., Heshi, K., & Mansoori, H. (2013). An introduction to Avicenna's thoughts on educational methods. *Journal of Education and Practice, 4*(9), 169–176.

Nucci, L., & Narvaez, D. (Eds.). (2008). *Handbook of moral and character education.* New York: Routledge. doi:10.4324/9780203931431

Nur Farhanah Amin. (2011). *Keberkesanan Kaedah Nyanyian Dalam Meningkatkan Ingatan Pelajar Tahun 5 Bagi Tajuk 'Kitaran Air'. Tesis Ijazah Sarjana Muda Perguruan (dengan Kepujian).* Institut Pendidikan Guru Dato' Razali Ismail.

Nurul Huda Adzis. (2004). *Nashid sebagai Hiburan alternatif dan peranannya dalam pembentukan peribadi remaja: kajian terhadap pelajar SPI, UTM.* Kertas Projek, Fakulti pendidikan Universiti Teknologi Malaysia.

Nuryatno, M. A. (2011). Islamic Education in A Pluralistic Society. *Al-Jami'ah. Journal of Islamic Studies, 49*(2), 411–431.

O'Grady, K. (2005). Professor Ninian Smart, phenomenology and religious education. *British Journal of Religious Education, 27*(3), 227–237. doi:10.1080/01416200500141249

Oloyede, I. O. (2004). The Place of Arabic and Islamic Studies in a Globalized Nation. *NATAIS Journal of the Nigeria Association of Teachers of Arabic and Islamic Studies, 7.*

Omar, A. M. (2010). *Dictionary of Holy Qur'an* (2nd ed.). NOOR Foundation, International Inc.

Önal, M. (2010). Wisdom (Hikmah) as a Holistic Basis for Inter-religious Education. In International Handbook of Inter-religious Education (pp. 221-234). Springer Netherlands.

Orak, J. (2016, April). Education from the perspective of Islamic and western scientists (Case study: Ghazali and Plato). *The Turkish Online Journal of Design, Art and Communication,* 127-135.

Osguthorpe, R. D. (2015). On the reasons we want teachers of good disposition and moral character. *Journal of Teacher Education, 59*(4), 288–299. doi:10.1177/0022487108321377

Osterman, K. (2010). Teacher practice and students' sense of belonging. In T. Lovat, R. Toomey & N. Clement (Eds.), International research handbook on values education and student wellbeing (pp. 239-260). Dordrecht, The Netherlands: Springer.

Othman, A., Hussien, S., Ahmad, I. S., Rashid, A. A., & Badzis, M. (2017). Islamic integrated education system model in the Malay archipelago: Implications for educational leadership. *Intellectual Discourse, 25*(1), 203–226. Retrieved from http://search.ebscohost.com/login.aspx ?direct=true&db=lxh&AN=123963599&site=ehost-live

Othman, M. S. B. A. (2004). Characteristics of Islamic management: principles and implementation. Brunei: Civil Service Institute.

Othman, N. S., & Ali, M. F. (2012). *Meningkatkan kemahiran mengingat nama-nama benua di dunia dan kedudukan Malaysia di peta dunia melalui kaedah nyanyian. Prosiding Seminar Penyelidikan Pendidikan IPG*. Kuala Lumpur: Institut Pendidikan Guru Malaysia.

Othman, R., Shahrill, M., Mundia, L., Tan, A., & Huda, M. (2016). Investigating the Relationship Between the Student's Ability and Learning Preferences: Evidence from Year 7 Mathematics Students. *The New Educational Review, 44*(2), 125–138.

Paramboor, J., & Ibrahim, M. B. (2014). Educational leadership as a manifestation of 'Adab' in education: Conception of Zarnuji. *International Journal of Education and Research, 2*(3), 1–12.

Parker, W. C. (2003). *Teaching democracy: Unity and diversity in public life*. New York: Teachers College Press.

Parrott, J. (2017). Al-Ghazali and the golden rule: Ethics of reciprocity in the works of a Muslim sage. *Journal of Religious & Theological Information, 16*(2), 68–78. doi:10.1080/10477845.2 017.1281067

Peleg, I., & Waxman, D. (2011). *Israeli's Palestinians: The conflict within*. New York: Cambridge University Press. doi:10.1017/CBO9780511852022

Pemerintah, P. (2010). PP Nomor 17 Tahun 2010 Paragraf 11 Pasal 97 tentang Kurikulum. *Pub., L*(97), 33.

Peters, R. S. (1981). *Moral development and moral education*. London: George Allen & Unwin.

Pinson, H. (2007). Inclusive curriculum? Challenges to the role of citizenship education in a Jewish and democratic state. *Curriculum Inquiry, 37*(4), 351–380. doi:10.1111/j.1467-873X.2007.00391.x

Pius Partanto & Dahlan Albari. (2001). *Kamus Ilmiah Populer*. Surabaya: Arloka.

Power, F. C., Higgins, A., & Kohlberg, L. (1989). *Lawrence Kohlberg's approach to moral education*. New York: Columbia Press.

Prain, V., Cox, P., Deed, C., Dorman, J., Edwards, D., Farrelly, C., ... Yagera, Z. (2013). Personalised learning: Lessons to be learnt. *British Educational Research Journal, 39*(4), 654–676.

Pritchard, A. (2017). *Ways of Learning* (4th ed.). Abingdon, UK: Routledge. doi:10.4324/9781315460611

Proctor, C. (2013). The Importance of Good Character. In Research, Applications, and Interventions for Children and Adolescents: A Positive Psychology Perspective (pp. 13–21). Academic Press. doi:10.1007/978-94-007-6398-2_2

Quraishi, M. A. (1983). *Some aspects of Muslim Education.* Universal Books.

Qureshi, O. A. (2016). Disciplinary and Islamic Education. In N. A. Memon & M. Zaman (Eds.), *Philosophies of Islamic Education: Historical Perspectives and Emerging Discourses.* New York: Routledge.

Rahim, A. A. (2013). Understanding Islamic Ethics and Its Significance on the Character Building. *International Journal of Social Science and Humanity, 3*(6), 508–513.

Rahman, A. A. & Rahman, M. A. (2013). Keberkesanan kaedah nyanyian dalam meningkatkan daya ingatan pelajar tahun empat bagi topik jenis-jenis rumah tradisional di Malaysia. *Penyelidikan Tindakan PISMP 2013, 2*(4).

Rahman, A. (1980). *Muḥammad the Educator of Mankind.* London: The Muslims Schools Trust.

Ramadan, T. (2004). *Western Muslims and the future of Islam.* Oxford, UK: Oxford University Press.

Rasyidah, R. (2012). Konstruksi makna budaya Islam pada masyarakat Aceh. *IBDA: Jurnal Kajian Islam dan Budaya, 10*(2), 218-230.

Rebstock, U. (2010). West Africa and its early empires. In M. Fierro (Ed.), *The New Cambridge History of Islam* (pp. 144–158). Cambridge, UK: Cambridge University Press. doi:10.1017/CHOL9780521839570.007

Recommendations of the Fourth World conference on Islamic Education. (1983). Makka Al-Mukarrama, Umm al-Qura University.

Reeves, M. (2000). *Muḥammad in Europe: A Thousand Years of Western Myth-making.* New York: New York University Press.

Rehman, A., Bilal, H. A., Sheikh, A., Bibi, N., & Nawaz, A. (2014). The role of motivation in learning English language for Pakistani learners. *International Journal of Humanities and Social Science, 4*(1), 254–258.

Reinders, H. (2014). Personal Learning Environments for Supporting Out-of-Class Language Learning. *English Teaching Forum, 52*(4), 14.

Richardson, J. T. E. (2005). Students' Approaches to Learning and Teacher's Approach to Teaching in Higher Education. *Educational Psychology, 25*(6), 673–680. doi:10.1080/01443410500344720

Rissanen, I. (2012). Teaching Islamic education in Finnish schools: A field of negotiations. *Teaching and Teacher Education, 28*(5), 740–749. doi:10.1016/j.tate.2012.02.001

Robinson, F. (1993). Technology and religious change: Islam and the impact of print. *Modern Asian Studies, 27*(01), 229–251. doi:10.1017/S0026749X00016127

Robinson, S. (2015). Islam, responsibility and business in the thought of Fethullah Gülen. *Journal of Business Ethics*, *128*(2), 369–381.

Robinson, S. J., & Smith, J. (2012). Exploring responsibility. *Journal of Global Responsibility*, *3*(1), 151–166.

Roorda, D. L., Koomen, H. M., Spilt, J. L., & Oort, F. J. (2011). The influence of affective teacher–student relationships on students' school engagement and achievement: A meta-analytic approach. *Review of Educational Research*, *81*(4), 493–529. doi:10.3102/0034654311421793

Rosenblith, S. (2008). Beyond coexistence: Toward a more reflective religious pluralism. *Theory and Research in Education*, *6*(1), 107–121. doi:10.1177/1477878507086733

Rosenblith, S., & Priestmanm, S. (2004). Problematizing religious truth: Implications for public education. *Educational Theory*, *54*(4), 365–380. doi:10.1111/j.0013-2004.2004.00025.x

Rosli, M. F., & Omar, B. (2013). Penggunaan teknik nyanyian dan Mnemonik (Ndm) dalam meningkatkan penguasaan kata sendi nama dari pelajar tahun tiga. *Kajian Tindakan PISMP 2013, 2*(7).

Rosli, M. R. B., Salamon, H. B., & Huda, M. (2018). Distribution Management of Zakat Fund: Recommended Proposal for Asnaf Riqab in Malaysia. *International Journal of Civil Engineering and Technology*, *9*(3), 56–64.

Roth, W. M., Tobin, K., & Zimmermann, A. (2002). Co-teaching/cogenerative dialoguing: Learning environments research as classroom praxis. *Learning Environments Research*, *5*(1), 1–28. doi:10.1023/A:1015662623784

Rowe, K. (2004). In good hands? The importance of teacher quality. *Educare News*, *149*, 4–14.

Royster, J. E. (1978). Muhammad as Teacher and Exemplar. *The Muslim World*, *68*(4), 235–258. doi:10.1111/j.1478-1913.1978.tb03359.x

Rudnitzky, A. (2014). The Arab citizens of Israel at the start of the twenty-first century. Tel Aviv: The Institute for National Security Studies. (in Hebrew)

Runesson, U. (2015). Pedagogical and learning theories and the improvement and development of lesson and learning studies. *International Journal for Lesson and Learning Studies*, *4*(3), 186–193. doi:10.1108/IJLLS-04-2015-0016

Rusman. (2009). Manajemen Kurikulum. Jakarta: Rajawali Press.

Sabani, N. (2016). Understandings of Islamic pedagogy for personalised learning. The International Journal of Information and Learning Technology. doi:10.1108/IJILT-01-2016-0003

Sabki, A. i., & Hardaker, G. (2013). The madrasah concept of Islamic pedagogy. *Educational Review*, *65*(3), 342–356. doi:10.1080/00131911.2012.668873

Sadaalah, S. (2004). Islamic orientations and education. In H. Daun & G. Walford (Eds.), *Educational strategies among Muslims in the context of globalization* (pp. 37–63). Boston: Brill.

Saeed, A. (2006). *Islamic thought: An introduction*. London: Routledge.

Safi, O. (2003). *Progressive Muslims on justice, gender, and pluralism*. Oxford, UK: Oneworld.

Sağlam, G., & Salı, P. (2013). The essentials of the foreign language learning environment: Through the eyes of the pre-service EFL teachers. *Procedia: Social and Behavioral Sciences*, *93*, 1121–1125. doi:10.1016/j.sbspro.2013.09.342

Sahin, A. (2013). *New Directions in Islamic education. Pedagogy and identity formation*. Kube Publishing Ltd.

Sahin, A. (2018). Critical issues in Islamic education studies: Rethinking Islamic and Western liberal secular values of education. *Religions*, *9*(11), 335. doi:10.3390/rel9110335

Sahlan, M. K., Abu-Hussin, M. F., & Hehsan, A. (2018). Market coopetition: Implications of religious identity in creating value added partnership within halal mart retailers. *Journal of Islamic Marketing*.

Saldana, J. (2009). *The coding manual for qualitative researchers*. London: Sage.

Salim, P. (1987). *The Contemporary English Indonesian Dictionary*. Jakarta: Modern English Press.

Salleh, M. A., Abu-Hussin, M. F., Azeez, Y. A., Adam, F., & Muhamad, N. H. N. (2015). The Emergence of Non-State Actors in Enhancing Malaysia's Relationship with the Gcc Countries. *Pertanika Journal of Social Science & Humanities*, *23*, 267–280.

Salleh, M. S. (2013a). Philosophical Foundations of Islamic Development : Khurshid Ahmad's Conception Revisited. *International Journal of Education and Research*, *1*(7), 1–16.

Salleh, M. S. (2013b). Strategizing Islamic Education. *International Journal of Education and Research*, *1*(6), 1–14.

Sallis, E. (2012). *Total Quality Management in Education*. Yogyakarta: Ircisod.

Samad, S. A. A. (2015). Pengaruh agama dalam tradisi mendidik anak di Aceh: Telaah terhadap masa sebelum dan pasca kelahiran. *Gender Equality: International Journal of Child and Gender Studies*, *1*(1), 111–124.

Sanneh, L. (1976). The origins of clericalism in West African Islam. *Journal of African History*, *17*(1), 49–72. doi:10.1017/S0021853700014766

Sardar, Z. (1983). The Future of Islamic Studies. *Islamic Culture, 57*(3).

Saud, L. (2013). Islamic Beliefs: The Development of Islamic Ideas. In A. B. McCloud, S. W. Hibbard, & L. Saud (Eds.), *An Introduction to Islam in the 21st Century* (pp. 51–80). Oxford, UK: Wiley-Blackwell.

Savignon, S. J. (1991). Communicative language teaching; state of the art. *TESOL Quarterly*, *25*(2), 261–277. doi:10.2307/3587463

Savin, C. F. (2001). *Tune-in to Biology: Music in the Science Classroom*. Retrieved from http://www.science.subaru.com/teaching_ideas/carolsavin

Schimmel, A. (1985). *And Muḥammad is His Messenger: The veneration of the Prophet on Islamic Piety*. Chapel Hill, NC: The University of North Carolina Press.

Selcuk, M. (2012). The contribution of religious education to democratic culture. In H. A. Alexander & A. K. Agbaria (Eds.), *Commitment, character, and citizenship: Religious education in liberal democracy* (pp. 215–225). New York: Routledge.

Seman, Z. C., Abdul, A. A. K., & Zaidul, A. S. A. (2014). *Nyanyian dan muzik mengikut pandangan hukum oleh Tuan Guru Hj. Abdul Rahman Pondok Sungai Durian Kuala Krai Kelantan*. International Research Management and Innovation Conference 2014 (IRMIC2014), Kuala Lumpur, Malaysia.

Shamal, S. (2000). Cultural shift: The case of Jewish religious education in Israel. *British Journal of Sociology of Education*, *21*(3), 401–417. doi:10.1080/713655352

Shams-ur-Rehman, T. (2008). Merging spirituality and religion: Developing an Islamic leadership theory. *IIUM Journal of Economics and Management*, *16*(1), 15–46.

Shen, L., & Su, A. (2019). Intervention of Smartphone Addiction. In *Multifaceted Approach to Digital Addiction and Its Treatment* (pp. 207–228). IGI Global. doi:10.4018/978-1-5225-8449-0.ch010

Sibai, M. (1987). *Mosque libraries: An Historical Study*. London: Mansell Publishing Limited.

Siddiqi, M. Z. (1961). Islamic Studies: Their Significance and Importance. *Islamic Culture, 35*.

Sidi, I. D. (2000). *Kebijakan Penyelenggaraan Otonomi Daerah Bidang Pendidikan (makalah)*. Bandung: UPI.

Sidiq, U., & Ikhwan, A. (2018). Local Government Policy Regarding Mandatory Students Diniyah Takmiliyah in Indramayu Regency. KARSA: Journal of Social and Islamic Culture. doi:10.19105/karsa.v26i1.1444

Siegel, H. (1988). *Educating reason*. New York: Routledge.

Sirtha, N. (2013, February 27). Menggali kearifan lokal untuk Ajeg Bali. *Bali Post*. Retrieved from http://www.balipos.co.id/baca/20130227/meggali-kearifan-lokal-untuk-ajeg-bali.html

Siti Suaini Yusoff & Mohamed Sulaiman@Wahid. (2012). Penggunaan teknik nyanyian untuk meningkatkan kelancaran membaca perkataan dua suku kata bagi pelajar 'Slow Learner'. *Prosiding Seminar Penyelidikan Tindakan PISMP, 3*(6).

Siti, S. M. S., & Muhamad, Z. A. M. (2014). Harmonizing al-Qabisy's view and practice of J-Qaf programme in malaysian primary school. *Asian Journal of Management Sciences & Education*, *3*(1), 153–162.

Siti, S. M. S., & Mustaffa, A. (2014). Guru bersahsiah mulia menurut pandangan Ibn Sahnun: Analisa buku Adab Mu'allimin. *The Online Journal of Islamic Education, 2*(2), 1–10.

Slade, S., & Prinsloo, P. (2013). Learning analytics, ethical issues, and dilemmas. *The American Behavioral Scientist, 57*(10), 1510–1529. doi:10.1177/0002764213479366

Smart, N. (1987). *Religion in the western mind.* New York: Macmillan. doi:10.1007/978-1-349-08772-3

Snorradóttir, A. B. (2014). *Language use in the English classroom: the role of students' first language in grades 9 and 10 in English classrooms in Iceland.* University of Iceland.

Sofian, K., Abu-Mokh, F. (2014). *The religious education book for the high school level: The first unit.* Haifa- Israel: Kul-Shee Library. (Arabic)

Sokol, B., Hammond, S., & Berkowitz, M. (2010). The developmental contours of character. In T. Lovat, R. Toomey & N. Clement (Eds.), International research handbook on values education and student wellbeing (pp. 579-604). Dordrecht, The Netherlands: Springer. doi:10.1007/978-90-481-8675-4_33

Stake, R. E. (1994). Case studies. In N. K. Denzin & Y. S. Lincoln (Eds.), *Handbook of qualitative research* (pp. 236–247). London: Sage.

Sternberg, R. (2007). *Wisdom, intelligence, and creativity synthesized.* New York: Cambridge University Press.

Sugiono, S. (2005). *Memahami Penelitian Kualitatif.* Bandung: Alfabeta.

Sugiyarti, E., Jasmi, K. A., Basiron, B., Huda, M., Shankar, K., & Maseleno, A. (2018). Decision support system of scholarship grantee selection using data mining. *International Journal of Pure and Applied Mathematics, 119*(15), 2239–2249.

Suhana Udin. (2012). Meningkatkan kemahiran mengingat huruf Idgham Maal Ghunnah menggunakan gabungan kaedah ilustrasi kartun, pergerakan dan nyanyian. Koleksi artikel penyelidikan tindakan PISMP pendidikan Islam. *Seminar Penyelidikan Tindakan IPG KBL Tahun 2012, 230-242.*

Suharto, T. (2018). Transnational Islamic education in Indonesia: An ideological perspective. *Contemporary Islam, 12*(2), 101–122. doi:10.100711562-017-0409-3

Suhnun, I. M. (1972). Adab al-Mu'allimin. Hasan Husni Abdul-Wahab.

Sulaiman, K. O. (2013). The Use of Instructional Materials for Effective Learning of Islamic Studies. *Jihāt Al-Islām, 6*(2).

Sultana, Q. (2012). Philosophy of education: An Islamic perspective. *Philosophy and Progress, 51-52,* 10–36.

Superka, D. P. (1976). *Values Education Sourcebook, Conceptual Approach, Material Analyses, and an Annotated Bibliography.* Social Science Eucation Consortium Inc.

Suryasa, W., Prayoga, G. P. A., & Werdistira, W. A. (2017). An analysis of students' motivation towards English learning as a second language among students in Pritchard English Academy. *International Journal of Social Science and Humanity*, (1): 2.

Suryobroto, B. (2004). *Manajemen Pendidikan di Sekolah*. Jakarta: Rieneka Cipta.

Susilowati, T., Dacholfany, M.I., Aminin, S., Ikhwan, A., Nasir, B.M., Huda, M., ... Wulandari. (2018b). Getting parents involved in child's school: using attendance application system based on SMS gateway. *International Journal of Engineering and Technology*, *7*(2.27), 167-174.

Susilowati, T., Teh, K.S.M., Nasir, B.M., Don, A.G., Huda, M., Hensafitri, T., ... Irawan, D. (2018c). Learning application of Lampung language based on multimedia software. *International Journal of Engineering and Technology, 7*(2.27), 175-181.

Susilowati, T., Jasmi, K.A., Basiron, B., Huda, M., Shankar, K., Maseleno, A., & Julia, A. (2018a). Determination of Scholarship Recipients Using Simple Additive Weighting Method. *International Journal of Pure and Applied Mathematics*, *119*(15), 2231–2238.

Swartwood, J. D. (2013). Wisdom as an Expert Skill. *Ethical Theory and Moral Practice*, *16*(3), 511–528. doi:10.100710677-012-9367-2

Swinton, J. (2001). Spirituality and Mental Health Care: Rediscovering a 'Forgotten' Dimension. Jessica Kingsley Publishers.

Tamam, E., & Krauss, S. E. (2017). Ethnic-related diversity engagement differences in intercultural sensitivity among Malaysian undergraduate students. *International Journal of Adolescence and Youth*, *22*(2), 137–150. doi:10.1080/02673843.2014.881295

Tan & Chin. (2012). Penggunaan Kaedah Nyanyian Untuk Meningkatkan Pengetahuan Tentang Cara Pengurusan Bahan Kitar Semula. *Persidangan Kebangsaan Pembangunan dan Pendidikan Lestari 2012*. Institut Pendidikan Guru Kampus Tuanku Bainun.

Tan, C. (2014). Rationality and autonomy from the enlightenment and Islamic perspectives. *Journal of Beliefs and Values, 35*(3), 327-39.

Tan, B. P., Naidu, N. B. M., & Jamil, Z. (2018). Moral values and good citizens in a multi-ethnic society: A content analysis of moral education textbooks in Malaysia. *Journal of Social Studies Research*, *42*(2), 119–134. doi:10.1016/j.jssr.2017.05.004

Tan, C. (2008). *Teaching without indoctrination: Implications for values education*. Rotterdam: Sense Publishers.

Tan, C. (2009). The reform agenda for madrasah education in Singapore. *Diaspora, Indigenous, and Minority Education*, *3*(2), 67–80. doi:10.1080/15595690902762068

Tan, C. (2011). *Islamic education and indoctrination: The case in Indonesia*. New York: Routledge.

Tan, C. (Ed.). (2014). *Reforms in Islamic education: International perspectives*. London: Bloomsbury. doi:10.5040/9781472593252

Tan, C., & Abbas, D. B. (2009). The 'Teach Less, Learn More' initiative in Singapore: New pedagogies for Islamic religious schools? *KEDI Journal of Educational Policy*, 6(1), 25–39.

Tan, C., & Abbas, D. B. (2012). Madrasahs and the state: Which worldview? In J. Tan (Ed.), *Education in Singapore at the beginning of the 2010s* (pp. 89–99). Singapore: Prentice Hall.

Tan, C., & Abbas, D. B. (2017). Reform in Madrasah education: The Singapore experience. In M. Abu Bakar (Ed.), *Rethinking madrasah education in the globalised world* (pp. 195–209). New York: Routledge.

Tan, C., & Ibrahim, A. (2017). Humanism, Islamic Education, and Confucian Education. *Religious Education (Chicago, Ill.)*, 112(4), 394–406. doi:10.1080/00344087.2016.1225247

Tang, C. M., & Chaw, L. Y. (2016). Digital Literacy: A Prerequisite for Effective Learning in a Blended Learning Environment? *Electronic Journal of E-learning*, 14(1), 54–65.

Taufiq, M. (n.d.). Al-Qur'an dan Terjemah; Al-Qur'an In Word. *Software Quran In Word*.

Thang, S. M., Ting, S. L., & Mohd Jaafar, N. (2011). Attitudes and Motivation of Malaysian Secondary Students towards learning English as a Second Language. *3L: The Southeast Asian Journal of English Language Studies, 17*(1).

Thang, S. M. (2004). Learning English in multicultural Malaysia: Are learners motivated? *Journal of Language and Learning*, 2(2).

Thang, S., Nambiar, R. K., Wong, F., Mohd Jaafar, N., & Amir, Z. (2015). A Clamour for More Technology in Universities: What Does an Investigation into the ICT Use and Learning Styles of Malaysian 'Digital Natives' Tell Us? *The Asia-Pacific Education Researcher*, 24(2), 353–361. doi:10.100740299-014-0185-2

Thiessen, E. J. (2012). Democratic schooling and the demands of religion. In H. A. Alexander & A. K. Agbaria (Eds.), *Commitment, character, and citizenship: Religious education in liberal democracy* (pp. 161–178). New York: Routledge.

Thomas, T., Wallace, J., Allen, P., Clark, J., Jones, A., Lawrence, J., ... Sheridan Burns, L. (2017). Strategies for leading academics to rethink humanities and social sciences curricula in the context of discipline standards. *The International Journal for Academic Development*, 22(2), 120–133. doi:10.1080/1360144X.2017.1285239

Thompson, G. L. (2015). Understanding the heritage language student: Proficiency and placement. *Journal of Hispanic Higher Education*, 14(1), 82–96. doi:10.1177/1538192714551277

Tibi, B. (2012). *Islamism and Islam*. New Haven, CT: Yale University Press.

Tichy, N. M., & Devanna, M. A. (1986). *The transformational leader*. New York: Wiley.

Tim Riset Penerbit Al-Qira'ah. (2010). Khitan dalam Perspektif Syari'at dan Kesehatan. Jakarta Timur: Pustaka Al-Kautsar.

Trimingham, J. S. (1980). *The Influence of Islam upon Africa*. London: Longman.

Compilation of References

Turner-Bisset, R. (2001). *Expert Teaching*. London: David Foulton.

Umam, C. (2014). Maintaining Islamic Values in English Language Teaching in Indonesian Pesantrens. *Didaktika Religia, 2*(1), 227–242.

Umi Kalsum Zakaria & Mohamed Sulaiman@Wahid. (2012). Aplikasi terapi permainan kerusi muzik dalam membantu pengecaman dan penyebutan suku kata KVKV. *Prosiding Seminar Penyelidikan Tindakan PISMP, 3*(6).

Veithzal, R. D. A. A. (2009). *Islamic leadership: Membangun superleadership melalui kecerdasan spiritual* [Islamic leadership: Super leadership through spiritual intelligences]. Jakarta: PT Bumi Aksara.

Victorian Curriculum and Assessment Authority (VCAA). (2015). *The Arts*. Retrieved from http://ausvels.vcaa.vic.edu.au/Overview/Strands-Domains-and-Dimensions

Waghid, Y. (2011). *Conceptions of Islamic education: Pedagogical framings*. New York: Peter Lang.

Waghid, Y., & Smeyers, P. (2014). Re-envisioning the future: Democratic citizenship education and Islamic education. *Journal of Philosophy of Education, 48*(4), 539–558. doi:10.1111/1467-9752.12118

Walker, R. (2010). The Conduct of Educational Case Study: Ethics, Theory and Procedures. In H. Torrance (Ed.), *Qualitative Research Methods in Education* (Vol. I, pp. 253–286). London: Sage Publications Ltd.

Wallace, A. R. (1863). On the physical geography of the Malay Archipelago. *Journal of the Royal Geographical Society of London, 33*, 217–234. doi:10.2307/1798448

Wallace, A. R. (1869). *The Malay Archipelago: the land of the orang-utan and the bird of paradise; a narrative of travel, with studies of man and nature*. London: Macmillan and Co.

Wane, N. N. (2011). Spirituality: A Philosophy and a Research Tool. In N. N. Wane, E. L. Manyimo, & E. J. Ritskes (Eds.), *Spirituality, Education & Society an Integrated Approach*. Sense Publishers. doi:10.1007/978-94-6091-603-8_5

Wani, H., Abdullah, R., & Chang, L. (2015). An Islamic perspective in managing religious diversity. *Religions, 6*(2), 642–656. doi:10.3390/rel6020642

Watt, W. M. (1961). *Muḥammad: Prophet and Statesman*. Oxford, UK: Oxford University Press.

Watt, W. M. (2017). *Islamic philosophy and theology*. Routledge.

Weinberger, A., Biedermann, H., Patry, J. L., & Weyringer, S. (Eds.). (2018). *Professionals' Ethos and Education for Responsibility*. BRILL.

Wenger, E. (2010). Communities of practice and social learning systems: the career of a concept. In *Social learning systems and communities of practice* (pp. 179–198). London: Springer. doi:10.1007/978-1-84996-133-2_11

Westheimer, J., & Kahne, J. (2004). What kind of citizen? The politics of educating for democracy. *American Educational Research Journal*, *41*(2), 237–269. doi:10.3102/00028312041002237

White, K. (2010). Asking sacred questions: Understanding religion's impact on teacher belief and action. *Religious Education (Chicago, Ill.)*, *37*(1), 40–59.

White, K. R. (2009). Connecting religion and teacher identity: The unexplored relationship between religion and teachers in public schools. *Teaching and Teacher Education*, *25*(6), 857–866. doi:10.1016/j.tate.2009.01.004

Wilkinson, M. L. N. (2013). Introducing Islamic critical realism. *Journal of Critical Realism*, *12*(4), 419–442. doi:10.1179/1476743013Z.00000000014

Wragg, T., & Brown, G. (1993). *Explaining*. London: Routledge. doi:10.4324/9780203308479

Wright, A. (2007). *Critical religious education, multiculturalism and the pursuit of truth*. Cardiff, UK: University of Wales Press.

Wright, R. (1996). Islam and liberal democracy: Two visions of reformation. *Journal of Democracy*, *7*(2), 64–75. doi:10.1353/jod.1996.0037

Wulandari, Aminin, S., Dacholfany, M.I., Mujib, A., Huda, M., Nasir, B.M., … Masrur, M. (2018). Design of library application system. *International Journal of Engineering and Technology*, *7*(2.27), 199-204.

Yahya, M. S. (2005). Atmosfir Akademis dan Nilai Estetik Kitab Taʿlīm al-Mutaʿallim [Academic atmosphere and ethical values of Taʿlīm al-Mutaʿallim]. *Journal Ibda*, *3*(2), 1–10.

Yin, R. K. (2009). *Case study research: Design and methods*. Thousand Oaks, CA: Sage Publications.

Yong, L. M. S., & Biramiah, K. (1996). *Dalam Guru Yang Kreatif: Isu-Isu Teoritikal dan Aplikasi Praktikal*. Kuala Lumpur: Arenabuku Sdn. Bhd.

Yukl, G. (2006). *Leadership in organisations* (6th ed.). Pearson Education.

Yun, Y. S. (2017). *Ritual Kematian di Aceh Barat Daya (Studi Etnografi di Gampong Kampung Tengah Kecamatan Kuala Batee)* (Unpublished Undergraduate Thesis). UIN Ar-Raniry.

Yunus, K., Mohamad, M., & Waelateh, B. (2016). The Breadth of Receptive Vocabulary Knowledge among English Major University Students. *Journal of Nusantara Studies*, *1*(1), 7–17. doi:10.24200/jonus.vol1iss1pp7-17

Yunus, M. (1990). *Kamus bahasa Arab- Indonesia* [A Dictionary of Arab to Indonesia]. Jakarta: Bulan Bintang.

Yusob, M. M., Salleh, M. A., Ariffin, M. R., & Mohamed, A. N. H. (2017). International Religious Freedom Act 1998 and the Issues of Religious Freedom in Muslim Countries. *Pertanika Journal of Social Science & Humanities*, *25*, 231–239.

Zakaria, T. R. (2000). Pendekatan Pendekatan Pendidikan Nilai dan Implementasi dalam Pendidikan Budi Pekerti. *Jurnal Pendidikan Dan Kebudayaan, 26*(2), 479–495.

Zaman, M., & Memon, N. A. (2016). *Philosophies of Islamic education: Historical perspectives and emerging discourses.* Routledge. doi:10.4324/9781315765501

Zamiri, A. (1998). *History of education of Iran and Islam.* Shiraz, Iran: Sasan Press.

Zarnuji. (1947). *The Instruction of the students: The Method of learning.* New York: King's Crown Press.

Zedan, A. M., Yusoff, M. Y. Z. B. M., & Mohamed, M. R. (2015). An Innovative Teaching Method in Islamic Studies: The Use of PowerPoint in University of Malaya as Case Study. *Procedia: Social and Behavioral Sciences, 182*, 543–549. doi:10.1016/j.sbspro.2015.04.776

Zia, R. (2007). Transmission of values in Muslim countries: Religious education and moral development in school curricula. In A. Benavot, C. Braslavsky, & N. Truong (Eds.), *School knowledge in comparative and historical perspective* (pp. 119–134). Springer. doi:10.1007/978-1-4020-5736-6_8

Zubairi, A. M., & Sarudin, I. (2009). Motivation to learn a foreign language in Malaysia. *GEMA Online Journal of Language Studies, 9*(2), 73-87.

About the Contributors

Miftachul Huda is a researcher at Faculty of Human Sciences, Universiti Pendidikan Sultan Idris, Malaysia. His research interest includes Islamic education, moral education and multicultural education, digital ethics and educational technology, learning and teaching theory, innovation. He has been experienced in working on research for more than five years. Contributing several works, he is currently the member of the advisory editorial board in some international journals. Traveling in some countries with scholarly intent makes him extensive experience on his research expertise in international trend and issues. Thus, he commits to contributing his knowledge to the benefit of society through professional and social activities.

Jimaain Safar is Associate Professor at Academy of Islamic Civilisation, Faculty of Social Sciences and Humanities, Universiti Teknologi Malaysia, Malaysia. His research interest includes Islamic education, Teaching and Learning, and Educational Evaluation. He has been working in teaching and research for more than twenty-five years.

Ahmad Kilani Mohamed is Associate Professor at Academy of Islamic Civilisation, Faculty of Social Sciences and Humanities, Universiti Teknologi Malaysia, Malaysia. His research expertise includes Islamic education, Arabic education, Sufism and Teaching and Learning. He has been working in research and teaching for more than twenty-five years.

Kamarul Azmi Jasmi is Associate Professor at Academy of Islamic Civilisation, Faculty of Social Sciences and Humanities, Universiti Teknologi Malaysia, Malaysia. His research interest includes Islamic Education & Arabic, Civilisation Studies, Islamic Education and Qualitative Research Approach at Universiti Teknologi Malaysia (UTM). He has been working in teaching for more than fifteen years and published books and referred journals. He is committed to continue his research and teaching as his contribution to the society through the professional and social activities.

Bushrah Basiron is a senior lecturer of comparative religion, innovations, learning and contemporary issues in digital age at faculty of Islamic Civilisation, Universiti Teknologi Malaysia (UTM). She has been working in teaching for more than fifteen years.

* * *

Diwi Abbas was a research assistant at the Nanyang Technological University for a funded project on madrasah education in Singapore.

Muhamad Mustaqim Ahmad is a teacher of Islamic education and got Master from Universiti Kebangsaan Malaysia, Malaysia.

Muhammad Talhah Ajmain received his primary & secondary education from Sekolah Islam Hidayah Johor. Obtained his Foundation and Degree from Akademi Pengajian Islam Universiti Malaya Kuala Lumpur (APIUM). He later completed his Masters in Islamic Education from Universiti Kebangsaan Malaysia (UKM) and is now currently furthering his Doctorate studies (Ph.D) in Akademi Tamadun Islam Universiti Teknologi Malaysia (UTM). He is passionate in the education field, being brought up in an environment with parents as educators themselves.

Benaouda Bensaid is Associate Professor at College of Humanities, Effat University, Jeddah Saudi Arabia. His research interest includes Islamic thought, spirituality and sustainability.

M. Ihsan Dacholfany is a senior lecturer at school of education, Universitas Muhammadiyah Metro Lampung, Indonesia. His teaching and research experience makes him aware of the need to contribute more to benefit for the societal life. Among his research interest includes educational studies, higher education and religion.

Ibrahima Diallo is Senior Lecturer at the University of South Australia.

AbdulGafar Olawale Fahm is a native of Nigeria. He received his B.A. in Islamic Studies from University of Ilorin, Nigeria. He obtained his M.A. from International Islamic University Malaysia and his Ph.D. in the same University. His areas of interest are Islamic Spiritual Culture, Contemporary Issues, and Islamic Thought. In addition, Dr. Fahm is a Lecturer in Department of Religions, University of Ilorin, Nigeria. He has published papers in various journals amongst which is "Islam as an Embodied Faith for the Young Minds: Aisha Lemu and Religious Education in Nigeria" in Journal of Religious Education and "Islamic Ethics and Stem Cell Research" published in Islam and Civilisational Renewal.

Azmil Hashim is associate professor of Islamic education at Universiti Pendidikan Sultan Idris (UPSI). He has been working in research and teaching for more than twenty years.

Hanin Naziha Hasnor is a lecturer in the Department of Culture and Language Studies at Curtin University, Malaysia. She holds a Bachelor and Master's Degree in Teaching English as A Second Language from Universiti Teknologi Mara (UiTM). Her research interest is in Scaffolding Language Learning and Early Childhood Education. She has been teaching for eight.

Mahyuddin Hassan is senior lecturer at Universiti Teknologi Malaysia, Malaysia.

Afiful Ikhwan is senior lecturer with the field of Doctor Management of Islamic education social science Islamic education integration of science and religion curriculum development at Universitas Muhammadiyah Ponorogo, Indonesia.

Noorhaswari Ismail is a teacher of secondary school and got Master from Universiti Teknologi Malaysia.

Anita Jimmie is a lecturer in the Department of Culture and Language Studies at Curtin University, Malaysia. She holds a Bachelor and Master's Degree in Teaching English as A Second Language from Universiti Teknologi Malaysia and obtained her PhD from Victoria University of Wellington, New Zealand. She has been teaching for 12 years and loves working with youths. Her area of interest includes Learner Engagement and Learner Experience in Higher Education and Learners' Resilience. She believes that learners who are engaged and immersed in various learning experiences will develop into successful learners, so she is driven in creating an encouraging environment for her students. Her other areas of interest include advancing and engaging in outreach projects for the local community.

Ju'subaidi Ju'subaidi is senior lecturer at State Institute of Islamic Studies (IAIN) Ponorogo, Indonesia. His research expertise includes Doctorate in education, education evaluation and education research methods.

Terence Lovat is Emeritus Professor in Theology and Education at University of Newcastle, Australia, Honorary Research Fellow at Oxford University, UK, Honorary Professor at Glasgow University, UK, and Adjunct Research Professor at Royal Roads University, Canada.

Salah Machouche is currently Assistant Professor at the International Islamic University Malaysia. He obtained his BA in philosophy (Algiers University, 1994), MA (Islamic Studies, 1998), and Ph D (Usul al-Din & Comparative Studies 2008) at international Islamic University. Author of "Tawhid and the making of human association science (Umran) in Ibn Khaldun's thought" in Arabic and few articles on human nature, thinking and learning. His field of research, human nature in Qur'an & Sunnah, Islamic theory of knowledge, Religion and Learning, and Ibn Khaldun's thought.

Abdul Manan, S, Ag, M.Sc., MA, Ph.D., was born in Alurambut, Manggeng district (now Lembah Sabil district), South West Aceh (Sumatra-Indonesia) on Juni 21st, 1972. His ethnicity is Acèhnese. He finished his Islamic Elementary School (MIN) Suakberumbang-South West Aceh in 1985, State Junior High School (Sekolah Menengah Pertama Negeri) Manggeng-South West Aceh in 1988, Teacher Training School (Sekolah Pendidikan Guru-SPG) Tapaktuan-South Aceh in 1991, Under Graduate Program of English Language Education at the State Institute for Islamic Studies Ar-Raniry (S.Ag) (now State Islamic University (UIN) Ar-Raniry) Banda Aceh in 1997, Master in Educational and Training System Design (M.Sc – Scholarship from Student Netherland (StuNED)) at the Faculty of Educational Science and Technology of the University of Twente, Enschede, Holland in 2001, Master in Islamic Studies (MA – Scholarship from Indonesian Cooperation in Islamic Studies (INIS) at the Faculty of Letters and Theology of the University of Leiden, Leiden, Holland (2003) and Dr. Phil – Scholarship from Deutscher Akademischer Austauschdienst (DAAD Bonn) in Ethnology at the Westfälische Wilhelms-Universität Münster, Germany in 2010. In 2015 again he got scholarship for alumni from DAAD Bonn called Wiedereinladung Scholarship for two months (June – July) to design his post-doctoral program proposal at the Institute for Ethnology at the Westfälische Wilhelms-Universität Münster, Germany. From 1995 – 1999 he worked as teaching staff of Language Development Centre of UIN Ar-Raniry. From 2004-2011 he worked as a methodology of Islamic Studies lecturer at Syaria Faculty of UIN Ar-Raniry and from 2012 till now he works as a cultural anthropology lecturer at Adab and Humanities Faculty of Universitas Islam Negeri (UIN) Ar-Raniry Banda Aceh.

Nurazmalail Marni is senior lecturer at Universiti Teknologi Malaysia, Malaysia.

Andino Maseleno is a visiting fellow at Universiti Tenaga Nasional, Malaysia. He received the B.S. in Informatics Engineering from UPN "Veteran" Yogyakarta, Indonesia, in 2005, M.Eng. in Electrical Engineering from Gadjah Mada University, Indonesia, in 2009 and Ph.D. in Computer Science from Universiti Brunei Darussalam, Brunei Darussalam, in 2015.

Imran Mogra is a senior lecturer in Religious Education and Professional Studies in the School of Education, Faculty of Health, Law and Social Sciences, Birmingham City University, England.

Elfi Mu'awanah is Associate professor of counseling guidance at State Institute of Islamic Studies (IAIN) Ponorogo, Indonesia.

Nasrul Hisyam Nor Muhamad is Associate Professor of religion and contemporary issues at Academy of Islamic Civilisation, Universiti Teknologi Malaysia, Malaysia.

M. Ikhsan Nawawi is senior lecturer at Institute for Islamic Studies Agus Salim, Lampung, Indonesia.

Widhiya Ninsiana is senior lecturer at State Islamic Institute of Metro Lampung Indonesia.

Madheil Azaeim Ahmad Puad is teacher of Islamic education at secondary school and got Master from Universiti Kebangsaan Malaysia, Malaysia.

Ali Rohmad is Senior Lecturer of Islamic Education at State Institute of Islamic Studies (IAIN) Ponorogo, Indonesia.

Mohd Hilmi Rozali is affiliated with Academy of Islamic Civilisation, Faculty of Social Sciences and Humanities, Universiti Teknologi Malaysia, Malaysia.

Najwan Saada is a lecturer of multicultural, citizenship, and religious (Islamic) education at Al-Qasemi Academic College of Education and Beit Berl College of Education, Israel. His research focuses on citizenship and religious (Islamic) education and the intersection of Islam, democracy and liberal education in western and Muslim-majority societies. Najwan's research has been published in Theory and Research in Social Education, International Journal of Religion and Spirituality in Society, Journal of Religious Education, Religious Education, and Education Review. Also, Najwan's interest includes critical and liberal Islamic education, values education, teachers' and students' religious identities, the social and philosophical foundations of education, and curriculum studies. Najwan's account on Academia https://independent.academia.edu/NajwanSaada. And he also has an account on Research Gate.

Noraisikin Sabani is a lecturer in the Department of Culture and Language Studies at Curtin University, Malaysia. Her educational background entails a B.Sc. in Teaching English as A Second Language from Universiti Malaysia Sarawak and a Master in Education from Edith Cowan University, Australia. She is currently pursuing her PhD in the Integration of Personalized Learning (Technology) and Islamic Pedagogy with Universiti Brunei Darussalam. She takes pleasure in engaging with youths and has been involved in formal and non-formal teaching for more than ten years. As a struggling learner in her past, she is passionate about researches that consist of aiding and engaging learners of all ages, including Higher Education. She believes in the possibility of growth in every learner, despite their individual challenges and pace of learning. Thus, she is also interested in undertakings projects relating to lifelong learning and learners' resilience.

Affandi Saleh is Associate Professor of Religion and International Relations at Universiti Sultan Zainal Abidin, Malaysia.

Maragustam Siregar is Professor of Islamic education at Universitas Islam Negeri Sunan Kalijaga, Yogyakarta, Indonesia.

Charlene Tan is an associate professor at the National Institute of Education, Nanyang Technological University, Singapore.

Index

Ensure Quality Research is Introduced to the Academic Community

Become an IGI Global Reviewer for Authored Book Projects

The overall success of an authored book project is dependent on quality and timely reviews.

In this competitive age of scholarly publishing, constructive and timely feedback significantly expedites the turnaround time of manuscripts from submission to acceptance, allowing the publication and discovery of forward-thinking research at a much more expeditious rate. Several IGI Global authored book projects are currently seeking highly-qualified experts in the field to fill vacancies on their respective editorial review boards:

Applications and Inquiries may be sent to:
development@igi-global.com

Applicants must have a doctorate (or an equivalent degree) as well as publishing and reviewing experience. Reviewers are asked to complete the open-ended evaluation questions with as much detail as possible in a timely, collegial, and constructive manner. All reviewers' tenures run for one-year terms on the editorial review boards and are expected to complete at least three reviews per term. Upon successful completion of this term, reviewers can be considered for an additional term.

If you have a colleague that may be interested in this opportunity,
we encourage you to share this information with them.

IGI Global Proudly Partners With eContent Pro International

Receive a 25% Discount on all Editorial Services

Editorial Services

IGI Global expects all final manuscripts submitted for publication to be in their final form. This means they must be reviewed, revised, and professionally copy edited prior to their final submission. Not only does this support with accelerating the publication process, but it also ensures that the highest quality scholarly work can be disseminated.

English Language Copy Editing

Let eContent Pro International's expert copy editors perform edits on your manuscript to resolve spelling, punctuaion, grammar, syntax, flow, formatting issues and more.

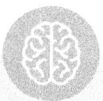

Scientific and Scholarly Editing

Allow colleagues in your research area to examine the content of your manuscript and provide you with valuable feedback and suggestions before submission.

Figure, Table, Chart & Equation Conversions

Do you have poor quality figures? Do you need visual elements in your manuscript created or converted? A design expert can help!

Translation

Need your documjent translated into English? eContent Pro International's expert translators are fluent in English and more than 40 different languages.

Email: customerservice@econtentpro.com   www.igi-global.com/editorial-service-partners

Lightning Source UK Ltd.
Milton Keynes UK
UKHW031011200820
368549UK00018B/2381